America and Guerrilla Warfare

America
and
Guerrilla
Warfare

Anthony James Joes

THE UNIVERSITY PRESS OF KENTUCKY

Scholarly publisher for the Commonwealth,
serving Bellarmine College, Berea College, Centre
College of Kentucky, Eastern Kentucky University,
The Filson Club Historical Society, Georgetown College,
Kentucky Historical Society, Kentucky State University,
Morehead State University, Transylvania University,
University of Kentucky, University of Louisville,
and Western Kentucky University.
All rights reserved.

Editorial and Sales Offices: The University Press of Kentucky
663 South Limestone Street, Lexington, Kentucky 40508-4008

04 03 02 01 00   5 4 3 2 1

Library of Congress Cataloging-in-Publication Data
Joes, Anthony James.
America and guerrilla warfare / Anthony James Joes.
p.   c.m.
Includes bibliographical references and index.
ISBN 0-8131-2181-7 (acid-free paper)
1. United States—History, Military—Case studies. 2. Guerrilla
warfare—History—Case studies. 3. United States—
Foreign relations—Case studies. I. Title.

E181.J64 2000
355'.02'18—dc21   00-028307

This book is printed on acid-free recycled paper meeting
the requirements of the American National Standard
for Permanence in Paper for Printed Library Materials.

Manufactured in the United States of America.

For Chris, AJ, and Vicky

Contents

Introduction

The Americans and Guerrilla Insurgency

The end of the Cold War did not mean the end of guerrilla insurgency.[1] The overthrow of the Ethiopian military regime in 1991 underlined the truth of that observation. And since then post–Cold War guerrilla conflict has flared from the Balkans to the Sudan, from Mexico to Mindanao.

Many factors account for this continuing and escalating pattern of internal violence. Most post–Cold War guerrilla conflicts have their roots in ethnic and religious tensions; the breakup of Cold War alignments has permitted many previously suppressed aspirations and hostilities of various groups to come to the surface. Much of the former Communist empire, the former "Second World," has been slipping, or plummeting, into Third World conditions. In most of those areas, elementary military training is widespread and modern weapons are abundant. Improved communications help to stir or reinforce discontent in poor countries or poor areas of countries. Exploding birthrates, especially in sub-Saharan Africa, are producing disproportionately youthful populations that tend to find frustrations intolerable and violence glamorous. The phenomenon of the "failed state," where a government collapses or disappears, opens the road to chronic organized violence. And although the USSR and its satellites are no longer available to supply arms to would-be revolutionaries, profits from the global drug trade buy great quantities of the newest weapons. Finally, the apparent need of not a few persons to find meaning in life through armed struggle against a perceived or defined evil guarantees that insurgency will always be occurring in some quarter, even if the particular socioeconomic problems there have been "solved."

It is almost certain that the United States will become involved in some of these guerrilla conflicts. Humanitarian impulses stimulated by sensational television coverage, the recurring American determination to make the world safe by spreading democracy, the participation of U.S. forces in UN peacekeeping or peacemaking missions—all these factors have been setting the stage for American troops to confront guerrillas. And the occasion may of course again arise when the United States wishes to assist guerrillas, on the model of the Afghan resistance to the Soviet invasion—perhaps on or within what China claims to be her borders, for example. Clearly, any decisions for U.S. involvement in a guerrilla conflict ought not to be made without due consideration of the experiences of the United States and of other major powers.

Perhaps the most important fact concerning the experiences of major powers when they have had to deal with guerrilla insurgencies is how very difficult, even dangerous, they found such challenges to be. Guerrilla warfare played a major role in the ending of the European colonial empires. Beyond that, in the twentieth century all of the great powers met frustration or even humiliation at the hands of guerrillas: the British in Ireland, the Germans in the Balkans, the Japanese in China, the Chinese in Tibet, the French and then the Americans in Vietnam,[2] and the Soviets in Afghanistan, and the Russians in Chechnya, to name only well-known instances.

Confronting guerrillas may present particular perils for the United States. Its armed forces are not as well prepared as they might be, psychologically or organizationally, to face guerrilla conflicts. Additional grave difficulties may well arise from the fact that many if not most guerrilla wars will derive from religious movements (notably but not exclusively Islamist) or from quasi-religious organizations like Peru's Sendero Luminoso. It is not clear that Americans—not just the armed forces but the political class, the electorate, and the media—are equipped to deal effectively with protracted, religiously inspired violence.[3] And by its very nature, guerrilla war is full of ugly incidents—just perfect for the American television industry.

The Nature of the Present Study

Dangers lie in the path ahead. To avert or at least prepare for them, Americans need to deepen and sharpen their understanding of what guerrilla war has meant and will mean. The principal method—however inadequate—for achieving this aim is analysis of experience. We need, of course, to exercise great caution in dealing with "the lessons of history": the past is littered with disastrous decisions and policies that were based on what were once considered to be convincing and even compelling analogies to previous situations. The full consequences of policies are notoriously hard to foresee, and interpretations of events and ideas change over time, often more than once.[4] The need is not for dogma, certainly not for maxims, but for insight that arises from careful analysis of each particular case in its particular context. It is especially important to look at the individual guerrilla conflict within its international political environment.[5] Another requirement is humility: the realization that we do not know all we need to know, and never shall, and that even the best-conceived and best-intentioned actions may produce consequences that are not only unforeseen but disastrous.

This volume examines nine cases of guerrilla conflict that involved the United States to a significant degree. Included are two cases in which the Americans themselves were the guerrillas (the American Revolution and the U.S. Civil War), three in which U.S. forces systematically engaged guerrillas on foreign soil (the post–Spanish War Philippines, Nicaragua, and Vietnam), three cases in which the United States assisted a foreign government challenged by guerrillas but did not deploy combat units (the post–World War II Philippines, Greece, and El Salvador), and one case in which the U.S. government aided a guerrilla movement abroad (Afghanistan).[6]

The number of cases is large enough to avoid the pitfalls awaiting those who derive conclusions from only one or two instances. But the number is not too big to prevent that consideration of detail and nuance that is so often lacking in large quantitative studies. The diverse settings of these wars, extending from the 1780s to the 1980s and from the Carolinas to the Philippines, permit comparisons between success and failure across time and across cultures. References to guerrilla conflicts that involved other great powers during and before the Cold War reinforce the comparative nature of this study.

I examine the configuration of these conflicts: their origins, why the Americans became involved, how they participated, and what patterns and deviations emerged from them. Perhaps one of the most notable aspects of the American involvement in guerrilla war suggested by this study is that the Americans have done well both in the role of guerrillas and in that of counterguerrillas, and it may be very useful for policymakers to reflect on that record. The war in Vietnam, the most distressing foreign conflict the Americans have ever engaged in, is profoundly atypical of U.S. experience in foreign guerrilla wars; our examination of events in the post-1898 Philippines and in 1920s Nicaragua underlines this. Of equal importance, the way the Americans dealt with the 1980s struggle in El Salvador—a reversion to the successful Greek-Philippine model—suggests that they indeed learned a few things from their agony in Vietnam.

1

American Guerrillas

The War of Independence

In their very first conflict as an independent people, the Americans displayed impressive prowess in guerrilla warfare. The contribution made by American guerrillas to the climactic events of the War of Independence, especially the bagging of Cornwallis at Yorktown, was substantial, even essential. Yet for some reason their story remains little known. In addition, the war suggests, across more than two centuries, certain fundamental difficulties impeding even great powers when they confront a major guerrilla challenge.

How the War Came About

The American struggle for independence from Britain had its origins above all in two key factors: the destruction of the French and Indian menace and the controversy over self-government. Before 1763 hardly a single American colonist would have desired independence from the British Empire, if only because of the menace to New England and other colonies presented by French power in Canada. The French incited their Indian allies to attack American farms and settlements. This brutal racial warfare left American colonists little choice but to look to the British army for protection (which in their view was often inadequate).[1]

The long struggle for control of North America between France and England and their respective Indian allies was played out in several acts: King William's War (1689–1697), Queen Anne's War (1702–1713), King George's War (1744–1748), and the French and Indian War (1754–1763), during which the young George Washing-

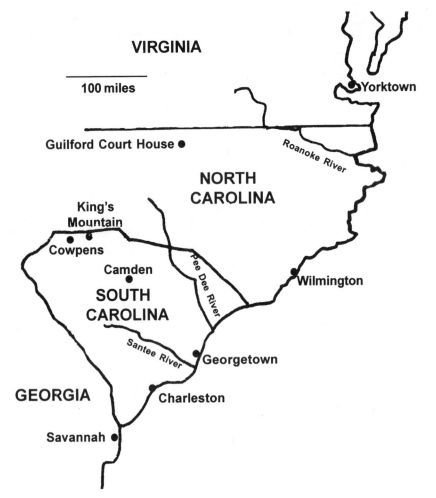

The Carolina Theater, circa 1780.

ton learned about leading men in combat.[2] For the most part these conflicts had been sideshows in a global struggle for empire among France, Britain, and Spain. But in the 1750s the great William Pitt convinced his countrymen that their main objective in this six-decade-old contest should be the final expulsion of French power from North America. His policy culminated in 1759 in the climactic British victory on the Plains of Abraham, in front of Quebec. By destroying the vast French empire in America—New France (Canada) and Louisiana (the Mississippi Valley)—the British set the stage for rebellion in their thirteen American colonies.

From the settlement of Jamestown in 1607 to the fall of Quebec in 1759, Britain's efforts to regulate life in its American colonies had been generally light-handed and intermittent. Out of this relative British neglect and the consequent necessity of self-reliance, a rarely articulated but constantly increasing sense of separateness had been developing in America, a growing apart from England in life and thought. With the final elimination of the French and Indian danger, American colonists became quite unreceptive to increased supervision from London.

"British subjects in America," a distinguished scholar wrote in 1965, "were then the freest people in the world, and in many respects were freer than anyone today."[3] But exactly at the time when its American colonists were feeling safe, expansive, and self-reliant, the government in London undertook to exercise greater control over them. The struggles in North America had cost the British government a lot of money. Since these wars, and especially the last one, had conferred inestimable benefits on the American colonists, Englishmen predictably concluded that the colonists should pay a fair share of the costs. This entirely comprehensible if lamentably inopportune intention to spread around the financial burden of a war from which all had gained produced in 1765 the notorious Stamp Act, the first direct internal tax ever laid by Parliament on the colonies. The money raised by the stamp law was earmarked for colonial defense, but it fell mainly on merchants, lawyers, and journalists and therefore raised a storm of protest. Representatives of nine colonies convened, full of indignation, in New York City for the so-called Stamp Act Congress. The next year, at the urging of Pitt, Parliament repealed the offensive legislation.

Reaction to the Stamp Act set loose a series of intertwined disputes that in a few years led to Lexington and to Yorktown. Where English politicians saw nothing more than a reasonable effort to rationalize relations within the empire, American colonists saw nothing less than a major step toward abolishing traditional and comfortable liberties. The vulgarized economic determinism that has so long pervaded American culture must not obscure the fact that it was never some piddling taxes on glass or documents or tea, or any other mere matter of government finance, that alarmed and mobilized the Americans. Rather it was the specter of Parliament's newly asserted right to do whatever it saw fit to do in the colonies and all the implications of that for the liberty of the Americans, their destiny, their self-image, and their self-respect.[4] To both the English and the American mind, property was inextricably intertwined with citizenship; hence questions of taxation—of whom, by whom—touched the very fabric of the polity. The freeborn English in America, newly emancipated from the dread vision of French and Indian depredations, awoke to find themselves confronted, as they thought, by a Parliament that considered them to be mere counters in a vast imperial game. They declined that role with vehemence. "Many revolutionaries believed that God had chosen America to preserve and to exemplify self-government for the world." But were the Americans really free, or were they, after all, pawns of a far-away Parliament, however enlightened and light-handed? And if one day that enlightened and light-handed Parliament should become benighted and rapacious—what then? Great principles were at stake. The American Revolution was "above all else an ideological, constitutional, political struggle."[5]

Many factors worked to widen the ideological fissures, including English domestic party politics. Above all, ignorance of American conditions and sentiments beclouded British policy, ignorance aggravated by slow and unreliable communications over the dangerous North Atlantic. Every difficulty, every controversy and rumor loomed more distorted and more menacing through an impenetrable oceanic fog of mutual incomprehension. Edmund Burke observed, "The Americans have made a discovery, or think they have made one, that we intend to oppress them; we have made a discovery, or think we have made one, that they intend to rise in rebellion against us."[6]

Even before the Second Continental Congress, with delegates

from all thirteen colonies, convened in Philadelphia on May 10, 1775, both sides had shed blood, at Lexington and Concord. Fort Ticonderoga fell to Ethan Allen's Vermonters in May 1775. The next month saw the sanguinary encounter called Bunker Hill. George Washington accepted the command of the "Continental Army" (which did not yet actually exist) in June.[7] Benedict Arnold began his march to Quebec in September.

Then, in a shocking and probably irreparable breach of the social contract, British authorities stirred up Indian tribes against the colonists. In January 1776 the cabinet compounded that error by hiring German troops to go to America and kill what in the British government's own eyes were British subjects on British soil. This last piece of foolishness simply appalled Americans (as well as many Englishmen in England); many who had up to then hoped and worked for reconciliation were pushed onto the side of revolution. A final rupture seemed inevitable. As the Declaration of Independence complained, "He [the King] is at this time transporting large armies of foreign mercenaries to complete the works of death, destruction and tyranny already begun." Hessian and other German troops in North America would eventually number twenty-nine thousand.[8] Armed conflict provoked a declaration of American independence, not the other way around.

Displaying in the course of these events a decent respect for the opinions of mankind, the Continental Congress, on July 4, 1776, declared the existence of a new nation. With deep misgivings, the British cabinet rejected this declaration, and so the war came.

Where Was the British Victory?

About three million persons lived in the mainly rural American colonies in 1776; of these about six hundred thousand were of African descent, most of them held in slavery. Large numbers of Americans were indifferent or actually hostile to the cause of independence. On the other side, the British were at least three times as numerous as the Americans, they had emerged from the Seven Years' War everywhere victorious over the puissant French, and they possessed both a relatively developed economy and a navy widely believed to be second to none. Yet these impressive disparities between the contestants failed to bring victory to the British. Factors that impeded or prevented the anticipated effects of British superiority require a brief review, both because of the influence they exerted on the overall conduct of the war and because of their role in the guerrilla conflict that developed in the Carolinas, the conflict that led to Yorktown.

The Disunited Kingdom

The decision to coerce the American colonists aroused misgivings and even open opposition within British society. After all, the American colonists were not only British subjects but, for the most part, fellow Englishmen. The Howe brothers (General William and Admiral Richard) were in command of British land and naval forces in America in 1776; both men sympathized with many of the colonists' complaints and spoke openly against a policy of severity. Several prominent army and navy commanders declined to serve against the Americans. Notable politicians opposed making war upon the colonists, including Charles James Fox, Edmund Burke, and the immortal Chatham (now old and quite ill). On hearing the news of the fighting at Lexington and Concord, Chatham exclaimed, "I rejoice that America has resisted!". Fox declared as early as November 1777 that America was too big and too far away to be conquered. The incitement of Indians against the colonists deeply distressed him; Indians were hard to control as allies and committed atrocities against civilians that provided excellent propaganda for the rebels. The cabinet, under Lord North, had the support of only a slender parliamentary majority, and North was consequently reluctant to undertake bold initiatives. Above all, the North cabinet was keenly aware that the British ruling classes had no intention of paying the financial and political costs of fighting a really serious war in America.[9] Consequently, the government needed to believe that restoration of order in the colonies would be relatively easy and cheap, that the American rebellion was the work of only a small minority who would soon give up—a belief constantly disappointed but constantly renewed, a belief that made possible the disaster at Yorktown.[10]

Strategic America

The war was going to be neither easy nor cheap, however, for reasons that many observers at the time were able to discern. In the first place, the very extent of the American colonies posed an impressive challenge to any campaign of coercion. Pennsylvania alone was nearly the size of England; South Carolina, one of the smaller colonies, was the size of all Ireland; North Carolina was twice as big as Belgium and the Netherlands combined. Boston was as far from Savannah as London was from Budapest, or Warsaw from Istanbul—and there was no air or rail or even reliable road transportation. A British attempt to subdue the American colonies would face many of the same difficulties as the later campaigns of Napoleon in Russia and the Japanese in China: the occupation of huge sectors of sprawl-ing territory would greatly tax the resources of the invading power but would not necessarily bring the end of the war any closer.[11]

The great size of the war theater would not have mattered so much if the British had been able to seize the brain center of the American rebellion. But no such place existed. Philadelphia, by far the largest American city, had 29,000 inhabitants (compared at the time to 250,000 in Moscow, 350,000 in Naples, 600,000 in Paris and 700,000 in London). The occupation of New York City, which in fact was in British hands for most of the war, could mean but little to the homespun frontiersmen of western Pennsylvania or the determined partisans of the Carolina Swamp Fox. And just as there was no all-important capital, there were no strategic fortresses whose fall would signal the eclipse of the rebellion: the British took Ticonderoga, called for some reason the "Gibraltar of America," with no discernible con-sequences.[12] Clearly, the British would accomplish little by captur-ing "key points."

Weakness in the Navy

Britain's supreme weapon should have been command of the sea. The asset of a large and habitually victorious navy should have al-lowed Britain to transport armies at will, keep those armies sup-plied, rescue forces that got into trouble, and isolate and bottle up the Americans. Yet the struggle that began as the American War of Independence was "the only war of the eighteenth century in which England failed to win ascendancy at sea."[13]

This absence of secure maritime supremacy had several sources. After the victory over the French in 1763, British cabinets had very shortsightedly allowed the navy to deteriorate. Diseases, especially scurvy, also weakened British naval power, even though the pre-ventive for scurvy was generally known and easily available. The ravages of disease are almost incredible to us today: of about 171,000 seamen who served in the Royal Navy during the war, less than 1 out of 140 died in combat, but 1 out of 9 died of disease (and 1 out of 4 deserted). There was in addition the problem, always so puzzling to civilians, of interservice rivalry and even hostility. As long as the Howe brothers were in command in America, cooperation between the military and the naval arms was quite adequate. But after Gen. Sir Henry Clinton took over the army command in the colonies, serious difficulties arose between him and the admirals, and many others as well. Then French intervention in the war drastically changed the entire maritime picture. The French navy, though lacking the size, skill, and self-confidence of its British counterpart, was nonetheless a formidable weapon. In the later years of the war, French naval power was augmented by the considerable fleets of the Spanish and the Dutch. All this caused the British greatly to fear an invasion of the home islands; hence they kept many ships in home waters, too many to allow them to maintain a constant naval supremacy in America. (If the British had bottled up the main French fleets at Brest and Toulon, the number of British vessels available for service in American waters would have been far fewer, but French soldiers and supplies would not have reached America; Yorktown would have been impossible. Nonetheless, such a sustained contest in European waters against the combined fleets of France and Spain was beyond the power of the Royal Navy in the 1770s.)[14]

Weakness in the Army

The principal instrument through which the subordination of vast America would have to be accomplished was of course the army. But the army was not in good condition. As an institution it was an object of distrust, ridicule, or aversion for many Englishmen, even for the government that maintained it. "Ever since Cromwell's time, the soldier had been regarded as the natural enemy of the liberties of the people." Partly because of this dour heritage, the British army in the eighteenth century had no serious organization above the regimental level; when a large force was required, regiments were simply thrown together. Of course, no professional staff existed. Army pay was low. There were no decorations for valor. Predictably, recruiting men to serve in the ranks was difficult. One method of getting men was to pardon criminals who would agree to join the army.

"In this way every gaol served as a recruiting depot."[15] Things were different, but not necessarily better, in the higher ranks: favoritism, connections, and money were the most important elements in the process of distributing commands (this was true in the navy as well).

Thus, the army was an object of distrust and dislike by many Englishmen of high and low estate, its recruits came too often from the most depressed social strata, and its leaders were men not necessarily distinguished for brilliance or even competence. In light of these distressing circumstances, it comes as no surprise that the army was also small. In December 1776 the British army counted 55,000 men, of whom some 21,000 were in North America along with Hessian and other German mercenaries. (Eventually almost half the troops sent to America were from German states. In 1775 the British government had tried to procure 20,000 Russian mercenaries, but Catherine the Great turned it down.) Even by September 1781, when Britain confronted not only the American rebellion but the combined hostility of the French, the Spanish, and the Dutch as well, the British army had only 149,000 soldiers, of whom 36,000 were militia in England; in all of North America and the West Indies, there were only 56,000 British troops. Thus, to the actual fighting in its thirteen North American colonies, Britain at no time committed as much as 1 percent of its total male population.[16]

In addition to being distrusted, poorly recruited, and small, the British army notably lacked anything approaching a decisive edge over its American opponents in terms of weapons. Eighteenth-century military technology was simple, inexpensive, and widely understood. The British had discipline and tradition, but they had no tactical or strategic airpower, no helicopter gunships, no tanks, no armored personnel carriers, not even repeating rifles. The principal weapon of all infantry regiments, even in Europe's most professional armies, was the musket. Having fired his musket once, the soldier had to reload: three shots a minute was considered a good rate of fire. (In order to appreciate the time lapse between shots, the reader is invited to hold his or her breath for twenty seconds.) The British musket had an optimal range of 40 yards. American guerrillas in Pennsylvania or Carolina often carried rifles, more sophisticated than the musket, with an effective range of 250 yards. Thus, even the sparse and mainly rural population of the revolted colonies could produce arms whose quality overmatched those of the best British regiments. And given the weaponry and tactics of the times, even very poor quality troops could inflict serious casualties on the enemy.[17]

The Puzzle of Supply

There was also a very serious question of supply. An army, especially one on campaign, has little or no ability to produce food or clothing or ammunition, yet it regularly consumes great quantities of those items, particularly food. Even at the end of the twentieth century, transporting a major military force across an ocean and supplying it once there is a formidable task. Two hundred years ago it was nearly impossible. A consideration of the problems involved in feeding and arming the king's soldiers in America illuminates our understanding of the British conduct of the war.

The needs of an eighteenth-century army were modest compared to those of a modern one, but they were still quite large. Every British soldier in America required 700 pounds of food a year, plus the casks and barrels in which that food was packed. A working horse needed 29 pounds of hay and oats every single day; the 4,000 British army horses in America in 1776 therefore required more than 14,000 tons of hay and 6,000 tons of oats annually. Even during the frightful winter of 1777–1778 at Valley Forge, the hungry little American army there consumed 2.25 tons of beef and 2.25 tons of flour (plus 15,000 gallons of rum and whiskey, assuredly for medicinal purposes).[18]

If asked where all these supplies for British forces in America were supposed to come from, a member of the British cabinet in 1776 would have answered, "from America." The Treasury contracted with London firms to supply the king's forces in America; these London firms subcontracted with groups in the colonies. But already in the spring of 1775 the system began to break down. The population of the colonies was relatively small and scattered, and much of it was hostile. Thus, the requisite quantities of supplies were not easy to assemble. And patriot groups in the colonies frequently prevented the acquisition and delivery of sufficient supplies. When British troops went out very far beyond the towns in search of sustenance, they often had to contend with bands of guerrillas, who removed foodstuffs from the path of British foraging parties and frequently attacked such parties, inflicting irreplaceable casualties on already inadequate British forces. If a British army controlled a small territory, it could not extract enough supplies from it; one could expand the food supply by expanding the amount of territory occupied, but that would require more soldiers, and more soldiers would require more supplies: "sufficiency was an ever-receding horizon."[19] Most of the food and other supplies for the British forces in America therefore had to come from England. That seemingly simple sentence actually bristles with unpleasant strategic implications.

The king's forces in America were at the far end of a tenuous supply lifeline: cumbersome vessels dependent on the wind, slowly and uncertainly moving across three thousand miles of the never hospitable and often tempestuous North Atlantic Ocean. Inauspicious winds and bureaucratic sloth usually prevented ships and fleets from beginning their voyages to America on schedule. Adverse weather could destroy well-built ships, and even a safe crossing sometimes required two full months. (News of the tremendously important battle of Saratoga, concluded by October 17, 1777, did not reach Benjamin Franklin, American envoy to the French government, until December 4). And because bad winds could easily blow a fleet far off course, it was not unusual that a ship carrying vital cargo to Boston would actually come to port at Charleston. Finally, the foodstuffs carried in these slow and vulnerable vessels were preserved by methods that had not improved in essentials since prehistoric times.[20] The long and dangerous distances across the North Atlantic had played their part in bringing on the war; they now compounded Britain's difficulties in waging that war.

The army's supply system was rife with fraud and embezzlement, a result of the patronage and amateurism of eighteenth-century British administration. Politicians who benefited from this system naturally opposed its reform.[21] Besides, any serious suggestion about improving the system of supply to British forces in America would collide with the myth that America itself would be able to supply the war (the same fatal myth shows up in British estimates of the political situation).

The British war effort, therefore, consistently displayed "the inability of the [British] army to obtain any dependable supply of provisions in North America." Serious consequences, both political and military, flowed from this inability. Poor logistics meant poor discipline. Since few professional British soldiers, and no German troops at all, were fighting in the colonies from motives of patriotism, the failure to furnish them adequate supplies encouraged desertion.

Another result was pillaging: soldiers showed scant respect for the property of disloyal civilians, but when they were hungry, soldiers took what they could from hapless farmers, regardless of their politics. This common practice turned loyal colonials into neutrals and neutral ones into rebels.[22] Moreover, if British forces moved away from the sea into the large, underdeveloped, and often hostile hinterland, they ran the risk of having their overland supply lines cut. So the king's troops usually stayed prudently close to navigable rivers or occupied port cities. The effective power of the Crown, that is, did not normally extend much beyond a relatively shallow group of coastal strongholds. Twice during the war British forces challenged these geographical realities; both instances ended in disaster, as will be seen shortly.

The dependence on local sources of supply is above all what made British forces so vulnerable to guerrilla attack. That dependence derived not only from the manifold difficulties of transatlantic transportation but also from the lamentable inability of the Royal Navy to maintain consistent control of American waters.

Political disarray inside Britain, the size of the American war zone and its distance from the mother country, the strategic dilemmas presented by an intercontinental naval war (including eventually the specter of a French invasion of England itself), the inadequate quantity and quality of troops available, and obstacles to the proper supply of those troops—all these factors operated powerfully to hobble the British effort to subdue the Americans, and they opened the path to American guerrillas.

British Options

The British clearly had impressive obstacles to confront, but they also had plausible courses of action to consider. First of all, they might have acquiesced in independence for the Americans, inviting them to enter into close commercial and military relations, rather than trying to coerce them into submission. Some sentiment did exist in governing circles for that course, but it would take another hundred years to develop the formula—peaceful independence and intimate links—for a British Commonwealth.

As a second possible course, rejecting American claims to independence and deciding to suppress them, the British might have concentrated every effort on destroying Washington's army, the rebellion's "center of gravity." That army numbered about eighteen thousand in 1776, peaked at twenty thousand in 1778, and then declined.[23] Certainly it would have been difficult to trap Washington in the wide spaces of America, especially since he himself understood the supreme importance of preserving his army no matter what. Nonetheless, such entrapment was not impossible: armies could find themselves caught, as Generals Burgoyne and Cornwallis would eventually come to understand. But instead of a strategy of destroying or dispersing Washington's army, the British settled on schemes of territorial conquest (the Saratoga and Carolina campaigns), which ended in disaster for them.

A third choice was to send enough troops to the colonies to overwhelm the rebellion, that is, to chase Washington's army into some remote hinterland, occupy the population centers, and hunt down guerrilla bands. But raising troops sufficient in number to accomplish these tasks was not feasible: early in the war it would have cost more money than the British wished to spend, and later it might well have precipitated a French invasion of England when it was denuded of troops. Consequently, British forces in America were always numerically inadequate; yet at the beginning of the war General Howe was in command on Staten Island of more than thirty thousand men (including Hessians), possibly the largest European expeditionary force of the entire eighteenth century.[24]

A fourth option, since the British did not want to send enough men of their own, was to get others do their fighting for them. They could have mobilized the significant elements in the colonies that desired to remain under the Crown—the loyalists—and provided them with the necessary training, equipment, and moral support. This line of action never received sufficiently realistic consideration. (But under this rubric of get-somebody-else-to-fight, the London government did adopt a typically disastrous half-measure: hiring German mercenary troops to fight in America. Of those, there were not nearly enough to suppress the rebellion, but there were more than enough to rouse Americans to bellicose indignation.)

Fifth, given their unwillingness to send enough troops to win the war and Washington's ability to avoid a decisive encounter, the British might have adopted what would in a later war be called an "enclave strategy": setting down small forces in the American population centers—the seaports—making them as impregnable as possible and gradually extending the territory under their control. In this way, without inflicting or suffering numerous casualties, they could have convinced the rebels that final victory was unattainable. A variation would have been to put into real effect Burgoyne's plan to split the colonies into two parts along New York State's eastern border (see the next section). Either of these alternatives would have given time and scope for corrosive quarrels and disintegrative jealousies among the Americans to have their inevitable effects. And once the French intervened in the conflict, an enclave strategy seems at least in hindsight to be the only one with any realistic hope of success. But a strategy of enclaves enjoyed little articulate support because it would have required too much time to become effective.

Sixth, the British might have selected some combination of those options: for instance, holding the larger southern centers with armed loyalists stiffened by some British regulars and protecting them with one sizable regular army, probably best based in Charleston. They approached this strategy in 1780 in South Carolina but soon abandoned it in pursuit of larger objectives (which also failed).

Thus, the British never adopted any of those six courses of action. In fact, they never developed any realistic or even coherent overall strategy for dealing with the rebellion.[25] With no Chatham to guide them, no Marlborough, no Wellington, directed (so to speak) by a cabinet of "mediocrities," the British embarked upon a distant and difficult conflict, "a war marked by all the folly of a Crusade, without the piety," stumbling on through one year after another, from one plan to another, while the number of their enemies increased and the prospects of their final victory diminished. "With all due credit to the Americans and their French allies, it is not too much to say that the British government and the British generals lost the Revolution for England."[26]

On to New York!

The confrontation at Yorktown had its origins in British plans for the conquest of the southern colonies. American guerrillas in the Carolinas played a decisive role in the failure of this British effort, a failure that led directly to Yorktown and the final triumph of the American cause. But the genesis of the British campaign in the Carolinas occurred far from those colonies. The invasion of the South was actually the second great British effort to break the rebellion; the first took place in New York and ended, as the southern campaign would end, in military disaster. The second (the southern) campaign would not (and could not) have taken place had it not been for the failure of the first (the northern) campaign, the culmination of which has gone into the books as the Battle of Saratoga. To appreciate not only the Carolina conflict with its climax at Yorktown, but also the British method of making war in America, we need to recall the events at Saratoga.

Accurately judging New England to be the heart of the rebellion, the British decided to isolate that region from the rest of the colonies. The essential plan was to establish a line of strong points and posts from Lake Champlain down the Hudson River to Albany and eventually extend it to New York City. This line would prevent or at least impede overland passage of supplies and troops between New England and the other colonies. Having geographically divided the rebels, the British could concentrate on subduing one group of colonies at a time; thus they would in effect nearly double their available forces. With one section of rebellious America having been subdued, the other sections would inevitably succumb as well.

John Burgoyne (1722–1792), soldier, parliamentarian, and playwright, was the principal author of what became the Saratoga campaign. In 1776 he sent the government his "Thoughts for Conducting the War from the Side of Canada." Burgoyne proposed to establish his base in Montreal and thence advance southward. A small diversionary force would march eastward from Oswego (on Lake Ontario) through the Mohawk River Valley. These moves would be supported by some sort of activity on the part of Howe's main army in New York City. All these forces would converge on Albany. But, according to most accounts of the campaign, Gen. William Howe, occupying New York City with a substantial force, was not originally supposed to march directly to Albany with anything like his whole army—or if he was, he was not aware of it.[27]

A noted historian of the Revolution calls the whole enterprise "stupid" because it diverted many troops away from the pursuit of Washington's army and because in the original versions Howe was not clearly responsible for giving support to Burgoyne until the latter had reached Albany. Moreover, even if Burgoyne's plan had been completely successful, the isolation of New England would have taken a very long time to become really effective. But leading military figures in London had for some time held the opinion that dividing the colonies in two along some line or other was possible and indeed would be the key to winning the war.[28] It was not unreasonable for them to believe that they could seal the eastern border of New York with small posts supported here and there by strong garrisons. Then New England, already blockaded by the Royal Navy, might have begun to suffocate.

General Howe, the British commander in New York City, was a Whig and had publicly opposed the policy of coercing the Americans. Nevertheless, he had long meditated on and even written to London about his plans to attack Philadelphia, the seat of the Continental Congress. Howe hoped that by threatening Philadelphia he would force Washington to stand and fight and inevitably be defeated. Thus the rebellion would (presumably) end. Howe knew that Burgoyne's operation was coming down into New York colony from Montreal, but he believed that Burgoyne could reach Albany without any direct assistance from New York City. So Howe and most of his army sailed away to the South on July 23. Several weeks before this, Lord George Germaine, the cabinet minister most directly concerned with American affairs, had concluded that Burgoyne's efforts toward Albany would require some support from Howe's forces. He therefore wrote Howe a letter directing him to send assistance up the Hudson River to Burgoyne. But it appears that the letter was mislaid; it never reached Howe. The question of the mislaid letter has always generated a good deal of controversy. In any case, instead of going up the Hudson to assist Burgoyne, Howe sailed off to the Chesapeake to trap Washington (who eluded him).[29]

The Burgoyne plan's other prop was supposed to be the diversionary march from Oswego eastward toward Albany through the valley of the Mohawk River. On July 26 that started out well enough, with Col. Barry St. Leger commanding a force of about 850 soldiers and loyal colonials and about 800 Indian allies. But colonial militia defeated them near Rome. Then, receiving news that Gen. Benedict Arnold was approaching, St. Leger's men panicked, for this Arnold "was feared by the white soldiers and the red warriors alike as was no other American officer."[30] St. Leger therefore retreated to Oswego and thence to Canada in August. With no support from either south or west, Burgoyne found himself and his army alone in the hostile wilderness. He had set out for Ticonderoga on July 1 with 7,700 troops and 500 Indians. Two thousand women accompanied his army in various capacities. After innumerable hardships and miscalculations and several small but sharp defeats at the hands of swarms of New England militia, with little food and less prospect of assistance, on October 17 Burgoyne surrendered his 3,500 men, all that remained to him, to the American general Horatio Gates near Saratoga.[31]

Burgoyne and St. Leger had committed the military mortal sin of despising and therefore underestimating their adversaries. They were not the first nor the last soldiers to fall into this error and to pay a high price for it.[32]

A French Alliance

The chanceries of Europe resounded with the news of Saratoga. Striking London like a thunderbolt, it shocked the cabinet into agreeing on a truly remarkable program. The British government now proposed to repeal all offensive legislation since 1763, renounce the right of Parliament to lay direct taxes on the colonies, recognize the legitimacy of the Continental Congress, and discuss the question of American representation in the House of Commons at Westminster. In June 1776 such a package would have stopped the Revolution cold. But before the plenipotentiaries carrying these offers from London could arrive in America, the Continental Congress had entered into a treaty of alliance with France. As the only condition of that alliance, the French had insisted that the Americans not make peace with England until the latter recognized their independence.[33] The British offer came too late.

Meanwhile, at Versailles, Louis XVI's foreign minister Charles, comte de Vergennes, had been carefully guiding his country's policy toward the American rebellion, biding his time, and arranging for secret assistance to be given to the rebels. Saratoga changed all this: it was "the sign for which France had waited."[34] On December 6, 1777, Louis XVI recognized the independence of the United States, and a military alliance soon followed. For the Americans, the French alliance meant an incalculable accession of strength. France had twenty-four million people to Britain's nine, a first-class army, and a considerable navy. True enough, France had suffered a decisive defeat by Britain in the Seven Years' War (what the Americans call the

French and Indian War), but what it had lost most was prestige, and that would be restored by a suitable humiliation of the English. Hence Vergennes's desire to assist the Americans. "Saratoga brought France into the war and thereby established the independence of the United States. If anyone doubts this and prefers to believe that our ancestors could have won through by their own efforts, he has only to consider the sequel. In the event, even after the intervention not only of France but later of Spain and Holland, the issue was long in doubt and Washington more than once feared the worst." Thus there can be no doubt that "the [British] defeat at Saratoga is the clearest turning of the war," one of the truly decisive battles in world history.[35]

The Franco-American combination was an odd one. The Americans had recently fought against the French; many Americans hated them, mainly because of atrocities committed by France's Indian allies. Influential persons on the French side also found the alliance unsettling. Although they sorely wished to harm England, were not the French in fact setting a very bad example in assisting rebels against a lawful king? Most of all, French help to the Americans and France's eventual full-scale entry into the war would throw the government's finances into chaos, a situation that would help lead them, just a few years after Yorktown, to a supreme crisis; indeed "the price to be paid for American independence was a French revolution."[36]

But the advisers of Louis XVI found Saratoga an irresistible temptation. With the British apparently bogged down in a difficult war in North America, France was free to strike at them when and as it pleased. Fortunately for the Americans, the French government had no way of knowing that, the victory at Saratoga notwithstanding, if General Howe had bestirred himself in the winter of 1777–1778, he could have destroyed Washington's desperate little army at Valley Forge.[37]

Without doubt, the most important consequence of the American victory at Saratoga and France's entry into the war, both immediately and in the long run, was that in the eyes of the London government, the major theater of combat was no longer in the American colonies. French intervention would mean a naval war for control of the West Indies and India, but above all it raised the dread prospect of an invasion of the home islands. France was the dominant power on the continent. Because Britain had no important allies in Europe, the French were free to contemplate a direct attack on the British Isles. And the eventual Spanish entry into the war further altered its strategic basis. Spain came in reluctantly, disliking the example a successful revolt by Britain's North American colonies would set for her own vast holdings in the New World. Spanish intervention in the conflict was therefore not on the side of the Americans but on the side of the French, and above all against the English. No longer a power of the first rank, Spain nevertheless possessed a sizable navy, a vast and rich colonial empire, and a faded but serviceable prestige. Now, with all her other worries, Britain would have to deal with a major threat to Gibraltar.

Thus, the consequences of Saratoga dramatically changed the way in which the British cabinet looked at the American war. First, as a result of France's entry into the conflict, British attention shifted from the North American war to the global conflict. Second, British hopes for the reconquest of America shifted from the Hudson Valley to the Carolinas. Many observers in London now believed that "the southern colonies were in many ways the soft underbelly of the rebellion." As 1780 dawned, the American war had been dragging on for almost five years and seemed far from an end. The British really had to try something new. Thus, Lord North's cabinet moved slowly but inexorably toward a new strategy: the reconquest of the colonies must begin in the South. The cabinet sent its thoughts on this grave matter to Howe's successor in America, Gen. Sir Henry Clinton.[38]

On to the Carolinas!

Throughout the American Revolution, a significant proportion of the colonial population remained loyal to the British Crown. The conflict, therefore, was not only a war of independence but a true civil war. But no widely recognized leader arose among the loyalists, and many of them fled to Canada during or after the Revolution. Little sympathy and less study has therefore been expended on those Americans who opposed the independence struggle. "The Loyalists in the American Revolution suffered a most abject kind of political failure, losing not only their argument, their war, and their place in American society, but even their proper place in history."[39] Nevertheless, the American loyalists were to play a signal role in the final years of the war.

The Loyalist Mirage

Concentrating resources on a reconquest of the southern colonies appealed to the British cabinet for several reasons. After Saratoga the government wanted to accomplish something somewhere. The southern colonies were supposed to have a beneficial climate and an abundance of food, and they were far from turbulent New England. But above all the South, it was widely repeated, was full of loyal subjects merely awaiting a sign, a rescuing act, by the mother country. Some in England who had originally opposed the coercion of the colonies as unjust or stupid underwent a change in their attitude because of their unwillingness to abandon the supposedly large numbers of suffering loyalists. Furthermore, growing opposition in Britain to sending any more soldiers to America would eventually force the recognition of colonial independence, unless troops could be obtained somewhere else—that is to say, from among loyal southerners. Therefore numerous southern loyalists must exist. The mantra of the loyalist hosts just waiting to be organized was the perfect answer to many problems. How to reconquer America? Simple: just get General Howe or somebody to chase away Washington's contemptible little army, and then the teeming loyalists would rise up to impose order on the rebel minority. This reputed abundance of loyal subjects was the decisive factor in the change in British strategy, because it would supposedly enable Britain to win the war, at least the southern war, cheaply.[40] (As a matter of fact, probably more New Yorkers were for the king than for the Continental Congress, but that had had precious little effect at Saratoga.)

General Cornwallis and other British commanders were always expecting to find these large numbers of loyalists who would join in the fight, and they were always disappointed.[41] British troops in the Carolinas did receive assistance from loyalist units, but often they were groups like the far-wandering New York Volunteers, or the Volunteers of Ireland, actually recruited in Philadelphia. The local loyalists were never numerous enough, nor were they employed with real effect. Where, then, were the great legions of loyal fighting men who needed just a little encouragement to subdue the small bands of rebellious malcontents in their midst? A partial answer: in the minds of British politicians, and nowhere else.

Twentieth-century estimates vary regarding the proportion of the American population that was loyalist. Perhaps about 20 percent of the white population in the thirteen colonies remained fundamentally attached to the old order, with a higher figure—from a quarter to close to a third of the population—for South Carolina, but these are informed guesses only.[42] Moreover, changing sides with the changing tides was not uncommon, especially in the Carolina partisan struggles. Who were these loyalists, called "Tories" by their opponents? Predictably, some of them were rich; also predictably, some were Anglican clergymen. But like support for the Revolution, support for the Crown cut across class lines. Poor backcountry farmers in North Carolina were loyalists because for years they had believed themselves oppressed by the coastal middle class that was leading the revolutionary cause. Other upcountry Carolina loyalists were smallholders who were suspicious of Whig (revolutionary) landowners or who felt the need of the Crown's military protection against hostile Indians, or both. Relations among these different colonial groups had been very tense since the 1760s.

Ethnicity also played a role in revolutionary politics. The "Scotch as a race generally remained loyal to the king of England and were the most important single group in North Carolina to do so."[43] In part the Scottish allegiance to the English monarch stemmed from religious principles: the Scots had taken an oath of fealty after the defeat of the Stuart rebellion of 1745. Many of the Scots believed that the English were invincible. And the Germans of South Carolina, especially in and around Orangeburg, were loyal to King George "of Hanover." In contrast, the Scotch-Irish who settled in the Carolinas nursed their ancient grudges against the English king and were therefore usually Whigs. Nevertheless, "the loyalists in the interior tended to be relatively recent immigrants who had moved into South Carolina . . . from northern Ireland or Germany, or from other colonies, particularly Virginia. The number of foreign and American loyalists with north Irish backgrounds suggests that caution should be exercised before accepting a simple 'Scotch-Irish' explanation of backcountry support for independence; it seems more likely that their relative newness to the areas in which they settled contributed to their indifference or hostility to the aggressive designs of the [South Carolina] Provincial Congress in 1775."[44] Thus, analysis of political disposition according to ethnic grouping is enlightening but inadequate.

But above all other aspects of the loyalist question, it is essential to keep in mind that sentiments of loyalty to the king and the old flag, however sincere, did not at all necessarily imply a willingness to bear arms against the Revolution.

So there were far fewer loyalists willing and able to fight than the king's ministers wished to believe. And besides the relative lack of numbers, other factors helped to restrain loyalist activism. For one thing, British commanders were loath to incorporate loyalist units into their own forces or to grant regular commissions to loyalist officers. For another, British soldiers were often looters—one more consequence of the supply problem—and were casual about discovering the political allegiances of those among whom they marched; the German mercenary troops were even worse because they could not even understand the protestations of their loyalist victims, assuming for the sake of argument that they would have paid any attention had such protestations been intelligible. Most of all, loyalists were reluctant to fight at the side of the British because they sensed, sometimes perhaps subconsciously, that the British troops could always decide to abandon them. This fear was well founded. The British had already undermined the confidence of loyalists in other colonies by their practice of occupying an area for a while, encouraging the local loyalists to publicly display their true sentiments, and then marching off. That is exactly what would happen to the loyalists of Georgia in 1780, and the Revolutionary forces almost always displayed more severity toward loyalists than toward British troops.[45] At a minimum, the British government and military never developed a clear idea of the place of the loyalists in the processes of reconquest and reconciliation. It can then be no surprise that even after the British victory at Guilford Court House (see the next section), the numerous loyalist recruits that were expected failed to turn out.

Despite its disastrous end, the Saratoga campaign had been fundamentally a good idea, because the real seat of the war was in the North. But the British belief in southern loyalism served their amour propre, justified their niggardliness, and suggested an easy way out of their several dilemmas. In overestimating the strength of southern loyalism, the British underestimated the weakness of their own position. And even if the southern colonies had contained great numbers of loyalists willing and able to bear arms, their mere mobilization would not in itself have ended the war: true peace, lasting peace would have required not only arming the loyalists but also reconciling the rebels.[46] In fact those two aims—militarizing the southern loyalists and pacifying the southern colonies—worked against one another. Shifting the emphasis to the southern theater was therefore a sign not of strategic rejuvenation but of strategic bankruptcy. In any event, the ill-founded and self-serving British belief in a sizable and available southern loyalism was the primary and decisive factor in the final and calamitous act.

The Invasion of the Carolinas

Aside from the mistaken expectation of loyalist support, concentrating efforts on the southern colonies was not in itself a terrible idea, if only because it would reduce the area over which the British had to deploy their less than abundant forces. And the British campaign to subdue the South opened brilliantly enough. There was in all the Carolinas only one real city, Charleston, the principal port south of Philadelphia, with a population of 14,000 people, of whom a third were slaves. Gen. Sir Henry Clinton attacked Charleston in February 1780. Given the population of South Carolina of that time, Clinton's army of more than 8,000 soldiers was equivalent to an American force of 400,000 landing in Cuba in 1999. Overconfident because they had repulsed a British amphibious attack in 1776, the American troops let themselves be trapped in Charleston, which fell on May 12, 1780, and 5,400 American soldiers became prisoners. It was "the greatest disaster suffered by the Americans throughout the war." British casualties were amazingly light, perhaps 268 killed and wounded; American casualties were not much higher.[47] The British did not leave the city until December 14, 1782, more than a year after Yorktown.

After the occupation of Charleston, Clinton returned to New York, leaving Gen. Charles Cornwallis in charge of about 8,300 British, Hessian, and loyalist troops.[48] In 1780 Cornwallis, at forty-three, was tall and handsome. He had fought in Europe during the Seven Years' War, becoming a colonel at age twenty-eight. A civilized man with the broad vision of a true statesman, while a member of Parliament he had opposed the tax measures that had helped bring on the American rebellion. Even as the conflict entered its fifth year, Cornwallis was convinced that reconciliation with the Americans was not only possible but imperative. Hence he hoped to win over the southern colonists, not to beat them, and certainly not to cow them into resentful submission. After all, the Americans were all the king's subjects, and most of them were of British stock, like Cornwallis himself (and weren't most of them loyalists, at least at heart?). Understanding Cornwallis's perspective explains a good deal about his military operations in the Carolinas.

Although they had taken Charleston with ease, the British still faced the inescapable facts of American geography. North Carolina, South Carolina, and Virginia together were larger than all Britain and Ireland combined, larger than post–World War II Poland, three times the size of the former East Germany. South Carolina alone, with thirty-one thousand square miles, was larger than Scotland, twice the size of Switzerland, and three-fifths the size of England itself. The population of South Carolina in 1780, however, amounted to only 180,000, and the majority were slaves. Along the coast were plantations with numerous slaves; in the interior were small farms worked almost exclusively by free men. It would not be easy for a substantial British force to find sufficient supplies in such circumstances—especially since the area was aswarm with guerrillas. Loyalist and patriot bands fought each other with fury: South Carolina after the British took Charleston was convulsed by "a civil war, and it was marked by bitterness, violence, and malevolence such as only a civil war can engender."[49]

Nevertheless, three months after the capture of Charleston, Cornwallis marched out of the city into the heart of South Carolina. At Camden on August 16, 1780, he encountered the army of General Gates, the man who had claimed most of the credit for the victory at Saratoga. The Battle of Camden turned into "the most disastrous defeat ever inflicted on an American army." Of the American force of 4,000, only 700 were later able to reassemble. British casualties totaled a derisory 324, of which 68 were mortal. Leaving his stricken soldiers behind, General Gates galloped away from the scene of the debacle and covered 180 miles in three days, surely something of a record in the annals of equestrian transport.[50] Soon there was not one single organized company of American troops to challenge the British enemy anywhere in all of South Carolina. Even the state's American governor had gone away.

Following the victory at Camden, General Clinton urged a conservative strategy: Cornwallis would hold South Carolina and Georgia, while Clinton himself continued to occupy New York City and its environs, until the rebels wore themselves out. Britain would thereby preserve some, and perhaps recoup all, of her colonies. In light of what transpired before and after, Clinton's conception was sound. But Cornwallis's thoughts had turned toward invading North Carolina. The smashing defeat of the rebel army at Camden had not put a lasting stop to resistance in South Carolina; Francis Marion and Thomas Sumter and other partisan chiefs stubbornly kept the war going (see the next section). Cornwallis reasoned that these guerrillas must be getting assistance from North Carolina, and so there he must go. Even before Camden, Cornwallis had been considering an invasion of the interior of North Carolina as the cheapest way to put an end to the guerrillas in South Carolina, cutting them off from supplies and recruits. And he would be able to chase away the little American army under Nathanael Greene, extinguishing the last flickering hope of the local guerrillas for assistance. He also expected to be able to harass Virginia from a new base in North Carolina. Inexorably his logic would lead him to conclude that permanent victory in North Carolina required the occupation of Virginia. "The cost of such an invasion he assessed lightly."[51] In this way Cornwallis was unwittingly—and literally—moving toward an acknowledgment that the true seat of the war did not lie in the southern colonies.

And so a British army embarked on a campaign that would take it far away from the coast of the Atlantic—the first such campaign since the disaster at Saratoga. Reaching Charlotte, North Carolina, early in October, Cornwallis heard the news of the battle at King's Mountain. There, on October 7, 1780, irregular American units had annihilated a British force of one thousand, mainly loyalists. The victors were guerillas and hastily summoned militia, and the battle of King's Mountain was in some senses "a sort of climax of the partisan [i.e., guerrilla] effort." Though an affair of relatively small numbers, the American victory "turned the tide of war in the south" because, filling the patriots of Carolina with fresh hope, it "set ablaze the back settlements."[52] King's Mountain was in effect the Saratoga of the South. Cornwallis prudently headed his army back to South Carolina.

Clinton penned a criticism of Cornwallis's return to South Carolina that is remarkably revealing: "The precipitancy with which this retrograde movement was made contributed, I fear, not a little to make the revolt more general and to increase the despondency of the King's friends, especially in North Carolina, where the loyalists whom [Cornwallis's] presence had encouraged to show themselves, being exposed to persecution and ruin by his retreat, *threw away forever all their confidence of support from the King's army.*"[53] Once again, the British had left their loyalist friends alone to face the Revolutionary music.

In any event, having reentered South Carolina, Cornwallis received reinforcements from Clinton. He now commanded about four thousand men, much better trained, armed, and equipped than Nathanael Greene's army of three thousand "tatterdemalions." Cornwallis divided his army, detaching a large force under Col. Banastre Tarleton to drive Gen. Daniel Morgan's Americans away from his flank while Cornwallis himself marched again into North Carolina to deal with Greene. Tarleton encountered General Morgan at the Battle of the Cowpens (January 17, 1781) and suffered an overwhelming defeat. The British lost 100 killed and 900 prisoners; American casualties were 72. It was the clearest American victory over regular British troops in the entire war. Cornwallis wrote of Cowpens, "The late affair has almost broke my heart." He then conceived the idea that Gen. Nathanael Greene was the mastermind behind all his troubles. Determined to pursue and catch Greene, Cornwallis threw the dice: he burned his own army's baggage train and, with the most minimal supplies, plunged deep into the Carolina interior to keep his rendezvous with destiny.[54]

Nathanael Greene, the target of Cornwallis's expedition, was a forty-year-old former Rhode Islander. The Quakers had expelled him from their midst because he attended a military parade in 1773. He was active in Washington's great Christmas Eve coup that netted numerous Hessian prisoners at Trenton in 1776. As quartermaster general of the Continental army, he had been "Washington's right arm," and after Gates's disgrace at Camden, Washington appointed Greene to command the southern forces. "In the opinion of some well-qualified judges [Greene] was Washington's superior both as strategist and as tactician."[55] The reconquest of Georgia and South Carolina in 1780 was the principal British accomplishment of the entire war; the reversal of the reconquest in 1781 would result from cooperation between General Greene and the southern guerrillas.

Deliberately leaving his supply train far behind, driving himself and his men to the full, Cornwallis caught Greene near Guilford Court House, North Carolina, on March 15, 1781. For Cornwallis, the battle of Guilford Court House was a tactical victory but a strategic defeat. That is, the British were left in possession of the field of combat while the Americans retreated. Technically Cornwallis had won a victory. But the American losses were relatively light and easily replaced, whereas Cornwallis's many casualties could not be replaced at all: "another such victory would mean the end of his army." Cornwallis could win at Camden, and again at Guilford Court House, but to what effect? When beaten, the Americans rose up to renew the struggle, while Cornwallis's own numbers dwindled in a bare and hostile landscape. "Again and again the Americans came forward to accept defeat. The Continental Army's power of recuperation was astounding, and in defeat it had nothing vital to yield." General Greene could suffer one tactical defeat after another, and the war would go on; but let Cornwallis be defeated only once, and British hopes to suppress the Revolution would be as good as finished. Greene is a classic example of a general who loses the battles and wins the war. One eminent authority writes of him, "His keen insight into the heart of Cornwallis's blunders and his skilful use of his guerrilla troops are the most notable features of his work and he seems to me to stand little if at all lower than Washington as a general in the field." He "remains alone as an American master developing a strategy of unconventional [i.e., guerrilla] war."[56] Greene's strategic vision—to wear down the British in cooperation with the guerrillas—was perfect. In the end, what was left of Cornwallis's army would be trapped and taken at Yorktown.[57]

But we are running ahead of the story. After his very costly victory at Guilford Court House, Cornwallis should have once again hastened back to his base in South Carolina—but he did not. And now the partisan war emerges into the center of the drama. In the eighteenth century they called the kind of war that was about to blaze across the Carolinas *la petite guerre*. But there was nothing petite about it in its effects on the outcome of the American Revolution.

Guerrilla War

Reflecting on the most effective way to achieve the pacification of an occupied country, Machiavelli wrote that "of all the methods that can be taken to gain the hearts of a people, none contribute so much as remarkable examples of continence and justice; such was the example of Scipio in Spain when he returned a most beautiful young lady safe and untouched to her father and her husband; this was a circumstance that was more conducive to the reduction of Spain than force of arms could ever have been. Caesar acquired such reputation for his justice in paying for the wood which he cut down to make palisades for his camps in Gaul that it greatly facilitated the conquest of that province." Or, in Shakespeare's words, "when lenity and cruelty play for a kingdom, / the gentler gamester is the soonest winner."[58]

The policies of the British and their loyalist allies were to diverge systematically and decisively from this advice. To begin with, on the morrow of his reconquest of South Carolina, General Clinton insisted that everybody come over openly to the loyalist side. This was a real error. Neutrality was almost as useful as open loyalism for the British war effort: after all, if every single American declared his neutrality, there would be no more war. But Clinton's heavy-handed insistence on forcing a public commitment pushed many neutrals onto the patriot side. "After the British had taken Charleston, many South Carolinians had sworn loyalty to the king. But when the British tried to force these people to fight for the king, the South Carolinians revealed their true loyalties and resisted the British army."[59]

Forcing all oath-takers to fight for the king or face arrest clearly made many recruits for the guerrillas.[60] But this was only the first entry in a list of true British blunders. Predictably, one of the major causes of the guerrilla war that swept across South Carolina after the battle of Camden (and even before) was the regrettable behavior of the British authorities. The Swamp Fox himself, Francis Marion, was deeply impressed with the help the British gave him in this way: "Had the British officers acted as became a wise and magnanimous enemy," he wrote, "they might easily have recovered the revolted colonies."[61] Consider the case of Andrew Pickens, a Revolutionary officer who, after the capture of Charleston, had given his parole to the British that he would fight no more and was living in peaceful quiet. British troops nonetheless came and burned his farm. Pickens thereupon publicly declared that this gratuitous outrage absolved him of his parole. He became a chief of the guerrillas and a sore affliction of the British.

This costly British vindictiveness had one of its main roots in the ever-present chimera of loyalist power. General Clinton sought to occupy all of South Carolina and then return to New York. But since he did not wish to leave behind him enough regular troops to garrison the state properly, he placed much of the responsibility for maintaining royal control in South Carolina in the hands of local loyalists. This was the Achilles' heel of the British plan to subdue the South on the cheap: not only were the loyalists much less numerous than the British had imagined, but also they were often members of marginal groups in society, and too often they were less interested in restoring the king's peace than in avenging themselves on their rebel neighbors. Under the protection of the British occupation, loyalists plundered the property of the patriots. They also liked to burn down churches, especially Presbyterian churches; southern loyalists bitterly viewed the Presbyterians as irredeemably seditious (it was no accident that Andrew Pickens was a Presbyterian elder). In imitation of General Clinton, loyalists insisted that there could be no valid neutrality: one was either openly for the king or else a traitor, to be dealt with as such.[62]

"Nowhere else," writes one distinguished student of these affairs, "did this war show its true character as a civil war so plainly." Indeed, "the bitterness of feeling between the two factions was carried to extremes beyond anything ever experienced in the northern colonies." When Burgoyne's men surrendered at Saratoga and were stacking their arms, General Gates would not let his troops look upon this humiliating act. But southern partisan warfare was a much different matter. "The war that blazed up in the summer of 1780 took on an aspect of vindictiveness and cruelty that at times appalled even the participants themselves."[63] Looting and destruction were common, looting by the loyalists from hostility, looting by the patriots from need. Plunder injured the plundering side, because many men would run straight home with their booty. Both sides carried off the slaves and horses of real or supposed enemies; loyalists and British soldiers often shot milk cows and bayoneted sheep.[64] When the revolutionary governor of South Carolina returned from Philadelphia, where he had been seeking aid, his first act was to issue a proclamation against plundering.

Closely following the looting and destruction of private property came blood reprisals and counterreprisals, in an endlessly escalating cycle. There were many cruel murders in the heat of battle and the chase. At the siege of Fort Balfour, partisans demanded that the British garrison surrender; the demand was rejected. The partisans thereupon stated that if forced to attack, they would give no quarter; with every reason to believe this threat, the commander and his ninety men surrendered. In this particular instance the captured men suffered no reprisals, but there were many other times when no pity was shown. "In the barbaric civil war in eastern Carolina, quarter was seldom asked or given."[65] The killing of fighting men after they had surrendered or asked for mercy was not uncommon: this savage practice was known sarcastically as "Tarleton's Quarter" (that is, "Tarleton's Mercy"); the British colonel Tarleton was notorious for ordering or permitting the killing of wounded and surrendered enemies. Often defectors were forced to prove their new allegiance by killing a member of the side from which they had deserted. One high-ranking British commander even had the corpse of a particular foe disinterred. Describing conditions in South Carolina in 1781, General Greene wrote that "the Whigs [patriots] seemed determined to extirpate the Tories [loyalists] and the Tories the Whigs. . . . If a stop cannot be put to these massacres the country will be depopulated in a few months more, as neither Whig nor Tory can live."[66]

Freebooters added an even more lurid hue to this distressing picture. These were men with no real political allegiance, who sought to take what they could in the general disorder. "There came with the true patriots a host of false friends and plunderers. And this was true of both sides in this terrible struggle. The outlaw Whig and the outlaw Tory, or rather the outlaws who were pretended Whigs and Tories as the occasion served, were laying waste the country almost as much as those who were fighting for the one side or the other." Of such freebooters Sumter wrote, "The dissoluteness of our pretended friends and the ravages committed by them are as alarming and distressing as that of having the enemy among us."[67]

The principal responsibility to stop all this fighting and pseudopolitical criminality rested on the British authorities, and from the beginning they should have exercised much greater control over the loyalists and their own troops. Had they acted thus, they would have been wielding a unique, powerful, but inexpensive weapon: constitutional legitimacy. The British government could claim very plausibly to be defending legality and order against the rule of force.

As in so many other cases, moral duty and strategic interest here coincided: "In the struggle for dominance against the backdrop of revolution, war becomes politics in that victory will be determined by the side that convinces people that it can protect lives and property. Generals who ignore this iron rule are foredoomed to failure."[68]

By allowing conditions in South Carolina and elsewhere to descend to an abysmal level, the British profoundly harmed their own cause, for they made guerrilla warfare inevitable. They trapped themselves in their pipe dream that the loyalists would fight and win the war for them. The loyalists were too few in numbers to carry out their assigned role and too violent not to provoke guerrilla uprisings. But beyond failing to fulfill the responsibilities of a civil government, the British also made their own particular contributions to the general breakdown of society. Not only had the name of one of their officers, Col. Banastre Tarleton, become a slang term for the murder of prisoners; in July 1781, in retribution for patriot plundering, the British burned down Georgetown, South Carolina. Later a British commander, a harbinger of Sherman, laid waste "a swathe fifteen miles wide on the seventy-five mile route from Kingstree to Cheraw." Many of those who joined the revolutionary partisan bands were intensely localist, disinclined to obey orders, opposed to long terms of service, and afraid of British bayonets.[69] But almost all Carolinians were skilled in the use of arms through the exigencies of everyday life and were adaptable and self-sufficient in the inhospitable and mosquito-bitten backcountry where their power lay. The British and their loyalist allies were not prepared for that kind of a conflict, and the flames of guerrilla resistance engulfed them. In the end, British failure to clothe themselves credibly in the robes of civilized lawfulness contributed as much to their undoing as any French fleet.

The guerrilla war in the Carolinas was fought out in "arduous campaigns almost unmentioned upon the pages of history." The battles had names like Nelson's Ferry, Fishdam Ford, Brake of Canes, Rocky Mount. The guerrillas usually went on horseback, giving them all-important mobility. But though they were mounted, they were not true cavalry: they dismounted to fight, often with rifles instead of muskets, which gave them a big advantage over the musket-carrying British infantry. In classic guerrilla style, they "fought only from cover, and ran away that they might live to fight another day." They could hide easily in the forested hills of western South Carolina. "Now they were numbered in hundreds, horse and foot; now, but a dozen bold and hardy followers, white and black. . . . at times they acted in concert with the Continental regulars, at others independently. They were always ready to attack a British outpost, cut off an enemy detachment, a foraging party or wagon train. If defeated, they scattered, took refuge in the swamps and forests, only to reassemble and carry on the fight as occasion served. It was such men that . . . kept the flame of resistance to tyranny alight in the South during the darkest days of the Revolution."[70] They were always short of ammunition, but in contrast to the normal condition in the British camps, the partisans usually had plenty of food: beef, fresh pork, hominy, corn, potatoes, peas.[71]

British and loyalist losses to the partisans after the fall of Charleston amounted to three thousand casualties and prisoners; partisan losses were perhaps one thousand. Eventually "the British conquest of South Carolina crumbled under the nerve-racking strain of a phantom enemy who lurked in every thicket, who struck communications, who always reassembled when dispersed, and who always made necessary the presence of British regulars everywhere at once." Thanks to the operations of the guerrillas, by the dawn of 1781 British pacification of the South had clearly failed; "it was doubtful that the British and Tories controlled ground beyond that upon which they stood."[72]

The Swamp Fox

Among the guerrilla chieftains who "kept the flame of resistance to tyranny alight in the South during the darkest days of the Revolution," the flame that illuminated the road to Yorktown, none is more deserving of an honored place in his country's history than Francis Marion, called the Swamp Fox.

Born about 1732, Marion served as an officer in the provincial forces and was elected to the South Carolina Provincial Congress late in 1774. In November 1776 he became a colonel of the South Carolina state troops. When Charleston and its garrison fell to the British on May 12, 1780, Marion was not present, because he had broken his ankle; by such brittle bones are the destinies of empires swayed. More than once Marion's command constituted the only organized patriot forces in all South Carolina. The British soon learned his name well. Right after the disaster at Camden, he and his men fell upon a detachment of British troops escorting 160 American prisoners to Charleston. Marion freed all the prisoners and made captives of their guards.

Almost as if born to be a famous guerrilla chieftain, Marion was "sparing of words, abstemious in his habits, a strict disciplinarian, ever vigilant and active, fertile of strategems and expedients that justified his nickname of Swamp Fox, quick in conception and equally swift in execution, unrelenting in the pursuit of his purposes, yet void of ruthlessness or cruelty to his victims." He possessed greater strategic sense than Thomas Sumter (see the next section) and was more cooperative toward other guerrilla leaders. Like a true fox of the Carolina swamps, Marion excelled at stealth; one of his favorite tactics was to approach the encamped enemy, send a group of his men to the right and another to the left, and then attack ahead with the main body. Gen. Henry Lee wrote, "Fertile in strategem, he struck unperceived; and retiring to those hidden retreats selected by himself, in the morasses of the Pedee and Black Rivers, he placed his corps not only out of the reach of his foe, but often out of the discovery of his friends."[73]

Revolted by the burning of houses, Marion forbade such activity to his men. In retaliation for British and loyalist house-burning and killing of livestock, especially by the notorious Colonel Tarleton, he permitted his men to kill enemy sentries—an act considered at the time to be quite barbarous. But Marion was not a cruel man. One of his own officers, who had broken with him over the explosive question of rank, nevertheless wrote of him, "He not only prevented cruelty in his own presence, but strictly forbade it in his absence."[74] Marion the warrior had deep religious sentiments and often led his men to church services.

With the insight of a true leader, he shared, and was seen to share, in the physical hardships of those in his charge: "since his men had no tents, he also slept in the open." But most of all, Marion was a cautious commander, very careful with the lives of his followers, "that kind of leader who attracts men, not by a convivial personality or generous nature, but because he wins, and his victories do not cost needless lives." His biographer wrote, "Marion's men loved him." Even Gen. Nathanael Greene, never one to exaggerate the value of guerrillas, wrote that Marion excelled "in all the qualities which form the consummate partisan—vigilance, promptitude, activity, energy, dauntless courage and unshaken self-control."[75]

But these words were penned after the war. In 1780 neither General Greene nor the Continental Congress nor even the South Carolina legislature appreciated the real worth of the partisans, and they gave the partisans no aid. The Swamp Fox and his men thus fought without pay, without recognition, often without ammunition; and many died for want of the most elementary medical attention.[76] Yet even in conditions of shortage and neglect, Marion's followers would distribute to needy civilians the precious salt that they had captured from the British.

Mobility—not for the first or last time—was the foundation of guerrilla success. Marion's "greatest strength was in keeping his men well-mounted, thereby frustrating the designs of a superior force to bring him to decisive action and destroy him." Lord Rawdon wrote to General Clinton on March 23, 1781: "Generals Sumter and Marion, commanding distinct corps, have made some efforts to excite insurrection in this province and to interrupt our supplies from Charleston. As the enemy are all mounted, we have never been able to force them to a decisive battle."[77]

Marion's mobility found its perfect foil in Cornwallis's strategy. In order to maintain at least some minimum of control over large areas of the South Carolina backcountry, General Cornwallis established a line of small forts through the interior of the state. That was not a bad idea in itself. However, the forts ultimately depended on Charleston for most of their supplies, and it was against these vital lines of communication that Marion repeatedly struck. Cornwallis eventually sent the notorious Colonel Tarleton—burner of homes and killer of prisoners—after him, but no one could catch the Swamp Fox. "With a force fluctuating from fifty to two hundred and fifty men, Marion . . . darted upon the enemy whenever an opportunity presented itself. He not only kept in check the small parties of the enemy, whom the want of forage and provisions, or the desire for plunder, occasionally urged into the region east and south of Camden, but he often passed the Santee [River], interrupting the communications with Charleston, and sometimes alarming the small posts in the vicinity . . . and eluded all the attempts made to entrap him." After the patriot victory at King's Mountain, Marion tirelessly roused South Carolina to revolt; he was close to cutting off communications between Charleston and Camden. In fact, "by the end of October [1780] their [the guerrillas'] activities made it impossible for the British to use the Santee River to transport material from the coast to the troops in the interior, a serious situation since Cornwallis was desperately short of wagons and horses." General Cornwallis's frustration is evident in his message to General Clinton of December 3, 1780: "Colonel Marion had so wrought the minds of the people, partly by the terror of his threats and cruelty of his punishments and partly by the promise of plunder, that there was scarce an inhabitant between the Santee and the Pedee that was not in arms against us. Some parties had even crossed the Santee and carried terror to the gates of Charleston."[78] Thus the Fox penned up the Lion.

In spite of these manifest successes, Marion had to cope with a frustrating pattern of patriot behavior: once they had subdued or chased out the local loyalists, many of his men would return to their homes for indefinite periods. He seldom commanded exactly the same men for more than two weeks at a time. Worn down by this indiscipline, as well as by all his other hardships and responsibilities, in May 1781 Marion was ready to lay aside his command. But General Greene successfully entreated him to carry on. Greene was setting forth the merest truth in a letter to Marion: "History affords no instance wherein an officer has kept possession of a country under so many disadvantages as you have. Surrounded on every side with a superior force, hunted from every quarter by veteran troops, you have found means to elude all their attempts, and to keep alive the expiring hopes of an oppressed militia, when all succour seemed to be cut off. To fight the enemy bravely with a prospect of victory is nothing; but to fight with intrepidity under the constant impression of defeat, and inspire irregular troops to do it, is a talent peculiar to yourself."[79]

The Gamecock

Another Carolina leader who emblazoned his name across the record of guerrilla warfare was Thomas Sumter. Born in 1734, near Charlottesville, Virginia, he received little formal schooling, not unusual for that time and place. Nor was it unusual, in speculative and underpopulated colonial South Carolina, that he did a couple of stints in jail for debt. Serving in the French and Indian War, he went to London in company with some Indian chiefs in 1762. A few years later he married a much-propertied widow a decade older than himself. As the American Revolution drew nearer, Sumter was a small plantation owner; he was also a Baptist—and an Episcopalian. No doubt this ecclesial broad-mindedness helped elect him to the First and the Second South Carolina Provincial Congresses in 1775 and 1776. Although he held a colonel's commission in the Continental army, he found his military activities frustrating and in 1778 retired to his plantation. But after the fall of Charleston in 1780, the British sacked and burned Sumter's house. Like an outraged lion he roared back into the conflict, to become "the hero who first had roused the Carolinians after the fall of Charleston."[80] The causes and consequences of Sumter's reentry into the fray, reminiscent of Andrew Pickens's, are surely unanswerable proofs that when those who claim lawful authority act in an illegal and vengeful manner, or permit their subordinates so to act, they are guilty of profound folly.

In June 1780 the South Carolina militia elected Sumter to be a general. The men under his command supposedly were enlisted "until the war was at an end or until their services were no longer necessary[;] they were to find their own horses, arms, clothing and all necessaries. It being absolutely necessary that they should act on horse back." But spring plowing was a job for men and horses, not wives and children, and so the partisans would have to go home for that. Nevertheless, Sumter often led several hundred men at a time into battle. At Hanging Rock, his men killed or captured more than 200 of the enemy, along with 100 horses and 250 muskets; partisan losses were but 20 killed and 40 wounded.[81]

As with the ancient Romans, so with the Carolina guerrillas (and General Greene, and indeed the American Revolutionaries in general), resilience was a major weapon. In August 1780, just days after the disaster at Camden, the British surprised Sumter in his camp at Fishing Creek. The Americans lost a stunning 450 casualties and prisoners. Yet within a week of the debacle, Sumter had reorganized his forces and was back in the field. He himself suffered wounds, and he carried a price of five hundred guineas on his head.[82]

The guerrillas never had enough ammunition. They sometimes employed squirrel rifles and homemade swords against British regulars. Cannons were usually unobtainable, even for an attack on a fortified post. Although Sumter was presumably ignorant of Roman siege methods, at least once he built a Roman-style tower of wooden rails, exposing to disconcerting fire British and loyalist troops who had imagined themselves safe behind the walls of their fort. He even made his men don wooden armor, which seems at least on occasion to have protected them from the fire of British and loyalist muskets. When not actually fighting or preparing to fight, the guerrillas needed to be kept active or they would drift back home. Rejecting the nonsense of close-order drilling, Sumter trained his men through swimming and running, leaping and wrestling.[83]

Like the Afghan mujahideen two centuries later, Sumter's partisans sometimes distributed food to the destitute civilian population. They employed Catawba Indians for the specialized service of tracking loyalists who lurked in the swamps. Sumter and his men furnished General Greene with valuable intelligence, priceless supplies, and tactical cover for the movements of his troops. Most of all, the guerrillas exhausted the British forces with ceaseless alarms and pursuits and searches. In these ways they made an effective British concentration against Greene's army nearly impossible. It was thus for good reason that in August 1780 Clinton received complaints from Cornwallis about the "indefatigable Sumter."[84]

The services rendered to the American cause by the Gamecock (as he came to be known) were significant. But so were his flaws. He did not submit with grace to authority. He and his men disliked the command of General Greene, and there was much misunderstanding and friction between regulars and guerrillas. In this Sumter and his men were not unique: "the Carolina Partisans were patriotic, but they were also independent, jealous, and self-willed." But there was more. Sumter paid his followers by taking the slaves from loyalists ("Sumter's Law") and distributing them among the guerrillas according to a fixed scale (three and a half for a colonel, one and a half for a lieutenant, one for a private). Marion the Swamp Fox deplored this depressing trade in human flesh because it was cruel and also because it stirred class hatred. Above all, Sumter was, in his biographer's words, "reckless of his own life and prodigal with the lives of his men."[85] Marion came to be very critical of Sumter's indifference to loss of life in his battles and declined ever to serve under his command. After the war Light Horse Harry Lee wrote: "He was not overly scrupulous as a soldier in his use of means and was apt to make considerable allowances for a state of war. . . . enchanted with the splendor of victory, he would wade through torrents of blood to obtain it." So it was that by the summer of 1781, at least in the eyes of some of his critics, "General Sumter [had] become almost universally odious."[86]

Clearly, Sumter had his share and more of shortcomings and even sins. But his portrait is in no way complete. There was in him as well an inclination to mercy toward the vanquished. A prisoner of his, for example, a wounded British officer, later wrote, "It is but doing bare justice to General Sumter to declare that the strictest humanity took place . . . [we] were supplied with every comfort in his power." Another time Sumter discovered that one of his prisoners—a loyalist officer, no less—was carrying a list of houses he had caused to be burned. Few would have condemned Sumter if he had handed this wretched man over to a certain lynching; instead, Sumter threw the paper into the fire.[87] And as the war wound to a close, Sumter often accepted repentant loyalist soldiers into his own ranks, probably preserving them from a harsh fate and certainly contributing to eventual reconciliation after the war.

Symbiotic cooperation between regular forces and guerrillas can generate tremendous power, and nothing better illustrates this principle than the Carolina campaign. Though the Afghan mujahideen brought their guerrilla war against the Soviet invaders to a successful conclusion without the presence of a friendly regular army, and Fidel Castro also won without such help, instances of this kind are rare. On the subject of guerrilla war, Greene wrote truly (if somewhat gracelessly): "The salvation of this country doesn't depend upon little strokes, nor should the great business of establishing a permanent army be neglected to pursue them . . . *You may strike a hundred strokes and reap little benefit unless you have a good army to take advantage of your success.*" Here is where Greene's regulars come into the guerrilla picture. In order to pursue and catch the guerrillas, British forces needed to subdivide themselves into compact, swiftly moving, long-ranging patrols. But with Greene's American army in the area, such roving bands of British or loyalist troops could fall prey to superior numbers. Thus the presence of Greene's forces—of a friendly regular army—in their vicinity protected the partisans. But in their turn the guerrillas were of incalculable benefit to Greene: they wore the enemy out in endless chases, inflicted small but accumulating numbers of casualties on them, and most of all prevented them from gathering sufficient provisions. Greene took a bold gamble and divided his army into two parts; he knew that Cornwallis, ea- ger to capture or disperse both wings of the American army, would do the same. But the division of British forces left each segment more vulnerable to guerrillas. So wide-ranging were Marion's men that the mere threat of them became almost as effective as their actual presence: never able to know where they would most likely strike next, the British were compelled to detach soldiers from their main force to strengthen isolated garrisons, provide convoy protection, or just limit the sweep of Marion's operations.[88] The fact is that "Greene could hardly have kept the field without the aid of Marion, Sumter, Pickens . . . and the Partisans." The result of this coopera- tion between Continental regulars and Carolina partisans was that "the [British] army was a ship; where it moved in power it com- manded, but around it was the hostile sea, parting in front but clos- ing in behind, and always probing for signs of weakness. . . . Whereas a defeated American army could melt back into the countryside from whence it came, a British force so circumscribed was likely to be totally lost."[89]

On to Yorktown

To review briefly: after General Clinton captured Charleston in May 1780, he returned to New York, while General Cornwallis remained in command of the southern army, made up of about 8,300 British, Hessian, and loyalist troops. In the following August these troops won another notable victory at Camden. But in October the Ameri- cans scored a resounding success at King's Mountain; then in Janu- ary 1781 the British suffered another disaster at the Cowpens. In reaction, later that same month Cornwallis burned his supply wag- ons and set out at the head of a part of his forces in pursuit of Gen- eral Greene's American army. Greene led Cornwallis into North Carolina and across it, farther and farther away from the Englishman's base of supply. Cornwallis expected (of course) to re- ceive crucial civilian support in North Carolina and met (of course) disappointment: the splendid vision of loyalist throngs had drawn the British first to Charleston and now deep into North Carolina.

Cornwallis won at Guilford Court House in March 1781, but with 500 British casualties out of an army of 1,900, his victory was again a Pyrrhic one.[90]

With his forces so depleted, Cornwallis was too weak to pursue and finish Greene. Like Hannibal in Italy, Cornwallis could best his enemies on the field but could not obtain adequate replacements. Winning battles but losing men, starved of supplies and deprived of rest by the ever-present partisans, his army was bleeding to death one drop at a time. "I have experienced the daggers and distresses of marching some hundreds of miles in a country chiefly hostile," he wrote, "without one active or useful friend [note well!], without intelligence, and without communications with any part of the country." Sickness and desertion were taking a mounting toll. And so Cornwallis retreated to the North Carolina coast, seeking refuge at Wilmington, which his army entered on April 7. The original purpose in invading North Carolina had been to catch Greene and to cut off assistance to the guerrillas in South Carolina. But in Wilmington Cornwallis changed his plan. He might have decided to return to South Carolina to bind up his army's wounds and solidify control of that state. Or he might have decided to stay along the North Carolina coast, resting his soldiers and building up supplies. Instead he gave up on the Carolinas altogether and marched into Virginia. Cornwallis's rationale for moving ever northward was this: Greene's army prevented Cornwallis from dealing effectively with the Carolina partisans; but Greene's army received supplies and recruits from Virginia; and so there Cornwallis would go. What he would do after that he probably had no idea. Abandoning the Carolinas for Virginia was a far cry from the original plan, by which he would first reconquer South Carolina and then move systematically north, to the heartfelt cheers of innumerable and generous loyalists, to subdue Virginia. And so "on May 13 [1781] he crossed his Rubicon, the Roanoke River (the boundary between North Carolina and Virginia)."[91] From there he would eventually march to the fateful precincts of Yorktown.

In leaving North Carolina before it had been pacified, Cornwallis was also leaving the British forces in South Carolina on their own. His invasion of Virginia thus doomed British control of South Carolina and of remote Georgia as well. Cornwallis had been relying on a string of small garrisons to hold South Carolina while he chased

Greene's army across North Carolina. But once Cornwallis abandoned North Carolina for Virginia, there was nothing to stop Greene from reentering South Carolina and gobbling up the British outposts there, which is exactly what he did. The British had fallen into the classic trap of those who would fight guerrillas: they built small outposts that they could not sustain. The smaller outposts could be starved out by Marion's partisans or overwhelmed by Greene's regulars. Of course the British were free to consolidate their small posts into larger ones, but the large garrisons would be neither numerous enough to prevent the partisans from controlling and organizing the countryside nor large enough to stand up individually to a determined assault by Greene. Thus, even though British forces in the province outnumbered his men, Greene was able to roll up their chain of outposts one link after another, capturing many British troops and sending the rest scurrying for safety into Charleston. These British troops had been too few to hold South Carolina, but they would have been of inestimable use to Cornwallis in North Carolina or Virginia. In the end "the British were pressed rapidly back until nothing remained of their southern conquests beyond the neighborhoods of Charleston and Savannah. These they held till the peace."[92]

Cornwallis had repaired to Yorktown to await succor from the invincible Royal Navy. Instead, he found himself facing a powerful French fleet that shut him off from the sea, and two armies, one French and one American (Washington's), that hemmed him in on the land side. Cornwallis surrendered at Yorktown exactly four years after Burgoyne had surrendered at Saratoga. A British relief force did indeed arrive at Yorktown by sea, but on October 24, just days too late to save Cornwallis. And when after their surrender the British forces left Virginia behind, they left many loyalists behind as well, this not for the first time.[93] Thus ended the second, and the last, of the great British campaigns to subdue the rebellious colonies.

The events at Yorktown, even more than those at Saratoga, produced consternation and exasperation in England. Prime Minister Lord North took the news "as he would have taken a ball in the breast."[94] The fall of Yorktown in 1781 had an effect similar to that of the fall of Dien Bien Phu in 1954. The British had lost only one of their three armies in America, and that was the smallest of them. Even without Cornwallis's seven thousand troops, they still had thirty thousand soldiers in America, and they held New York, Savannah, and Charleston. Moreover, the American forces themselves faced many serious problems, military, political and financial. But the shock of Yorktown came after many years of fighting a less than glorious and less than popular war. And it came at a time when Fortune had deserted the British in other places: they had tasted defeat not only in Virginia but also in India and the Caribbean; furthermore, there was the perpetual fear of an invasion of England itself. England was fighting a world war alone, while the number of her enemies—the Americans, the French, the Spanish, the Dutch— was growing. British-American peace negotiations began soon after Yorktown, producing a preliminary treaty in November 1782 and the final Treaty of Paris in September 1783.

Yorktown, where Britain's American empire had its end, is about sixteen miles from Jamestown, where it had had its beginning.

Instead of holding Cornwallis responsible for the debacle at Yorktown, after the American war the British twice made him governor general of India and also viceroy of Ireland. He died in 1805. The British reluctance to blame their American defeat on a particular military leader indicates a conclusion on their part that the conflict had been ill-starred from the beginning.

Gen. Nathanael Greene's untimely death in 1786, before his forty-fourth birthday, undoubtedly deprived his country of important services, including much good advice during the War of 1812.

After the Revolution the South Carolina legislature passed bills to protect former guerrilla leaders from lawsuits arising out of the wartime destruction. Francis Marion had emerged from the war in seriously straitened financial circumstances. He nevertheless refused to accept this legal protection, declaring that during the conflict he had acted rightly, and if not, then he must make restitution. Marion served in the South Carolina constitutional convention of 1790 and later in the state senate. He died in 1795. South Carolina named a county in his honor.

As for the Gamecock, after the Revolution Thomas Sumter's neighbors elected him to the Continental Congress, an honor that he declined. He later spent several terms in the South Carolina House of Representatives. And eventually he did go on to the national Congress, serving in the first U.S. House of Representatives in 1789 and in the U.S. Senate from 1801 to 1810. Afterward he was President

Madison's ambassador to Brazil. Sumter lived to be almost one hundred years old, surviving the battle of Yorktown by half a century. He was the last of the Revolutionary commanders to die. Like Marion, Sumter had a county in South Carolina named after him. But what most indelibly inscribed Sumter's name on the pages of American history was a fort in Charleston Harbor.

Reflection

In 1776 the Americans were few in number, scattered along the edges of an undeveloped continent, and deeply divided on the issue of independence. For them to win their struggle against the mighty British empire, many factors clearly had to come together. Any list of the most crucial of these factors would include disquiet regarding the conflict within England itself; the vast extent of the American colonies; their distance from the mother country in an age of tenuous communications; the relative technological parity between the British and Continental armies; and perhaps above all the quality of American leadership, most especially that of George Washington: clearsighted in strategy, steadfast in defeat, trusted by all.[95]

But for the purposes of this study, two other aspects of the conflict stand out. The first is foreign assistance to the forces of independence. There is probably no more clear-cut example of the importance of outside help to the success of an insurgency than the American War of Independence. And there is no better demonstration of the value of that help than the battle of Yorktown, in which Cornwallis faced nine thousand American and eight thousand French troops, while a powerful French fleet under Adm. le comte de Grasse closed off any possibility of either escape or rescue. The French navy indeed played a role of greatest significance in the American Revolution. Its vessels carried French troops to America as well as gold, clothing, and cannons to Washington's army. French warships kept the specter of invasion luridly before British eyes, and they often interrupted the already quite tenuous system whereby the British supplied their forces in America. The unreliability of supply in turn forced British armies to stay fairly close to the seacoast most of the time; this did little for their self-confidence, and when the French navy was in a position to operate in American waters in strength, the result was disaster for the British. And of course important British military and naval units were unavailable for service in America because of hostilities not only with France but also with Spain and the Netherlands. The Spanish operated against Gibraltar and augmented the French invasion threat against England, and the fiercest naval battle of the war took place between British and Dutch squadrons off the Dogger Bank in 1781.[96] It is difficult to grasp why the British cabinet failed to see the inevitability of foreign intervention and the decisive effects it must have on the course of the American war, but the British would repay the French a quarter-century later in Spain.

A second aspect of supreme importance was systematic British miscalculation about the kind of challenge they were facing in America. It was clear from the beginning that the British ruling classes did not want to pay very much for the suppression of the Americans; in other words, they did not want to send Clinton and Cornwallis enough soldiers with which to get on with their tasks. The defeat at Saratoga sent a clear message to London about the nature of the war, but the cabinet did not wish to receive it: refusing to recognize the seriousness of the war, they failed to put up the money and effort to win it. By 1780 the meaning of the war was clearer than ever, and the British government should have made peace either with the Americans or with the French.[97] Instead, unwilling to grapple with grim financial, geographical, and strategic facts, they sought solace in their mantras about submerged but potent popular support and invaded the Carolinas.

And by this route we come, as Cornwallis did, to the American guerrillas. Unsung then as now, they nonetheless stand in the center of the Carolina campaign, which played such a signal role in the outcome of the war. In the dark night following the American catastrophe at Camden, they alone kept the flame of resistance alive. When General Greene arrived to take command of the small regular American forces in the South, the guerrillas were ready to cooperate with him. And on notable occasions many guerrillas fought as regular formations within his army, as at Eutaw Springs, "bloodiest battle of the southern campaign."[98]

One cannot sufficiently stress the importance to the final victory of the symbiotic relationship between Greene's regulars and the Carolina partisans. The presence of Greene's army prevented the British from dispersing into small groups to hunt down the guerrillas. In turn the guerrillas both cowed the loyalists and buzzed around the fringes of the British forces, harassing their communications, inflicting casualties, depriving of them of food and rest, wearing them down. General Cornwallis identified Greene's little army as his strategic target, but he lacked sufficient troops to simultaneously defeat Greene and hold South Carolina against the partisans. In short, the guerrilla bands both distracted Cornwallis from his main objective and rendered merely nominal his control of the Carolinas. The unreliability and inadequacy of supplies and replacements from England magnified the importance of the guerrillas, who operated so effectively against the foraging efforts of British troops. It was primarily the unrelenting guerrilla activity after Camden that convinced Cornwallis to make his fateful incursion into North Carolina, and then the same conditions drew him farther north into Virginia—into Yorktown.[99]

The guerrillas had "by their own unaided efforts, broken up the plans of the enemy, and disconcerted their schemes of campaign for the whole country. The advantages of their uprising had not been confined to South Carolina or even the South. It is not presumptuous to say that they had done as much to save Washington's army from destruction in its time of weakness, and to render Yorktown possible."[100] That is the truth, simple and incalculable, about the Swamp Fox, the Gamecock, and the guerrillas of Carolina.

IOWA

NEBRASKA

● St. Joseph

Missouri River

Centralia ●

Topeka
●

● Independence

Lecompton ●

● Kansas City

Lawrence ●

Jefferson City ●

KANSAS

MISSOURI

———
25 miles

Baxter Springs ●

OKLAHOMA

ARKANSAS

Map produced by Anne Szewczyk.

The Missouri-Kansas Border, circa 1861.

2

Confederate Guerrillas

The War of Secession

On December 3, 1861, President Abraham Lincoln sent his annual message to Congress, expressing the hope that the war, already nearly a year old, would not descend into a "violent and remorseless revolutionary struggle." Yet that was exactly the sort of struggle that would emerge, in the form of Emancipation, Sherman's campaigns through Georgia and Carolina, and guerrilla warfare.[1]

Slowly falling back in the face of Union advances, Confederate forces in the West moved closer to their bases of supply and were in friendly territory. In contrast, as the Federal armies inexorably advanced into rebel territory, they moved farther away from their bases. Thus, the longer the war continued, the longer became the communications lines of the Union forces. The railways made steady Federal movement into the South possible, but they were vulnerable to disruption and destruction by Southern guerrillas. The Confederacy, with its great spaces, rural society, and rudimentary transportation system, was close to ideal for guerrillas; their raids against railway supply lines forced the Federals to use great numbers of troops to guard their rear areas.[2] Guerrilla operations of this type were more important in Tennessee and adjacent areas than in Virginia because supply lines for both sides were shorter in Virginia.

On February 17, 1863, President Lincoln wrote to Gen. William Rosecrans, "In no way does the enemy give us so much trouble, at so little expense to himself, as by the raids of rapidly-moving small bodies of troops (largely if not wholly mounted) harassing and discouraging loyal residents, supplying themselves with provisions, clothing, horses and the like, surprising and capturing small detachments of our forces, and breaking our communications." General Sherman seconded Lincoln's observation: "Though our armies pass across and through the land, the war closes in behind and leaves the same enemy behind."[3]

Efforts to ward off guerrilla raids caused a tremendous dispersion of Federal forces. At the height of the crucial Vicksburg campaign in 1863, General Grant had 60,000 men at the battlefront while fully an additional 40,000 were employed against guerrillas and raiders. And in the worst days of the counterguerrilla campaign in Missouri (see the section titled "The Engulfing Flames" below), the activities of 3,000 or 4,000 partisans absorbed the attention of 60,000 Union soldiers.[4] Clearly, Confederate guerrilla warfare diverted many Union soldiers from the principal fronts. Two aspects of this guerrilla warfare are especially noteworthy: Confederate regulars employing guerrilla tactics behind Union lines in northern Virginia; and pro-Confederate civilian insurgents in Kansas and Missouri engaging in the notorious "border war."

Mosby in Virginia

Among Confederate guerrilla leaders, perhaps the most successful, and certainly one of the most famous, was John Singleton Mosby. Born in Powhatan County, Virginia, on December 6, 1833, as a youth he was of very delicate health; many who knew him in his teens predicted that his life would not be a long one. But near the end of an exceptionally long life, he wrote triumphantly, "I have outlived nearly all the contemporaries of my youth."[5] Mosby attended the University of Virginia for a while, where he excelled in languages and literature but not in mathematics. In the years before the war, he successfully practiced law in Virginia, despite (or perhaps because of) having had to serve a term in prison in 1853 for wounding a local bully.

As the clouds of secession gathered, the young Virginia attorney strongly supported Stephen Douglas and the Union. A friend once asked what he would do if South Carolina were to secede: "I told him I would be on the side of the Union."[6] But when Virginia went out, John Mosby, like Robert E. Lee and so many others, went out with it, enlisting as a private in the state army. Federal troops took Mosby prisoner in July 1862; they exchanged him for a Union lieutenant (who was never heard of again). Surely the freeing of Mosby must rank not far below the shooting of Stonewall Jackson in the list of fateful accidents of the war.

Military life agreed with Mosby. Certainly it did not depress his intellectual appetite: a December 1862 letter to his wife asks her to send him his copies of Plutarch, Macaulay, Scott, Shakespeare, and Byron.[7]

Early in 1863 Gen. Jeb Stuart sent Mosby with 15 men to operate behind Union lines. From this little band would evolve the Forty-third Battalion of Virginia Cavalry, soon to be known as Mosby's Partisan Rangers. During the course of the war, Mosby enrolled a total of 1,900 men into his Partisan Rangers; when the war finally ended, he still commanded about 700. Mosby apparently never employed more than 300 men in a single operation because a larger movement would have been too easy for the Federals to detect and intercept.

Mosby's Men

What kind of men were Mosby's Rangers? Mostly they were "farmers, carpenters, livestock breeders, teachers, merchants and business men." A few, like Mosby himself, were lawyers, and at least one was a Baptist minister. Most of them were in their teens or early twenties; Mosby observed, "They haven't the sense to know danger when they see it."[8] Mosby operated mainly in Loudon and Fauquier Counties in northern Virginia, and over 80 percent of his recruits came from that state. The terrain in that part of the Old Dominion was well suited to guerrilla operations.

"The military value of a partisan's work," Mosby wrote, "is not measured by the amount of property destroyed or the number of men killed or captured, but in the number [of enemy soldiers] he keeps watching."[9] The aim of Mosby's Rangers therefore became rendering any movement in their area so dangerous that Union troops would be able to pass through safely only in large numbers. "In general it was my purpose to threaten and harass the enemy on the border and in this way compel him to withdraw troops from his front to guard the lines of the Potomac and Washington. This would greatly diminish his offensive power." Mosby also liked to derail and loot trains, even if they carried numerous armed guards. But so many Union soldiers were deployed to protect Gen. George Meade's railway supply line in northern Virginia that Mosby's campaign to disrupt it was not a success.[10]

Fame attached to Mosby and his Rangers with the capture of Brig. Gen. Edwin H. Stoughton in a daring nighttime raid near Fairfax Courthouse in March 1863. On another occasion he and five of his men rode right into Union-occupied Alexandria in an attempt to kidnap the Unionist governor of West Virginia. But the normal warfare of the Partisan Rangers consisted of small, sharp actions. For example, in July 1863 Mosby's men captured 186 Union soldiers, 123 horses and mules, and a great quantity of weapons. On one raid they grabbed $173,000 cash; they took another $112,000 from a military wagon train. Mosby's style was exceedingly aggressive. He once wrote, "If you are going to fight, then be the attacker."[11] Mosby's men were mounted on good horses. The standard civil war image of mounted combat calls to mind sabres glistening in the sun, but the usual armament of the Rangers consisted of two .44 caliber Army Colt revolvers. Armed with their pistols, Mosby said, "my men were as little impressed by a body of men charging them with sabres as though they had been armed with cornstalks." To be effective, Colt revolvers had to be used at fairly close quarters; in this context it deserves notice that, unlike other guerrillas, Mosby's rangers never wore Federal disguise.[12]

Mosby often violated one of the most sacred of guerrilla principles, by leading his men in attacks on Union targets even when they were outnumbered, relying on surprise or entrapment. For instance, a few of Mosby's men would fire some shots at a group of Federals, who would then pursue them only to fall into a two-sided trap. In this way Mosby defeated a superior force of Michigan cavalry at Rector's Crossroads in June 1863. In January 1864 he attacked 300 Federals with only 100 of his own men. On that particular occasion, because the winter weather was harsh, the Union soldiers had posted no outside sentries! This appalling breach of standard procedure and good sense was apparently common on both sides. As late as January 1865, about 40 Partisans successfully attacked close to 100 Pennsylvania cavalry.[13] More than once such habitual bravado caused Mosby to suffer a serious wound.

Intelligence naturally played a vital role in the guerrilla struggle. Mosby collected much information from local young women who patriotically flirted with Union officers.[14] On the other side, Federal partisan-hunters picked up valuable leads from former Rangers who had turned against the Confederate cause or nursed some grudge against Mosby.

Union commanders in northern Virginia never committed enough men to deal with Mosby; they had bigger fish to fry in front of Richmond. But inevitably, Mosby's activities brought down retaliation by Union troops upon the heads of the local population. In August 1864 Maj. Gen. Christopher Augur, commander of the Washington area, told his troops to "destroy, as far as possible, the sources from which Mosby draws men, horses, and support." The Federals burned houses known to be used for rendezvous by Mosby's men. In November 1864 General Sheridan ordered a wide swath of northwest Virginia cleared of all sustenance. He forbade the burning of houses or the killing of civilians, but crops and barns were given the torch. Many who suffered these losses were Unionists or peaceful Quakers. Mosby's men often shot captured Federal farm-burners with his approval. Nevertheless, Federal destructiveness caused many civilians in the area to turn away from Mosby and his men, who eventually found themselves without sufficient provisions. As the frightfulness of the war inexorably increased, Gen. Henry Halleck gave approval to the summary execution of captured guerrillas as well as their known sympathizers.[15] Grant told Sheridan, "Wherever any of Mosby's men are caught, hang them without trial." But Sheridan did not always follow this order. And in November 1864 Mosby and Sheridan agreed through correspondence not to kill prisoners.[16]

Mosby's Confederate Critics

The Confederacy could never finally decide how it felt about its own guerrillas. In April 1862 the Confederate Congress enacted laws on the status of partisans. One result was that Mosby's band became a unit of the Army of Northern Virginia, under Lee's command. In March 1863 Mosby received the rank of major. From that time he usually signed his communications to his superiors "Major of Partisan Rangers." Nevertheless, the upper ranks of the Confederate officer corps looked upon guerrillas, including Mosby and his men, with distaste and even apprehension. In their view guerrillas were hard to control and did not always share the concepts or aims of those supposedly directing them—even on so fundamental a question as "who is the enemy." For example, Mosby's men sometimes fought against other groups of Confederate guerrillas who inhabited the mountainous areas of northwest Virginia and whom the Rangers looked upon as undisciplined. Regular officers also criticized the Rangers because they believed that the partisans' relaxed and romantic lifestyle undermined discipline among regular troops. For instance, Rangers kept a great deal of the plunder from their raids. Although that was in accordance with Confederate law, some observers believed the hope of plunder to be "the cohesive force of the Ranger service."[17] When not actually fighting, they were at leisure, which was most of the time. Perhaps most irritating to the regulars, Mosby's men often stayed overnight or longer with civilians in their homes in northern Virginia. It was particularly in these unmilitary circumstances that surprise Union sweeps would capture groups of Rangers. During one such operation the Federals rounded up no less than twenty-eight of Mosby's men. In December 1864 Federal searchers surprised Mosby himself in a private home; the partisan leader narrowly escaped arrest and suffered a gunshot wound. The Federal unit most successful against Mosby's Rangers was known as Blazer's Scouts. These guerrilla-chasers acted with decency toward the civilians of Virginia, who consequently did not automatically flee when the Scouts approached; thus, Blazer's men often entered guerrilla areas without a general alarm being raised and apprehended quite a few of Mosby's men.[18]

Some critics of the Rangers maintained that they actually assisted the Union side because their presence in an area discouraged Yankee soldiers from straggling or deserting. In 1864 Robert E. Lee wrote, "Experience has convinced me that it is impossible under the best officers even, to have discipline in these bands of Partisan Rangers, or to prevent them from becoming an injury instead of a benefit to the service." In the face of such general disapproval, in February 1864 the Confederate Congress repealed the legal authorization for partisans. All guerrillas were now to become affiliated with regular Confederate army units—but not Mosby's Rangers. The Congress specifically exempted his group, plus one other partisan band.[19]

The noted Civil War historian Bruce Catton wrote that the guerrillas prolonged the war in the eastern theater by eight or nine months.[20] Mosby himself firmly believed that the activities of his unit extended the life of the Confederacy. Some authors dispute these beliefs. It is perhaps not possible to settle the question of the exact military value of Confederate guerrillas definitively. On the subject of their bravery and dash, however, there is much agreement. Even the skeptical Wert concluded that "John Mosby and the 43d Battalion had no equals as guerrillas during the Civil War."[21] And no less an authority than J.E.B. Stuart wrote of Mosby that "his exploits are not surpassed in daring and enterprise by those of petite guerre in any age." Another distinguished student-practitioner of the art of war wrote that "there were probably but few men in the South who could have commanded successfully a separate detachment in the rear of an opposing army and so near the border of hostilities, as long as [Mosby] did without losing his entire command." The writer was Ulysses Simpson Grant.[22]

John Mosby never surrendered. Instead, shortly after Appomattox, he simply disbanded his men. On the direct orders of General Grant, Mosby received a parole in June 1865. He was not yet thirty-two years old. After the war Mosby told Southerners that they should have no doubt in their minds that they had suffered a defeat both decisive and irreversible. The tasks ahead were now to reinsert the South into the life of the nation and to regain influence in Washington. For this reason, and because of his personal knowledge that Grant was a generous foe, Mosby joined the Republican party as a Grant supporter.[23] He served as U.S. Consul in Hong Kong and as an attorney in the Department of Justice. Mosby outlived the Confederacy by more than half a century and died in Washington in 1916. Quite a record for a sickly youth.

Quantrill in Missouri

At the opposite end of the war from Mosby, geographically and morally, stands another Confederate guerrilla leader, the most notorious of all the bloodstained characters churned up by the dread struggle: the sociopath William Clarke Quantrill.

Controversy surrounds the details of his early life. He was born in Ohio in 1837, the son of a schoolteacher who embezzled school funds and tried to kill one of his accusers. Quantrill himself may have held several midwestern schoolteacher posts. He went to Kansas Territory in 1857, where he took part in the pre–Civil War fighting, rustling cattle and killing at least one man: "Quantrill's year of banditry in Kansas was his apprenticeship."[24]

Early in the war, former Missouri governor Sterling Price organized a small Confederate army, which Quantrill joined as a private soldier, but he soon ran off. Marked out to be a leader of guerrillas by his natural intelligence, his relative education, and his skill with horse and pistol, he formed his own armed band. Missourians like Cole Younger and Frank James had authentic grievances against the Union authorities, but Quantrill "chose to fight for the Confederacy because it was a chance to hit back at the people of Kansas," who before the war had issued warrants for his arrest.[25] Quantrill's forces were often quite large—several hundred—and he led them through subchiefs. His men called themselves "bushwhackers."

Most Union cavalrymen serving on the border carried only single-shot muzzle loaders, whereas the principal weapon of Quantrill's men was the Colt revolver. Each guerrilla carried three or four of these guns, and their wild charges against Union formations had devastating firepower. In addition, the Union cavalry had a very difficult time catching Quantrill's men. The nature of the terrain favored guerrilla war, the partisans knew the land thoroughly, and their mounts were often superior to those of the Federal troops. Members of Quantrill's original band "came from some of the best rural families of western Missouri, the majority of them driven to insurrection by the treatment their people had received from the Union troops that occupied the area." They thus enjoyed the sympathy of many rural folk. And the guerrillas' awareness that if captured they were almost certain to be shot concentrated their attention and sharpened their determination. Nevertheless, during 1862 alone Quantrill's band was taken by surprise at least three times by Union attacks; those who escaped were able to do so only because of the incompetence of their assailants.[26]

The Lawrence Raid

All of Quantrill's operations were wild and bloody, but it is with the ferocious events in the town of Lawrence, Kansas, that his name is forever linked. On August 21, 1863, Quantrill led a force of close to five hundred partisans into the community. He targeted Lawrence for several reasons. Founded in 1854, the town had been the center of the Free State Party during the days of Bleeding Kansas;

"Lawrence, Kansas, epitomized everything the South despised about the North." But a decisive descent upon the town would also allow Quantrill an opportunity to take "revenge on individuals who might know too much of his past."[27] Whatever the reasons, Quantrill's raid on Lawrence would be the culmination, the last dreadful act, of a decade of Kansas violence.

In the days leading up to the attack, several persons reported seeing large bands of guerrillas, almost certainly Quantrill's men, along the eastern fringes of the Kansas border, but nobody imagined they were headed for Lawrence. Quantrill forced ten Kansas farmers to guide them toward Lawrence and murdered the farmers when they were no longer needed. Then the hundreds of guerrillas, including Frank James and Cole Younger, later notorious bank- and train-robbers, galloped into the unprepared town. There they proceeded systematically to gun down 180 unarmed men and boys. U.S. senator Jim Lane of Kansas was in the town when Quantrill struck, and he escaped capture and certain torture and death only by luck. The guerrillas also set the torch to most of the buildings. The terrified Kansans hardly fought back; apparently only one guerrilla was killed in the raid, although in subsequent days Union cavalry captured several wounded guerrillas.[28]

Incredibly, not a single woman was killed or even seriously injured during the Lawrence massacre.[29] The reluctance to harm women that characterizes the Kansas-Missouri border war, even during the slaughter at Lawrence, contrasts dramatically with the subhuman ferocity against them displayed by troops in the Vendée and Spain. The guerrilla war could not have continued without the support of women. "By using women as their final screen, guerrillas had created a situation in which Union troops would have to war on women in order to destroy guerrillas." But few Union officers and men could bring themselves to take reprisals against women. "At the most women were tormented, arrested, or sent into exile." Everyone in Missouri knew about the extreme reluctance of Federal soldiers to punish even those women known to be actively assisting the guerrillas. This was one more reason why the guerrilla war could not be ended.[30] The partisans, with hardly any exceptions, displayed the same behavior. "Primary in the code of these guerrillas was an injunction against harming women and children. Guerrillas were the protectors not the despoilers of home and family."[31]

Nevertheless, the massacre at Lawrence was "the most atrocious single event of the entire Civil War," "a diabolical, unpardonable massacre, one which has no parallel in the Civil War." Without doubt "the butchery of Lawrence shocked the whole nation."[32] The Union response was swift and fearsome: Brig. Gen. Thomas Ewing ordered that within fifteen days all civilians must evacuate Bates, Cass, and Jackson counties, plus most of Vernon county, the general area from which Quantrill had launched his raid. Fully 20,000 Missouri civilians had to leave their homes, most of which were then burned by Kansas troops. Cass county, which before the war had had 10,000 inhabitants, was soon down to a pitiful 600. These frightful events provoked a great public outcry: after all, Missouri was a Union state, not some newly occupied rebel province. The widespread revulsion at Ewing's ferocity caused the suspension of his order in November, but many of the banished civilians did not return to their homes until after the war. The forced depopulation of these Missouri counties constituted the most drastic action by Union forces against large numbers of civilians until General Sherman (Ewing's brother-in-law) went marching through Georgia—which after all was, unlike Missouri, a rebel state.[33]

Quantrill and the Confederacy

Quantrill liked to show a paper that he claimed was his commission as a captain in the Confederate forces. After a stormy interview in Richmond with the Confederate secretary of war, he began to call himself colonel and was sometimes so addressed by officers of the regular Confederate army. Yet even before Lawrence, Confederate military leaders "had rejected the guerrillas themselves for their indiscipline and brutality." Thomas Reynolds, the "Confederate Governor of Missouri in exile," wrote to Confederate military authorities that he completely opposed guerrilla war.[34] Gen. Edmund Kirby Smith believed that the guerrillas in Missouri caused useless suffering. The events at Lawrence ruined Quantrill's reputation among the Confederate forces. Gen. Henry McCulloch wrote to Gen. Kirby Smith that Quantrill's men were "the wildest savages" and that their bloody acts "should be disavowed by our [Confederate] Government."[35]

Not long after the destruction of Lawrence, Quantrill and his men wiped out the Union garrison at Baxter Springs, Kansas, killing seventy-eight Union soldiers and civilian captives with the loss of only two guerrillas. They then went south to Texas, where they had some trouble with local Confederate military authorities who apparently tried to arrest them. Quantrill's band was beginning to split apart: jealous confrontations broke out over the division of spoils, as the impending defeat of the South grew ever clearer. And the atrocities at Lawrence had been distasteful to some of Quantrill's followers. (The last man killed on the Lawrence raid had been a Mr. Rothrock, a Dunkard minister. Some of Quantrill's men came up to his house, ten miles south of Lawrence, and made the women there cook them breakfast. Upon learning that Rothrock was a minister, they shot him several times and rode off.) Losing control over his men and finding critics and enemies everywhere, in June 1864 Quantrill took a few followers and headed for new fields in Kentucky; he was thus unavailable to participate in Price's invasion of Missouri (see the section titled "Society Disintegrates" in this chapter). Some have expressed the belief that Quantrill's intention was to go to all the way to Washington and kill President Lincoln. Perhaps; but in January 1865 Quantrill led a raid on Danville, Kentucky. Later he joined his men with those of a small Kentucky guerrilla band. In May 1865 Quantrill, seriously wounded, was taken prisoner in Spencer County, Kentucky. He died on June 6, 1865. Having on his deathbed accepted baptism into the Catholic Church, he received burial in the Louisville Catholic Cemetery. In his will he bequeathed to his girlfriend Kate Clarke a sum of money with which she opened a brothel in Saint Louis.[36]

The Agony of Missouri

In Virginia, Confederate guerrillas were regular soldiers employing partisan tactics behind or on the flanks of Union armies in a much-fought-over battle zone, in support of large conventional armies. In contrast, guerrillas in Missouri were hardly ever regular soldiers, they operated over a much larger area, and they played an incomparably more visible role, in a state that most of the time was behind the Union lines. The typical figure of the Virginia guerrilla war was John Mosby, who, with a few cosmetic touches, could pass for a sort of latter-day cavalier; the typical figure thrown up by the strife in

Missouri turned out to be somebody remarkably, frighteningly different, the blood-soaked Quantrill. But there was, sadly, much more to the story of guerrilla warfare in Missouri than Quantrill alone. Missouri offers a lurid picture of how guerrilla warfare draws into itself civilians who wish only to be neutral; events there highlight the disintegrative effects that prolonged combat of this kind can have on human society. What happened to the "family-centered, property-owning farmers, evangelical Christians, and lovers of law and order" in Missouri is a truly disturbing page in American history.[37]

Missouri became American territory in 1803, part of the Louisiana Purchase. It was admitted as the twenty-fourth state in 1821 through the famous Missouri Compromise, that ultimately unsuccessful effort to calm the nation's first major crisis over slavery—a crisis Jefferson called a "firebell in the night." Missouri entered the Union as a slave state, and it was such in 1861. Most of its inhabitants, however, were neither slave-owners nor slaves, but small farmers. Many were German immigrants or their immediate descendants; Saint Louis, with an 1860 population of 167,000, was 60 percent foreign born, the largest percentage of any American city. Slave or free, black persons accounted for less than a tenth of the state's population of 1.2 million. In March 1861, in the heat of the secession crisis, Missouri voters elected delegates to a convention that would decide the state's future course; Unionist candidates outpolled secessionist candidates 77 percent to 23 percent. Many Missourians were sympathetic to the perplexities of the white South; almost certainly a majority of them were troubled by Lincoln's policy of military resistance to secession. Yet, "if they had had a truly free choice, most Missourians would have remained neutral during the war." Instead, the unhappy state became the scene of "the worst guerrilla war in American history."[38]

"A Nasty War"

The conflict in Missouri "was not a stand-up war with uniformed, flag-carrying massed troops charging one another in open combat nor even the confusion of a typically disorganized battlefield; it was thousands of brutal moments when small groups of men destroyed homes, food supplies, stray soldiers, and civilian lives and morale." Missourians were engulfed by a "war of ten thousand nasty incidents." "At the core of the guerrilla war experience for all fighters was the deep need for taking blood revenge." In its essence the Missouri struggle became a war of reprisal and counterreprisal. On October 5, 1863, Lincoln described that guerrilla war to a group from Missouri and Kansas: "Each man feels an impulse to kill his neighbor lest he be first killed by him. . . . Every foul bird comes abroad, and every dirty reptile rises up. . . . Murders for old grudges, and murders for pelf, proceed under any cloak that will best cover for the occasion. These causes amply account for what has occurred in Missouri."[39]

The roots of this ugly war lay in the Kansas-Nebraska Act. Sen. Stephen Douglas of Illinois led the enactment of that law in May 1854. His bill explicitly repealed the Missouri Compromise, under the provisions of which the Territory[40] of Kansas would have automatically been free, that is, closed to slavery. In place of the Compromise, Douglas's bill established the principle of "popular sovereignty," whereby the new settlers of Kansas would themselves decide whether it would be slave or free.

The repeal of the Missouri Compromise seemed to open up the entire West to the curse of slavery. It thus produced a terrific uproar in the Northern states and led to the founding of the Republican Party. Pro- and antislavery forces all over the country competed with one another in rushing settlers to what would soon become known as "Bleeding Kansas." In May 1856 marauders sacked the antislavery capital of Lawrence (Quantrill's descent was still to come), and John Brown, calling himself God's chosen instrument, with the help of his sons hacked five sleeping proslavery men to pieces with sabres. Missourians, from Washington politicians to "border ruffians," played the leading role in the violence that racked Kansas. The Buchanan administration sanctioned egregious vote frauds so that Kansas might enter the Union as a slave state; these false elections, as much as any other single factor, brought about a major split within the ruling Democratic Party and all the consequences stemming from that fateful schism. The violence in Kansas was a true dress rehearsal for the coming War of Secession.[41] And the poisonous fruits of the ugly little war in Kansas would be copiously consumed in western Missouri.

Long ago a distinguished historian of the Missouri guerrilla conflict wrote that "the most direct factor contributing to the great insurrection which took place on the western border after 1861 lay in the abuses visited upon the civil population by the Union military forces."[42] There is truth in that observation, but not the whole truth, as will become evident. Many Union soldiers in Missouri, officers and enlisted, were from out of state. Remembering "Bleeding Kansas," they regarded white Missourians as trash and referred to them as "pukes." General Halleck, in his General Orders of January 1, 1862, branded all guerrillas as "freebooters and banditti"; when captured they were to receive no mercy. Apprehended guerrillas or suspects would therefore often suffer execution right on the spot. Of course the guerrillas often practiced the same policy, and "take no prisoners" became the cry on both sides.[43] But General Halleck went far beyond that. He declared that "those who are not for us will be regarded as against us. . . . *There can be no individual neutrality in Missouri.*" This was a sentence of doom for many helpless civilians. Acting in the spirit of the theory that any Missourian was a rebel sympathizer unless proved otherwise, Union general John Pope declared that local communities were responsible for the safety of any stretches of railroad in their vicinity. After guerrillas attacked a train near the town of Palmyra, Pope ordered the townspeople to pay damages. When the town council imprudently refused, Pope turned his men loose on the helpless community.[44]

Soldiers from Kansas, admitted as a free state in 1861, predictably behaved with special harshness in Missouri. Seeking to pay off old grudges, they tended to treat all Missourians as rebels. U.S. senator Jim Lane led the Kansas Brigade into the town of Osceola and plundered it. In the words of one historian, "Most of the troopers of the Seventh Kansas Cavalry were simply thieves." Gen. Henry Halleck, commander of the Department of Missouri, wrote to Gen. George McClellan in December 1861 that "the conduct of the forces under Lane . . . has done more for the enemy in this State than could have been accomplished by 20,000 of his own [the enemy's] army." Thus, "the population which was to create and support guerrilla warfare against the Union had grown larger and larger during the summer and winter of 1861–1862 because of the outrages perpetrated against the people of Missouri by occupying Union forces." But in profound contrast to Mosby's practice in Virginia, Missouri guerrillas often wore Federal uniforms, an illegal deception that permitted them to approach the enemy very closely. As a result of this practice, Union soldiers understandably became tense, resentful, and trigger-happy.[45]

The Engulfing Flames

Guerrilla war spread into more and more areas of the state. Mountainous southern Missouri was especially good territory for guerrillas, but Jackson county, on the Kansas border, the site of Kansas City and Independence, was the most guerrilla-infested of all. Unlike Mosby's men in Virginia, Missouri guerrillas hardly ever faced Federal troops unless they were overwhelmingly strong. Guerrilla bands composed mainly of quite young men raided towns, attacked wagon trains and river steamboats, ambushed Federal patrols, burned Unionist houses, wrecked bridges, and tore up railways and telegraph lines. "By the end of June 1864 transportation had become so hazardous on the Missouri [River] that it was difficult to find pilots and crews." In July 1864 Union military authorities felt compelled to halt all river traffic in the state.[46] The *Kansas City Journal* described the situation in classic terms: "The rebels hold the countryside, while the loyal people are besieged in the towns."[47] Union commanders therefore tried hard to keep large numbers of soldiers within the state and away from the big war in Tennessee and Virginia. (But it was of course in the big war in the East that the fate of Missouri would ultimately be decided.)

Eccentric and vicious characters always come to the surface in guerrilla conflicts, and the increasingly barbarous struggle in Missouri facilitated this tendency. Some guerrillas wore human scalps on their bridles.[48] At Centralia, Missouri, in September 1864, having massacred 150 Union soldiers, the guerrillas sliced off the ears of some and the genitals of others and mounted several heads on poles.

The commander of the Union garrison at Independence wrote to headquarters in Saint Louis that nothing could be done about the situation unless the government dispatched ten soldiers for every guerrilla. But of course Federal commanders in the state were always under pressure to send their best men to the "real war" in the East. Hence, Union troops in Missouri were as a rule second rate, and there were never enough even of those. Federal authorities therefore had to try to meet the guerrilla challenge by using vengeful and poorly disciplined local militia. As early as July 1862, Gen. John

Schofield issued General Orders 19: all able-bodied men capable of bearing arms had to report to the nearest military post, there to be organized for fighting guerrillas. Many who were subject to the order ran away and joined the rebels, but more came to the Union ranks: 52,000 by the end of 1862, a number that should have sufficed to deal with the guerrillas. Eventually there would be perhaps 10,000 Missouri state militia and another 50,000 unpaid local emergency forces. The system did not work very well. In more than one locale the militia came to a live-and-let-live understanding with guerrillas. The so-called Paw-Paw regiments, composed of former Confederate soldiers or sympathizers who had taken a loyalty oath to the Union, were, with reason, looked upon as unreliable. In July 1864 about 1,500 Paw-Paws defected en masse to the Confederate side.[49]

Society Disintegrates

The guerrilla war engulfed the civilian population. Guerrillas often took what they needed or wanted from civilians, or even killed them, without the merest pretense of trying to discover the political sympathies of their victims. Despite declared policies forbidding reprisals against civilians, Union forces also became increasingly harsh in their conduct toward them. The grim conditions of a guerrilla conflict within a civil war naturally opened the door for unscrupulous or demoralized Federal soldiers to intimidate, rob, or even kill civilians on the pretext that they were guerrillas.[50] But eventually even Union soldiers who had been originally well disposed toward civilians came to view them, snug and safe in their houses, as persons probably aiding the guerrillas and hence their mortal enemies.

Many factors hardened the attitude of Union soldiers toward the civil population of Missouri. First, there were not enough troops to properly contain the guerrillas or even adequately defend their own outposts, and they thus felt insecure and threatened by seen and unseen enemies. In addition, "the knowledge that their guerrilla enemies took no prisoners and warred on civilians all the time weakened local Union commanders' demands for good conduct from their subordinates." Another factor that helped undermine official Union prohibitions against mistreatment of civilians was the manner of recruiting Union soldiers. Many units had been raised within a specific locale and had elected their own officers, who not only knew their men but naturally shared their values and fears. This made it very difficult for officers to enforce discipline regarding the treatment of local civilians. "The primary community for soldiers was their own platoon or company, thirty to ninety men stationed at a barely secure outpost surrounded by a dangerous countryside where guerrillas lay in wait to pick them off and where many of those friendly-acting farmers were agents of the enemy. It is no wonder that field officers identified with and defended their men against all outsiders, which tended to mean everyone—the guerrillas, the Union brass, and all local citizens."[51]

By adopting the belief that reprisal was the only effective way to fight guerrillas, the Union forces descended into the worst modes of partisan warfare. Yet many Union soldiers viewed their actions not as wanton or unwarranted but rather as an unavoidable and indeed rational response to what they considered, with good cause, to be the uncivilized and despicable methods of warfare used by the guerrillas. The truth is that "in Missouri-style warfare, the southern guerrillas had determined how the Federal troops would fight."[52] In the heartland of Jefferson's republic, the forces defending the constitutional order grew more and more indistinguishable in their behavior from robbers and assassins. Civilization itself was tottering on the edge of the abyss.

Thus, it was the civilian population of Missouri, much more than the Federal troops or the guerrillas, that paid the price for the progressive disintegration of legality and morality. Civilians would encounter guerrillas dressed in Union uniforms and Union troops dressed as civilians. Under such circumstances no one knew what to say or whom to trust. Expecting that Federal troops would protect them, civilians would often suffer violence at their hands. "Now civilians were isolated and ravaged from all sides; for them, violent attacks punctuated endless days and nights of anxiety. What did loyalty and justice mean to them now? How could they respond to such chaos? Where could they turn for protection?" Amid these dreadful conditions and facing the threat of even worse things to come, large numbers of Missouri folk naturally thought of seeking safety by fleeing their homes and even their state. But for many, leaving might be worse than staying. One could not carry away one's home and fields; but because house-burning by both sides was so very common, few wanted to buy any property in Missouri, and prices were deflated anyway. And one's chances of being robbed or killed on the way to some other county or state were frighteningly high. Nevertheless, "eventually *most rural Missourians did become refugees;*" hundreds of thousands sought to flee the omnipresent, unpredictable, escalating violence, leaving whole counties desolate.[53]

Then in September 1864 came Confederate major general Sterling Price's long-awaited invasion of Missouri. From his base in northern Arkansas, Price led about 12,000 men into the state. Confederate leaders hoped that 100,000 Missourians would rise up and join Price, taking over the state and thus outflanking Kentucky and Tennessee, a great coup that might reverse the tide of the war. Price urged Missouri guerrillas to help his invasion by creating havoc north of the Missouri river, burning bridges and cutting transportation lines. But the much-anticipated great Missouri uprising never materialized. Perhaps 5,000 joined in the effort, and most of those deserted as soon as they perceived that the invasion would fail.[54] Price himself, after an epic march of two months through Missouri, Kansas, and Oklahoma, ended up back in southern Arkansas, having lost half of his original invasion force.

Union efforts to rid Missouri of guerrillas continued. In 1864 there was a new plan: every county seat and large town would have a permanent garrison; every railroad bridge would have a blockhouse to defend it; constant patrols would comb the areas between one post and another. But these Union tactics, along with selective banishment and executions, "might at best partially contain a guerrilla war but could never uproot it."[55] Meanwhile Union cavalry sweeps resulted in great destruction but little injury to guerrillas. Because of the great size of the state, the demands on manpower from more vital theaters of the war, and the desperation of the guerrillas, who knew that they might be shot down on the spot if taken, the Union authorities never came up with a really effective plan of counterinsurgency. There was no clear-cut defeat of the guerrillas; the little war in Missouri ended only when the big war in the East ended. Many guerillas had in fact been killed. Of the survivors, some, such as the James brothers, became permanent outlaws, but the great majority returned to civil society. "Most ex-guerrillas . . . went back to the farm, raised corn and children, and attended the Methodist Church (Southern) on Sundays."[56]

The Absent Guerrilla War

When General Lee surrendered his Army of Northern Virginia at Appomattox in April 1865, for all practical purposes the American Civil War came to an end. But *why* did it end? After the defeat of their armies by Napoleon's forces, the people of Spain had erupted into partisan war and inflicted great costs on the invaders. Southerners had fought with historic effect as guerrillas during the American War of Independence; indeed, Southern guerrillas became important in that conflict *after* the regular American forces had suffered catastrophic defeat. Confederate guerrillas had given much trouble to Union forces in Virginia, Missouri, and elsewhere. At least one student of the subject has maintained that from the very beginning the South chose the wrong kind of war; the Confederacy should have opted immediately to wear down the Union forces and public opinion through guerrilla conflict.[57]

Abraham Lincoln always feared that the longer the war went on and the harsher it became, the greater the possibility that when the rebel armies had been beaten, Southerners would turn to guerrilla warfare, a massive, remorseless, unending struggle. As the Civil War neared its end, General Grant had no plans to defeat or even to cope with a massive guerrilla movement. Later he wrote: "I saw clearly . . . that Lee must surrender or break and run into the mountains— break in all directions and leave us a dozen guerrilla bands to fight. To overcome a truly national, popular resistance in a vast territory without the employment of truly overwhelming force is probably impossible." As a matter of fact, guerrilla units were the last Confederate forces to lay down their arms. Some Confederates did call for a massive guerrilla war in 1864–1865; and since there were still one hundred thousand Confederates under arms after Lee surrendered, such an undertaking was certainly possible in theory.[58] Yet, after having raged for four years across a vast landscape, within a few weeks of Lee's surrender the fighting came to an almost total halt. Why did a passionate minority of the former Confederate armies not continue the struggle in which they had fought so long and sacrificed so much? Why did the War of Secession not continue after 1865 in an implacable guerrilla struggle?

The short answer, which is true enough, is that the commitment by Southerners to the cause of an independent Southern nation was not strong enough to sustain continued resistance in the face of the overwhelming Federal victories. Surrender was preferable to further struggle. But that is not a sufficient answer. After such frightful sacrifices, *why* did Southerners "prefer surrender to struggle?" After the war the former Confederate senator Benjamin Hill wrote, "All physical advantages are insufficient to account for our failure; the truth is we failed because too many of our people were not determined to win."[59] Despite the overstatement, there is truth here; material factors are not the determining ones in war, as Sun Tzu, Washington, Napoleon, and Mao Tse-tung have variously attested. The fact that guerrilla war did not blaze across the South after Lee's surrender suggests that Confederate defeat was moral as well as material. Among the factors that helped produce moral defeat were widespread misgivings within the South over secession, the unexpected sufferings of the war, resentment of compulsory military service and government requisitions, increasingly embittered Confederate factionalism, profound uneasiness about the institution of slavery, and—not nearly least—the adroit policies of President Lincoln.

Opposition to Secession

A key to understanding why peace returned after April 1865 can be found in the actual process of secession, well before the first gun was fired at Fort Sumter. The immediate cause, or excuse, for secession was of course the election of Abraham Lincoln of Illinois as president in the autumn of 1860. There had been four major candidates in the campaign: Lincoln, the candidate of the young Republican Party, which was committed to preventing the expansion of slave territory; Stephen Douglas, also of Illinois, paladin of pro-Union Democrats; Vice President John Breckinridge of Kentucky, the choice of the southern wing of the Democratic Party, which would later support secession (although Breckinridge himself did not advocate secession during the campaign); and John Bell of Tennessee, former Speaker of the House and a Unionist in the venerable Whig tradition.

Three of the candidates—Lincoln, Douglas, and Bell—were avowedly Unionists; thus, we may reasonably construe votes for them as votes unfriendly to secession, at least secession in the foreseeable future. When the ballots had been counted, the three pro-Union presidential tickets had done very well in what would shortly become Confederate states: in Georgia, Louisiana, Tennessee, and Virginia, Bell alone or Bell and Douglas together received over half of the popular vote; in North Carolina these two pro-Union candidates obtained almost half the votes. Clearly, in broad stretches of what would soon become the Confederacy, Unionist sentiment was quite considerable and often dominant.

After Lincoln's victory in the presidential contest, most of the future Confederate states held conventions to determine their relationship with the Union. Almost invariably the turnout in these state elections was lower than in the presidential contest, and the method of selection of delegates was usually weighted in favor of large slaveholders. The cause of secession, moreover—this is a crucial point—received much impetus from the widely propagated belief that the process would be peaceful: that is, that the Federal government would not attempt to use coercion to preserve the Union.[60] The Buchanan administration held that secession was unlawful but so was Federal resistance to it. And even if the Lincoln Republican administration, blinded by passion or hysteria, should attempt to coerce the South, surely the contest would quickly end in the complete military humiliation of the Federal side. In a word, secession would cost little fighting, probably none at all.

Nevertheless, in many Southern states the process of secession was slow and faced determined and often ardent resistance, especially by nonslaveholders. Consider this sequence of events. South Carolina declared its secession on December 20, 1860; several other Deep South states followed shortly; Jefferson Davis of Mississippi was chosen Provisional President of the Confederate government in early February 1861; Fort Sumter came under attack on April 12, and three days later President Lincoln called on the nation to provide seventy-five thousand volunteers to preserve the Union. Yet, despite all these dramatic events, North Carolina did not finally secede until May 21, Virginia until May 23, and Tennessee until June 8. North Carolina's governor, Zebulon Vance, resisted secession right up until Lincoln's call for volunteers to invade the South. The Virginia convention voted to leave the Union by only eighty-eight votes to fifty-three, and that was after actual fighting had begun. Robert E.

Lee resigned from the Federal army only because Virginia seceded. Later he wrote that "the act of Virginia in withdrawing herself from the United States carried me along as a citizen of Virginia."[61]

Virginia's secession immediately provoked a countermovement in its western counties, where pro-Union citizens began organizing what eventually emerged as the state of West Virginia. By June 1863, over 11,000 West Virginia volunteers were in the Union Army, more than the number from several individual Northern states, including Connecticut. Union soldiers from West Virginia number 32,000 by war's end. Had Federal troops been within striking distance, the eastern counties of Tennessee might well have imitated the western counties of Virginia and withdrawn from their state in order to remain in the Union. Tennessee senator Andrew Johnson refused to recognize the secession of his state and retained his seat until he was appointed military governor of Tennessee by President Lincoln in March 1862. And fully 30,000 East Tennesseans eventually volunteered for service in the Union armies, a larger force than Lee commanded at the time of his surrender at Appomattox.[62] In all perhaps 100,000 white Southerners served under the Union flag, a number that must be subtracted from the potential ranks of the Confederacy, thus making a difference of 200,000 men between the two sides.

The Unexpected War

Many who had supported or accepted secession had done so in the belief that it would cost nothing, that the Federal government would not be able to resist, and that if resistance occurred it would end in a brilliant Southern victory. "It is doubtful that any people ever went to war with greater enthusiasm than did Confederates in 1861." Some who did foresee a serious conflict could not possibly have calculated just how protracted and terrible the struggle would be or how every passing year would make clearer the coming Union triumph. So eager were the Confederates to have some sort of battle, some sort of glory, before the war came to its speedy and predetermined end, that they fired on Fort Sumter in Charleston Harbor even though the commander there had said he would surrender in two days. All the fashionable of Charleston watched the assault as if it were a fireworks display. Then the first big battle of the war, at Bull Run in July 1861, was a deceptively easy Confederate victory, confirming to

Southerners, as if confirmation were needed, that they were all brave, that Northerners were all poltroons, and that the war was going to be short and even exciting.[63]

Soon, however, these Southern delusions began to explode like artillery shells. Fort Sumter indeed fell easily to the dashing Confederates, but the attack shocked and enraged Northern opinion, and Bull Run gave Unionists a much more realistic grasp of the grim task before them. Then in February 1862 really ominous news began to roll in: Nashville became the first Confederate state capital to be occupied by Union forces. New Orleans, the largest city and the chief port of the Confederacy, fell to the enemy the following April, Baton Rouge (another state capital) in May, and Memphis in June. Psychological depression was already setting in. One historian sees the reverses of early 1862 as the real crisis, even worse than the one that followed the defeats of the summer of 1863.[64] Whatever the merits of that view, Southerners were convinced that the Confederacy had done its very best in the invasion of Pennsylvania, only to suffer a stunning repulse at Gettysburg, while the Union had stood firm, able to call on vast resources yet untapped.

From the shattered belief in a short and glorious war would stem all the other internal afflictions of the Confederacy.

What is the explanation for the widespread belief in the South that the Federal government would not be able to thwart secession? That belief seems especially bizarre in academic discussions of the American Civil War, which revolve around statistics establishing the inferiority of the Confederacy to the Union both in population and in economic strength. Once this relationship has been established, the obvious conclusion is supposed to emerge: disparities in wealth and population between the two sides made the defeat of the Confederacy "inevitable."

Yet all sorts of questions arise from such a mechanistic analysis. First of all, if the hopelessness of their cause is so easily established, why did the Southern leaders go ahead with secession? Were they ignorant of such readily available comparative statistics, or were they crazed fanatics impervious to logical argument, or were they merely stupid? To assume a necessary Federal triumph is also to insult the most sophisticated political leaders of Europe, almost all of whom expected (and desired) a Confederate victory. And there were many dark days, many dark months, when to the eyes of President

Abraham Lincoln, his cabinet, and his supporters, a final triumph for the Union appeared to be anything but inevitable. Surely, reflecting on their Vietnam experience, Americans should be skeptical of any insistence that one side must prevail over the other because it is larger and richer.

Union Resources

True, the Union enjoyed certain superiorities that were impressive on paper. The population of the loyal states was 23 million, as against only 9 million in the Confederate states, and fully 3.5 million of the latter were slaves. But the Union figure includes the 3 million inhabitants of the border states: Missouri, Kentucky, Maryland, and Delaware. In all four of those states, slavery was legal. Few of their inhabitants had voted for Lincoln in the 1860 presidential contest. Few were enthusiastic for a Federal war of conquest, and many thousands from these border states would serve in the armies of the Confederacy (although a substantial majority of border state white men who fought in the war fought for the Union side).[65] Moreover, Lincoln faced an obstreperous Democratic Party that had exercised a nearly exclusive hold on power at the national level between 1800 and 1860. It contained numerous elements that were fully prepared to resist any provocative measures taken by the Republican president. Even among Lincoln's own followers, there was widespread uneasiness over waging an aggressive war against fellow Americans who had assumed a defensive posture. When on April 12, 1861, the Confederates committed the incalculable blunder of firing on the American flag flying over Fort Sumter in Charleston harbor, they united most of the public opinion in the Northern states behind Lincoln's policy of military coercion *for the time being.*

Further, the dramatically different strategic tasks facing the two sides had a very important bearing on the apparent disparity in numbers. In order to win its objective, the Confederacy needed not to defeat the Union but only to survive. In contrast, the goal of the Lincoln administration—preservation of the Union—meant the complete political reincorporation of the seceded states. That objective would require not merely a victory here or there, however spectacular, nor even a string of such victories (which were close to impossible anyway; battles of annihilation were rare because the defeated army was almost always able to retreat). No, complete restoration of the seceded states to the Union required the total military conquest and occupation of the territory of the Confederacy, a sprawling empire without an adequate railway network or even a reliable highway system that conquering armies could use.

The army that would be called upon to accomplish this tremendous agenda was at the time of secession quite small, even before Southern officers and men withdrew from it. In addition, the Americans had no experience of a really long and sanguinary war, certainly not the Americans of 1861. Their experience of conventional war was the Battle of New Orleans in 1815 or the Battle of Buena Vista in 1847: one brave fight and the issue was decided.[66] True to this tradition of the decisive battle, in the spring of 1861 President Lincoln federalized seventy-five thousand militia for *ninety days service*. Clearly, the Unionists as well as the Confederates had little idea of what lay in store for them.

To return to the question of Union superiority: the Confederacy mobilized a much greater proportion of its military-age males than the Union did. Hence, at their peak, the Union armies mustered one million men; the highest figure for the Confederacy was around six hundred thousand. The ratio in favor of the Union was thus only five to three, a thoroughly inadequate superiority if the Union was going to have to assume and remain on the strategic offensive throughout the war.[67] This inadequacy of the Union advantage in numbers is heavily underlined when one contemplates the vast size of the Confederacy. It is farther from Dallas to Atlanta than from Berlin to Rome, farther from Richmond to New Orleans than from Warsaw to Istanbul, farther from El Paso to Charleston than from Paris to Athens or Lhasa to Bangkok. The state of Georgia alone is as large as England and Wales; Arkansas is as large as present-day Greece. The Confederacy of 1861 was larger than the 1999 combined areas of France, Germany, Italy, Poland, Spain, and Switzerland.

Fighting across this extensive Southern empire, moving ever farther from their bases in the North, the Union armies would need very long logistical tails: they eventually had to devote a great deal of their energy and personnel to the delivery and safeguarding of supplies. Considerable numbers of troops had to be peeled off at intervals to garrison occupied territory and to guard vital railways

against guerrilla raids, tasks from which by and large the Confederates were free. The various Federal armies were often widely sepa-
rated from each other, with no telephones or radios. Real coordination
among them remained only an aspiration until the beginning of the
fourth year of the war, when President Lincoln entrusted command
of all the national armies to Gen. Ulysses Grant.[68]

But the Lincoln administration faced a task that was yet more
gargantuan than this discussion suggests. The Federal armies had
to subjugate the South not only completely but also *quickly*, for at
least two reasons. First, if public support in the Union states should
weaken or evaporate before the final conquest, all might be forever
lost. Second, if the fighting was too protracted, even if the Federal
armies were completely victorious, the conflict might leave vast strata
of Southern society so alienated, so irreconcilable, that reunion would
become nominal at best. Embittered Confederates might bide their
time until an opportunity arose to renew the war; the Union victory
would be worse than hollow. Or the conventional war might end
only to be succeeded by a desperate guerrilla resistance as implacable as it was destructive.[69]

Apparent Southern Advantages

The leaders of the Confederacy certainly did not believe that their
defeat was inevitable; on the contrary they had high hopes for success. It was not at all clear, at least not before Fort Sumter, that public
opinion in the North would endorse, much less sustain, a war of conquest of the South. Even if the Lincoln administration did organize
substantial forces for an invasion of the Confederacy, the waterways
and rail lines along which such armies would most likely move were
so obvious that it would be easy for the Confederates to block them.
After all, the officer corps of both armies had been trained at the same
military academy and tested in the same Mexican War. The Confederacy would assume the strategic defensive: that is, in order to win
the war, the Union armies would have to invade, conquer, and hold
the sprawling territories of the South, every single state. In contrast,
for the Confederacy to win, it needed only to survive, just hanging
on until Northern public opinion turned against the costs of the
struggle. The Union had to win, and win utterly; the Confederacy
had merely not to lose. And the weapons technology of the 1860s

definitely favored tactics of defense: during the war the majority of the battles were won by the force that was on the defensive.[70]

Furthermore, Confederate leaders had high expectations that Europe, especially Britain and France, would recognize Southern independence and intervene together decisively to end the fighting. Europe had to have the Southern cotton crop. After all, was not cotton king? This dramatic overestimation of European dependence on Southern cotton was indeed one of the most serious delusions on either side. Nevertheless, powerful political forces in Europe did hope to see the American republic ripped in two, and they watched for their opportunity. Thus, the Confederacy could have fought a defensive war, preserving its manpower, exhausting Unionist patience, and working for foreign intervention.[71]

Contrasting Strategies

Aware of these dangers, Gen. Winfield Scott, the commander of Union forces at the outbreak of the fighting, presented to President Lincoln a strategy for restoring the Union by emphasizing the long-term superiority of Federal resources, a strategy that came to be called (usually in derision) the Anaconda Plan. Scott proposed to develop a tight blockade by land and sea to squeeze the economic life of the Confederacy; meanwhile the Federal government would build and train powerful armies that would eventually advance systematically by means of river routes and occupy the South one section at a time. This was a sound plan, but it would require a long time—perhaps two full years—to implement. It therefore ran immediately afoul of that Northern popular impatience that led to the disaster of Bull Run. But after 1861—after Northern "On to Richmond" illusions had been shattered—the fundamental Union strategy evolved into a variation of Scott's Anaconda: shut the Southern ports, pin Lee down in Virginia, wage offensive war in the West.

The strategic conceptions of Gen. Robert E. Lee, the premier paladin of the Southern cause, appeared able to counter the Yankee Anaconda. Lee believed that if the Confederacy remained on the strategic defensive, the numerically superior Union armies, backed by the agriculture and industrial resources of the Northern states, would be able to nibble the Confederacy away, state by state. The Confederacy could not pursue a strategy similar to that of the Russians in

1812 and retreat ever deeper into their vast territory; the most productive and populous areas of the Confederacy were Virginia and Tennessee, directly subject to Union invasion. In Lee's view, to defeat the enemy's strategy of strangulation and amputation, the South must, while most of its territory still remained unoccupied, break the commitment of the Unionists to persist in the war. He inexorably concluded that in order to shatter the Northern will and sustain the Southern faith, he must concentrate all available forces in one place against one opponent and achieve some major victory on Northern soil, a Napoleonic victory of annihilation, followed perhaps by the occupation or destruction of Philadelphia or some other principal Northern city.[72]

Such an offensive posture was questionable strategy. The Confederates did not have to win great victories (or any victories at all) in order to achieve their aims. Moreover, during the Civil War, battles of annihilation were nearly impossible because of the tactical advantages of the defensive army, as well as the ability of the defeated army to retreat (both truths were made painfully clear to Lee at Gettysburg). Above all, Lee's concepts meant that the Confederacy would pursue a strategy inappropriate to it as the side weaker in manpower. Nevertheless, Lee's Napoleonic vision prevailed. Out of it arose his invasion of Maryland in 1862 and Pennsylvania in 1863. Each ended badly. His retreat from Anteitam both forestalled British recognition of the Confederacy and provided Lincoln the opportunity he needed to issue the Emancipation Proclamation; Gettysburg broke the spiritual heart of the South. But these costly eastern failures were not the whole price of Lee's offensive vision: his belief in the principle of concentration, and his Virginia parochialism, led him to virtually ignore Union military progress in the western parts of the Confederacy, and it was there—at Nashville, New Orleans, Vicksburg, Chattanooga—that the Union won the war. And even if Lee had had his battle of annihilation, his Cannae, what then? Strategically, the shattering of one army would not have much impaired the North's ability to wage war, just as Napoleon's stupendous victories did not in the end save him from Saint Helena. We cannot know what the moral effect on Northern opinion would have been if Lee had smashed a Federal army in a Northern state and had gone on to partially or completely destroy some great Northern city. But just as Hannibal's crushing triumph at Cannae did not break the Roman will, neither did the enormous Union casualties at Fredericksburg and Chancellorsville destroy Unionist sentiment. And there is this also: between September 1862 and July 1863, as Lee pursued his vision of the great decisive battle from Antietam through Fredericksburg and Chancellorsville to Gettysburg, his Army of Northern Virginia suffered the loss of sixty thousand in casualties and personnel missing; these lost soldiers alone would have constituted an army considerably larger than that which Lee had actually commanded at Antietam. Thus, Lee rejected the plausible hopes of a strategy of defense without being able to replace them with tangible gains from a strategy of offense.[73]

Meanwhile, determined to derive advantage from such numerical superiority as the Union possessed, Lincoln wished to press all along the boundaries of the Confederacy until a breakthrough was made somewhere. By increasing Union pressure in the West (Tennessee and Mississippi) he was concentrating against the enemy's weakness and reinforcing Union success. The ever-more-effective Union blockade complemented that strategy. But Lincoln's generals, schooled in the teachings of Jomini, dismissed these ideas as ignorant; like Lee, they believed in placing overwhelming numbers of troops at the crucial point, which they considered to be northern Virginia.[74] Thus for years they played to Lee's strengths, and the terrible war ground on. Lincoln's grasp of strategy was much superior to that of his generals, until he finally found Grant.

Conscription

In its previous nineteenth-century conflicts (the War of 1812 and the Mexican War), the United States had relied upon volunteers to fill the ranks of its armed forces. But in the Civil War, volunteering soon proved to be an inadequate source of manpower. Accordingly, on March 3, 1863, Congress passed the Enrollment Act. This law was hardly a dragnet. It permitted drafted men to avoid service by paying a "commutation" of three hundred dollars or by providing a substitute, a person who was not subject to the draft (less than twenty years old, for example, or an alien).[75] The real intention behind Federal conscription was to spur men to volunteer and thus avoid the stigma of the draft (which it did). With the options of commutation, substitution, and volunteering, only a very small proportion of draftable men in Union states were actually conscripted.

In the beginning the Confederacy also relied on volunteers, but "the unexpected length and magnitude of the struggle"—a telling phrase—soon rendered that source inadequate.[76] So the Confederates resorted to a draft law in April 1862, a year before the Union draft. In the Confederate states as in the Union, the principal effect of conscription was to drive up voluntary enlistments; during the Civil War conscription per se produced very little new manpower for the armies.

But within the Confederacy the price paid for conscription was especially high. Its draft laws exempted large social categories. State and national officials were immune, as were members of numerous skilled vocations; almost immediately men flocked to join those exempt vocations, and large numbers secured enrollment in them by bribing officials (who were also draft exempt). Because one could be drafted only in his state of domicile, many men simply began to roam across the South. But most notably exempted from conscription were otherwise draftable persons who owned twenty slaves. Predictably, this provision caused profound bitterness. Many were the soldiers "who openly complain[ed] that they [were] torn from their homes, and their families consigned to starvation, solely in order that they may protect the property of slaveholders [who stayed home] in quiet enjoyment of luxuriant ease." And even when members of the planter class did serve in the armies, and many did, they often refused to accept discipline from or show deference to officers of higher military rank but lower social status.[77]

Vice President Alexander Stephens and other powerful Confederate politicians openly and bitterly opposed the draft; to them conscription seemed to conflict with the whole states' rights philosophy, which for them legitimated the war. Angry arguments over the draft repeatedly broke out between the central government and state officials, especially in North Carolina. "Conscription was the most unpopular act of the Confederate government. Yeoman farmers who could not buy their way out of the army voted with their feet and escaped to the woods or swamps. Enrollment officers met bitter resistance in the upcountry and in other regions of lukewarm or nonexistent commitment to the Confederacy."[78] Many Southern

Unionists drafted into the Confederate ranks deserted to the Federal side when the opportunity arose.

Requisitions

Soon the Confederate government began to take things as well as men. As the needs of the fighting forces increased, the availability of key commodities decreased. Thus the government at Richmond found itself forced to resort to requisitions among the civil population. In many instances palpable injustice and even brutality were involved; Confederate agents, unsupervised, often subject to bribes and pressures, seized grain at below market value. "No other one thing, not even conscription, caused so much discontent and produced so much resentment toward the Confederacy." As early as August 1862 this chilling observation appeared in the *Richmond Enquirer*: "We often hear persons say, 'The Yankees cannot do to us any more harm than our own soldiers have done.'"[79] Indeed, with the government forcibly confiscating goods, property, and later slaves, the Confederacy "was becoming, in large areas, a police state." Understandably, ominously, "the universal hatred of impressment [requisitions] became comingled with the widespread hostility to President Davis."[80]

The Union blockade aggravated the growing economic misery. The American maritime tradition, experience, and manpower were located in the East, not the South, a fact that would become increasingly important in the conflict. The Confederacy had three thousand miles of coastline, with innumerable inlets. Yet there were few important ports, and of those only six, including New Orleans, Mobile, and Charleston, had interstate rail connections. The major ports that the Union armies could not occupy the Union navy effectively shut down. By the end of 1862 the blockade was no longer a "paper" one, but quite real. In 1861 Southern port cities had shipped 3.5 million cotton bales to Europe; in 1863 the number was down to 168,000. In an effort to break the suffocating blockade, the Confederates developed their ironclad warships, beginning with the famous *Virginia* (originally the *Merrimac*). The effort failed resoundingly. Many daring blockade runners, specially built craft, slim and swift, darted through the Union stranglehold; their captains and crews wrote an impressive record of romantic daring and also amassed great profits. Too often, however, their cargoes consisted of luxury goods instead of the weapons and medicines for which there was more need but less profit.[81]

Another serious effect of the blockade was a drastically increasing inflation. By December 1864 in Charleston, it took forty-two Confederate dollars to buy one dollar in gold. The unexpectedly long war also produced the unforeseen problem of refugees. The movement of these unfortunate people from one state to another increased the pressure on dwindling supplies of food and housing. As early as the spring of 1863, a violent bread riot broke out in Richmond itself and was only partially calmed when President Davis himself addressed the turbulent citizenry.[82]

The inexorable approach of Federal armies, the tightening blockade, the requisitions and the conscription, the absence of the men from so many rural families, all resulted in serious deprivation for ordinary people, and especially for the poor, in terms of food and basic household needs. The well-known sufferings of soldiers' families increased the incidence of desertion; Gen. Joseph Johnston stated that he did not blame his men for deserting, when letters from home were telling the soldiers that their families were destitute because of the omnivorous Confederate requisitions agents. More gall was poured into the Confederate cup by the widespread belief that the rich were not bearing their fair burden of the draft, the length and the condition of military service, or physical deprivation. Predictably, the autumn 1863 elections saw the defeat of several fire-eating secessionist congressmen and their replacement by former Whigs and conciliationists. This phenomenon was especially notable in North Carolina, where a largely Democratic House delegation was replaced with one that was almost completely Whig. After the 1863 elections, the pro-Davis majority in the Confederate House of Representatives was sustained by the votes of members "representing" Missouri and Kentucky, which had never seceded, and districts in Tennessee and Louisiana under Union occupation.[83]

No doubt Southerners could have more cheerfully borne their sufferings if they had had some real conviction that they would not eventually turn out to have been in vain. But the resounding reelection victory of Lincoln in November 1864 destroyed hopes for a negotiated peace; the hope for a military victory had long since turned cold.[84]

Desertion

Many in the South realized that Gettysburg and Vicksburg spelled the doom of their independence: those twin disasters of July 1863 produced "an epidemic of desertion." A few weeks after Gettysburg, General Lee wrote President Davis that unless the number of desertions could be reduced or made up, "I fear success in the field will be seriously endangered."[85] The Confederate Congress passed amnesty measures for draft dodgers on three separate occasions, with little result.

Consider the case of North Carolina. That state seceded on May 21, 1861, a full five months after South Carolina and three months after the presidential inauguration of Jefferson Davis; it was nearly the last state to enter the Confederacy. With only one-ninth of the total Confederate population, North Carolina furnished one-sixth of the entire Confederate army, and one-fourth of all Confederate battle fatalities were troops from North Carolina. Twenty thousand of its soldiers died as a result of combat and another twenty thousand of disease; it had the highest death total of any Confederate state. These figures might seem to indicate that North Carolinians gave the last full measure of devotion to the Confederate cause, but that is far from the truth. Unionist sentiment in North Carolina was widespread; nearly half its voters in the presidential contest of 1860 had opted for pro-Union candidates. The state's western counties were especially unsympathetic to secession. Such feelings received great stimulation in April 1862 with the passage of the Confederate draft law, from which Confederate and state officials received exemptions (of course). In the lower house of the Confederate Congress in Richmond, the only two votes cast against the draft law came from western North Carolina. Soon thereafter the Chief Justice of North Carolina pronounced the Conscription Acts unconstitutional.[86]

During the war North Carolina had by far the largest number of deserters from the Confederate armies, almost twenty-four thousand, twice the number of the next highest state, Tennessee (which also had strong Union attachments). In the spring of 1863—*before* Gettysburg—the number of desertions from North Carolina regiments had alarmed General Lee. The state home guards were quite unreliable, and deserters and draft refusers swarmed among the western mountains. "By 1864 there were so many deserters in West

North Carolina that there was no stigma attached to desertion; and because of the warm welcome accorded them and the safety assured them, deserters not only from North Carolina but from practically every state in the Confederacy lurked in the mountains and plundered, murdered, or drove out the loyal citizens as they pleased." Confederate troops hunting for deserters and guerrillas in western North Carolina burned homes, slaughtered livestock, and arrested the families of suspects, promising the release of the latter if the wanted men turned themselves in. They beat mountain women and sometimes hanged them—not quite to the point of death—to force them to give information against relatives and neighbors.[87]

Desertion rates in the Union forces were high as well. The largest battle ever fought on the North American continent took place at Gettysburg. When on the eve of that battle General Meade arrived to take over the command of the Union's chief force, the Army of the Potomac, he expected to find 160,000 men. He found instead only 75,000; the other 85,000 were absent without leave.[88] Yet the comparison of Union and Confederate desertion rates is misleading. It was not the Northern states that were being invaded, and it was not their soldiers, their people, who might face severe punishment as a consequence of defeat.

Confederate Disunity

The citizens of the seceded states were decisively a minority of the American population. Any contest, political or military, with the rest of the nation would demand of Southerners that they display monolithic unity, at least for a while. Yet secession had enjoyed nothing approaching unanimous support. And after the war had begun, profound disquiet over secession was followed by deep division over numerous other issues.

The many heavy burdens that Southerners carried through the struggle, which eventually crushed them, would doubtless have been borne more easily and perhaps more successfully if the burdens had been counterbalanced by a feeling among Southerners that the Confederacy was their true nation. Certainly such a feeling would have been essential to any effort to continue the struggle after Appomattox. But how to turn what had always before been a geographical expression ("The South"), or a section of a nation, into a nation? Clearly, to emerge successful from a long war, the secessionist effort would require a sustaining ideology. Just as clearly, the defense of the institution of slavery would not satisfy that requirement.

President Davis's first ideological pronouncements derived from his view of the Confederacy as the last true resting place of American liberty and independence. But by emphasizing and idealizing particularism, such a view actually worked against the emergence of a Southern nationalism. Similarly, there was at least an embryonic secessionist ideology available in the doctrine of states' rights, but that doctrine itself undermined any nascent Confederate nationalism. Many Southerners chastised Davis for daring to use the expression "southern nation." Nor was this concept likely to stir the blood of ordinary yeomen-turned-soldiers. There was true Union nationalism, mainly (but not exclusively) in the Northern states, and there was state patriotism, especially in the South, but it seems to be almost incontestable that there was no effective Confederate nationalism. The Confederacy was not a nation, not a patria, but only a constitutional arrangement, without the legitimacy of age, without the catalyst of a foreign foe, and without the support of a unified population. The very name Confederate States reveals—emphasizes—its nature as an alliance of disparate elements.[89]

The emergence of Confederate nationalism confronted impressive obstacles: persisting Unionist sentiment in many of the seceded states, increasing physical hardship, combustible class resentments, the concept of state sovereignty itself, and above all the spreading conviction after mid-1863 that the war was lost. And supporters of the Confederacy knew that under Lincoln's amnesty proclamations they could return, almost at will, to their membership in what had been until recently—and all their lives—their true national home.[90]

From the start, the absence of a pervasive conviction of Confederate nationalism showed itself in the conflict between the central government and the states. That conflict grew more intense as the condition of the Confederacy grew more desperate. The Confederacy was fighting for survival itself; logic and experience demanded a greater concentration of power in the center, and in the center a greater concentration in the executive, at least for the duration of the emergency. This did not happen; on the contrary, the "Confederacy tried to operate on the basis of eleven separate conflicts instead of merging its resources into one great centrally-directed war."[91] For example, Governor Vance of North Carolina hoarded ninety-two thousand uniforms and countless blankets while Lee's soldiers went ragged. Sen. George Davis of North Carolina wrote in April 1863, "I have for a long time been very indignant at the appointment of persons from other states to command North Carolina troops."[92] The governors of Mississippi and Georgia enrolled state militias that they forbade to the Confederate authorities; these thousands of men were thus useless to the defense of the South. (If one adds the members of these sacrosanct state militias to the Southerners serving in the Union armies and deserters from the Confederate ranks, the loss of manpower to the Southern cause is remarkable.)

Lincoln found himself bedeviled by both abolitionists and copperheads, but his domestic political troubles were not comparable to the divisiveness that was disintegrating the Confederacy. Conflicts among its leaders grew hotter even as the war turned against them: conflicts between President Davis and Vice President Stephens, between Davis and Congress (many Confederate congressmen pursued a real vendetta against him), between Davis and his generals (most notably Beauregard and Johnston), between Davis and state governors, between governors and generals, and on and on. Although leading what was in fact a revolution, Jefferson Davis was no Cromwell, certainly no Robespierre, but in truth a conservative. He did not know how to rally the Southern people. Had Davis possessed true political insight, he would have offered Lincoln a cease-fire between the 1864 Democratic Convention and the fall of Atlanta, in order to discuss peace; if the guns had once been quieted, it is questionable that Northern opinion could have again been rallied. Yet in his experience, his integrity, and his devotion to Southern independence, Davis was almost certainly the best of the Southern statesmen. It is not at all clear that anyone from the ranks of those who sought to displace him would have done a better or even a comparable job (a consideration with many implications).[93]

Nevertheless, Davis increasingly became the object of the most intense vituperation by his enemies in Congress and in the press. He "did not know how to deal with the politicians." Consequently, "his path became stony with needless quarrels," resulting, for example, in his appointing no less than six successive secretaries of war in four years. Throughout the entire war, Lincoln vetoed exactly three bills; Davis vetoed thirty-eight—and the Confederate Congress overrode his vetoes on all of them but one. More and more of Davis's opponents accused him of dictatorship. Congressman William Boyce of South Carolina wrote to Davis in October 1864, "Suppose there were no States, only provinces . . . what greater power would you exercise than you do now? . . . Our government exercises the powers of a central despotism." Vice President Stephens was such an implacable critic of Davis that General Sherman actually approached him and Governor Brown with the proposition that Georgia secede from the Confederacy.[94] "One who delves deeply into the literature of the period may easily conclude that Southerners hated each other more than they did the Yankees." These divisions and hatreds "sapped the South's vitality and hastened Northern victory."[95]

This destructive internecine fighting of course reflected the approach of defeat. But it also reveals the unimpressive quality of the political (as distinguished from the military) leadership of the Confederacy in all branches and at all levels. The Confederate Congress was "far inferior in brains and character to its counterpart in Washington, and far less effective in supporting the Executive." Most Confederate leaders had spent their entire adult lives as oppositionists; by 1861 it was too late to acquire the habits of government. Besides that, they had been educated in a political culture that tended to identify political criticism as willful malice and indeed as a reflection upon the intelligence or even the integrity of the one criticized.[96]

It must be kept in mind that, as far as the leaders of the Confederacy knew, there was always more than a theoretical possibility that if they lost the war they would all be hanged. Nevertheless, as the tide of war clearly turned against them, the political infighting at all levels in the Confederacy grew ever more bitter and personal. Does not this bizarre contentiousness, this remarkable inability to submerge provincial agendas, individual ambitions, and personal rivalries in the interest of pure survival—especially when viewed in conjunction with the truculent recklessness displayed at Fort Sumter—turn a most revealing light on the inner reality of the secession movement, indeed on the entire "states' rights and Southern liberties" issue that led to war itself?[97]

The disparity in the quality of political talent available to the

Union and to the Confederacy was actually a major factor in the war's outcome, a factor for some reason usually neglected. Certainly it is no accident that the supreme embodiment of the Confederacy has always been the soldier Robert E. Lee, whereas the supreme embodiment of the Union cause has always been the politician Abraham Lincoln.[98] At any rate, the divisive and vituperative style of Confederate politics manifested itself even in the question of slavery.

Slavery: From Cornerstone to Millstone

The causes of the American Civil War are numerous and complicated, as are the causes of Union victory and Confederate defeat. But one cause stands out above all others for both Southern secession and Southern defeat: the institution of slavery. "Nobody who has read the letters, state papers, newspapers, and other surviving literature of the generation before 1861," writes Samuel Eliot Morison, "can honestly deny that the one main, fundamental reason for secession in the original states which formed the Southern Confederacy was to protect, expand and perpetuate the slavery of the Negro race." Lincoln said in his second Inaugural address: "Slavery constituted the peculiar and powerful interest. All knew that this interest was, somehow, the cause of the war. To strengthen, perpetuate and extend this interest was the object for which the insurgents would rend the Union, even by war." And R.M.T. Hunter of Virginia, Confederate secretary of state and former Speaker of the U.S. House of Representatives, exclaimed, "What did we secede for if not to save our slaves?"[99]

One often reads that secession occurred because the Republican victory in 1860 threatened the safety of the institution of slavery within the Southern states. But that is misleading. Secessionist threats had resounded in the South for more than two decades before the founding of the Republican party. As early as 1832, President Andrew Jackson, himself a Tennessee slaveholder, had threatened to hang South Carolina fire-eaters. The 1860 Republican platform pledged to respect slavery in those states where it existed by vote of the legislature; Lincoln had for years made abundantly clear his view that the Constitution did not allow Congress to interfere with slavery *in a state*. More to the point, after the 1860 elections the Republicans were a minority in both houses of the Congress (and on the

Supreme Court as well). Advocates of secession were alarmed not because of anything the Republican platform said or Lincoln did, but because of what could eventually happen after two or three more Republican administrations: the slow, gradual, legal erosion of slavery to the point of extinction, first in the border states and then ultimately in the Deep South.[100]

The more exuberant apologists for slavery found such a prospect or even possibility intolerable. During the 1850s they began to expound the argument that slavery, far from being a necessary or inescapable evil, was in fact a positive good, a good that required not merely protection but propagation. It was this increasingly aggressive determination not only to preserve but also *to extend* slavery that led to demands for the reopening of the slave trade (specifically prohibited by the Constitution), the spectacle of Bleeding Kansas, the Dred Scott fiasco, and the deliberate shattering of the Democratic Party. To advanced proponents of slavery, it was clear that the Southern states must free themselves from the menacing incubus of the increasingly democratic and industrializing Federal Union; then they would become the nucleus of a great tropical slave empire eventually embracing Mexico and the entire Caribbean. It is undeniable that the ardent proslavery men, the fire-eaters, plunged their country and their section into disunion and invited civil war before any overt act of hostility toward slavery by the Lincoln administration, indeed even before Lincoln had been inaugurated.

Slavery created the Confederacy. Could slavery then sustain it? Could slavery justify all the sacrifices that would be imposed upon the whites of the seceded states, even though only about 6 percent of them were slave-owners?

The True Price of Slavery

From the first, the hopes of secession were pinned on foreign intervention. Of course, effective British recognition would have involved a confrontation with the growing Union navy. But slavery as well as American maritime power restrained the British government. William Gladstone at first portrayed the embattled Southerners as merely one more oppressed people valiantly struggling for independence, for freedom. However, the Emancipation Proclamation, issued in September 1862 after Lee's reverse at Anteitam, made it impossible to sustain such a view any longer. Just as Lincoln had intended and foreseen, the proclamation fused the cause of preserving the Union with the cause of extending human liberty. Henceforth the victory of the Confederacy must mean a victory for human slavery. Nearly all reformist opinion in England rallied against intervention. John Bright declared that "the Confederates were the worst foes of freedom that the world has ever seen." John Stuart Mill believed that the breakup of the Union "would be a victory of the powers of evil which would give courage to the enemies of progress and damp the spirits of its friends all over the civilized world." The first Confederate commissioners sent to Britain to negotiate recognition wrote home to say that slavery was very unpopular in Britain; "the sincerity and universality of this feeling embarrass the Government in dealing with the question of our recognition."[101]

Slavery was a problem inside the Confederate house as well. Committing a propaganda disaster incredible but not unique, Confederate vice president Alexander Stephens defiantly proclaimed that "this stone [slavery] which was rejected by the first builders, is become the chief stone of the corner of our new edifice." In fact Stephens was saying more than he perhaps realized.[102] The stone of slavery had indeed been rejected by the "first builders," the men of the Philadelphia Constitutional Convention, prominent among whom were many Southerners. In the springtime of the republic, almost everyone, slaveholders included, viewed slavery as either a great evil or a great misfortune. The founding fathers hoped that it was on the way to extinction. That is why the words "slave" and "slavery" do not appear in the original Constitution, so that they—artifacts of a benighted era—would not be found there after slavery had become extinct; the Constitutional circumlocution for slaves was "all other persons." Why would Southerners have submitted to a Constitution that made participation in the slave trade a felony if they believed slavery was anything other than an unfortunate and hopefully temporary condition?

And before the Constitution, when the American states governed themselves under the old Articles of Confederation, the Northwest Ordinance of 1787, based on proposals of the Virginian Thomas Jefferson, proclaimed the vast empire between the Ohio River and the Great Lakes closed to slavery. Jefferson also advanced plans for the gradual emancipation of the slaves, to be followed by their training in useful crafts at public expense. His *Notes on the State of Virginia* depicts slavery as degrading to slave and master alike. Another Virginian, James Madison, the "Father of the Constitution" and the fourth president of the United States, hoped that by destroying the slave trade the Americans "might save themselves from reproaches and our posterity from the imbecility ever attendant on a country filled with slaves." George Washington attributed the alleged inferiority of blacks not to their genes but to their chains. He freed his own slaves, saying, "I can clearly foresee that nothing but the rooting out of slavery can perpetuate the existence of our union, by consolidating it in a common bond of principle."[103]

Sixty years after Washington's pronouncement, on the outbreak of the Civil War, Robert E. Lee told Gen. Winfield Scott that if he owned every slave in the South, he would gladly free them all to ensure peace. And in 1856 Lee had written: "There are few, I believe, in this enlightened age, who will not acknowledge that slavery as an institution is a moral and political evil. . . . *a greater evil to the white than to the colored race.*" All educated southerners (at least) were uncomfortably aware that slavery carried the condemnation of the whole Christian world. Indeed, the Constitution of the Confederacy itself prohibited the international slave trade. And many in the South would interpret the military defeat of the Confederacy as God's judgment on the sin of slavery.[104]

To achieve their ends, the leaders of secession would have to destroy the Union that Washington and Madison and Jefferson—all Southerners—had so mightily labored to build. They would also destroy the lives of scores of thousands of fine young men from every state of that Union. But why must the Confederacy pursue this bloody destruction? Southern apologists said they were fighting for liberty. But it was not the liberty their fathers had fought for, the liberty to govern themselves as free men. It was not the liberty the Vendéans had fought for, liberty to worship God. It was not the liberty the Spaniards had fought for, liberty from a cruel foreign overlord. What was it, then? Confederate liberty meant this: the liberty of a small minority within the South to hold millions of men, women, and children in perpetual slavery. Here was the unspoken paradox, the key contradiction, of the Confederate position—fundamental, inescapable, corrosive, and fatal.[105]

An Army of Slaves

Of all the manifestations of the general uneasiness among the Confederates about this paradox of slavery, the most intriguing and revealing was the issue of saving the rebellion by arming the slaves.

The inexorable advance of Union armies into Confederate territory, the unabating stubbornness and tactical genius of Robert E. Lee, and the wide-ranging activities of Confederate guerrillas all combined to create a critical demand for more Federal manpower. The urgency of the need helped lead Lincoln to approve the formation of military units composed of black men, including former slaves. Properly trained, such units could take over the troop-consuming tasks of holding forts and guarding junctions behind the lines, freeing experienced white soldiers for combat, including guerrilla-hunting. Lincoln of course had to move cautiously in this matter, an exceedingly sensitive one in Union slaveholding states like Kentucky, even though black troops were deployed against guerrillas in Missouri as early as October 1862.[106]

The formation of black Federal units created consternation among the Confederates. They threatened to execute any captured white officer who had been in command of black troops "for inciting servile insurrection." President Lincoln knew how to deal with that kind of threat: in July 1863 he announced that for every Union officer-prisoner illegally executed by the Confederacy, he would hang one Confederate officer.[107] In all, about 180,000 blacks served with the Union forces, approximately one out of every ten men who donned the uniform of the United States during the war.

For decades before the war, thousands of free persons of color had lived in the South. But the conditions of these persons were in many areas so bad that they often petitioned the courts to be allowed to return themselves to slavery under a master of their own choosing. Nevertheless, companies of free black soldiers had organized in New Orleans as early as 1861. Apparently their services were not accepted. But the unexpectedly long and costly war, which like every major war was also a social revolution, was already causing Confederates to tamper with that institution in the name of whose inviolability they had plunged a nation into civil carnage. Mississippi passed legislation freeing any slave who defended white women or helped his master who was wounded in battle.[108] And, more pertinently in view of what was eventually to come, the Confederate government had from the first days of the war hired slaves from their masters and set them to erecting fortifications and other war-related work. It is notable that the Confederacy felt able to conscript the services of free white men, but not unfree black men, who constituted 40 percent of the Southern labor force and were largely left to the disposition of their owners.

"If Slaves Make Good Soldiers"

As defeat for the Confederate cause undeniably loomed, demands arose for desperate measures to stave off that dread outcome. The South must cast everything into the fire to keep the engine of war going—*everything including slavery itself.* Gov. Henry Allen of Louisiana declared his belief that the Confederacy should arm every Negro male, put him in the army, and then emancipate him after final victory had been achieved.[109] By late 1864 Robert E. Lee and even Jefferson Davis had expressed themselves in favor of arming and freeing at least some slaves. Lee had apparently been in favor of arming slaves since Gettysburg.

Even to talk about arming and freeing Negro slaves shook Southern morale to its foundations. Such proposals of course provoked ferocious opposition. If the Confederacy were to arm its slaves, then what in heaven's name was the war all about? In January 1865 the legislature of South Carolina vigorously condemned any arming of slaves. Senator Hunter of Virginia pointed out with unsettling logic, "If we are right in passing this measure [to arm slaves and promise them freedom] we were wrong in denying to the old [Federal] government the right to interfere with the institution of slavery and to emancipate slaves." Or more succinctly, in the words of Maj. Gen. Howell Cobb, a former U.S. congressman: "*If slaves make good soldiers, then our whole theory of slavery is wrong.*"[110] Indeed.

But, as Robert E. Lee rightly observed, slavery would surely be extinguished, if not by the Confederacy then by the Union. The only real question was, Who would get the benefit of arming the blacks? Lee wanted black troops. "My own opinion," he wrote, "is that we should employ them without delay. I believe that with proper regulations they can be made efficient soldiers." Lee advocated emancipation for any slave who joined the army, and emancipation for his family if the black soldier did his duty. If the Confederacy did not arm the slaves, everything would be lost; if it did arm them, something (not least the property and the personal freedom of the leaders of rebellion) might be saved.[111]

Accordingly, in March 1865 (five minutes to midnight on history's clock), the Confederate Congress, by a vote of 9 to 8 in the Senate and 40 to 37 in the House of Representatives, passed a bill calling for the creation of slave military formations (to enroll up to three hundred thousand men!).[112] In 1861 the seceded states had begun the war in order to continue slavery; by 1865 they would end slavery in order to continue the war. Truly, war is revolution.

Marching through Georgia

A *strategy of attrition* is an effort to defeat the enemy by inflicting unacceptably high numbers of casualties on them; a *strategy of exhaustion* is an effort to defeat the enemy by depriving them of the means to continue the struggle. An example of President Lincoln's strategy of exhaustion is the Union blockade. Other instances are the occupation by Federal troops of ever-larger chunks of the Confederacy, the emancipation of slaves in rebellious areas, and the induction of former slaves into the Union armies. General Sherman's deliberately destructive march through Georgia and South Carolina is a further instance of this strategy and suggests the concept of *political* exhaustion: making it plain to Southerners that the Confederacy could no longer protect anybody anywhere. Sherman's march was aimed at Confederate morale. Lincoln also sought to employ political exhaustion against the rebels, and he did so with great effect, as will be seen.

The notoriety of General Sherman's march "from Atlanta to the sea" is deserved, but his continuance of the campaign into South Carolina was even more devastating than the better-known Georgia episode. House-burning was much more common in the South Carolina campaign; many Union officers and soldiers wrote home that they found it supremely fitting to visit destruction upon the state that had been the first to secede and the first to fire on the American flag. Columbia, the handsome state capital, suffered severely from several major fires. General Sherman always denied, with vehemence, that these fires resulted from his orders, and the evidence sustains his denial.[113]

The unprecedented path of desolation Sherman was cutting through the Southern heartland caused some desertions from Lee's army in Virginia by men anxious to go home and safeguard their families. In fact, Confederate soldiers from regions occupied by Union troops had been leaving the army to care for their families long before Sherman ever saw Georgia. The campaign also brought home to large strata of the civil population just how far the Confederacy's military position had deteriorated, how utterly unable their government was to protect them: "Sherman's march to Savannah had shown the Confederate defenses to be an eggshell." Yet, the devastation of Southern agricultural capacity, a main justification of the march, seems to have had little effect on Lee's army, which lacked not foodstuffs but the means to transport them. Lee's men were hungry at Appomattox, and Grant fed them, but this had little to do with Sherman.[114]

The deliberate destructiveness of Sherman's troops caused despair in the South. It also engendered a profound and lasting bitterness against the Union, against Northerners in general, a bitterness that delayed postwar reconciliation by decades and distorted the political and social development of the Southern states for a century. Sherman argued, in the manner of Julius Caesar, that his policy of destruction in fact saved lives and suffering because it shortened the war. In this and other ways his march foreshadowed Allied strategic bombing of German and Japanese cities during World War II. It is interesting that William Sherman's detractors heap execration upon him for destroying property, as if that were unquestionably worse than destroying lives. His men committed little rape and less murder. One finds nothing, absolutely nothing, in Sherman's march to compare to the systematic atrocities in the Vendée or in Bonapartist Spain. That he bore no personal hatred toward Southerners in general is shown by his exceedingly generous surrender terms to the army of General Johnston. During the negotiations for that surrender, Sherman offered Confederate general John Breckinridge a ship to carry the fugitive Jefferson Davis and his family to safety outside the United States. And in the period of Reconstruction, Sherman repeatedly expressed his distaste for punitive measures against his ex-Confederate foes. For Sherman, total war and total forgiveness were different sides of one coin.[115]

With Malice toward None:
Lincoln and the Politics of Victory

Whatever one's opinion of Sherman, his ruthless pursuit of the strategy of exhaustion provided a dramatic backdrop for President Lincoln's policy of clemency toward repentant Confederates and the smooth reincorporation of seceded states into the Union. Halfway through 1864 at the latest, most Confederates knew that they faced a clear choice: continue to suffer in a losing war, or find shelter in a forgiving peace.

The powerful military weapons of the Lincoln government included an increasingly effective blockade; notable improvements in Union army leadership, discipline, and armament; and the steady transfer of manpower from the Confederate to the Union side through the flight of slaves to the Union lines and the creation of black military units. Lincoln augmented this impressive armory with potent political weapons. One was the Emancipation Proclamation, which destroyed any chance of European intervention on behalf of the South. Another was the constant promise of a moderate peace, which fanned the already-bright flames of division among the foe. It was no accident that Lincoln's running mate in 1864 was the Tennessean Andrew Johnson.

At the end of 1863 President Lincoln issued a Proclamation of Amnesty and Reconstruction. It was "a device to shorten the war and solidify white support for emancipation." Under this proclamation any Confederate, with the exception of certain high political and military officers, who agreed to take an oath of renewed allegiance to the United States and pledged to accept the end of slavery would receive full restoration of rights. When the number of such oath-takers in any formerly seceded state equaled 10 percent of the vote cast in the election of 1860, they could reorganize their state government and receive the recognition of the Federal administration. Even before Appomattox, such governments were functioning in Tennessee, Arkansas, and Louisiana. And in February 1863 the

House of Representatives seated two newly elected members from Louisiana.[116]

The attitudes of Grant and Sherman toward their defeated opponents reflected Lincoln's leniency. Grant's generosity to Lee and his soldiers unquestionably helped prevent an outbreak of serious guerrilla fighting. A week and a half after Lee surrendered at Appomattox, with the Confederacy clearly drawing its last painful breath and *only a few days after Lincoln had been murdered*, Sherman offered very moderate terms to Joseph Johnston's army in North Carolina, in part because he did not want that army to scatter and turn to guerrilla war. Similarly, Union military authorities "granted truly generous terms, in view of their bloody record" to Missouri partisans.[117]

The Prospects for Guerrilla Resistance

What if, in spite of the ever-tightening blockade, the inexorable advance of the Union armies, the utter extinction of the hope of foreign intervention, the crushing fatigue produced by years of sacrifice, the grotesque inadequacy of slavery as a rallying symbol, the complete absence of any other sustaining ideology, and the easy peace proffered by Lincoln—what if in spite of all this, large numbers of Confederates were in the spring of 1865 actually giving serious thought to continuing the fight by turning to guerrilla tactics? Surely they would have had to confront the following disheartening considerations.

First, the efforts of Confederate guerrillas, however chivalrous or sanguinary, had not been decisive when those guerrillas had had the support of large armies fighting in the field. How then could one rationally hope for a more favorable outcome after those field armies had been defeated and dispersed?

Second, nearly every single successful guerrilla movement in history has received assistance from the outside. French help was of incalculable importance to the American Revolution; Wellington brought essential support to the Spanish guerrillas.[118] But to whom could Confederate guerrillas look for assistance in 1865? The Great Powers had declined to recognize the Confederacy in its full flower; would they then risk the wrath of a triumphant and puissant Union by aiding the guerrilla remnant of a thoroughly defeated cause—

assuming for the moment that any substantial amount of aid would get through the Union blockade?

Third, a protracted Confederate guerrilla resistance rooted in popular support would need a proper enemy. But such an enemy was absent. For Southerners to undertake and to sustain a bloody guerrilla resistance, in defiance of all arguments and handicaps, it would surely have required the most powerful consciousness of national identity—an inescapable conviction of the foreignness of the foe, his manifest, irredeemable, repellant otherness. The great guerrilla wars of history have burst forth against foreign invaders who were wantonly murderous (China, Yugoslavia), racially alien (Vietnam, Tibet), or religiously obnoxious (Spain, Afghanistan). Merely to mention such cases is to underline their profound and unbridgeable contrasts with the American conflict. The relationship of Pennsylvanians to Virginians was not even remotely comparable to that of German to Serb. On the contrary, Pennsylvanians and Virginians shared ethnicity, language, religion, historical experience, patriotic symbols, and political convictions. Sherman and Sheridan did not preside over systematic sacrilege and wholesale executions as their Napoleonic counterparts in Spain did; even the mentally unbalanced Quantrill never descended to the mass rapes and murders of women and children that befouled the revolutionary troops in the Vendée.[119] To say the least, Southern separatists lacked a satisfactorily alien foe against whom to define themselves.

To the degree that a Southern patriotism existed at all, it was rooted in the fact of slavery. Slavery was at the very heart of the war. But slavery, which had created the Confederacy, could not sustain it. Even in 1861 "Long live slavery!" would have been a public relations disaster. With slavery clearly doomed by 1865, why should the war continue? And if, nevertheless, large segments of the white South had undertaken guerrilla war after 1865, almost certainly Union forces in the South would have increasingly come to consist of black soldiers, with the effect that Southern blacks would have become not only emancipated legally but also dominant militarily and thus politically.

If, instead, Confederates bowed to the surrender of General Lee, if they admitted the failure of the cause, what fate awaited them? Did they face sweeping confiscations, mass deportations, countless hangings, Vendéan drownings, the Gulag Archipelago, the Katyn Forest? No. This alone awaited them: they would enter into civil relations with the administration of Abraham Lincoln, the legitimate government of the United States, put in office by a free election in which Confederates themselves had participated hardly fifty months before. And they could participate in similar elections if they would accept amnesty and help to bind up the nation's wounds.

Confederate leaders were familiar with the dread consequences of the Spanish guerrilla resistance against Napoleon. More to the point, they had before them the grim example of Missouri. The South proved to be no Spain. The leaders of the Confederacy—almost all of them, with the notable exception of President Davis himself—urged their followers to take the path of peace. In his last wartime message to President Davis, April 20, 1865, General Lee wrote: "As far as I know the condition of affairs, the country east of the Mississippi is morally and physically unable to maintain the contest unaided with any hope of ultimate success. *A partisan war may be continued, and hostilities protracted, causing individual suffering and the devastation of the country, but I see no prospect by that means of achieving a separate independence.* . . . To save useless effusion of blood, I would recommend measures be taken for suspension of hostilities and the restoration of peace."[120]

The Weariness of the South

During the American Revolution, southern guerrillas arose and flourished in those darkest hours after the British had shattered the regular American army in the area and when prospects of immediate assistance were remote. Spain erupted into guerrilla resistance after the armies of Napoleon had swept aside its regular forces. These guerrilla wars followed upon a period of conventional armed conflict that was relatively brief. The case of the Confederacy was much different.

The soldiers of the Confederacy had been told at the beginning that secession would be peaceful. That expectation proving naive, they were then told that the war would be short and victorious. All too soon the whole idea of peaceful or easy secession was exposed as foolishness. The proportion of casualties to total population in the Civil War was higher than in Britain or France during World War I. In addition, the fundamental Confederate strategy of avoiding defeat had turned the South into the theater of the war, with all its attendant calamities. As early Confederate victories evaporated under a waxing Unionist sun, enthusiasm for an independent Southern commonwealth based on slavery began to evaporate with them, while internecine hatreds boiled over in frightening implacability. For at least two years before Appomattox, and especially after the summer of 1863, Southerners experienced a growing, dreadful conviction that the frightful slaughter of their young men and their deep and increasing material privations were after all to be in vain. After the reelection of President Lincoln, desertions from the Confederate armies increased dramatically.[121] Even in Lee's Army of Northern Virginia, the embodiment of heroic and effective resistance, desertion became very serious during 1864 and reached crisis proportions by March 1865.

The Confederacy's thorough, undeniable defeat after almost four years of bloody combat had understandably deprived it of the spiritual as well as physical stamina to carry on the conventional war, much less to undertake a massive guerrilla struggle. An exhausted South, facing on the one hand certain defeat (made more terrible by Sherman's calculated destructiveness) and on the other hand Lincoln's sincere stance of malice toward none and charity for all—how could this South possibly have fought on? A few handfuls of Confederates who would not accept surrender went by way of Texas into Mexico and the army of the emperor Maximilian (another lost cause); some other irreconcilables found their way to Brazil. It is emblematic of the unwillingness of Confederate leaders to continue the war after Appomattox that John Mosby, the most famous of the guerrilla leaders, not only advocated reconciliation with the victorious Union but embraced the Republican Party of General Grant.[122]

Reflection

It was an incalculable blessing upon everyone that a massive guerrilla war did not break out across the post-Appomattox South. The containment of fifty thousand Confederate guerrillas would have required the protracted occupation of the South by a half million

Union soldiers: the Missouri horrors multiplied by eleven. How, after such a conflict, reunification of the country in any meaningful sense could have been effected in less than a century, if ever, is difficult to imagine. But following the formal surrenders of Generals Lee and Johnston, there was peace, a lasting peace.[123] No Southern guerrilla movement could be sustained in the face of the undeniable defeat of the Confederate armies and the generous peace terms of President Lincoln and Generals Grant and Sherman.

Six hundred thousand American combatants perished in the War of Secession—more than in World War I, World War II, and Korea combined. The billions of dollars spent by the Federal government would have been more than enough to peacefully purchase the freedom of every single slave. So all-consuming, so revolutionary did the conflict become that toward the end the Confederates were prepared to cast the edifice of slavery into the furnace of war. And on the same day that the American flag was once again raised over Fort Sumter, the war claimed the life of Abraham Lincoln. But the republic had safely passed through its fiery trial.

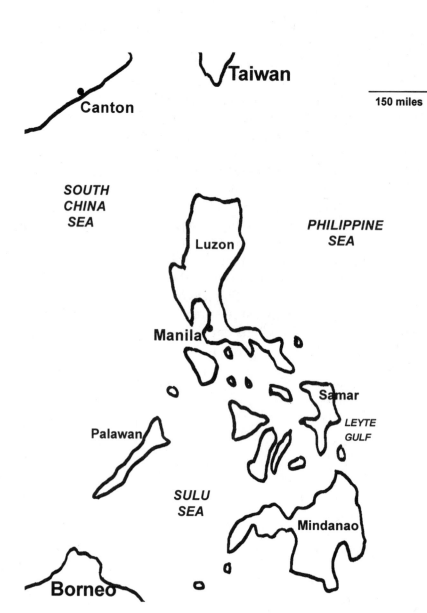

Taiwan

Canton

150 miles

SOUTH
CHINA
SEA

Luzon

PHILIPPINE
SEA

Manila

Samar

LEYTE
GULF

Palawan

SULU
SEA

Mindanao

Borneo

Map produced by Anne Szewczyk.

The Philippines, 1898.

3

The Philippine War

Forgotten Victory

In the twenty-first century the Filipinos and the Americans continue to be, as they long have been, old friends, trading partners, and military allies. Their intimate links include memories of a gratifyingly victorious struggle against a common foe during World War II. The Constitution of the United States provided the model for that of the Philippines, and most Filipinos speak the language their ancestors learned from the Americans. And for students of insurgency, twentieth-century Philippine history provides two instructive examples of how to defeat a guerrilla movement, one with direct and the other with indirect American participation. We consider the former case here and the latter in chapter 6.

The Archipelago

The Philippine archipelago comprises more than seven thousand islands; only three thousand of them have names. They stretch from north to south for almost a thousand miles, the distance from Madrid to Vienna or from Seattle to Los Angeles. The 116,000-square-mile area of the country equals that of Arizona or Italy. The largest of the islands is Luzon, about the size of Kentucky or the former East Germany. Damp and warm, the Philippines produce rice, hemp, coconuts, and sugarcane.

The archipelago has been conquered in turn by the Spanish, the Americans, the Japanese, and the Americans again. Magellan, the circumnavigator, arrived in the islands as early as 1521, to meet his death. The Philippines received their name in 1542, in honor of the prince who as Philip II would one day rule an immense empire and launch the ill-named Invincible Armada. But effective Spanish occupation of the islands did not begin until the 1560s, and Manila was not founded until 1571.

Spanish rule united the islands for the first time in their history; today's Filipino nation took its shape from yesterday's Spanish colony.[1] The Spanish conquest of the Philippines was relatively bloodless, because of the dispersion of the population, the absence of strong native states, and linguistic differences among the islands. But the Spaniards had not thoroughly subdued the large southern island of Mindanao even by 1898.

Along with administrative unity, the Spanish imposed their economic system, including large estates owned by religious orders. But what most profoundly and permanently shaped the culture of the Filipinos was the propagation of Catholic Christianity in its Iberian Reconquista version. "A striking feature of Spanish imperialism was the inseparable union of the Church and the state." Bringing the true religion to the benighted islanders was the main justification for imperialism, an effective answer even to those churchmen who questioned the rightness of conquering the Philippines: "Spain's mission was to forge the spiritual unity of all mankind by ... spreading the gospel among the infidels of America and Asia." Aside from missionaries, relatively few Spaniards came to settle in the islands, and as late as 1898 only one in ten among the native population spoke Spanish. Thus, "the Spaniards put a heavy emphasis on Christianization as the most effective means of incorporating the Filipinos into Spanish culture, and the Filipinos themselves responded enthusiastically to the multiform appeal of the new religion." Consequently, "Catholicism provided the cement of social unity."[2]

The evangelization of the Philippines was no small task. The population was geographically dispersed and spoke a bewildering variety of languages utterly unknown to Europeans. Before 1700 there were few missionary priests in the islands, mostly members of the great orders: Jesuits, Dominicans, Franciscans, Augustinians. Nevertheless, the ceaseless efforts to spread the Christian religion achieved successes that were great and lasting. Spanish priests also relentlessly attacked the native practice of ritual drunkenness, the eradication of which contributed to the sobriety that characterizes the Filipinos to this day.

Christianity brought the Philippines into the orbit of Western civilization, where they have remained ever since. Today the Republic of the Philippines is the only Christian nation in all of East Asia; "the Filipinos are [also] unique for being the only oriental people profoundly and consistently influenced by Occidental culture for the last four centuries."[3]

However one may evaluate the cultural effects of Spanish rule, it promoted neither economic development nor self-government. By the dawn of the nineteenth century, Filipinos of education and prominence, called ilustrados, were chafing under the discrimination against them by Spaniards with regard to appointments in church and state. The Spanish were pursuing similar policies in their Latin American domains, setting creoles against peninsulares. Resentment was also high against the enormous financial and political power of the monastic orders. Late in the nineteenth century some ilustrados founded the Katipunan, a secret society whose purpose was to work toward the overthrow of Spanish power. Emilio Aguinaldo, born in 1869, became head of the Katipunan in Cavite (on Luzon) and eventually throughout all of the islands.[4]

The Americans Arrive

In the summer of 1896, the Katipunan launched a major rebellion. It lasted only about a year, because Aguinaldo and several other prominent rebel leaders agreed to go into exile in Hong Kong in return for the promise of a substantial payment to them by the royal government. Underlying discontents, however, were not addressed, and so rebellion broke out again in March 1898. But within a few weeks, Spain and the United States were at war.[5]

Affairs in the Philippines had very little to do with the outbreak of the Spanish-American War, but the effects of that war on the islands would be profound indeed. The U.S. Asiatic Squadron, under Como. George Dewey on his flagship the *Olympia*, sailed from Nagasaki to Manila Bay. There, on May 1, Dewey won his total victory against the Spanish fleet under Adm. Patricio Montojo. And on May 19 Dewey had Aguinaldo brought back to the islands (to Cavite).

A few days later Aguinaldo proclaimed himself dictator of the provisional government of an independent Philippine Republic. By the end of June, most of the key island of Luzon (but not Manila) was in the hands of his adherents, and Aguinaldo apparently believed that Washington would recognize his government.[6]

Dewey's naval triumph did not mean that the fighting in the islands was over. The first units of the U.S. Army began arriving on June 30, 1898; Manila fell to the Americans on August 13. These American troops were ten thousand miles from Washington, D.C. They were deploying in an archipelago made up of thousands of islands with perhaps ten million inhabitants[7] (nobody knew for sure) who displayed a vast cultural diversity, from Hispanicized Manilans at one extreme to the pagan tribes of the Luzon mountains at the other. Because no one in the Philippines knew what President McKinley's policy toward the islands was or would be, the U.S. Army leaders on the scene refused to allow Aguinaldo's forces to enter Manila in strength. Nevertheless, the army stood by while many small Spanish garrisons and outposts outside Manila, cut off from supplies and instructions from Madrid, surrendered to Aguinaldo's men. Had they been able to look into the near future, the Americans would have wanted to capture those posts themselves.

Although the United States had gone to war with Spain over Cuba, Dewey's unexpectedly lopsided victory in Manila Bay meant that the American government now had to decide the fate of the Philippines. At the beginning of the war, President McKinley had nothing remotely approximating a policy for the islands. For the Americans to return control of the Philippines to the Spanish after having conquered them seemed dishonorable, as well as cruel to the Filipinos, who would pay a dread price for their rebellion. But many in Washington (and elsewhere) believed that the islands were not ready to govern themselves. Philippine independence would most probably dissolve into civil war and anarchy. Such conditions would tempt other powers with imperial holdings in the Western Pacific (such as Japan or Germany)[8] to occupy the islands. Considerations like these began to move McKinley's advisers toward the idea of a temporary American possession of the whole archipelago.

The predictable end of the Spanish-American war came on December 10, 1898, with the signing of the Treaty of Paris. Among other provisions, Spain sold the Philippine Islands to the United States for twenty million dollars. By that time the American government had adopted the position that the Filipinos could not protect their own independence. Washington hoped that the promise of benevolent and efficient administration at the hands of Americans, plus a definite guarantee of independence at some future date, would calm and even placate most of the inhabitants of the archipelago.[9]

Insurgency

In February 1899 about fifteen thousand American troops held Manila, under the command of Gen. Elwell S. Otis. These men were mostly volunteers; a few months previously they had been civilians. At various points around the capital were about thirty thousand soldiers more or less loyal to Aguinaldo. Relations between the two forces were rapidly deteriorating. Actual fighting between the U.S. Army in Manila and Aguinaldo's troops began on February 4, 1899.[10]

A month later a presidential commission arrived in the islands. Jacob Gould Schurman, president of Cornell University, headed the commission, which also included Dean C. Worcester, a University of Michigan sociologist and veteran of several scientific expeditions to the islands. The commissioners published a proclamation to the Filipinos setting forth the benevolent intentions of the U.S. government. The document pledged that government to protect the Filipinos "in their just privileges and immunities," to "accustom them to free self-government in an ever-increasing measure," and to "encourage them in . . . democratic aspirations, sentiments, and ideals." Some members of Aguinaldo's self-proclaimed government wished to accept the terms of this April proclamation; they were stopped only by the vigorous intervention of his troops.[11] The American forces were perplexed to find that even by the end of the year, many Filipinos had not even heard of the April proclamation. Nevertheless, respected Filipinos who had been members of the insurgent congress went over to the American side, and Filipinos had begun to join American-sponsored police units on Luzon and Negros Islands and to act as scouts and interpreters for the U.S. Army.

In command of the only organized armed force that operated

throughout the length of the islands, Aguinaldo also possessed in the Katipunan an infrastructure that could provide his troops with information and money, distribute propaganda among the civilian population, and punish defectors. Aguinaldo's movement received vital support as well from elements of the native Catholic clergy. Yet it would be anachronistic to assume that Aguinaldo was the leader of a movement of full-fledged Filipino nationalism. In the first place, he had achieved supreme leadership over the insurgency only after his followers had executed Andres Bonifacio, founder of the Katipunan. This act disillusioned many who might otherwise have rallied around a nationalist banner. Furthermore, many of the social elite of the islands were reluctant to assist the rebellion. But of supreme importance in limiting support for the insurgents were the ethnic divisions within Philippine society. The center of the revolt was in the Tagalog-speaking regions around Manila. Aguinaldo and a disproportionately large number of the other principal leaders of the insurgency were Tagalog. But Gen. Antonio Luna, perhaps the best officer in the nationalist army, was an Ilocano. The murder of Luna at Aguinaldo's headquarters under very suspicious circumstances exacerbated ethnic tensions throughout the islands. Aguinaldo's soldiers engaged in a lot of indiscriminate pillaging, but probably no group suffered more from this sort of activity than the numerous Chinese minority. The Americans soon learned to take advantage of these conditions by employing non-Tagalog Filipinos in their paramilitary forces.

A Guerrilla Conflict

The Americans sought to involve key elements of the population in their own defense, and they set up civil administrations to incorporate prominent local citizens into the American scheme. These projects were sometimes successful. But more than occasionally, the guerrillas killed persons who worked with the Americans, and there were instances in which Filipinos outwardly cooperated with the Americans but secretly aided the guerrillas. As with every other aspect of the Philippine struggle, the situation varied greatly from one region to another. Nevertheless, it was not uncommon that "while American troops were occupying towns and establishing municipal governments with the natives holding offices, the Insurgents arranged a parallel organization, in many cases employing the same natives who held office under the Americans. The towns were taxed, contributions and supplies collected, and recruits for the guerrilla forces enlisted right under the noses of the unsuspecting Americans."[12]

For much of the time, the American effort amounted to a war of attrition: they killed a few guerrillas here, captured some rifles there, destroyed a food dump someplace else. Frequent patrols and rapid response to any guerrilla action began to exhaust the insurgents. Because of the nature of the terrain and the state of communications—many islands, many villages, no radio, no helicopters—it became possible, indeed imperative, for local U.S. commanders to adjust their tactics to the local situation. In addition, particular units tended to remain in the same area for extended periods. Such decentralization in the counterinsurgency effort—local tactics adapted to local conditions—eventually paid great dividends.[13]

As the 2000s dawn, U.S. forces seem to have become reluctant, in the view of a noted authority on the Philippine insurgency, to mount operations against guerrillas during a rainy season, because airpower then becomes less reliable. But the evidence from the Philippine conflict strongly suggests that rainy seasons are at least as hard on poorly equipped and supplied guerrillas as on regular troops. The Americans built all-weather roads in the Philippines, increasing their mobility without appreciably helping the guerrillas.[14] In any event, the United States won its complete victory over the guerrillas without any air force at all, rainy season or no.

Intelligence became an ever-sharper weapon in American hands. When U.S. Army units remained in an area for an extended period, they were often able, through close observation, to identify and arrest supporters of the insurgency. Bribery helped too: several local commanders paid handsome rewards to Filipinos who would furnish information about the rebel organization in a village or town. Guerrillas who took advantage of amnesties often provided much interesting information; prisoners obtained their freedom if they agreed to identify former comrades or lead U.S. solders to their hiding places.[15] And of course the army recruited a growing number of Filipino scouts from ethnic groups opposed to the Tagalog-dominated guerrillas, men familiar with the countryside and the sympathies of its inhabitants.

Next to the guerrillas, the most important quarry for American troops was rifles: finding, capturing, or buying them from the locals. Rifles were relatively scarce among the guerrillas to begin with, and of course no fresh supplies were coming in from outside. The Americans paid good money to anyone turning in a rifle, with no questions asked. And in lieu of cash, any Filipino who turned in a rifle or any other serious weapon at an army base could secure the release of a prisoner of war. Gen. Arthur MacArthur (who succeeded Otis as commander in the Philippines) called this prisoners-for-rifles trade one of his "most important policies."[16] The resulting constant loss of firearms, through battle, discovery, or cash rewards, gravely undermined the ability of the guerrillas to carry on their struggle.

In the later stages of the conflict, food became as problematical for the insurgents as rifles. The Americans devoted increasingly successful efforts to cutting off food supplies to the guerrillas, scouring a given territory for hidden fields and storehouses. Constant American patrolling kept the guerrillas on the move and uncovered many food caches. Men had to shift their attention and activity from fighting the Americans to getting or growing or stealing food. The American food-denial campaign seriously hurt both the guerrillas' morale and their health; guerrilla life in any country and any conflict is often filled with hardships; for the Philippine insurgents, the lack of medical facilities and the decreasing food supplies meant increasing illness.

The food-denial campaign inevitably led the Americans to develop plans for concentrating the rural population. The idea for concentration arose late in the conflict in those areas where the remaining guerrilla groups seemed determined to fight on indefinitely, even though it had become perfectly clear to all observers that they could not possibly be victorious over the Americans, and despite repeated American requests that they accept honorable surrender. Something drastic had to be done.

Concentration worked generally in this way: the civil population of a given region received instructions to move into a designated town by a particular date, bringing all family members, animals, and foodstuffs with them. After that date any goods or animals found outside the town were liable to confiscation, and men were liable to arrest on suspicion of being guerrillas. Food shipments between towns were subject to very strict controls. (Almost fifty years later the British would impose similar policies in their conflict with Communist guerrillas in Malaya.) The U.S. Army carried out large numbers of vaccinations, sought to ensure adequate food supplies for the concentration areas, and tried to provide adequate jobs for civilians on public works projects. Nevertheless, hardships, injustices, and suffering were inevitable. Proper sanitation became a serious problem, with the consequent health dangers. Perhaps eleven thousand Filipinos died as result of poor conditions in the concentration areas. At almost exactly the same time, the very large-scale British efforts to concentrate the Boer civilian population in the South African War was resulting in a much higher loss of life, mainly from typhoid fever.[17]

War Crimes

The image of the American army in the Philippines as composed mainly of brutal racists wading through a swamp of atrocities has found its way into some of the books, and even to a degree into the collective memory of the U.S. Army itself. Such an image does not fit comfortably with the available evidence.[18]

Most American soldiers in the Philippines were very young, under twenty-five; most had never been away from home, or at least away from their native states, before. Hardly a single one arrived with even a rudimentary knowledge of Tagalog, not to mention the languages spoken by remote minorities. They were fighting an unseen enemy in a unhealthful climate that many found maddeningly oppressive. And it is the very essence of guerrilla war that occupation troops often find it nearly impossible to distinguish friend or neutral from enemy; when soldiers and civilians are racially alien to one another, the situation becomes even more explosive. Thus the stage was lavishly set for a volcanic eruption of abuses and crimes.

During the first year of the conflict, the Americans usually released prisoners once they had been disarmed. As a rule they did not punish villagers even when there was evidence that they had cooperated with the insurgents. The Americans offered the Filipinos many inducements to support American rule but exacted few real penalties for opposing it. All this was in accordance with the aim of eventual reconciliation. After the middle of 1900, however, ideas began to change. Many Americans had come to believe that the policy of benevolence toward the guerrillas and their sympathizers had produced a situation in which the population feared the rebels much more than they feared the Americans.[19] The opinion was widespread that even those Filipinos who were well disposed toward the Americans viewed the policy of restraint as proof of an essential lack of seriousness. Reprisals, by demonstrating the prohibitive costs of further resistance, would shorten the war and save lives, both American and Filipino. Hence a new attitude appeared among the Americans: benevolence to those who were peaceable but severity to those who persisted in obviously useless violence.

Believing that time was clearly on the side of the Americans, General MacArthur resisted pressures from below for a harsher policy. There had previously been instances of misbehavior by American soldiers in certain areas, even the looting of some churches; General Otis and his subcommanders sought to punish those who committed such acts. Brig. Gen. J. Franklin Bell actually forbade his troops to enter civilian houses, and he insisted that all supplies, whatever their source or quantity, be paid for. Nevertheless, by the summer of 1900, some American units were burning down any barrio within whose precincts an ambush or an act of terror or sabotage had occurred. The "water cure," getting information from a captured guerrilla by forcing him to drink water through a tube until he gave in, was becoming a common practice.[20] There is no doubt that during the year 1900 abuses by American forces increased; rebel propaganda efforts were unsparing in their depiction of the Americans as steeped in atrocities, and some of this propaganda reached the United States.

Evidence exists of an inverse relationship between breaches committed by American troops and the length of time those troops had spent in a given area. Gen. Frederick Funston, the captor (later) of Aguinaldo, believed it was essential to maintain troops at the company level in the same place for a long time, in order to learn both the terrain and the people. In the key province of Batangas, in southern Luzon, American troops were mainly volunteers, many of them only in their teens and most of the rest in their twenties; they were white, single, and had little formal education and often less than six weeks of military training. This was a perfect setup for real trouble;

nevertheless, soldiers in the town garrisons were involved in many fewer incidents with civilians or prisoners than soldiers on field duty.[21]

Many insurgents also committed crimes. During 1899 numerous peasants leveled accusations of robbery, rape, and murder against the forces of Aguinaldo. Sometimes these incidents reflected the ethnic divisions of the islands, a predictable situation since Aguinaldo and most other leaders of the rebellion were Tagalogs from central Luzon. Sometimes guerrillas struck at those who had been their personal enemies before the war. Later in the struggle, Aguinaldo's followers sought to impose discipline on the civilian population through such acts as setting whole villages on fire. Occasionally this sort of behavior was effective, but often it backfired, creating much hostility toward the insurgents.[22]

As 1900 wore on, the tide was obviously turning decisively against the insurgents; the Americans were on the move, and great numbers of guerrillas, including officers, were defecting. Desperate to reinstill discipline into their supporters, the guerrillas resorted more frequently to terrorist acts; killings of the officials of American-established municipal governments increased, and guerrilla units even threatened that any town that cooperated with the Americans would be burned down and all its male inhabitants put to the sword. American forces thereafter intensified their efforts to protect villagers from guerrilla reprisals. Quite understandably, the local population often turned against the guerrillas, either because they resented guerrilla terrorism or because they did not want guerrillas to draw American troops into their districts.[23]

Whatever may be the exact balance with regard to violations of the laws of war or of humanity, it is clear that after the conflict was over—and indeed while it was at its height—good relations between Filipinos and Americans flourished. Even Emilio Aguinaldo, who had lost more as a result of the conflict than perhaps anyone else, in later years wrote many admiring words about his former American foes. Most notably, he pronounced it a good thing that the United States had established its rule over the Philippines, because otherwise the islands probably would have been partitioned among several foreign powers and thus almost certainly would never have become united.[24]

The Americans Attract Support

Many American officers in the Philippines were of the same Progressive persuasion as their relatives back home in the States: they believed in honest government, fair taxes, free education, and public health measures, and they believed in the power and the duty of enlightened government to uplift those in its care. They soon showed that they grasped the connection between the present conduct of the army and the future reconciliation between Americans and Filipinos. One American general said, "We have got to live among these people, we have got to govern them. Government by force alone cannot be satisfactory to Americans." General Otis, in command of American ground forces, "for all his faults as a troop commander, recognized that the problem facing the Americans in the Philippines was in reality a political one."[25] That is, Otis understood that his task was not only to defeat the rebels but also to set the stage for pacification and reconciliation.

Quite aside from waging war against the insurgents, the U.S. Army faced a daunting task in the Manila of 1899. The city, which with its immediate environs was home to four hundred thousand persons, was woefully overcrowded. Schools were closed, the port was not operating, rubbish and garbage went uncollected in the streets, and the Aguinaldo forces had cut off the water supply. The city was on the verge of epidemic and anarchy. The Americans began by cleaning up the filth in the streets. They then appointed municipal health officials and offered free medical care to the many indigent inhabitants of the capital. Launching a campaign to vaccinate thousands first in Manila and then in the countryside, the army eventually reduced smallpox from a scourge to a problem. As the American forces moved out from the capital, they distributed food, set up municipal governments, and attacked the deplorable sanitary conditions. They reformed the prison system, releasing many who had languished untried in jail for years. They built or rebuilt schools, often with soldiers as instructors, and taught many children; this was one of the most popular American programs among a population hungry for education. The Americans also gave the same care to wounded Filipino prisoners as to their own wounded. The undeniable and growing success of this American "policy of attraction" deeply disconcerted the insurgent leaders.

The Presidential Election of 1900

Aguinaldo's fundamental plan was to protract the conflict until American troops began to break down from disease and exhaustion or until opinion in the United States turned against the war, or both. A guerrilla pamphlet declared, "We repeat that we must not give or accept combat with such a powerful foe if we have not the greatest chance of success. . . . Let us wait for the deadly climate to decimate his [ranks] and never forget that our object is only to protract the state of war."[26] Aguinaldo and his lieutenants concocted a strategy against the Americans that North Vietnamese general Vo Nguyen Giap would employ seven decades later (with immeasurably more success).

Although the U.S. Senate passed the treaty with Spain providing for the annexation of the Philippines, agitation against the war continued in certain American circles. U.S. soldiers in the islands believed that the guerrilla resistance took courage from the speeches of members of so-called anti- imperialist leagues, and also from the correspondence between such persons and Philippine guerrilla chiefs. Activists in the United States even sent propaganda to American soldiers in the islands, urging them to abandon this brutal imperialistic war. The announced object of the guerrilla leadership—to tire the Americans by making their occupation of the islands as costly as possible—was thus more than a mere pipe dream. Meanwhile both Filipino guerrillas and American anti-imperialists looked forward eagerly to the victory in the approaching presidential election of William Jennings Bryan.[27]

Former "Boy Orator of the River Platte," evangelist, prohibitionist, future crusader against Darwinism in the famous Scopes "Monkey" trial, in 1900 William Jennings Bryan was indeed the Democratic presidential standard-bearer (for the second but not the last time), running on an "anti-imperialist" platform. The specter of a Bryan victory seriously hobbled American efforts in the Philippines: fearing that a Bryan presidency would mean an immediate pullout of U.S. forces from the islands, many Filipinos shied away from cooperating with the Americans.

Even though Aguinaldo desperately needed a Bryan victory, the Philippine insurgent later described the American politician as "nearsighted, selfish and unstatesmanlike." Aguinaldo was well aware that Bryan wanted the United States to annex the Philippines so that there would be a war that he could blame on McKinley. Bryan did in fact go to Washington and ordered Democratic senators to vote for McKinley's annexation treaty, which he later denounced during the campaign.[28]

But this Machiavellian medicine show was all in vain: Bryan suffered a rebuff from the American electorate even more decisive than that of 1896. The effects of his defeat reverberated across the Pacific. Many Filipinos had wished to make peace with the Americans but had hung back from fear of guerrilla reprisals if the Americans abandoned the islands. The reelection of McKinley destroyed this possibility, and large numbers of Filipinos rallied to the American side and to the newly formed pro-American Federal Party. The election certainly wounded the morale of the Aguinaldo supporters, sustained as they had been by the mirage of a coming Bryan triumph; the amount of money and food turned over to the guerrillas declined sharply. Nevertheless, the massive postelection surrenders that American forces had been hoping for did not materialize.[29]

At the same time, it was becoming apparent that General Otis, a conscientious and hardworking officer, was not cut out to fight guerrillas in the jungle. He relied on sweeps and other time-wasting tactics. Over and over his forces would occupy a village for a time and then withdraw, allowing the guerrillas to reenter the place. Otis himself was not unaware that he was making little progress, and he asked to be relieved. In May 1900 Gen. Arthur MacArthur took over as commander of the U.S. Army in the Philippines. Within a month MacArthur issued a proclamation of amnesty for guerrillas. Meanwhile he developed plans for an offensive against remaining insurgent forces. McKinley's decisive defeat of Bryan was the signal to go ahead. MacArthur launched the offensive in December, involving the majority of his seventy thousand troops. The Americans initiated many small-scale clashes, increased the number of towns with permanent garrisons, and began to gather into those towns the outlying population in areas where guerrillas were active.

The End in Sight

After the presidential election of 1900, General MacArthur responded to growing demands for a more vigorously punitive policy toward guerrilla sympathizers. Henceforth even those men who were only part-time insurgents would receive harsh treatment when captured. The army would no longer accept compulsion or intimidation as excuses for acts in support of the rebels. The Americans also stopped releasing prisoners and began instead to send captured guerrillas to detention on Guam.

The Americans had not been idle with regard to improving their intelligence activities against the insurgents. Between late 1900 and early 1901, they made a serious and fairly successful effort to break up the revolutionary organization in Manila. Then, on March 23, 1901, a week after Aguinaldo's second in command had surrendered, the Americans achieved the greatest intelligence coup of the war: American army officer Frederick Funston captured Aguinaldo himself.[30] A few weeks later that guerrilla leader swore an oath of allegiance to the United States and urged his followers to lay down their arms.

The insurgents were really becoming desperate now; during 1901 the number of whole barrios put to the torch by guerrillas greatly increased. Predictably, many Filipinos responded to such acts by joining in active cooperation with the Americans. By mid-1901 more than fifty-four hundred were serving as army scouts or police (notably, almost all were non-Tagalog).

The founding of the Filipino Federal Party at the end of 1900 was another response to insurgent terrorism. The party sought to rally their countrymen around a program of conciliation with the Americans and eventual independence. Some supported the Federal Party because they believed that what the Philippines needed was not independence but modernization, and a period of rule by the United States would bring exactly that. Immediately recognizing that the Federal Party's peaceful road toward independence was a major threat to them, the insurgents vowed to execute party members without trial.[31]

It was clear that the insurgency could not last much longer. American "propaganda of the deed" such as the schools program, the increasing number of permanently garrisoned towns, the aggressive actions by army units that gave the rebels no respite, the growing involvement of Filipinos in peacekeeping activities (such as the Philippine Constabulary, a mobile force of three thousand, mainly under American officers), the efforts of the Federal Party, the capture of Aguinaldo, all resulted in the surrender of larger and larger numbers of guerrillas. In March and April 1901 alone, surrenders totaled thirteen thousand.

In the spring of 1901, Secretary of War Elihu Root became convinced that the fighting was nearly finished. Wishing to establish closer civilian control over the U.S. Army in the Philippines, and believing he would have an easier time of it with a commander who had not exercised the vast powers of MacArthur, Root replaced him with Brig. Gen. Adna R. Chaffee, who came to the Philippines after seeing action against the Boxer Rebellion.

By summer of the same year, southern Luzon Island remained the area of highest guerrilla activity. The population was quite dense, the terrain was ideal for guerrillas, and diseases were rampant. The people were mostly Tagalog; hence U.S. forces found few members of minority ethnic groups to recruit as scouts and informants. The guerrillas in the area were under the command of thirty-six-year-old Maj. Gen. Miguel Malvar: "charismatic, a dedicated patriot, and an able organizer, he was probably the most capable adversary the Americans faced in the Philippine war."[32] In June, however, the able Gen. Juan Cailles surrendered to the Americans, bringing with him about 100 officers, 500 men, 140 civilian officials, and 400 invaluable rifles. This major haul of prisoners and weapons began the death knell of organized rebellion on Luzon.

At the same time, U.S. casualty rates went steadily downward.[33] And on the Fourth of July, William Howard Taft, future president and future chief justice of the United States, took the oath as civil governor of the Philippines.

As the summer of 1901 drew to a close, everything seemed to be going in the Americans' favor. But toward the end of September, an event occurred that seemed likely to undo much of the Americans' success in winning over the Filipinos. Samar was a jungle-covered island with a population of only 250,000, plus a small number of American troops. In the town of Balangiga, insurgents succeeded through treachery in massacring and mutilating a company of the U.S. Ninth Infantry. Because the guerrillas had executed this grisly butchery at a stage in the conflict when it was obvious that their cause could not possibly be victorious, it provoked a furious reaction among American troops on Samar. To them it seemed not a justifiable act of war but plain murder. Brig. Gen. Jacob Smith, in charge of pacification of the island, vowed to turn the interior of Samar into "a howling wilderness."[34] Smith's punitive campaign on the island involved many violations of the general U.S. policy of benevolence that had seemed to be working so well after three years.

While Smith carried out his drastic campaign against the guerrillas on Samar, Gen. Franklin Bell captured the last insurgent stronghold on southern Luzon, in Batangas province. Bell then ordered his subordinate commanders to establish security perimeters around the numerous towns and bring all the inhabitants of the area to live inside these perimeters. Soldiers confiscated any food found outside the lines. Eventually more than three hundred thousand people were gathered inside the designated boundaries. To further isolate the guerrillas, Bell instituted a pass system for civilians. By the spring of 1902 Batangas was calm.

On the Fourth of July 1902 the Americans offered another amnesty for all remaining guerrillas except for a few accused felons. By year's end the number of U.S. Army troops in the islands was down to fifteen thousand. Though not happy about the American occupation, most politically concerned Filipinos appeared ready to submit to U.S. administration and work peacefully toward independence.

An Authentic Victory over Guerrillas

Aguinaldo's followers were fighting in their home territory, on terrain favorable to guerrilla tactics, under the banner of national independence and defense of religion. This has been the classic formula for a powerful and persisting guerrilla movement through the ages and across the continents.

On the other side, the Americans were a truly foreign force in every way: racially, culturally, linguistically, and religiously. They had no familiarity with the peoples among whom they were fighting or the places where the fighting occurred, no long colonial experience to guide them, and no adequate defense against many of the maladies to which the climate of the Philippines exposed them. Far from home, the Americans were also few in number: with the task of pacifying a vast archipelago with 10 million inhabitants, the American forces totaled 20,000 early in 1899, peaked at 70,000 late in 1900, then quickly declined to 42,000 by mid-1901[35] and sank to a mere

15,000 by the end of 1902. And of course these troops completely lacked that airpower which Americans have come to regard as the indispensable key to victory in all circumstances. Looking back at the Philippine struggle from the vantage point of a hundred years, therefore, it approaches understatement to observe that the situation overflowed with possibilities for disaster.

In the end the Philippine insurrection cost the Americans more casualties (4,200 killed, 2,800 wounded) than the war with Spain and, when it came to dollars, several times the original price paid to Spain for the islands.[36] Even so, for the three and a half years of the conflict, the number of American fatalities averaged only about 100 per month. The Americans won a clear-cut and relatively bloodless victory in a short period of time and in a manner that laid the foundation for a close future friendship between two peoples on opposite sides of the vast Pacific.

How did they accomplish all this?

A decisive feature of the Philippine insurgency was that the guerrillas received no assistance from outside. Hence, they started out poorly armed and stayed that way. At one point Aguinaldo said he hoped for help from "perhaps Germany." Maybe he thought the Germans would help him for nothing, or that the Philippines would be better off under Wilhelm II. More importantly, members of the Japanese army officer corps wished to assist Aguinaldo: "Asia for the Asians!" Some Japanese officers did manage to get to Luzon to offer their services, and there was at least one unsuccessful attempt to send the insurgents a shipload of weapons and ammunition from Japan.[37] But the Imperial Foreign Ministry was opposed to such potentially explosive actions and was able to enforce its will, more or less. Moreover, any serious outside intervention would have to confront the U.S. Navy. As it turned out, not a single foreign state granted recognition to Aguinaldo's self-proclaimed government.

This isolation of the battlefield was clearly very important; it helped set certain limits to the entire scope of the war. But other elements played their powerful roles as well. Above all, the American victory in the Philippines illuminates with perfect clarity the decisive influence of political factors on the outcome of this type of struggle. Consider first that, as the leader of resistance to a foreign occupation, Aguinaldo had in his favor—at least in theory—the mighty weapon of nationalism, of hatred for the alien invader. But he was never able to wield this weapon effectively. A broad Philippine national consciousness did not exist. Most of the inhabitants of the islands were simple peasants who concerned themselves with family, village, and church, not with political abstractions. Besides that, there were many ethnic tensions and rivalries within Filipino society, which the insurgency aggravated rather than suppressed, and which the Americans were quick to perceive and exploit.

The support of the landowning notables could have been invaluable to Aguinaldo, because they exerted great influence over their numerous tenants and servants. But Aguinaldo's social conservatism did not win him the reliable support of these traditional elites. Most of them seem to have grasped very early that Aguinaldo could not defeat the Americans; consequently, they feared that if they openly supported Aguinaldo, the Americans might confiscate their property or hand the running of the country over to some other group lower down on the social scale. Such fears had solid foundation. The U.S. Army arrested notables who supported Aguinaldo and seized their estates; in some areas Filipinos friendly to the Americans were permitted to harvest the crops of known supporters of the insurgency. Thus, the upper classes, with whatever reluctance, turned away from Aguinaldo.

Aguinaldo might then have looked for help in the opposite direction, seeking to arouse the peasantry by waving the banner of social revolution. But he was much too conservative to unleash such an appeal, with all its consequences, foreseeable and otherwise. Aguinaldo's insurgency never was and never could have been a Maoist "people's war." But if—or rather, since—the victory of a guerrilla movement friendly to the upper classes offered little promise of improvement in the lives of ordinary peasants, why should they endanger themselves for the cause? And almost as if they wished to make all these facts perfectly clear to the peasantry, the guerrillas practiced impressment, taking young men by compulsion into their ranks, unless their parents or an employer were willing and able to secure their release for a substantial cash payment.[38]

Instead of social revolution, Aguinaldo offered the Filipinos political aims that were cloudy at best. At one point during the conflict, he declared that he wanted the Philippines to be a U.S.

protectorate while developing into a free republic—but that was exactly what the U.S. government had promised. He wrote that he and his followers "neither hoped for victory over the Americans nor hated them. But we wanted to gain their respect," and "it was our hope that, if we should perish . . . we would at least earn the respect . . . of the Americans."[39] Reviewing these pronouncements, Aguinaldo later wrote, "I must admit that there was some ambiguity and perhaps even inconsistency in our position." Years later, Aguinaldo ran for the presidency of the Philippine Commonwealth against Manuel Quezon. He was badly beaten.

Aguinaldo and his followers faced daunting obstacles in their efforts to rally the inhabitants of the Philippines around them. And in the light of the actual historical record, it would be all too easy to assume that American victory was demanded, so to speak, by the circumstances, all too easy to forget that the American forces might have done Aguinaldo's job for him: that is, they might have conducted themselves in such a manner as to provoke a furious national resistance, forcing the Filipinos to overcome their ethnic and social divisions, at least for the time being, and unite against the foreigner. But in fact the Americans behaved, for the most part, in ways that did not arouse the rage or desperation of the Filipinos and make recruits for Aguinaldo.

Winning the Peace

Foreign conquerors though they surely were, the Americans were not easy to hate. Aguinaldo had warned his countrymen that the Americans had come to enslave the Filipinos and abolish Catholicism. That kind of propaganda backfired badly. It soon became clear that the Americans had not come to uproot religion and trample the defenseless. At the minimum, with their schools and sanitation programs and free inoculations, the Americans were undeniably a tremendous improvement over the Spanish. Revolutionaries often promise, and sometimes provide, literacy and health care to the lower classes; in the Philippines the Americans did both. In a real sense they were the revolutionaries, not Aguinaldo.

And even on the issue of Philippine independence, what the Americans and the insurgents disputed was not the right to independence but merely the timing of it. If one's understanding of the term *colony* derives from Vietnam or Algeria under the French, or Ireland or India under the British, then the Americans never intended the Philippines to be a colony. From almost the earliest days of American rule, plans were set in motion for self-government, resulting in an elected legislature in 1907, the very first in Southeast Asia. In 1934, hardly three decades after the Americans had taken control of the islands, the U.S. Congress established that Philippine independence should occur one decade later. And having early made clear their commitment to self-government, the Americans did not debar former guerrillas from participation in public life; this decision not to look closely into the wartime activities of former insurgents helped greatly in the general reconciliation after 1902.[40] Some ex-revolutionary leaders actually received posts in the American civil government after their surrender, and the first president of the Philippine Commonwealth was the former insurgent Maj. Manuel Quezon.

The unmistakable steps taken by the Americans to improve the lives and prepare for the independence of the Filipinos found their all-important counterpoint in the American style of fighting the guerrillas. There were no screaming jets accidentally bombing helpless villages, no B-52s, no napalm, no routine artillery barrages, no "collateral damage." Instead, the Americans conducted a decentralized war of small mobile units armed mainly with rifles and aided by native Filipinos, hunting guerrillas who were increasingly isolated both by the indifference or hostility of much of the population and by the concentration of scattered peasant groups into larger settlements.

Ethnic tensions within the archipelago, along with the social conservatism of the insurgents and their uninspiring political aims, severely limited their domestic support, and they could find no sustenance from overseas. These grave weaknesses had their effects multiplied by the American policy of rectitude and reconciliation. For most Filipinos, the Americans were, at the very minimum, not irritating enough to justify fighting them.

Out of his long experience in dealing with guerrillas, the noted French colonial commander Louis Lyautey developed a general strategy of counterinsurgency that emphasized limiting damage to the civilian economy and winning over the local population through minimal force and good administration. The key concept of this strategy was to hold territory rather than to kill guerrillas. In their conflict with the Philippine insurgency, the Americans came to many of the same conclusions as Lyautey about how to fight guerrillas; consequently, "after 1900 the American stress on the isolation of the guerrilla and the protection of townspeople from terrorism and intimidation was an important element in the success of pacification operations."[41]

Perhaps the major lesson of the Philippine war is that a complete and lasting American victory derived from the combination of increasingly effective counterguerrilla tactics with an intelligent program of improving society and reconciling opponents. One element without the other would surely not have worked as well, and might not have worked at all.[42]

The Moro War

In addition to the followers of Aguinaldo, U.S. forces in the Philippines had other opponents to contend with. These were the Moros, concentrated on Mindanao and a few other islands. The conflict with the Moros was distinct from the struggle against Aguinaldo in a number of ways. The areas where most of the Moros lived were far from the centers of Aguinaldo's main support. Although racially indistinguishable from other Filipinos, the Moros' adherence to Islam had long before consolidated them into a separate element, hostile to the Christian Filipino majority in general and to Aguinaldo's movement in particular. Mainly for the latter reason, the American authorities did not turn their attention to affairs in the Moro territories until Aguinaldo's followers had ceased their resistance. Yet, when fighting broke out between American forces and the Moros, it continued for almost a decade.

The Moros were "a society based on war." Indeed, war, slaveholding, and piracy shaped Moro society as much as Islam did. As late as 1908, after a decade of U.S. occupation, the straits of Basilan were known to be full of pirates. And even in 1936 (if not later), women could still be openly bought and sold in Mindanao and Sulu.[43]

For centuries the Moros fought outsiders: the Spanish, the Christian Filipinos, the Americans, the Japanese, the Philippine republic.

In contrast to the dispersed organization elsewhere in the pre-Spanish Philippines, the Moros had imported an Islamic state system; this, along with their religion, was the basis of their resistance to Spain. The first Muslim missionaries arrived in the southern islands around 1380, and the first sultan of Sulu established his capital at Jolo in 1450. Spanish forces had arrived in the Philippines shortly after their last great victory over the forces of Iberian Islam, at Granada, at the very time when Islamic missionaries were making great strides in the archipelago. "Spanish expansion overseas retained many of the characteristics of the centuries long reconquista of Spain from the Moors,"[44] and the Philippines provided the setting for the last major encounter between the Reconquista and Islam. The Spanish called the Muslims of the Philippines Moros ("moors"), after the Saracens who invaded Spain from northern Africa in the eighth century.

The Spanish found perhaps 250,000 Moros on Mindanao. Under their sultans, and in the name of the true religion, the Moros resisted Spanish incursions with ferocity and success. They raided and destroyed Christian Filipino settlements adjacent to Mindanao; over the decades they took uncounted thousands of Christian Filipinos as their slaves. Moro hostility and depredations kindled and strengthened the loyalty of the non-Islamic Filipino majority to Spain; for centuries, the Spanish army recruited Christian Filipino troops, especially from Pampanga.[45] The conflict with the Moros never experienced a decisive moment, in large part because the numerically inadequate Spanish forces on Mindanao usually waged war in defensive style, from inside small forts, in which the garrisons were often decimated by malaria and malnutrition. Even as late as the outbreak of the Spanish-American War, the authority of Spain over much of the Moro territories remained purely nominal.

In the summer of 1898 the Moro population approximated four hundred thousand, spread over Mindanao, Sula, Basilan, and Palawan. The island of Mindanao itself, thirty-six thousand square miles, is the size of Portugal or Indiana. The Moro leaders challenged the right of the United States to receive title to the Philippines from Spain; in their eyes the extinction of Spanish rule meant the independence of the islands, or at least of the Moros. Nevertheless, on August 20, 1899, Gen. John C. Bates signed an agreement with the sultan of Sulu, whereby the latter acknowledged U.S. sovereignty, in return for an American subsidy and guarantees of the sultan's religious primacy and trade rights. The so-called Bates Agreement recognized the sultan of Sulu as the religious, not the political, leader of the Moros.[46]

Almost unanimously, the Moro leaders on Mindanao hated the Filipino nationalist movement. They offered their cooperation to American forces in eliminating armed bands of Aguinaldo's followers. As late as 1902 and 1903, relations between the Moros and U.S. troops were mostly friendly; American officers made several visits to and explorations of Moro country either alone or with small escorts.[47]

Things began to change dramatically with the arrival of Maj. Gen. Leonard Wood, newly appointed governor of the vast Moro Province (Mindanao plus Basilan, Palawan, and the Sulu Archipelago). Wood established himself in his provincial capital of Zamboanga in August 1903. He was dismayed at conditions in Moro society, where slavery, polygamy, and tribal warfare were openly practiced and where murders were punished with a trifling monetary fine. Despite the implicit promises in the Bates Agreement, Wood refused to recognize slavery in his province, and the Moros would not accept any interference with that practice. Consequently, during the thirty-two months Wood served as governor, American troops and Moro warriors fought many engagements against each other; usually it was guerrilla combat, but sometimes pitched battles involving hundreds of Moros. The Americans benefited from the assistance of the Muslim Provincial Constabulary; established by Wood in September 1903, its membership rendered valuable services.[48]

As they searched for Moro rebels on Mindanao, American detachments made nightly camps, in the fashion of Roman legions on campaign. The camps usually measured forty by twenty yards; before nightfall, the soldiers would clear the surrounding underbrush for fifty yards around and pile up the brush around the perimeter of the camp as a protective screen. During these months the U.S. Army replaced the .38 caliber pistol with the .45, because the former weapon could not stop the *juramentados*, individual warriors who were sworn to give their lives in exchange for the lives of Christians (which all Americans were in Moro eyes). Often one or two enraged juramentados would attack a small party of American soldiers and trade lives.

General Wood thought that the Moros, although undeniably brave, were no real threat to American control of the islands. When confronted by U.S. regulars, a common tactic of the Moros was to withdraw into their fortified houses, where they were completely vulnerable to artillery.[49] This method of warfare necessarily involved the death of women and children because when locked up inside their fortress-houses, the Moros refused to surrender; furthermore, the women often fought beside their men.

The Americans finally defeated the Moros, but they were able to maintain fairly good relations with their former enemies because they acted as a barrier between the Muslims and the encroaching Christian majority. A notable advantage the Americans had in dealing with the Moros that the former Spanish overlords had lacked was the sincere promise of religious freedom. During the fighting, the young John J. Pershing worked hard to win Moro friendship by stressing that the Americans would not try to impose Christianity on them.[50]

Afterward

The Moros preferred being ruled by Americans to being ruled by Christian Filipinos. Nevertheless, most Moros refused to learn English and shunned American public schools as being "Christian." Hence the Moros remained isolated and backward, while civil service positions necessarily went to educated Christian Filipinos from outside of Mindanao.

After the establishment of the Philippine Republic in 1946, outbreaks of Moro resistance occurred sporadically. A serious rebellion broke out in 1971, under the general leadership of the Moro National Liberation Front (MNLF), which aimed ultimately to establish an independent Muslim state on Mindanao. To counter Moro charges that his government was committing genocide against the Muslim population, Philippine president Ferdinand Marcos allowed teams of Islamic ambassadors, foreign ministers, and other high dignitaries to tour Mindanao in 1973 and 1974. Their reports consistently discounted charges of religious persecution, attributing the conflict between the Moros and the Manila government to socioeconomic and leadership problems, not to religion per se. Accordingly, the 1974 Islamic Foreign Ministers' Conference in Kuala Lumpur refused to admit the MNLF even as observers.[51] Potentially sympathetic Arab countries such as Libya were far away, and furthermore the Manila government often earned the gratitude of the Arab bloc by supporting it on international questions.

Cut off from any prospect of obtaining serious aid from Middle Eastern states, the rebellion also suffered from grave divisions within Moro society. Some prominent leaders of the MNLF espoused Marxist doctrines, thus alienating the more traditional sectors of the Moro population. But even if they were unanimous in their views and actions, the Moros would still constitute only a small minority, less than one-third, of the population of Mindanao, which much of the world assumes to be the stronghold of Philippine Islam.

Yet the principal obstacle confronting armed Moro rebellion against Manila is not isolation from outside help nor numerical inferiority nor internal divisions. Beyond all these weaknesses, devastating as they are, any Moro independence movement contains within itself a fundamental strategic weakness that is permanent and fatal. Whatever its institutional origins or political coloration, no Philippine government can possibly countenance partition of the country—especially a partition that would abandon millions of non-Muslim Filipinos to a Moro regime. Therefore the MNLF cannot achieve its aims by relying on a war of exhaustion (a strategy that always has double effects anyway): the government will not, because it cannot, grow tired of a war to preserve the territorial integrity of the country. To win independence, therefore, the Moros would have to carry the war directly and successfully into the heavily populated areas of Luzon. But for the MNLF to wage effective guerrilla war outside of predominantly Muslim areas is impossible.[52] By its very self-definition, a Moro insurgency can seek support only among a well-defined constituency which is concentrated far from the seat of national power in a limited geographical area, and even in that area it is a minority of the population. The Moros cannot win. Nevertheless, bloody attacks on local authorities, kidnappings of foreigners, and murders of Catholic church workers by Moro guerrillas continued through the 1990s.

A final note: those Japanese military and naval officers who wished in 1899 to go to the Philippines and fight the Americans saw their desires frustrated, but not permanently. By occupying the Philippines, the Americans had placed themselves athwart the high road to the Imperial vision of a Japan- dominated Southeast Asia. Four decades later, this awkward juxtaposition would lead to Pearl Harbor, the Japanese occupation of the Philippines, and the islands' eventual liberation (by another General MacArthur). Three years of Japanese rule sharpened the insights of many Filipinos into the essential nature of American administration.

Central America, 1929.

Map produced by Anne Szewczyk.

4

Nicaragua

A Training Ground

To many observers, the republics of Central America might seem to constitute a fairly homogeneous entity. Their people speak a common language and profess a common religion. They all experienced centuries of Spanish administration, and they began their careers as independent states at the same time. Together they form a relatively compact isthmus of 188,000 square miles, somewhat bigger than the state of California.

Nevertheless, the appearance of Central American homogeneity can be deceptive. After winning independence from Spain and deciding not to throw in their lot with Mexico, the original five Central American republics—Guatemala, Honduras, El Salvador, Nicaragua, and Costa Rica (Panama remained a province of Colombia until 1903)—attempted to form a federation. That experiment in union lasted from 1825 to 1838. It broke apart amid discord and violence for several reasons, including disparity in the size of the constituent republics' populations, diversity in their racial composition, incompatibility among their economies, controversy within the Catholic Church regarding the desirability of union, hostility between the various Conservative and Liberal parties as well as between rival political personalities, and the reluctance of the Costa Ricans to link their future to societies they looked upon as less stable and less civilized.[1] After the collapse of federation, several efforts followed to restore it by force; all were unsuccessful and served only to increase suspicions and hostilities in the Central American region.

In the particular case of Nicaragua, its achievement of independence from Spain removed such restraints as had previously existed on domestic violence and external intervention. For the first hundred years of statehood, Nicaragua was the scene of endemic civil conflict, usually in the form of warfare between the Liberal and the Conservative Parties, which was often a cover for rivalry between the leading cities of Leon and Managua. Nicaraguan society was so invertebrate and its government so weak that in 1855 a North American adventurer named William Walker could land in the country in command of a force of fifty-seven men and, in alliance with some prominent leaders of the Liberal Party, make himself president and remain in office until his regime collapsed in 1857.[2]

The United States and Nicaragua

In 1912 Nicaraguan president Adolfo Diaz, faced with yet another of his country's innumerable rebellions, asked the United States to help restore order. In the summer two thousand U.S. sailors and Marines landed in Nicaragua. They established a semblance of peace at the cost of thirty-seven Marine casualties. The Marines were to remain in Nicaragua most of the time until 1925, although after 1912 the American presence usually consisted of no more than a one-hundred-man detachment guarding the U.S. legation in Managua. This was indeed a minuscule force to "occupy" a country whose population approached seven hundred thousand, in an area of almost forty-six thousand square miles, the size of Pennsylvania. The purpose of this Marine legation guard was to serve as a warning that renewed revolution or civil war could prompt another American intervention; nevertheless, a few weeks after the withdrawal of the main body of Marines in 1912, widespread civil violence again wracked Nicaragua. In 1923 the U.S. Department of State announced that the legation guard in Managua would be removed following the 1924 elections, which the Liberal Party had implored the Americans to supervise. Thus the United States innocently and ominously advanced more deeply into "the arcane and unpredictable world of isthmian politics." In 1924 the Liberals emerged victorious in "the most nearly honest elections in the history of the country." In Washington's view, the few-score Marine presence should now be brought home; "peaceful habits seemed so well established that in 1925 [President] Coolidge deemed it safe to remove this symbol of American power."[3] The last Marines left Nicaragua that summer.

The following year, Conservative Party leader Emiliano Chamorro seized the government and the Liberals revolted. Another Nicaraguan-style civil war—violence between powerful families assisted by client systems dignified by the name of parties—blazed across the country. The Mexican government sent weapons and volunteers to help the Liberals. And U.S. Marines again landed in the tormented country to protect the lives and property of Americans and other foreigners, since nobody in Nicaragua could guarantee their safety. The problem facing the U.S. government was stark and simple: if the Americans refused to maintain order and supervise elections, the incumbents would rig the balloting and the losers would take up arms; the resulting civil war could well spill over into neighboring countries, including strategic Panama. President Coolidge placed the Nicaraguan nettle in the hands of Henry L. Stimson, who was "determined that the United States see to it that the election of 1928 be completely free."[4] Under American supervision, the elections produced another easy Liberal victory.

Why, beginning with the administration of President Taft and continuing through the administrations of Presidents Wilson, Harding, Coolidge, and Hoover, were U.S. troops—however few in number—stationed in Nicaragua? The least important reason was to protect American investments there, which were very small. Of more importance was a (naive) belief that a period of American occupation would help stabilize Nicaraguan political life. The decisive reasons, however, were two. First, the United States wished to provide security for the Panama Canal Zone; violence within Nicaragua or any other Central American state had a tendency to spill across borders. In addition, strife in Nicaragua might invite European or Mexican intervention. Second, the Americans were determined to prevent the construction of any future interoceanic canal in Nicaragua from falling to a German or a Japanese firm. The Bryan-Chamorro Treaty, signed in August 1914 and proclaimed in June 1916, granted the United States the perpetual and exclusive right to construct an interoceanic canal in Nicaragua, along with the right to build a naval base on the Gulf of Fonseca, in return for the payment of $3 million. Washington further sought to increase stability within Central America by convincing the Mexican government to join in guaranteeing the neutrality of Honduras.[5]

The Guardia

In spite of these plausible justifications, any U.S. military presence in Nicaragua provoked much adverse criticism at home. Thus, the Coolidge administration faced a real problem in January 1925 when newly inaugurated Nicaraguan president Carlos Solorzano asked the State Department to keep U.S. troops in his country. Washington found an apparent solution by undertaking to train a group of Nicaraguans and form them into a nonpartisan, professional constabulary that would maintain the peace in Nicaragua and perhaps serve as a model for other countries in the Caribbean area.

The State Department submitted to the Nicaraguan government a plan (which was accepted) for a force of 410 men, with retired U.S. Army major Calvin Carter, who had helped train soldiers in the Philippines, as commander. All recruits were to be volunteers. They would wear uniforms and receive regular pay, training, and discipline. Most of all, they were to be above politics, loyal not to this or that regional caudillo but to the nation. But no party or faction in Nicaragua, then or thereafter, ever really accepted the nonpartisan nature and purpose of the constabulary, and that is the essential reason why things went fundamentally wrong. Indeed, by 1926 the U.S. minister in Managua reported that the new constabulary, the Guardia Nacional, was disintegrating into a partisan force in the service of Conservative president Emiliano Chamorro. The Guardia was thereupon disbanded. Nevertheless, pressure to develop a reliable force continued both in Nicaragua and in Washington, and fresh recruiting for a new Guardia began in May 1927 under the supervision of Marine colonel Robert Rhea.[6]

The U.S. government assumed the responsibility for building up a new Guardia Nacional for two main reasons. First, it wished—against all local tradition—"to transform Nicaragua's armed forces into a nonpolitical force, dedicated to defending constitutional order and guaranteeing free elections."[7] Second, it wanted a body of men capable of restoring order in the northern countryside by defeating the Liberal Party insurgent leader Augusto Sandino (of whom, more is to come).

The Americans soon found it necessary to send several specially trained medical personnel to help with the Guardia. Syphilis and malaria were rampant in the country. Recruits often suffered simultaneously from several venereal diseases, whose symptoms they stoically accepted as an unavoidable part of life. Neither lectures nor U.S. Marine Corps prophylactics were able to accomplish great changes in this department. The Marines were far more successful in their national campaign against smallpox and typhoid.[8]

Originally all recruits for the Guardia had to be at least eighteen years old and literate. This second requirement had to be dropped in order to obtain enough men to maintain order in the 1928 presidential election. (U.S. supervision of that election took place at the request of the opposition Liberal Party, several elements of which had openly rebelled against the Conservative regime of Emiliano Chamorro.)

In the early years of the Guardia Nacional, almost all the officers were U.S. Marines. The author of the major study of the Guardia (and a relentless critic of U.S. policy in Nicaragua) wrote, "The marines did surprisingly well, transforming their raw recruits within a few months into the best trained, disciplined and equipped force in Nicaraguan history."[9] Life in the Guardia was no bed of roses for the enlisted men, but the regular pay, uniforms, food, and medical treatment, together with the respect for Nicaraguan fighting qualities that many Marine officers developed, made conditions highly acceptable for most recruits.

In the late 1920s the Guardia under its Marine officers found it necessary to take over many police duties, especially in the city of Managua. They acted with great efficiency in making arrests and in collecting fines. Undoubtedly, the Managua municipal treasury benefited from their actions, and street crime was kept to a minimum, but the Guardia's efficiency probably did not endear it to every element of the population.

By the time the 1928 elections rolled around, Guardia strength was at eighteen hundred officers and soldiers; most of the American officers in the Guardia were Marine noncommissioned officers. Guardia supervision of the presidential election of 1928 seems to have been nearly impeccable. To prevent multiple voting, the fingers of voters were dipped in Mercurochrome; the followers of Sandino (who, in contrast to most of the other Liberals, did not accept U.S. supervision of the election) told the people that the Mercurochrome was poison. Ninety percent of the eligible voters went to the polls anyway, and Liberal candidate Gen. José Maria

Moncada won a clear victory. Even the Conservatives acknowledged that they had been defeated fairly. For the first time in Nicaraguan history, the ruling party had lost an election. At the insistence of the Conservative Party, the United States oversaw the elections of 1930 and 1932 as well. The fairness of the Marine supervision of each of these elections receives important confirmation from the fact that they were all won by the Liberal Party, traditionally the anti-U.S. and pro-Mexican faction in Nicaragua. In spite of all this, the revolt of Sandino and his band continued.[10] Following the 1928 elections, the Marines reduced their activities in the northern provinces, where Sandino was active, and returned to mainly garrison duties in the large towns, although skirmishes between Marine-led Guardia patrols and Sandino bands occurred through 1932.

Despite their good work against disease and election disorders, the mere presence of Americans in Nicaragua was being denounced throughout Latin America and in the United States as well. In the Senate the attack on American involvement was led by the country's leading isolationist, William E. Borah of Idaho. Another isolationist, Burton K. Wheeler of Montana, advised his fellow senators that if the Marines were going to be used to fight bandits, they should be sent not to Managua but to Chicago. Increasing pressure on the United States for the Marines to withdraw would eventually force the Guardia into combat on its own before it was ready; the Marines simply had not had time to train enough officer replacements. Thus, the door was left wide open for the politicization of the Guardia once the Marines left. This outcome was made almost inevitable by the quixotic crusade of the renegade Liberal politico and warlord Augusto Sandino.

Sandino

Born in 1895, Augusto Sandino was the son of a local landowner and an Indian woman. As a young man he had had to flee the country after wounding someone in a brawl. He went to Mexico, and while there became a member of the fiercely anti-Catholic Freemasons. He affected the middle name of Cesar. Sandino's father was a member of the Liberal Party, and so young Augusto decided to be a Liberal as well. Returning to Nicaragua in 1926 and joining the rebellion of the Liberals against President Chamorro, Sandino soon achieved a position of leadership and assumed the rank of general in the Liberal army under General Moncada in 1927.

By the Peace of Tipitapa, arranged by Henry Stimson and signed in May 1927, the leaders of the Liberal and Conservative Parties agreed to stop the fighting. Fully thirteen Liberal generals signed the agreement, but not Sandino. He apparently wanted U.S. supervision of the 1928 elections but did not like the arrangements under which it was to be carried out. According to some sources, Sandino declared himself ready to lay down his arms if the United States agreed to establish a military government that would ensure free elections.[11]

Within two months of the Peace of Tipitapa, the Marine presence had been reduced from 3,300 men to 1,500. Then, on July 16, 1927, Sandino sent his followers to attack the Guardia Nacional post and Marine barracks at Ocotal. The town was infiltrated by six hundred of Sandino's men at dawn. The thirty-nine Marines and forty-seven Guardia members succeeded in repulsing the onslaught after hard fighting. In what may have been the first dive-bombing action in history, five Marine aircraft strafed and bombed the Sandino forces. When the besieged Marines and National Guards sortied from their barracks, the attackers withdrew. The defenders had suffered one dead and five wounded.[12]

After his defeat at Ocotal, Sandino realized that the only way he and his followers could keep fighting was to take the path of guerrilla war. So began the five-year conflict that was to shape so much of Nicaraguan politics for the next six decades.

There is merit in the idea that "Sandino was one of the precursors of modern revolutionary guerrilla warfare—the process used to seize political control of an entire country by guerrilla action, without resort to conventional military operations except perhaps in the final stage of the struggle when the guerrilla army has acquired many of the characteristics of a regular army." This approach to power is certainly not that of Marx or Lenin; neither is it that of Mao or Giap. In any event, although Augusto Sandino can perhaps be classified (with generosity) as a nationalist, he was certainly no Communist. On the contrary, he boasted of how he frustrated the efforts of Farabundo Marti to take over his movement "for the Comintern." He stated, "There is no need for the class struggle in Nicaragua because here the worker lives well; he struggles only against the American intervention."[13]

And the struggle went on. Beginning in December 1927, two hundred Marines and National Guards found and attacked Sandino's headquarters at El Chipote and pursued its occupants, but most of the Sandino forces escaped. Between the attack on Ocotal and the spring of 1929, Guardia patrols made at least thirteen contacts with Sandino bands, mixed Marine-Guardia patrols thirty-two contacts, and solely Marine patrols another fifty-nine, more than one hundred encounters in all. During that two-year period the Marines suffered seventy casualties.[14]

Sandino had gone to Mexico by way of Honduras in 1929. Returning the following year, he divided his army into eight columns of seventy-five to one hundred men. In response, the Marines trained an elite Guardia battalion whose elements would carry out extended patrols and persistent hunts for the guerrillas; such tactics frightened Sandino, but they were not enough to overcome guerrilla advantages and Marine handicaps. Sandino's men, with rifles and machine guns, were as well armed as the Marines. They could escape the Marines in the northern wilds, where the population was friendly to them, or slip across the Honduran border.

As for the Marines and the Guardia, they lacked sufficient numbers to hold fixed posts and at the same time hunt the guerrillas effectively; there was too much territory to patrol. Their food and equipment, as well as fodder for their horses, had to be carried on mule-back, for the countryside was too poor for foraging. True enough, the Marines were better trained and better marksmen than the guerrillas. They also had the advantage of aircraft, which could provide them with close combat support, emergency supplies, and medical evacuation. Aircraft also helped the small groups of Marines in the field to stay in contact with their headquarters. But aircraft over a given area also alerted the guerrillas to the possible presence of Marines. Moreover, the Sandino soldiers learned how to negate Marine air support at least to a substantial degree, by restricting daylight movements, refraining from firing at airplanes, and camouflaging their camps.

Sandino also benefited from his international connections. Some of Sandino's followers said that the Mexican government was considering a treaty with Sandino for the building of an interoceanic canal in which the Imperial Japanese Government would have the major share; Mexican officers would take over the training of a new Nicaraguan army.[15]

Casualties during the conflict were not numerous, but encounters between the two sides were often grisly. The Sandino bands not only executed prisoners but did it in notably cruel ways, with the approval of their leader. The official seal of the Sandino forces pictured a guerrilla with a machete beheading a prostrate Marine.[16]

On June 18, 1930, Sandino led four hundred men in an attack on Jinotega; this was the "most formidable guerrilla force assembled in Nicaragua up to that time." On the last day of the year, guerrillas ambushed a party of ten Marines repairing telephone lines and killed all but two of them, an event that caused a sensation in Congress. And perhaps a new plateau in the conflict was reached in April 1931, when Sandino forces seized the headquarters of the Bragman's Bluff Lumber Company, "massacring the American and British [civilian] employees and sacking the company town."[17]

By the end of 1930, the Guardia numbered 160 officers and 1,650 men. Because of the Sandino revolt, the Guardia had become larger and more militarized than was originally planned.[18] At the same time, domestic pressure inside the United States to withdraw the Marines meant that the Guardia did not receive sufficient training and indoctrination to ensure that it would remain truly neutral politically.

As 1932 dawned, leaders of both Nicaraguan parties had expressed their desire that U.S. Marines remain in the country. In almost everyone's eyes, "the marines . . . symbolized order in a disorderly society." Nevertheless, President Hoover was eager to wind up the Nicaraguan involvement. Congressional criticism of the intervention was growing ever more strident; Hoover and his advisers were well aware that a complete and final U.S. military victory in Nicaragua would not be possible unless several thousand troops were sent there; and finally, Secretary of State Stimson believed (illogically, perhaps) that he could not effectively criticize the Japanese invasion and occupation of Manchuria while U.S. Marines remained in Nicaragua. Stimson accordingly announced that all parties had agreed that the last Marines would leave after Nicaragua's 1932 elections. (Both the Liberals and the Conservatives had requested U.S. electoral supervision for one last time).[19] Once again, in honest elections, the Liberals won a clear victory.

Having handed over command of the Guardia to their Nicaraguan successors on January 1, 1933, the last Marines left Nicaragua
from the port of Corinto the following day. During more than five
years, seventy-five Nicaraguan National Guards and forty-seven
Marines had lost their lives in or as a result of combat. Another eighty-
nine from both groups had died of disease, accident, or suicide. Ten
mutinies among Guardia units had resulted in the deaths of seven
Marine officers. If figures from Haiti and the Dominican Republic
are added in, the Marines had suffered a total loss of seventy-nine
officers and men killed in action or dead of wounds in the entire
Caribbean area.[20]

Lessons

Before, during, and after the decade of the twenties, significant elements in Nicaragua desired and requested a U.S. military presence
in their country. These elements notably included most of the leadership, civilian and military, of both the Conservative and the traditionally anti-U.S. Liberal Party, the party to which Augusto Sandino
had always belonged. In his long rebellion against the American
presence in his country, Sandino received the support of only a minority of his countrymen; despite the fact that his men were well
armed, Sandino's guerrilla "revolution" was never able to deploy
even as many as one out of a thousand Nicaraguans. How, then,
could the Sandino insurgency survive? When hard pressed,
Sandino's bands were able to escape across the Honduran border,
and they also obtained valuable aid and advice from Mexican dictator Plutarco Calles and his handpicked successors. Clearly these were
major assets. But by far the principal reason Sandino was able to
stay in the field so long against his foes was not some widespread
nationalist revulsion against American imperialism but rather the
inadequate numbers of the Marines and National Guards who had
the responsibility of controlling him. In December 1929, for example,
the U.S. military presence in Nicaragua was only eighteen hundred
men, a figure derisively below the ten-to-one ratio of soldiers to
guerrillas called for in most studies of counterinsurgency.[21]

Nevertheless, despite their scant numbers—or perhaps because
of them—service in Nicaragua taught or retaught the U.S. Marines

many interesting lessons about how to combat guerrillas. First and most obvious was the absolute necessity for constant training. But the Marines also proved to themselves that large search-and-destroy sweeping movements were generally useless. Sustained patrolling was much more effective against the guerrillas. Under most circumstances, the best tactics consisted of small independent patrols that went out on extended hunts for guerrillas: twenty men, sacrificing everything to speed and therefore carrying very little with them, could cover up to thirty miles a day. "Nothing upsets a guerrilla band more than to be chased by a compact, fast-moving patrol of soldiers who are familiar with the people and terrain of the area of operations, and are willing to stay in the field until decisive contact is made."[22]

The Marines were quick to take advantage of the Indian dislike of ethnic Nicaraguans, especially on the part of the Miskito tribe. They also discovered the benefits of mixed-nationality combined units, in which Nicaraguans of the Guardia received on-the-job training from the Marines while the latter obtained valuable instruction in the nature of the countryside and its inhabitants. "American officers shared with Nicaraguan enlisted men the hardships and dangers of life on the trail, and more often than not formed bonds of comradeship with the native soldiers. Together they trudged through sweltering valleys, endured torrential downpours, forded swirling rivers, inched their way up precipitous mountainsides, and shivered through the night in rain- or sweat-soaked clothing—lying in hammocks rocked by tropical breezes that could seem as cold as an arctic blast."[23]

Often subjected to enemy ambushes, the Marines eventually concluded that the most effective response in such situations was to return a great volume of automatic-weapon fire. They also confirmed the value of close air support: indeed, "Marine aviation came of age in its support of ground troops in Nicaragua." Above all, perhaps, the Marine commanders of the Guardia Nacional "learned that a successful operation was one in which the enemy suffered casualties and they had none."[24]

Out of their experiences in Nicaragua and other countries of the Caribbean, the U.S. Marines distilled some principles of counterinsurgency that appeared in their *Small Wars Manual* of 1940. Examples of these principles, striking for their simplicity and insight, deserve quotation here:

The occupying force must be strong enough to hold all the strategical points of the country, protect its communications, and at the same time furnish an operating force sufficient to overcome the opposition wherever it appears. . . . While curbing the passions of the people, courtesy, friendliness, justice, and firmness should be exhibited.[25]

When the patrol leader demands information, the peasant should not be misjudged for failure to comply with the request, when by doing so, he is signing his own death warrant.[26]

In small wars, caution must be exercised, and instead of striving to generate the maximum power with forces available, the goal is to gain decisive results with the least application of force and the consequent minimum loss of life.[27]

Members of the United States forces should avoid any attitude that tends to indicate criticism or lack of respect for the religious beliefs and practices observed by the native inhabitants.[28]

In small wars, tolerance, sympathy and kindliness should be the keynote of our relationship with the mass of the population.[29]

At least one further general observation needs to be made in this context. While they were active in Nicaragua, the U.S. Marines controlled virtually the whole armed effort against the guerrillas, training and leading the Guardia units until enough Nicaraguan officers became available. This state of affairs contrasts dramatically with the situation American forces faced in South Vietnam more than thirty years later.

Afterword

Following the 1932 presidential election victory of the Liberals, the leaders of the two parties entered into a fateful agreement: once the Marines were gone, officerships in the Guardia were to be divided equally between the parties. This decision was absolutely contrary to the aims of the American advisers, which had been to produce not a bipartisan but a nonpartisan constabulary.[30] Anastasio Somoza Garcia, a leading Liberal, a general in the old army, and a protégé of the outgoing Liberal president, Moncada, was designated as commander-in-chief of the Guardia Nacional.

As soon as the Marines had left Nicaragua, negotiations began in earnest between the Managua government and Sandino, who came to the capital city by plane early in February 1933. A signed agreement provided for a cease-fire, amnesty for Sandino's men, and the handing over by them of a certain number of their arms. In addition, Sandino retained the right to keep a force of one hundred armed men in his base along the northern border, these men to be paid by the government. Sandino publicly embraced Guardia commander Somoza.[31]

Yet all was not well. It soon became clear that Sandino's followers were not handing over arms as had been promised in the agreement; Sandino also began speaking of the Guardia Nacional as an unconstitutional body. When the treaty was nearing its expiration date (February 1934) General Somoza declared that the Sandino bands must give up all their arms, after which many of them would be incorporated, if they wished, into the Guardia as regular members; then everybody would live in peace, presumably. Sandino ignored these proposals.

The Liberal president, Juan Sacasa, invited Sandino to come again to the capital and discuss matters. Sandino arrived there on February 16, 1934, without incident, and remained in the city for several days. But on February 21, members of the Guardia removed Sandino and some of his aides from the car in which they were traveling; they were then driven to the airfield and killed. Apparently, some bitterly anti-Sandino officers had forced Somoza to consent to these murders, which were publicly denounced by the U.S. ambassador. At the same time, the Sandino camp at Wiwili was surrounded, and the troops there were disarmed. In 1936 General Somoza ran successfully for the presidency with Guardia backing. He thus combined the presidential office with the command of the Guardia, and the Somoza family dictatorship began. Many must have believed at the time that the Sandino episode was over, but in fact "Sandino's ghost . . . haunted the Somozas ever [after]."[32]

Reflecting on these events, Undersecretary of State Sumner Welles commented, "Over twenty years of attempted assistance [by the American government] . . . had brought benefits neither to Nicaragua nor to the United States."[33]

Greece, 1947.

5

Greece

Civil War into Cold War

Greece provided the stage for the first armed conflict of the Cold War. Thus, the forty-year contest that would strain the power and wisdom of the democracies to their limits found its first battleground in the very birthplace of democracy.[1] In fact the beginnings of the Greek struggle antedated the coining of the term *Cold War*. This first military confrontation between the Communist East and the democratic West provoked the proclamation of the Truman Doctrine and served as a major catalyst of the Containment Policy.

Greece had for long ages been too poor to support all her numerous progeny, but the Greek conflict was not a conflict of classes; both sides drew supporters from all social strata. The war was above all an ideological struggle, a symbol and a microcosm of the great global confrontation that, from the mountains of Greece to the mountains of Afghanistan, from Berlin and Budapest to Seoul and Saigon, would overshadow the human race for forty years.[2]

Covered by rugged mountains, lacking a modern road network, Greece seemed to be a perfect setting for waging guerrilla war. Nevertheless, by 1949 a well-armed Communist guerrilla movement had suffered an unequivocal defeat at the hands of the Greek government, sustained by American and British assistance. But the simultaneous victory of Mao Tse-tung halfway around the globe completely stole the attention of Washington away from these auspicious Hellenic events. And soon another, more dramatic conflict was raging in Korea. So the Americans never had the chance to absorb lessons from the Greek conflict that could have saved blood, tears, and treasure a decade and a half later in Vietnam.

A Poor and Turbulent Land

Today Greece comprises about fifty-one thousand square miles, the size of Virginia and Maryland combined. Much of this territory has been Greek only since the end of the Second Balkan War in 1913. In her great days Greece wrote a record of incomparable glory. But since well before the Christian era and until the early nineteenth century, Greece had been merely a part of another empire: first the Roman, then the Byzantine,[3] then the Turkish. Their Turkish overlords allowed the Greeks a measure of religious freedom, but otherwise their rule was oppressive and obscurantist, and Greece sank slowly and deeply into economic and cultural depression. Many viewed the civil war of the 1940s as an effort to make Greece a province of yet another empire, Stalin's.

The French Revolution, the sympathy of the Russian Crown for Greek aspirations, and Russia's victories over the Turks all greatly stimulated Greek nationalism. A guerrilla war of independence against the Turks began in 1821. The Greeks enjoyed the moral support of all Europe; volunteers came to fight for free Greece, including George Gordon, Lord Byron, who died there. In 1828 Russia declared war against Turkey. The following year the Turks recognized the independence of the Peloponnesus and the southern mainland.[4] Thus, when the Greek Communists began their attempt at armed conquest, Greece had been an independent state for only a little more than a century.

Greece's victories in the Balkan Wars of 1912 (against Turkey) and 1913 (against Bulgaria) had more than doubled its territory. By revealing the true weakness of Germany's protégé Turkey, these Balkan clashes helped provoke World War I. In 1917 Greece entered that conflict on the side of the Allies under Prime Minister Eleutherios Venizelos, after the pro-German King Constantine had been forced to abdicate in favor of his son.[5] With the end of World War I, Greece obtained most of Thrace (including Bulgaria's southern coastline). Claiming a substantial area in Asia Minor, the Greeks invaded the Turkish mainland, but Turkish forces under the celebrated Kemal Ataturk bloodily repulsed them in 1922. Greece was saddled with the repatriation of 1.5 million Greeks from Turkish territory. Virtual civil war followed this double catastrophe; in 1924 republican forces exiled King George and proclaimed a republic. After many convulsions, the monarchy returned in 1935. None of these turbulent events strengthened the prestige of parliamentary institutions.

The Communist Party

In its early years, the Greek Communist Party (KKE) was a marginal element in the national life. It seemed to many Greeks the agent of a foreign power; its advocacy of independence for Greek Macedonia, so recently acquired in the Balkan Wars, further damaged its electoral prospects. Following World War I and the calamitous defeat at the hands of the Turks in 1922, economic conditions in the country were terrible. Nonetheless, membership in the party in the 1920s never exceeded 2,500.[6] In 1930 there were only about 1,700 Greek Communists, with fewer than 200 in Athens, the country's only large city.

Gen. Ioannis Metaxas, a staunch monarchist and an enemy of Venizelos, exercised dictatorial powers under King George II from 1936 to 1941. Metaxas nearly extinguished the Greek Communist Party. He offered amnesty to party members who would publicly testify about their subversive activities. In response to lurid revelations, other members also recanted their errors. The government then organized its "own" Communist Party; the resulting confusion and dissension wreaked havoc in what was left of Greek Communism.[7] Because Hitler and Stalin were partners in 1940, the party was about to administer the coup de grace to itself by stupidly choosing to collaborate with the Italian and German invaders of Greece. Hitler saved the Communists (and not only in Greece) from that miserable fate by attacking Stalin's Russia on June 22, 1941. The German invasion of Greece and the Soviet Union transformed the numerically tiny, intellectually sterile, and morally bankrupt Greek Communist Party into an organization capable of attempting to impose itself on the nation by force of arms.

The National Liberation Front

Greece was an important conduit of supplies from Germany to Field Marshal Erwin Rommel's army in North Africa. To protect these supply routes, and because Hitler was sure that Greece, and not Italy, would be the scene of the Allied invasion of southern Europe, the

Germans maintained substantial forces in the country. By 1944, 180,000 Axis troops occupied Greece, 100,000 of them German and the rest mainly Bulgarian and Italian.[8]

The Communists took the lead in organizing the anti-Axis National Liberation Front (EAM) in September 1941. "Fronts"—broad coalitions under attractive slogans—were a standard Communist tactic all over the world, devices by which Communists could organize and manipulate people who would not otherwise have joined any group known to be under the domination of Communists. The EAM platform therefore said nothing about any proletarian revolution or dictatorship; its purpose, according to its leaders, was strictly and simply to organize the population for resistance to the Axis occupation. In the face of the German invasion, the king and his cabinet had retreated to the island of Crete, and then to Egypt, under British protection. So the EAM came into existence during a national leadership vacuum. Avoiding any allusions to class struggle, the EAM became for many a beacon of leadership at a time of deep national suffering. It also exposed numerous republican and socialist elements in the country to Communist infiltration.[9]

For a long time, the EAM did not create a serious fighting force. Not until December 1942 did its leaders announce the formation of the National Liberation Army, ELAS (similar to "Hellas," the national name for Greece).[10] When during the Russian Civil War Leon Trotsky built the first Red Army, he imposed on every unit a double-headed command structure: the orders of the military commander were subject to veto by the political officer representing the Communist leadership. ELAS units adopted the same structure.

Procuring weapons was not a difficult task for ELAS. Before it disintegrated in the face of the Nazi invasion in 1941, the Greek Army had hidden stocks of small arms, many of which were revealed to ELAS. With little attention to possible postwar consequences, the British also began to supply weapons to the various guerrilla formations, including ELAS. In fact, the British insistence that all guerrilla forces unite under a single overarching command often meant that noncommunist and anticommunist guerrilla bands had to subordinate themselves to regional ELAS forces or even accept amalgamation with them.

When the Italian government surrendered to the Allies in September 1943, ELAS persuaded the British to order Italian forces in Greece to break up into small units, which ELAS then disarmed. In this way ELAS came into possession of many heavy and light weapons, becoming independent of its British suppliers. And when in 1944 the German Army decided to abandon Greece, it left behind great stores of weapons and ammunition, doubtless in the hope that ELAS would one day use them to resist the returning British.[11]

"Topographically, [Greece] provides almost optimum conditions for waging guerrilla warfare."[12] The most attractive and important target for guerrilla forces in a poor country is almost always the transportation system, because any disruption in it is a major one. With few paved roads and only one main railroad line, the Greek communications network was totally vulnerable to guerrilla action, and so were the Germans who used it.

By January 1944 ELAS counted almost 25,000 full-time fighters with perhaps another 40,000 reserves. Nevertheless, ELAS accomplished little: its most spectacular action was the blowing up (under British supervision) of the Gorgopotamos railway viaduct. It was not the conflict at hand but rather the power vacuum that would surely come into existence at war's end that preoccupied the Communist leaders. The expansion of ELAS and the elimination of rival resistance groups were the main objectives; fighting the Axis came third on their list of priorities. Consequently, "only a small fraction of the armed manpower of ELAS was ever in action against the Germans. The rest were reserved for purposes of political control." ELAS units confined themselves largely to the mountains. The Germans employed with some success specially trained guerrilla-hunting units that operated in guerrilla dress. But their principal tactic against guerrillas was wide encirclement, an operation requiring secrecy and a great deal of time and manpower to make sure there were no gaps in the circle. Despite careful planning, breakthroughs almost always occur during such operations. Furthermore, the Germans cared less about guerrillas in the mountains than transit through the valleys; German troops in Greece therefore did not pursue ELAS units with much energy.[13] They turned their energy elsewhere.

The suffering of Greece during World War II was greater than that of most European nations. Deaths alone amounted to 8 percent of the population; the destruction of the already quite limited material wealth of the country was hard to calculate. Much of that destruction was the result of German policy. The Germans did not commit enough strength in Greece to pursue guerrillas systematically, so they resorted to reprisals against civilians as their main counterguerrilla method (as the Soviets would do forty years later in Afghanistan). ELAS units would carry out an operation in full knowledge that the German authorities would hold responsible the entire community in whose neighborhood the act occurred. The Germans destroyed more than two thousand villages in whole or in part. They machine-gunned civilian prisoners by the hundreds. In July 1944 they locked hundreds of women and children of one unfortunate town in a building and then set it on fire. The savagery of their reprisals, the indiscriminate killing of civilians and burning of dwellings, turned men loose from their destroyed villages to become new recruits for ELAS. In areas where guerrillas operated, the German refusal to distinguish between pro- and antiguerrilla Greeks meant that it was actually safer to be a guerrilla than a peaceful civilian. But many who suffered loss of family or property, or both, from German reprisals blamed their losses on ELAS policies.[14]

The peasants had to endure not only reprisals by the Germans but depredations by ELAS. The guerrillas forcibly requisitioned food from the barely surviving villagers and compelled boys and girls to join their ranks. Throughout the war ELAS employed terror tactics against its Greek opponents or suspected sympathizers of their opponents. ELAS did not have a monopoly on anti-German resistance; notable among the non-ELAS guerrilla forces was EDES, the Greek National Republican League, led by the dashing Col. Napoleon Zervas. The Communists feared and hated EDES. In the autumn of 1943, with the war in Europe reaching a crescendo, ELAS chose to launch major attacks against EDES and other nonsubmissive guerrilla forces.[15] This campaign to destroy EDES was the real beginning of the civil war.

This growing Communist-dominated armed force, so circumspect toward the Germans and so violent toward fellow countrymen, filled many Greeks with dismay. They feared that the clearly doomed Hitlerite occupation would give way to a permanent Stalinist dictatorship before Allied troops were able to arrive in numbers. In the midst of these lawless and violent conditions, armed citizens' units called Security Battalions appeared in the summer of

1943. The main function of these units was to try to maintain order in their local areas with the acquiescence of German military authorities. The Security Battalions never enrolled many more than perhaps fifteen thousand men. Some joined in reaction to depredations by ELAS. Other recruits were former members of EDES and similar guerrilla organizations that ELAS had attacked and dispersed. Still others joined out of fear of or sympathy for the Germans. For large numbers of Greeks, whether one joined ELAS or EDES or a Security Battalion largely depended on the accident of who was in control of the area in which one happened to live.[16] And for some, joining a Security Battalion was a conscious decision about what kind of Greece should emerge from the war. Before the middle of 1943, Germany was clearly headed for defeat; many Greeks therefore preferred temporary collaboration with the Germans to permanent subordination to the EAM and its foreign masters.

Of course, in the view of the EAM, Security Battalion members and their families were nothing but collaborators and fascists, and hence legitimate targets for assassination. When German troops began their pullout from the Peloponnesus, ELAS units there murdered many civilians.[17] Soon ferocious encounters between Communists and noncommunists blazed all over the country.

The Battle for Athens

In order to avoid being cut off by military developments elsewhere in Europe, German and other Axis forces withdrew from Greece in October 1944. In other words, Greece was evacuated, not "liberated." This opened the way for the return of the royal government from Cairo to Athens. Throughout the war Communist agents had stirred up dissent and mutinies inside the armed forces of the Greek government-in-exile. Their agitation was so successful that the British authorities in Egypt were forced to disband most of the units of the Royal Greek Army, so that by April 1944 "the Greek armed forces in the Middle East were a thing of the past." The Communist plan was simple: at the end of the war, with the Germans gone, rival guerrilla forces destroyed, and the exile government lacking prestige and military resources, ELAS would face no serious rivals for power. When the royal government landed at Athens on October 18, 1944 (without the king, George II, who said he would return if a plebiscite called him), it brought with it only about three thousand troops, a large proportion of them officers. At that point ELAS already controlled three-quarters of the territory and about one-third of the population of Greece. A few weeks later a brigade of soldiers of the royal government marched through Athens. They received a tumultuous welcome, attributed to widespread popular fear of ELAS. These Greek soldiers were eventually reinforced by some British units, but only a small proportion of the latter were combat troops.[18]

When the first small detachments of British troops landed near Athens in the autumn of 1944, ELAS offered no resistance. This may have been the major mistake of the entire civil war; anticommunist forces would never again be so weak as they were in those days. The EAM nevertheless went ahead with preparations for an uprising. It ordered general strikes throughout the country to prevent distribution of United Nations Relief and Rehabilitation Administration (UNRRA) supplies and thus increase the level of economic misery. ELAS units converged toward the capital.[19]

In the first days of December, the Communists made their grab for power. They lost the conflict from the very first day. Instead of storming central Athens, they contented themselves with numerous minor successes in outlying areas, overcoming police posts or annihilating surviving pockets of EDES supporters in Epirus.[20] During most of the fighting, major ELAS forces were in Thessaly, several days' march away from Athens. Thus, the British were granted precious time in which to reinforce the capital. Moreover, the very concept of confronting the British was a flawed one. ELAS was in essence a hit-and-run guerrilla force that had seen little action against regular troops in its two years of existence. By ordering the uprising, the Communist leadership was in effect demanding that ELAS turn itself overnight into a regular combat force, prepared to take and hold territory and expel British and Greek national forces from Athens and Salonika. And this was not to be the last fateful error made by the Communist leaders.

After fighting had raged for a week, Field Marshal Harold Alexander, supreme Allied commander in the Mediterranean Theater, came to Athens to observe the situation. A few days later ELAS mounted new attacks on the city. The British repulsed these assaults, even though ELAS managed to overrun a Royal Air Force detachment outside the main British defense perimeter. On Christmas Day Prime Minister Winston Churchill himself arrived in beleaguered Athens. Churchill met with leaders of the Greek government and of ELAS, but the fighting went on. There were by then 60,000 British troops in the Athens area, rising eventually to 75,000, of whom 2,100 became casualties. By mid-January ELAS was in full retreat and agreed to a truce starting January 15. Meanwhile, ELAS units in other parts of Greece were busy attacking rival guerrilla bands. EDES suffered a severe shortage of ammunition; ELAS destroyed it as a fighting force.[21]

During the battle for Athens, ELAS had rounded up thousands of hostages. Before abandoning the outskirts of the city, ELAS began killing these captives; British forces found many mutilated bodies, victims of Communist "People's Courts." Much of the deep popular animosity toward ELAS, especially in the Athens area, home in those days to one Greek in every seven, dates from these savage events. Among those killed by ELAS were noncommunist trade union leaders; their murders caused prominent Socialist politicians to abandon the EAM. Sympathy for the EAM also precipitously decreased in British left-wing circles. The hostage killings caused numerous middle-class Greeks to seek insurance against a Communist victory through cash payments and other services to the guerrillas. In later years the Athens Communist Party organization admitted that killing the hostages had been a devastating error.[22]

In February 1945 the Varkiza Agreement brought the fighting to a halt. The Greek Communist Party was recognized as a legal entity and allowed to publish newspapers freely and continue to operate EAM. In return, ELAS agreed to hand over a large quantity of arms and did so. However, most of the weapons it surrendered were old Italian pieces; ELAS kept hidden the good weapons that the evacuating Germans had left behind.

Until the secret records of the Kremlin have been thoroughly searched, no one can be sure of the level of Soviet involvement in the EAM uprising. It nevertheless seems doubtful that Stalin, who neither knew nor cared very much about Greece, instigated these events. A small Soviet military mission had parachuted into ELAS headquarters in midsummer 1944; it was apparently unimpressed with ELAS, because no aid was forthcoming from Stalin. At the

Tehran Conference in November 1943, Churchill, Roosevelt, and Stalin had decided against any large-scale operations in the Balkans. In October 1944, with tacit American approval, the British and the Soviets had divided up that area: Rumania and Bulgaria were to fall under Soviet control, while Greece remained under British influence. Even after the EAM's open rebellion, Stalin sent and maintained an ambassador to the royal government in Athens, thus explicitly recognizing its legitimacy and also signaling less than total confidence in the Greek Communist insurgency.[23]

The Parliamentary Setting

National elections took place for a new Parliament in March 1946. The Communists boycotted these elections, despite the desperate problems of postwar adjustment and despite (or because of) the presence of hundreds of election observers from France, Britain, and elsewhere. (There were no observers from the Soviet Union; Moscow wanted no precedent for outside observers of elections in its newly acquired Central European empire.) The Communists abstained from the elections for two reasons. First, the KKE did not wish to reveal to the world how low its electoral appeal actually was.[24] Second, the Communists had decided to try again to come to power by force. To this end, the KKE had already established a guerrilla training base at Bulkes, northwest of Belgrade in Tito's Yugoslavia, at that time the Communist satellite most vocally loyal to Stalin. It was also counting on support from Communist regimes in neighboring Albania and Bulgaria. Thus, just as conservative and moderate parties were winning an overwhelming victory at the polls, Communist forces attacked the village of Litokhoron, on the slope of Mount Olympus, an assault generally considered the beginning of the second phase of the war.

The Athens government held very few good cards. The anticommunist side suffered not only from grave military weaknesses but also from deep political fissures. Students of revolution from Plato to Brinton have pointed to divisions within the governing class as a prime condition for revolution. Bitterness between monarchists and republicans had been poisoning Greek political life for more than a generation before the German invasion. After World War II, in the midst of devastation and insurgency, this hostility reasserted itself

as if nothing had changed. With at least one eye on electoral considerations, many leftist and liberal politicians in Greece were more
susceptible to offers of compromise from the EAM than to exhortations to pursue victory over the Communist-led insurrection. On
the other side, elements on the extreme right of the majority Popu-
list (monarchist) Party had discredited themselves by committing
atrocities against Communists and other enemies. Dwight Griswold,
the Nebraska Republican who headed the U.S. aid mission to Greece,
told Washington: "You cannot build a government on the rightist
parties and [expect to] establish peace and quiet in Greece. There is
too much of a tendency in those groups to carry on a blood feud
against all Greeks who do not agree with them politically."[25] The
partisanship. selfishness, nepotism, and "inveterate pettiness" of
Greek politicians discredited the parliamentary system, increased
the attractiveness of the insurgency, exasperated the Americans, and
hampered a successful anticommunist effort.[26]

Renewed War

The Communist guerrilla campaign began with the murders of local officials and civilians known to be friendly to the government.
Then came attacks on small police stations; to avoid the loss of such
vulnerable outposts, the government began consolidating them into
larger and fewer positions. The guerrillas would then raid the villages where the police posts had just been abandoned, seeking supplies and recruits. Finally came attacks on larger police posts (thirty
to forty men), forcing them also to be consolidated. By the late autumn of 1946, only the large towns, as a rule, were under government control; vast areas of the countryside were wide open to
guerrilla activities. When finally the National Army was called in,
the guerrillas employed the same general tactics against it: they attacked small army posts along the frontier with Yugoslavia and Albania, which the army leadership then consolidated into ever-larger,
ever-fewer positions, leaving wide gaps along the borders through
which the guerrillas freely passed back and forth. On October 28,
1946, Markos Vafiades, the principal leader of the Communist armed
forces, announced the new name of the insurgents: the Democratic
Army. Its slogan was "By Fire and Axe."[27]

Commentators on guerrilla warfare often observe that the thorough defeat of an insurgency requires a ten-to-one ratio of government troops to guerrillas. At the beginning of 1947, the guerrillas had 13,000 members operating inside Greece, with another 12,000 across the three borders. Against them the National Army could muster 90,000, with the national police (gendarmerie) adding another 30,000. By the autumn of 1947, the National Army had grown to about 135,000 men, while the Democratic Army counted perhaps 23,000, not including reserves across the frontiers. Clearly the numbers of the government forces were inadequate, especially to impede the passage of guerrilla units across Greece's more than six hundred miles of frontier with her Communist neighbors. The mountains along these northern borders were main areas of guerrilla operations for more than the obvious strategic reasons; farther south, in Athens and the Peleponnesus, most of the people feared and hated the guerrillas because of ELAS provocations and atrocities during the German occupation and above all because of the killing of hostages in the Athens area from December 1944 to January 1945.[28]

Who Were the Insurgents?

For its war against the parliamentary government in Athens, the Democratic Army (that is, the Communist-led guerrillas) gathered its members from four principal sources. First among them were members of the KKE—the Greek Communist Party—and their sympathizers. Most of these were city dwellers with above-average education, often fanatically devoted to the party's vision of a New Greece, which they of course would rule.

Former members of ELAS were a second key group in the Democratic Army. Greece had too many people; for large numbers of Greeks, the main aspects of village life were omnipresent poverty, class tensions, and a bleak future.[29] Many villagers, therefore, had seen the wartime resistance experience as both a welcome escape from an unrewarding existence and an opportunity to display heroism, all under the rubric of struggling for justice and a better life. For such individuals the end of World War II had been a letdown, a return to an uneventful, unrewarding routine. When in the spring of 1946 the Communists began widespread recruiting of guerrillas, many former resistance fighters welcomed the chance to turn back the clock to more fulfilling days.

Macedonian separatists made up another major constituent. The Turks had misruled Macedonia until the Balkan Wars of 1912–1913. When the civil war broke out, Greece possessed 13,000 square miles of Macedonia, while Bulgaria and Yugoslavia divided another 12,000. The KKE pledged that after a Communist military victory, Greek Macedonia would be allowed to go its separate way, presumably to become the nucleus of an independent Macedonian state that would include territories in Yugoslavia and Bulgaria. Only a minority of the Macedonians in the Democratic Army appear to have been convinced Communists.[30]

Forced recruits and abductees, often teenagers (of both sexes), composed the fourth and largest element of the guerrilla ranks. As the conflict ground on, the Communists relied more and more on compulsory recruitment and kidnappings. After the insurgency had been defeated, the principal military leader of the Democratic Army wrote that from the middle of 1947, almost all new guerrillas had been brought into the ranks by compulsion. The reader may immediately suspect that forced recruits would make poor fighters. Sometimes that was the case. But the usual way the Democratic Army obtained the services of such persons was to threaten them and their family members with death if they refused to serve or tried to desert; these forced recruits were always well aware of how vulnerable they and their families were to reprisals. In addition, the dangerous life of the guerrillas often forced them, especially very young ones who had never lived outside their parents' houses before, to turn to each other for support and loyalty. Finally, the KKE placed great stress on the political indoctrination of all Democratic Army members, not without effect. All these powerful pressures produced military units that, from conviction or desperation, often fought well enough.[31]

Though increasingly unable to attract volunteers, the Democratic Army nevertheless found many factors operating in its favor. A tradition of guerrilla warfare went far back into Greek history, into the long night of Turkish occupation. The general poverty of the rural areas and the great devastation wrought by World War II had created a population capable of withstanding the physical hardships of guerrilla life. The EAM still basked in the afterglow of the resistance to the detested Germans, whereas in contrast the royal government had spent most of those bitter years outside the country. The National Army had superior equipment, but the country's difficult terrain and primitive transportation system favored the lightly armed and tactically flexible guerrillas. The guerrillas had no responsibility for holding or defending particular territory. If pressed by government troops, even if surrounded, they simply broke up into smaller units and (usually) escaped their enemies. The classic guerrilla tactic of mining roads was especially suited to Greece; by 1947 mines had become "the most effective single weapon in the guerrilla arsenal."[32] They greatly hampered the movement of the National Army but had little effect on the guerrillas, who possessed no tanks and few trucks.

Another source of Communist strength was the Communist vision of a Bright New Greece in which everyone's desires would find fulfillment. In contrast, the government seemed able to offer nothing more than a dreary status quo. No charismatic hero arose to propound a shining vision of a noncommunist Greece; in fact, the government seemed unable to deal with even the most pressing and mundane economic and social problems—problems greatly aggravated by the fighting in the mountains that produced a flood of seven hundred thousand refugees, one Greek in ten, pouring into the cities and exhausting the government's scant resources.[33]

The contrast between the bleak today offered by the government and the bright tomorrow offered by the Communists and their fellow travelers was able to win for the latter, at least in the early stages of the civil war, the support of roughly a fifth of the population. In most parts of Greece, the KKE was able to operate a well-articulated underground organization called the Yiafaka, built upon the infrastructure the EAM had created in many parts of the country during the German occupation. Yiafaka had perhaps fifty thousand active members by 1947. This network of agents and sympathizers helped provide food for the guerrillas. Above all, Yiafaka supplied intelligence, having infiltrated both the National Army and the civil service. The Democratic Army therefore often had a good idea of the plans of its enemies.[34]

In addition, Greece's Communist neighbors had been quite openly providing help to the guerrillas since July 1946. During 1947 the guerrillas greatly benefited from the arrival of men trained in military institutions in Albania, Bulgaria, and Yugoslavia. The Yugoslavs sent a great quantity of weapons; they also attached a general and a small staff to the headquarters of the Democratic Army. Even the skeptical Soviets eventually sent some 105 mm howitzers.[35] National Army efforts to intercept supplies for the insurgents coming from the northern neighbors were only partly effective.

Without doubt, these sanctuaries across the rugged frontiers were the most serious tactical challenge confronting the national government and army. Time after time, the National Army would corner insurgent units in the North, only to watch in frustration as they escaped over the border into a Communist state. For example, the guerrillas maintained a major stronghold in the Grammos Mountain area, along the Greek-Albanian border. In June 1948 the Greek National Army launched the biggest operation of the entire war against this Grammos base. After a tremendous battle, in which eventually perhaps half of the total number of guerrillas in the entire country participated (around 12,000), the National Army was able to occupy Mount Grammos. Guerrilla losses were severe: those killed or captured amounted to almost 4,000.[36] However, most of the guerrilla forces on Grammos retreated into Albania, and after a march through southern Yugoslavia, they appeared again on Greek soil in Macedonia. This proximity to any Democratic Army unit of sanctuary inside one of the three Communist neighbor states meant that for the most part the guerrillas were free to fight only when and where they chose. The Greek government made constant appeals to the United Nations to remedy the constant violation of its borders; little resulted other than the usual waterfall of words. No wonder that the morale of the National Army was sinking.

The Greek Army

When the Communists began the major phase of the civil war in 1946, the Greek National Army (GNA) was in real trouble. During the Axis occupation (1941–1944) the army, except for some units in Egypt, did not exist. Soldiers and officers alike lost their skills and their traditions. The new army that came into existence after 1945 was poorly trained. There was little time for training in the midst of civil war, and so basic deficiencies in operations remained uncorrected almost until the end. The equipment of the GNA was inadequate, with a pronounced shortage of mountain artillery. The Royal

Hellenic Air Force monopolized the skies of Greece, but in the early years of the civil war that was of little benefit to the government because there were so few planes and trained pilots.

In war, the proportion of morale factors to material factors, according to Napoleon, is three to one. In the GNA of 1947, if equipment was poor and training was sketchy, morale was nearly disastrous. This dangerous situation arose from problems in the officer corps, inattention to the requirements of enlisted men, and faulty disposition of military resources. First and foremost, the GNA faced an acute shortage of good-quality officers. The German conquest of Greece, the government's flight into exile, and the political divisions within the army had demoralized and disintegrated the officer corps. In the reconstituted army, professional training was low. For attracting the attention of one's superiors and obtaining promotion, skill or bravery counted less than political connections. Political interference led to the promotion of unsuitable officers and encouraged insubordination. Incompetence or fear of making mistakes inhibited the aggressiveness of many officers toward the enemy. Yet it was extremely difficult to remove poor or insubordinate officers because of the same plague of political interference with army personnel matters that had led to their promotion in the first place. Not surprisingly, the army had three different chiefs of staff during 1947 alone. Nevertheless, only a very small number of GNA officers defected to the Democratic Army—perhaps no more than twenty-seven.[37]

Poor morale among the enlisted men derived from the perception of multiple inequities. The first classes of draftees into the new National Army were veterans of the Albanian War of 1940; they could not understand why they were called to the colors while younger men were left at home. Most of these draftees were family men, and army pay was so low and government services so poor that their families were often in a state of real want. The rich and the politically well connected were able to obtain exemptions from military service. Those few high-ranking officers who bothered to listen to the problems of their men knew that poor morale also resulted from too few decorations for bravery, an inadequate promotion policy, haphazard punishment for those who avoided military service, and the government's failure to arm loyal but defenseless villagers.[38]

The GNA style of warfare did nothing for morale either. Greece's frontiers with her Communist neighbors extended for several hundred miles, very long borders in comparison to the total area of the country. Under the best of circumstances, the GNA would have found it extremely difficult to control the length of the borders as well as to protect major urban centers, patrol important highways, guard essential crops, guarantee public services, and pursue guerrilla bands. What rendered the satisfactory performance of these tasks quite impossible was that influential politicians demanded the stationing of troops in their constituencies.[39] The GNA responded to these many pressures by adopting a posture of static defense: an attempt to occupy every place of any potential value to the government or to the insurgents. This was the worst possible approach to fighting guerrillas, because it permitted the guerrillas, by assembling units from several different districts, to attain numerical superiority over the government troops at a particular point of attack. Meanwhile, the GNA could not take the offensive because it lacked the manpower to protect every sensitive point in the country and still maintain mobile attack units.

The GNA temporarily broke out of its defensive posture in April 1947 and attempted a major cleanup of Central Greece, with the idea of pushing guerrilla units toward the northern frontiers. The campaign failed for several revealing reasons. First was the insufficiency of competent officers. Another was the self-imposed time limit on these clearing operations. There were not enough troops to garrison all sensitive places, including important politicians' bailiwicks, and at the same time carry out aggressive mobile clearing operations. Hence, only a limited amount of time—a few weeks or a few days, depending on its size—was allocated to the "cleaning" of any particular area. When the allocated time had expired, army units in that area moved on to some other designated place, even if all the guerrillas in the first area had not been driven out.[40]

The guerrillas killed local officials and unfriendly civilians, both in the mountains and in the larger towns. This practice undercut their support; so did the kidnapping of thousands of children to be sent to Soviet satellites, there to be trained as good citizens of a new, Communist Europe.[41] But these were weaknesses of the insurgency rather than strengths of the government, and they paled when compared to the advantages enjoyed by the guerrillas. During 1946 and

1947, therefore, the Communists were making significant tactical and psychological gains; in contrast, belief in the victory—even the survival—of the government was evaporating.

During the first year and a half of the conflict, although there was never a real danger that Democratic Army forces would successfully attack Athens, the government's inability to defeat the guerrillas meant that time was working against it. Without some unforeseeable, drastic alteration in the struggle, a Communist victory, and consequently the Stalinization of Greece, seemed inevitable to many. Yet as 1947 drew to a close, the beleaguered government in Athens was about to see the scales of war tip undramatically but unmistakably in its favor. A new national defense corps was taking form, whose mission was to prevent the reinfiltration of areas that had been cleared of guerrillas. And the morale of both the government and the GNA rose with the arrival of the first group of officers from the U.S. Army.[42]

The Truman Doctrine

Between the battle for Athens and the renewal of the civil war, the British Labour Government under Clement Attlee undertook to train the new Greek National Army. Including national guard units, the GNA grew from 30,000 in February 1945 to 75,000 by the end of the year. Until the spring of 1947, Britain also maintained 143,000 of its own troops in Greece, not counting the 1,400 officers and enlisted men involved in training the GNA. On February 21, 1947, however, the Attlee government informed the Truman administration that Britain could no longer afford to support her clients in Greece, nor in Turkey either. This information reached Washington at a crucial point in the reassessment of U.S. foreign policy that had been under way since the surrender of Japan. The administration had been fairly well informed about events in Greece during World War II, but Secretary of State Cordell Hull and his successor, E.R. Stettinius Jr., had no wish to become embroiled in what they judged to be unpalatable controversies of old-world imperialist politics. Thus, up to the very eve of the Cold War, the U.S. government did not develop a real policy regarding Greece.[43]

Nevertheless, late in February 1947, Gen. George Marshall gave

President Truman a blunt message: although no one could guarantee that with U.S. aid Greece would be definitely saved, he could guarantee that without U.S. aid Greece would be definitely lost. At the same time, Dean Acheson stated his belief that the loss of Greece would eventually result in the Communization of all of the Balkans and most of the Middle East and North Africa as well. Reflecting on the fermentation of thought in that crucial late winter and early spring of 1947, George Kennan wrote: "People in Western Europe did not, by and large, want Communist control. But this did not mean that they would not trim their sails and even abet its coming if they gained the impression that it was inevitable. This was why the shock of a Communist success in Greece could not be risked."[44]

The Truman administration became interested in Greece mainly because of its belief that the Soviets were involved in the insurgency. The exact degree of such involvement may never be known.[45] Nor is it necessary to thrash out here the question of whether Soviet foreign policy was prompted by a desire for expansion or a quest for security: from Stalin through Brezhnev the results were the same. A distinguished historian of U.S. foreign policy has elaborated and summarized the view from Washington: "The United States had no choice but to act in this situation. The results of inaction were only too clear: the collapse of Europe's flank in the Eastern Mediterranean, establishment of Communist dominance in the Middle East, and a Soviet breakthrough into South Asia and North Africa. The psychological impact upon Europe of such a tremendous Soviet victory over the West would have been disastrous. For Europeans already psychologically demoralized by their sufferings and fall from power and prestige, this would have been the final blow. In short, what was at stake in Greece was America's survival itself."[46]

In Washington there was considerable opposition to any overt U.S. participation in Greek affairs. Many felt that such an involvement would mean "pulling British chestnuts out of the fire."[47] Nevertheless, three weeks after being informed by the British that they could not sustain their commitments in Greece, President Truman went before a joint session of Congress and delivered one of the most important speeches in the history of the United States, an address that laid the foundations of American foreign policy for what would become known ever after as the Cold War: "I believe," Truman said, "that it must be the policy of the United States to support free peoples who are resisting attempted subjugation by armed minorities or by outside pressures.

"I believe that we must assist free peoples to work out their own destinies in their own way.

"I believe that our help should be primarily through economic and financial aid which is essential to economic stability and orderly political processes. . . . Should we fail to aid Greece and Turkey in this fateful hour, the effect will be far-reaching to the West as well as to the East."

Some weeks later, the terse presidential sentences, soon to be known as the Truman Doctrine, were effectively elaborated in an article by George Kennan in the influential journal *Foreign Affairs*. Kennan saw Soviet policy as "a fluid stream which moves constantly, wherever it is permitted to move, toward a given goal. Its main concern is to make sure that it has filled every nook and cranny available to it in the basin of world power." He therefore recommended to the American people "a policy of firm containment, designed to confront the Russians with unalterable counterforce at every point where they show signs of encroaching upon the interest of a peaceful and stable world." This containment policy would both defend the territory of the West and "promote tendencies which must eventually find their outlet in either the breakup or the gradual mellowing of Soviet power."[48]

Secretary of State Marshall identified U.S. objectives in Greece more specifically. American assistance must aim at maintaining the independence and territorial integrity of that nation; to that end it was necessary to develop the Greek economy, raise the general living standard, distribute the tax burden more equitably, and eliminate corruption as far as possible.[49]

American Aid

When the austere cadences of President Truman's March address to Congress had died away, Americans began to confront the implications of the task they had undertaken. In his report to the National Security Council in January 1948, former Director of Central Intelligence Sidney Souers stated: "The Greek government rests on a weak foundation and Greece is in a deplorable economic state. There are general fear and a feeling of insecurity among the people, friction among short-sighted political factions, selfishness and corruption in government, and a dearth of effective leaders. The Armed Forces of Greece are hampered in their efforts to eliminate Communist guerrillas by lack of offensive spirit, by political interference, by disposition of units as static forces and by poor leadership." Nevertheless, the report continued, the United States had to make the effort. "The defeat of Soviet efforts to destroy the political independence and territorial integrity of Greece is necessary in order to preserve the security of the whole Eastern Mediterranean and Middle East, which is vital to the security of the United States."[50]

At the same time, the director of the State Department's Office of Near Eastern and African Affairs warned that the Kremlin undoubtedly planned to wear down U.S. willpower in Greece: "If it should be decided that we are not capable as a country of dogged determination we should review our whole foreign policy in order to make sure that, in view of our inherent psychological weakness, it might be better for us to return to isolationism and abandon a policy in world affairs which we are not capable of carrying on."[51]

The urgency of Greek affairs was heavily underlined shortly after the Souers report when Communists in Czechoslovakia brutally destroyed that country's democratic institutions. And soon after that the Soviets imposed the Berlin Blockade. Now the Cold War was really on, and Greece was emerging as a major battleground. Secretary of State Marshall rightly observed that the reestablishment of order in Greece did not require the destruction of all the guerrillas, which in any case might be impossible.[52] It required instead a well-led, aggressive army capable of pushing the guerrillas back from the centers of Greek life and keeping them away—quite an order.

Toward the end of 1947, the United States had shipped 174,000 tons of military supplies to Greece. Soon the United States was spending about ten thousand dollars to eliminate one guerrilla. The guerrilla movement, however, was not suffering visible defeat; on the contrary, the overextended GNA, penetrated by Communist agents, was effectively in control of only about a fifth of the territory of the country. American military leaders such as Maj. Gen. Stephen Chamberlin, director of army intelligence, believed that the problem with the GNA was not its size but its leadership and tactics. The Americans asked the British to provide direct operational guidance to Greek units; the British were unwilling to comply, suggesting that the Americans take on the task.[53]

Washington then established the Joint U.S. Military Advisory and Planning Group (JUSMAPG) to assist the GNA with planning and leadership development. Marshall chose Gen. James Van Fleet to direct this group. No desk-bound commander, Van Fleet was often on the front lines observing the good and bad features of the GNA's antiguerrilla campaigns. He also kept up a constant barrage of requests for more American help for the Greek Army. About a year after the proclamation of the Truman Doctrine, there were 250 U.S. officers in Greece with JUSMAPG; some of them participated in a joint Greek-U.S. staff formed to plan and supply combat operations. The joint staff had a bracing effect on the Greek army: because the Americans were less knowledgeable of and less sensitive to the nuances of Greek politics, they were able to bring more strictly military considerations to bear on operational planning than Greek officers had been accustomed to.

Greek Politics as Usual

Certainly those Americans who opposed, for whatever reasons, the effort to defeat the Greek Communist insurgency could find plenty of opportunities to criticize the government in Athens, particularly regarding the rivalry and hostility between the major Greek political parties. High American officials in Greece especially disliked the leader of the conservative Populists, Constantine Tsaldaris. They wanted to avoid making the United States too dependent on his party even though it had won a majority of parliamentary seats in the 1946 elections. Also, in order to gather as much support as possible for the anticommunist effort, Secretary of State Marshall from the beginning wanted Greece to be governed by a broad coalition.[54]

Such a coalition proved difficult both to construct and to preserve. Greek politicians felt that they could continue in their old partisan ways, scheming in the corridors and cafés of Athens while an armed revolutionary challenge crackled all around them, because U.S. assistance guaranteed ultimate victory. Hence they seem to have felt absolved from having to mute their internal squabbles and give serious and sustained attention to painful decisions about reforming the government and the economy. Indeed, many Greeks, not just politicians but citizens and soldiers as well, were apathetic in the face of the mortal challenges facing them, believing that outside factors in the civil war were so massive that their own efforts were puny and inconsequential in comparison.[55]

Within the Truman administration, impatience with the shortcomings of the Athens politicians was rising. In November 1948 a Policy Planning Staff report suggested that the Secretary of State make it clear that there were limits to U.S. aid, and if the Greek government was not willing to implement certain economic and military changes, the United States might conclude that it had better places to spend its money. The U.S. Embassy in Athens pointed out, however, that the Greek government was being severely damaged by propaganda emanating from the Soviet Union and eagerly repeated by Communist and sympathizer elements in the United States and Western Europe, propaganda magnifying Greece's admittedly serious problems and the shortcomings of the government. Furthermore, many of these problems and shortcomings stemmed from the existence of foreign-fueled civil war.[56]

Nonetheless, the grave crisis confronting Greece clearly meant that "a parochial, narrow-minded leadership, with anti-Communism its only credential, [could] not possibly provide the required foundations for a successful war against a Communist guerrilla offensive." Seeming to realize this, many national party leaders did eventually manage to put aside the worst of their partisan belligerence. The old Venezelist warhorse Themistocles Sophoulis, leader of the minority Liberal Party, agreed to preside over a coalition cabinet consisting mainly of his perennial foes, the Populists. Constantine Tsaldaris was the leader of the majority party and therefore the parliamentarian with the most right to be prime minister; he nevertheless agreed to accept a subordinate post in the Sophoulis cabinet. This coalition guided the nation through the worst days of the civil war to victory, from September 1947 to June 1949, when Sophoulis, close to ninety, passed away.[57]

American Troops to Greece?

The Truman administration emphasized from the start that any U.S. military personnel sent to Greece would have solely an advisory, not a combat, role. Nevertheless, from the very beginning of open

U.S. involvement in the conflict, pressures began to build toward commitment of American ground combat forces. An internal State Department memorandum noted that "Greek officials are obsessed with the idea of getting the United States so deeply committed in Greece that it will be unable to withdraw if the Greeks themselves lie down on the job." Constantine Tsaldaris suggested throughout 1947 that the U.S. send a small number of combat troops to bolster the morale of the GNA.[58]

The situation in Greece looked very dark in the winter of 1947–1948, and the administration contemplated an expansion of the American military role. In December 1947 the State Department's Loy Henderson expressed his belief that if Greece's Communist neighbors recognized a guerrilla counterstate within Greece and sent assistance to it, or if they introduced their own troops into the fighting, then the United States should at least call on the United Nations to authorize the dispatch of armed forces to assist the legitimate government. In a top-secret memorandum, Maj. Gen. A.V. Arnold declared that sending two American army divisions to Thrace could make a vital contribution to ending the war. Arnold and the State Department's Robert Lovett discussed this possibility with George Kennan. Kennan appeared not to oppose the idea of U.S. troops as part of a United Nations force to seal the northern borders, but he thought that if American soldiers went to Greece to fight, the Peloponnesus might be an easier place to defend.[59] (This conversation is not found in Kennan's memoirs.)

Nevertheless, such powerful opposition arose to any proposal for sending U.S. ground combat units to Greece that a real debate never developed. In August 1947 John Foster Dulles, the principal Republican spokesman on foreign affairs, opposed deploying U.S. combat troops for the purpose of closing the northern frontiers (which of course would have been, next to preventing the fall of Athens itself, the most serious justification for the insertion of American troops). U.S. ambassador Lincoln MacVeagh, described by Dean Acheson as "wise and first-rate," believed that the GNA could achieve control of the situation with better tactics and leadership. And Dwight Griswold also came out vigorously against the use of U.S. combat units. "Defeat of Communism," he wrote, "is not solely a question of military action as demonstrated in Germany, France and elsewhere. In Greece, the military and economic fronts are of equal importance." Therefore he "would oppose the use of even a single American officer or soldier against the Greek bandits [guerrillas]." In the autumn of 1948 the National Security Council received a draft report from the Department of State warning that the introduction of American combat units might serve the Kremlin as an excuse to send Soviet forces into formerly subservient and now rebellious Yugoslavia. During the winter of 1948–1949, when many in Washington were gloomy about the course of the war, General Marshall flew to Athens to get a better grasp of the situation. He returned home sharing the view of the U.S. ambassador that it was not the size of the Greek Army but its effectiveness that needed to be increased.[60]

Some of the most telling opposition to deploying American combat troops in Greece came from the U.S. military. In September 1947 Undersecretary of War Kenneth Royall told Marshall that the introduction of such units would be "disturbing and provocative." About a month later, Maj. Gen. Stephen Chamberlin, who had headed a special military mission to Greece, expressed his conviction that the Greek Army should be able to cope with the guerrillas, provided there was no overt intervention from the north. General Marshall feared that the dispatch of combat troops to Greece would result in a buildup of forces there larger than the United States should commit to one place or that it might lead to their withdrawal under unpropitious and unheroic circumstances. Maj. Gen. A.M. Harper described sending American troops to Greece as putting them in a strategic "mousetrap." Any sizable commitment of U.S. ground troops to Greece would mean stripping American forces from other places; even then, such forces would be numerically inferior not only to those the Soviets could potentially commit but even to the forces of Greece's immediate Communist neighbors. The Joint Chiefs went on record against such a deployment unless it was preceded by national mobilization. That was hardly likely in 1947 with the vast postwar demobilization still going on. In mid-1945, the U.S. armed forces totaled 12 million men and women; by mid-1947 they were less than 1.6 million. The number of U.S. Army combat personnel would not be sufficient to repel a large-scale invasion of Greece by her northern neighbors.[61] Tensions with the Soviet Union were rising, and in the spring of 1948 the Americans would have to deal with the Berlin Blockade. And the signing of the NATO Treaty was coming up, vastly extending American military commitments.

Almost unanimously, high-ranking military leaders who publicly expressed views on this question opposed assigning U.S. combat forces to Greece. They believed the Greek Army was big enough to do the job, that there were other important demands on the slender U.S. forces, and that American troops would find themselves in an untenable position in the event of a Soviet invasion of Greece. Finally, the British informed Washington in early 1948 that they would continue to keep a considerable number of their troops in Greece, thus allowing the United States to concentrate on economic aid and military supplies.

Reflecting these points of view, Souers told the National Security Council in May 1948 that "the United States should not now send armed forces to Greece as token forces or for military operations." Consequently, a year and a half after the enunciation of the Truman Doctrine, there were no more than 450 U.S. military personnel in Greece providing operational advice, and this at the division level. (Of those, three American officers were to lose their lives.)[62] Maj. Gen. James Van Fleet became commander of JUSMAPG in February 1948; he and the head of the British Military Mission acted as advisers to the Greek National Defence Council.

The Growth of the National Army

As 1948 wore on, neither the Greek nor the American government suspected the gravity of the problems confronting the insurgents. On the contrary, a feeling of despondency began to envelop the Greek government and army and their supporters in Washington. In a major change of tactics, the GNA had launched massive assaults against guerrilla base areas on Grammos and Vitsi Mountains, cutting off insurgent supply routes. The attacks were costly, and in the end the guerrillas escaped into Albania and eventually returned to Grammos. The GNA was suffering eighteen hundred casualties a month, yet nothing much seemed to be getting accomplished: "two years of hard and bloody effort seemed to have ended in failure." In General Marshall's view, the Greek Army was worn out from fighting, it had no time to train its soldiers adequately, and there was no end in sight as long as the guerrillas could escape over the frontiers. In November 1948 the Policy Planning Staff of the State Department produced an analysis of the military situation in Greece along the same lines. The inefficiency of the Greek National Army, it stated, was partly the result of physical and mental exhaustion. Conventional combat, military occupation, and insurgency had been battering Greece ever since 1940. For the GNA soldier, the fighting seemed to stretch on endlessly, because the enemy had the ability to escape across the borders. The guerrillas, in contrast, could find rest and supplies on non-Greek territory whenever necessary. In addition, the proportion of guerrilla troops who were in combat units was very high compared to that of the GNA, because medical care, supply and training facilities, and personnel were to a large degree furnished to the guerrillas by the neighboring Soviet satellites. The report emphasized the need to get rid of incompetent GNA officers and improve training.[63]

Henry F. Grady, U.S. ambassador in Athens, also contributed some trenchant observations on the disappointing course of the conflict. He disagreed strongly with General Van Fleet's requests for more men, more money, and more arms for the GNA. To Grady the real solution lay elsewhere. He pointed out that "the bandit [Democratic] land army is not backed by a single airplane, heavy gun [sic], or naval vessel." In his view the GNA was already too big, draining the economy of manpower and money. Greece required not a bigger and bigger army, but a stronger, more united, and more efficient government in Athens. Victory demanded "spirit and leadership," and the Americans could not provide these things to the Greeks. An army smaller in size but better trained, better fed, stripped of its old worn-out soldiers and political officers could wage a more aggressive campaign against the guerrillas, especially in winter, which in a country like Greece could actually be an ally of the government. Grady had put his finger on a number of important, if sensitive, spots. The leaders of the GNA were slow to grasp the fact that one of their allies was the weather. Most guerrillas operated in the mountain areas. During the winter they suffered from cold and lack of supplies. Many died of exposure. And the guerrillas could be tracked in the snow. The winter also impeded the GNA's use of trucks and heavy equipment, but with its regular supply lines and relatively unlimited food and medicine, the individual GNA soldier suffered much less than the guerrillas. In countries with harsh winters, governments need to grasp the potential payoffs of winter operations.[64]

Substantial changes did occur in the organization and tactics of the Greek National Army during 1948. The government began deploying the National Defense Corps, civilians organized into one hundred battalions of five hundred men each. The original plan was for these battalions to act as minutemen in support of the GNA, but eventually they were turned into full-time soldiers. In addition, with U.S. aid the army established commando units specially trained for difficult operations.[65] The government also abandoned the policy of inducting only politically reliable young men into the ranks of the GNA. The policy of selective recruitment had left politically disloyal elements free to engage in subversion or even to join the guerrillas. Under the new system, all eligible males were drafted, with the less reliable stationed in the less vital posts. The worst cases were sent to the island of Makronisos for political education.

The GNA also began the practice of removing civilians from the vicinity of insurgent strongholds targeted for attack. This imposed a temporary hardship on the villagers involved, but it also deprived the Communists of intelligence and food. One keen student of the war has identified the removal of the population from around guerrilla-controlled areas as a secret of the success of the Greek government. Of equal importance, the GNA became more attentive to the fact that it was not enough simply to chase armed guerrillas out of an area; the civilian infrastructure also had to be uprooted if government success was to be lasting.[66] Thanks to improved intelligence, the government found it easier to infiltrate its agents into the Yiafaka organization.

All these changes, along with American assistance, were bringing the GNA into good material and moral shape. From mid-1948, therefore, the GNA's real need was not to increase its numbers and equipment but rather to use them with greater efficiency and determination. Above all, the GNA required skilled and aggressive leadership: "all depended on leadership and morale."[67] And in that crucial sphere, improvement was on the way: in January 1949 the king appointed Gen. Alexander Papagos as commander in chief of the Greek armed forces.

Papagos, a successful commander in the Albanian war of 1940, had sufficient seniority and prestige to overcome the habitual indiscipline among high Greek Army officers. He had refused to accept appointment as commander in chief unless he was given supreme power to remove incompetent or disobedient officers. His self-confidence and spirit of aggressiveness, his attention to detail and determination to have his orders strictly complied with gave army operations the unity and vigor they had previously lacked.[68]

The systematic clearing out of both the guerrillas and the Yiafaka infrastructure from southern and central Greece was a high priority for Papagos. This was strategically a sound choice, owing to that region's distance from the Communist borders and its conservative sympathies. Once the GNA had chased out the guerrillas and broken the Yiafaka in the south, Papagos repeated the operation in other regions. His intention was to pin the Democratic Army against the northern borders while depriving it of its network of civilian sympathizers and agents, so that it would become like a great tree with withered roots. Meanwhile, the British and American military missions gave Papagos good advice, partly because they could speak to him not from the point of view of domestic Greek politics (the plague of the GNA), but as detached professionals. In essence, though, General (later Field Marshal) Papagos simply forced the GNA to do what it had the capability to do, and that turned out to be enough.[69] His task was made very much easier by the mistakes of his opponents on both sides of the border.

As 1949 dawned, although no one in Athens or Washington knew it for sure, the Democratic Army was on the verge of defeat.[70] U.S. assistance, increased unity among the noncommunist political forces, and the leadership of General Papagos were all playing essential roles in bringing it to this point. Even more important, however, were two crucial decisions of the insurgent leadership: to terrorize the peasantry and to conventionalize their tactics.

The Communists and the People

Relations between the guerrillas and the peasantry underwent a profound change between the end of the German occupation and the height of the insurgency. ELAS had stressed united resistance to the Germans. Many peasants had responded, providing food, shelter, and information. But during the civil war, the Democratic Army was getting supplies from across the frontiers and thus felt itself less dependent on peasant goodwill. At the same time, peasants who had been willing to give some help against the Germans were reluctant to participate in an uprising against a Greek government.

Under these circumstances, the fact that most of the leadership of the Democratic Army was made up of Communists became crucial. The segment of the population that was attracted into the Communist Party was not only numerically slender but also sociologically unrepresentative. The leadership was drawn from lower-middle-class intellectuals; most of the members either came from areas only recently acquired by Greece or were students, tobacco workers, or seamen, socially marginal groups in a predominantly peasant country. As the conflict wore on, Communist behavior toward the peasants deteriorated. Supplied with information about the identities of nationalist sympathizers and the location of their homes, Democratic Army units would swoop down upon a village or small town and kill those suspects and their families. Then they would carry off scarce foodstuffs, forced recruits, and hostages. Further, the insurgents often deliberately destroyed whole villages for no other purpose than to create hungry refugees that the government would be hard pressed to feed and house. Sometimes they committed atrocities with no discernible explanation at all. In addition, children were taken from their homes and sent to be trained as guerrillas or Communist functionaries in Eastern Europe. Of the twenty-eight thousand children thus removed from Greece, only about half were ever repatriated.[71] Later efforts of the International Red Cross to obtain information on the missing children had little success.

The guerrillas, by thus antagonizing the mountain people, undercut themselves in their own immediate theater of operations, destroying their last chance to build up a reliable base populated with supportive civilians. By mid-1948 at the latest, it had become evident that the insurgency had few followers in the cities; in Athens, the scene of many grisly hostage murders in 1945, even the small proletariat was apathetic. The purging of the entire Communist leadership group in the capital city produced no beneficial change. And in the Peloponnesus, guerrilla activity had never been very successful, because of both the relatively adequate transportation system and the conservative sentiment of the region.

The principal objectives of the KKE and the Democratic Army had been to bring the economy crashing down and to break the GNA. American assistance removed any serious chance of attaining either of these objectives; moreover, Communist economic warfare had alienated large numbers of originally neutral civilians and filled all Greece with fear of a Communist victory.[72] One ominous consequence of these serious and self-inflicted political wounds was that help from the neighboring Communist regimes was becoming ever more crucial to the insurgents.

Adopting Conventional Tactics

Sometime in early 1947, the Communist leadership decided to erect a counterstate, a "Free Greece." A state needs a permanent territory and a capital city to receive accredited foreign diplomats; hence, in late May 1947 the Democratic Army sought to capture and hold the town of Florina, near the Albanian border. After severe fighting the insurgents withdrew, defeated. Nevertheless, the desire to set up a counterstate endured, and the insurgents actually proclaimed its birth on December 24, 1947. That was a mistake; when neither the Soviets nor any satellite state recognized the existence of Free Greece, the project suffered a grave moral setback. And to get themselves a capital, the insurgents again decided to abandon their largely successful guerrilla tactics and launch a major conventional attack on a suitably sized town. They chose Konitsa, only five miles from the Albanian border. On December 25, 1947, about 5,000 insurgents vigorously attacked the town and its 1,300 GNA defenders. Konitsa was soon surrounded, and Greek aircraft had to drop supplies into it. The government placed tremendous importance on this battle: Queen Frederika herself flew into the besieged town to hearten the defenders. On January 4 the attack was broken off, with Konitsa still in national hands. Soon thereafter Parliament outlawed the Communist Party.[73]

The best commander in the Democratic Army was Markos Vafiades. Usually called simply Markos, he had come to Greece from his birthplace in Anatolia as a teenager in 1923 and shortly thereafter joined the KKE. It was mainly because of his leadership that the insurgents had been able to take control of so much Greek territory and avoid costly confrontations with major elements of the GNA.

Markos had objected to the assault on Konitsa; after the defeat there in January 1948, he wanted to return to guerrilla tactics. Communist Party boss Nikos Zachariades, however, opposed such a return. He instead pressed more and more insistently for a permanent switch to conventional war in order to break the GNA and open the road to Athens. A schoolteacher, born like Markos in Anatolia, Zachariades had gone to Moscow for training in the arts of Communist subversion. He installed himself, on Kremlin orders, as secretary general of the Greek Communist Party in 1931. He spent most of World War II in the infamous Nazi concentration camp at Dachau; both inside and outside the party, questions arose as to exactly how he had managed to emerge alive from that hellhole.[74]

Following the GNA assault on Mount Grammos in June 1948, Markos had extricated his followers from their precarious position and led them into Albania. But Zachariades continued to demand that the Democratic Army adopt conventional tactics, that is, seizing and holding territory even in the face of GNA counterattacks. In November 1948 Zachariades finally succeeded in ousting Markos from command of the Democratic Army and also from his seat on the KKE Central Committee. (Zachariades told Markos: "You will become a worm and crawl before me.")[75] Retaining his direction of the KKE, he now exercised control over the Democratic Army as well. Zachariades used his dictatorial power to turn the Democratic Army away from guerrilla warfare, which had brought it control of most of the territory of the country, to conventional warfare, which would throw it directly against the numerically superior and better-equipped Greek National Army.

Many students of the Greek civil war maintain that the insurgents turned to conventional warfare too early. One could argue, however, that the switch was made much too late. Whatever one's opinion on that score, by the second half of 1948, defeat for the insurgency was already looming. But when the insurgents, who lacked an air force among other things, engaged in positional warfare with a Greek Army that was improving every month in training, tactics, numbers, equipment, and morale, their defeat became inevitable.

Why Zachariades made this fateful decision is not entirely clear. True, he was unfamiliar with the nature of guerrilla warfare, having been in prison during the ELAS period. And he was not well informed about the improvement in training and morale that the GNA had been experiencing during 1948. Other possible explanations include his evaluation of the current strategic situation faced by the Democratic Army. The main object of the guerrillas had been to disrupt the Greek economy to the breaking point; but the inflow of economic aid from the United States had short-circuited that strategic aim. The increasingly bitter dispute between Tito and Stalin (the Cominform expelled Tito on June 28, 1948) and the decision by Zachariades that the Greek Communists would support Stalin meant that the loss of the Yugoslav sanctuary was only a matter of time. Clearly, the sands of the insurgency were running out. Perhaps jealousy of the heroic and popular figure of Markos also motivated Zachariades. He saw to it that no one from the ranks of ELAS was ever again allowed to attain an important post within the party. Later on, he would personally engineer the expulsion from the party of all the most successful guerrilla leaders.[76]

Whatever caused Zachariades to fire his best military commander and impose conventional warfare tactics on the Democratic Army, the result was disaster. It ranks with the terrorism against the rural population as an explanation of the ultimate defeat of the Communist insurgency.

Under the new policy of Zachariades, in December 1948 and January 1949 the Democratic Army mounted several major conventional attacks on sizable villages and towns, seizing a lot of food and taking many young men and women as hostages. Such assaults made it necessary for the guerrillas to assemble in large columns, a procedure that of course rendered them vulnerable to attacks by the ever-improving Royal Greek Air Force and to encircling movements by the GNA. In February 1949 Zachariades directed a renewed attack against Florina, in which the Democratic Army employed heavy artillery on a large scale. Nevertheless, the attack failed, and the insurgents suffered numerous casualties, perhaps as many as half their forces. By this time two-thirds of the Democratic Army was composed of Macedonians.[77]

Morale within the Democratic Army began to sink. One reason for this, of course, was the very high rate of casualties resulting from the change to conventional warfare. Another was that in the late winter of 1948 the Cominform, under Stalin's orders, proclaimed its support for an independent Macedonia. This announcement caused consternation within Greece and within the Greek Communist Party as well. The hostile reaction only increased, if possible, when Zachariades forced the politburo of the KKE to endorse the Moscow line.

Intended to hurt Yugoslavia's Tito, Moscow's Macedonian maneuver undermined what little prestige remained to the Democratic Army, and desertions from it accelerated. The Democratic Army was more and more composed of forced recruits. Macedonians were the other major component, in part because an increasingly better-trained GNA, employing steadily improving tactics, was destroying or otherwise eliminating guerrilla units in southern Greece. The Democratic Army still had about 25,000 men and women by the end of 1948; by mid-1949 that number was down to around 20,000, of whom seven in ten were Macedonians. Most of the time only about half of the insurgents were inside Greece.[78]

At the same time, the national armed forces were growing ever stronger. They now included 150,000 regular troops, plus 50,000 members of the National Defense Corps (whose main function was to take over positions of static defense in order to release GNA troops for active combat), along with 25,000 in the paramilitary gendarmerie. The unified command under Papagos, the gradual weeding out of incompetent officers, the spreading effects of American aid, and, not least, the deepening conviction that its members were fighting not only about forms of government but for the very territorial integrity of the motherland (i.e., to keep Macedonia Greek)—all these factors helped to solidify the Greek armed forces into a power that the physically and morally diminishing Democratic Army had little hope of withstanding. But perhaps nothing raised the morale of the government side and withered that of the insurgents more than the disappearance of the Yugoslav sanctuary.

Tito Closes the Border

For months, the Yugoslav dictator Tito had been imposing more and more restrictions on the movements of the insurgents. Finally, in July 1949, he closed the border to the guerrillas.[79] Tito's move against the Democratic Army and the KKE behind it, as well as his break with Stalin, would hardly have been possible if Britain and America had not assisted the Greek national government. If the Democratic Army had won in Greece, Tito would have found himself almost completely surrounded by Moscow's satellites, an untenable position from which to defy the Kremlin.

Closing the border to the guerrillas hurt them in several ways. In the first place, the guerrillas in most of northern Greece no longer had shelter from pursuing GNA troops. From now on, guerrillas who found themselves pressed against the Yugoslav frontier would face either capture or death. GNA operations, so frustrated for years by the open border, would now almost always bear fruit.

A second consequence was that ending the free passage of armed units from Yugoslavia to Greece and back again in effect sealed several thousand Greek guerrillas inside Yugoslavia, where they could render no assistance at all to the Democratic Army in Greece itself.

Third, that part of Greece lying between the Yugoslav border and the Aegean Sea was under the fairly firm control of the GNA. Hence, guerrilla units in Thrace (the area of Greece closest to Bulgaria) were now cut off from the rest of Greece. The GNA could destroy them or drive them into Bulgaria at leisure. The isolation of the guerrillas inside Yugoslavia and in Thrace reduced for practical purposes the number of the Democratic Army's fighting personnel by almost a third.[80]

Fourth, and certainly not least, Tito's move had shut down a major lifeline, cutting off most supplies to the Democratic Army that had come not only from Yugoslavia but also from Albania. Albanian territory was still available as a sanctuary, but most of the supplies that had flowed across the Greek-Albanian border had had their origin in Yugoslavia, or at least had passed through that country. This compounded the disaster for the Democratic Army, because at least three-quarters of its weapons and all of its heavy equipment (mortars, antitank guns, and so on) came from across the borders. With the Yugoslav frontier closed, the sealing of the Albanian border became the primary strategic objective of the GNA. It was all over but the last act.

Some students of the war have maintained that although the Democratic Army would probably have given up the struggle long before it did had there been no open frontiers, closing the Yugoslav border in 1949 was not as decisive as is sometimes thought, because the Democratic Army had clearly lost the war before the closing occurred.[81] Perhaps; nevertheless, it is not unreasonable to believe that if the frontiers had remained open to the insurgents and they had persisted in guerrilla tactics, the conflict could have gone on for a much longer time.[82]

Finale

Still insisting that the Communists must abandon guerrilla tactics for conventional combat, Zachariades erected another "impregnable" bastion in the Grammos Mountain area. There he conveniently assembled 12,000 insurgents for the GNA to attack. The final GNA offensive against the Grammos stronghold began in August 1949, with the assistance of 50 ex–U.S. Navy Helldiver aircraft. The Democratic Army lost more than 2,000 killed, captured, or surrendered. On August 31, for the last time, sizable guerrilla units scuttled back across the Albanian frontier. The Albanian government announced that they would be disarmed and detained.[83]

And in those same days, Zachariades accused high-ranking leaders of the KKE of being lifelong traitors and agents of the hated British. Zachariades knew that Marxism-Leninism could never be wrong; nor could those who opposed Greek Communism possibly have been popular and strong. He therefore looked elsewhere for the explanation of Communist defeat. He believed (or at least proclaimed) that he found it in a colossal conspiracy of false Communists to betray the revolution.[84]

Radio Free Greece, the voice of the Communist insurgents, announced on October 16, 1949, that military operations were being suspended. And on November 28 President Truman informed Congress that the Greek government had emerged victorious from the civil war.

Casualty figures vary from source to source. A reasonable estimate of casualties for Greek national forces, including the gendarmerie, would be 17,000 dead and 40,000 wounded or unaccounted for. The guerrillas executed more than 4,000 civilians and burned twelve thousand homes and ninety-eight railroad stations.[85] Greek government forces killed at least 37,000 guerrillas and captured another 20,000.

Learning from the Greek War

On the one hand, even before the outbreak of the civil war, the Greek economy, underdeveloped to begin with, had been ravaged by years of foreign war and occupation. Defeat and exile had disintegrated the old army. The new army, badly equipped and poorly trained, seethed with political intrigues and personal rivalries. Disputes between monarchists and republicans bitterly divided the political leadership. On the other hand, with its rugged topography, primitive communications, and guerrilla tradition, Greece was a country eminently fitted for insurgency. Several years of struggle against the Germans and EDES had helped the insurgents to develop and perfect their organization and tactics. And they possessed sanctuaries across the border that were not only places of safety and sources of supply; they were also the outward sign of their alliance with international Communism, a political force that seemed to many in those days to be the wave of the future. With all these advantages, how did the insurgency fail?

Although it was not at all clear at the time, the Greek civil war turned out to be "a textbook case of everything that can go wrong in an insurgency."[86] Some of the problems of the insurgents arose uncontrollably from their environment, others were of their own making, and certain of their weaknesses had at first been mistaken for strengths. Although students of the war dispute their relative weight, probably all would agree that a list of major causes of the insurgency's defeat must include two external factors—foreign assistance to the Greek government and the closing of the Yugoslav border—and two self-destructive errors by the KKE: the badly timed adoption of conventional warfare and the alienation of the Greek people.

Foreign Help for the Greek Government

After World War II, guerrilla movements, or revolutionary armies founded on guerrilla movements, came to power in Yugoslavia, China, and Vietnam. In those countries the authority of the previous government had been destroyed by foreign invaders, and then those invaders were themselves defeated by other foreign states, leaving a power vacuum for the insurgents to fill. Greece escaped that pattern. Outside intervention foiled the Communist takeover of Greece not once but twice: intervention by the British in 1944–1945 and by the Americans after 1947.

The Royal Greek Government's dependence on foreign advice and support apparently did its cause no harm. That was so for two reasons. First, Britain had long been the patron and protector of Greek independence and territorial aspirations, and the United States was a land to which many Greeks had emigrated and from which the émigrés kept in close contact with relatives and friends left behind in the mother country. A second reason was of course that the public associated the Greek Communists with the Soviet Union. The Greek Communist Party profited little from this identification. Stalin in effect left the Greek Communists to fend for themselves when the proclamation of the Truman Doctrine made it clear that if the war continued, U.S. involvement in the Balkans would deepen and thus complicate Soviet relations with other Communist states in that region. And Stalin did not even think it worthwhile to invite the KKE to the 1947 founding meeting of the Cominform.[87]

But quite beyond the Soviet question, many ordinary Greeks identified the insurgents, and especially their leadership, with the country's national enemies, notably Bulgaria and Yugoslavia. However convenient the foreign sanctuaries were to the insurgents, their open dependence on Greece's northern neighbors must in the final analysis be accounted a net loss for them. It was especially damaging when the Soviet Union began trumpeting the idea of detaching Macedonia from Greece and as Macedonians increasingly predominated in the ranks of the insurgent forces. That the KKE endorsed (with reluctance) the Soviet policy of a "free" Macedonia only underlined the connections between the insurgents and foreign powers who wished Greece little good.

The United States gave substantial help to the Athens government; in fact, more American aid went to Greece per capita than to any other country.[88] One distinguished Greek student of the conflict maintains that American material help arrived too late to be a major reason for the guerrillas' defeat. But a widespread view, especially among Western analysts, is that "it was above all America's dispatch of military advisers, its reorganization of the Greek army, its donation of enormous military supplies, its granting of economic aid, and even its intervention in internal political affairs, that kept this key position on the southern flank of Europe out of Russian control."[89]

Economic and military aid from the United States allowed the Greeks to increase the size of their army and upgrade its equipment without greatly disrupting the nation's economy. The United States provided both the pressure and the means for the GNA to improve its operations. And as the conflict developed, American aid to the government increased while Communist help to the guerrillas declined (precisely the reverse of what would happen in South Vietnam twenty-five years later).

It is nevertheless worthwhile to reflect that in important ways Greece was a nearly ideal setting for a major U.S. effort to stop Communist subversion. The Greek government was highly receptive to American advice as well as aid, and the large majority of Greeks were anticommunist, or at least not procommunist. American assistance would certainly have had little effect if substantial segments of the Greek population had not been resolved to resist the insurgents.[90]

Abandoning Guerrilla Tactics

Guerrilla warfare is the strategy of the weaker side, of those who cannot openly confront the superior numbers, training, and equipment of the opponent's regular armed forces. According to the classic Maoist formulation, the destiny of guerrillas is to grow in strength until they can wage conventional war, that is, assemble in large numbers to occupy and hold specific territory against whatever attack the enemy forces may mount, and then seek out those enemy forces and bring them to battle. When guerrilla forces adopt conventional tactics, by definition they throw away their great advantages of mobility and surprise and give the regular army time to bring its (presumably superior) numbers and equipment to bear. Clearly, then, the switch from guerrilla to conventional war ought to occur only when (and if) the insurgents are gaining physical and moral strength and the government forces are losing both. The Democratic Army had experimented with conventional tactics in the assaults on Florina and Konitsa in 1947. Even though at that time the Greek National Army was perhaps in its worst condition, the results had been bad for the insurgents. To confront the GNA directly in the winter of

1948–1949, with American help coming into play and the insurgency clearly in decline, was a most egregious error.

Losing the Yugoslav Sanctuary

In the age of aircraft, Greece was arguably too small for classical guerrilla warfare. Sanctuary in the Communist states to the north, therefore, provided the insurgents with that space without which they probably would not have been able to function for long. Certainly the ability of the insurgents, when pressed by the GNA, to retreat across friendly borders and receive shelter, training, and medical attention was a major factor in sustaining the insurgency, despite its more subtle negative aspects. One may perhaps better appreciate the importance of the Yugoslav border closing by trying to imagine the consequences in South Vietnam if the borders of Laos had been closed to the movement of troops and supplies from North Vietnam.

The history of guerrilla conflict suggests the general rule that guerrillas ought wherever possible to operate close to international borders. Nevertheless, the Greek case proves that the possession of sanctuaries may not always be an unmixed blessing. Dependence on Greece's Communist neighbors identified the guerrillas in the minds of many as an antinationalist element, and nowhere have Communist insurgents come to power without having first succeeded in wrapping themselves, however uncomfortably, incongruously, and impermanently, in the banners of nationalism.[91] In Greece nationalism clearly worked against the Communist side. Moreover, the availability of escape across friendly borders caused the Greek guerrillas to develop a particular mode of fighting; even when it had become apparent that the Yugoslav frontier would soon be closed to them, they were unable to adapt. And lastly, secure in their possession of across-border sanctuaries, many guerrillas no doubt felt freer than they otherwise might have to express their profound hostility toward their peasant countrymen. Thus in the end sanctuaries, much to be desired in theory, helped to undermine the guerrillas.

Alienating the Peasantry

Yet, in spite of all these errors and setbacks, could the Democratic Army not have recommitted itself to guerrilla tactics, learned to live without its Yugoslav sanctuary, and thus hung on until the Americans lost interest in Greece—until, for example, the outbreak of the Korean War? The answer is Possibly—if the insurgents retained or developed the support of a substantial share of the population.

Such support, however, did not exist, certainly not by 1949. After the fighting had abated, elections in 1949 and 1950 showed the Communists with about 10 percent of the electorate, a sufficient pool from which to have drawn guerrillas but not nearly enough to have overthrown even the wobbly Greek state. That is why the Communist Party's repeated calls for an uprising of the urban masses never produced a response. Confronted by this uncanny, un-Marxist indifference to the cause of revolution shown by the citizens of Athens, the party fired the whole leadership in that city. The great majority of the population declined to answer the repeated summons to revolution for at least two good reasons. First, although from a military point of view Greece was a nearly ideal locus for a guerrilla-based revolutionary effort, from a political standpoint it was much less than that. Some observers believe that democratic governments, at least in the short term, are not very efficient at coping with insurgency. That may be true. But it is certainly true that to overthrow by internal rebellion a government based on popular consent, or even with the trappings of such consent, is very difficult. That is because many who might long for profound changes in the life of the society cannot be mobilized for armed struggle and fratricidal destruction if there exists, or seems to exist, a nonviolent path to the desired changes.[92] Parliamentary government provides such a path, and Greece possessed a parliamentary government, however threadbare.

But surely, in a country like postwar Greece, with so much poverty and so many tensions, the existence of a parliamentary government did not have to be an insuperable handicap. The Communists should have been able to build outward from their hard core, gathering support with a program of radical redistribution. At the very least they could have amassed a large following among the peasants in the mountainous districts that the insurgents controlled most of the time. But that did not happen. And here we have the second reason why the revolutionary appeals of the KKE fell on barren soil, indeed the key to the defeat of the insurgents: "The rebels failed because the mass of the people was against them."[93] As the conflict went on, support for the Democratic Army and the KKE behind it withered, especially in the villages.

How did the withering occur? After the end of the civil war, a member of the KKE Politburo provided an explanation: the defeat of the Communists was the bitter fruit of "the policy of devastation of the countryside." And how to account for this "policy of devastation?" The guerrillas had safe supply sources over the frontiers and thus were relatively independent of the peasantry. But clearly not all guerrilla movements that have enjoyed sanctuaries (such as the Afghan mujahideen) have antagonized the civilians among whom they operated. The answer lies in the character of the driving force behind the insurgency in Greece: the Communist Party. The party's hard core was not merely unrepresentative of the majority of Greeks; it was *profoundly hostile* to them. Communist activists were contemptuous and ashamed of the mass of the peasantry, whom they viewed as ignorant, superstitious, and irredeemably petit-bourgeois. Here lies the root of the conscious and unconscious policy of trying to elicit cooperation or passivity in the villages through terror.[94]

The years of the German occupation witnessed the beginnings of this epiphany of hostility: ELAS guerrillas deliberately brought down the Nazi wrath upon helpless villagers. The fratricidal propensities of ELAS were even more strikingly revealed during the 1944 fighting in Athens, when "the Communists, whose many atrocities were perpetrated mostly upon innocent and defenseless hostages, came to be hated with a passion rare in the nation's history." Finally, the hostility of the KKE toward the common folk attained its full dimensions during the civil war in the policy of gaining power by destroying the economic life of the nation at whatever cost to the peasants. In a Brave New Stalinist Greece, the fate of the peasants was to be not liberation but liquidation. Thus the Communists, by their brutality against the peasants, poisoned the waters in which they had to swim.[95]

American assistance enabled the Greek Army to hold together and grow stronger. Closing the Yugoslav frontier shortened the conflict. But the insurgents themselves violated the two must fundamental rules of guerrilla warfare: make friends with the civilians among whom you must exist, and never fight unless you are certain to win. In these ways they became the principal architects of their own defeat.

Under unpropitious circumstances, in a poor and devastated land hedged by Soviet satellite states and within striking distance of the Soviet Army, the United States helped to achieve the total defeat of a major Communist insurgency without committing its own combat troops. The outcome of the Greek conflict must be accounted a major triumph of U.S. policy.

Yet, suppose the leadership of the Greek Communist party had been a bit more sagacious. Specifically, what if it had had the simple common sense not to terrorize the peasantry among whom it had to operate? And suppose further that a better-directed Communist insurgency had manifested itself at a time when American political leaders believed (as they did not in 1947) that the United States possessed sufficient armed forces to sustain a significant intervention on the ground? What would have happened then?

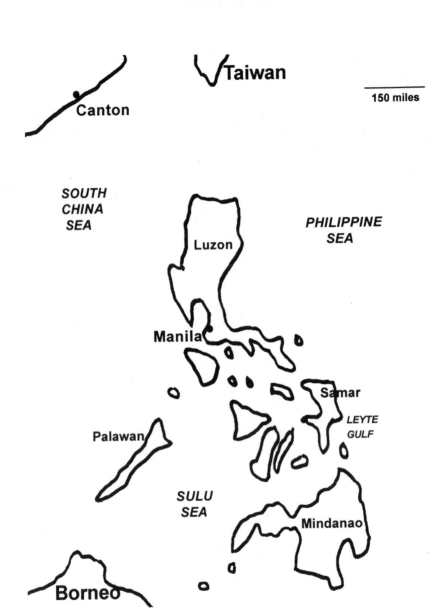

The Philippines, 1946.

Map produced by Anne Szewczyk.

6

Back to the Philippines

The Huks

A traumatic Japanese occupation of the Philippines during World War II provided the opportunity for a Communist-organized attempt to take over political power in that country by force of arms. The attempt ended in frustration, in part because of American policies. The Philippines became the first republic in Asia to defeat a Communist insurgency.

The Japanese Occupation

The Republic of the Philippines celebrated its first Independence Day on July 4, 1946. On that day Manuel Roxas was sworn in as the new republic's first president. The country over which he presided had a population of about 20 million.

It was less than a year since World War II had ended, and the Philippine republic was celebrating its birthday amid great devastation. In the eyes of many Japanese, the Pacific War had been the latest and greatest episode in the epic confrontation between the European and the Asian races. In the Russo-Japanese War of 1904–1905, for the first time in modern history an oriental nation dealt a decisive defeat to a major occidental power. That conflict had provided compelling evidence to Japanese expansionists that it was their nation's destiny to put an end one day to white domination over Asia. From Shanghai to Sumatra, Imperial Japan must destroy Caucasian colonialism and gather all the teeming lands of the East into the Greater East Asia Co-Prosperity Sphere. Nevertheless, in their three-and-a-half-year occupation of the Philippines, the Japanese committed appalling atrocities against its Asian inhabitants. Carlos P. Romulo, who after the war became foreign minister of the Philippines, wrote that the brutal behavior of the Japanese arose from the frustration and outrage they felt when so many Filipinos openly sided with the Americans, the white enemy.[1] Besides experiencing an exceedingly cruel occupation, the Philippines saw some of the hardest fighting in all of World War II, including the Battle of Leyte Gulf, the largest naval engagement in the history of the planet. At the war's end, widespread social disorganization and serious economic hardship confronted the fledgling republic, and 70 percent of Manila lay destroyed.

Many Filipinos had organized to resist the Japanese occupation. In March 1942 a mainly Communist group founded the People's Army Against Japan. The Tagalog acronym of this group was Hukbalahap, hence the nickname Huks. By late 1943 there were perhaps ten thousand Huks. At the end of the war they were well equipped with Japanese or American weapons. As in German-occupied Greece, the Communist-directed guerrilla bands in the Philippines looked to the postwar period; they fought not only the Japanese but also guerrilla units loyal to the United States. With the end of the war, the Japanese departed, but the Huks did not lay down their arms. Tensions increased between the Huks and the authorities of the new Philippine republic. The U.S. Army was reluctant to confer any legal status on the Huks or to pay them for their alleged wartime services. Furthermore, the Huks wanted severe punishment for all Filipinos who had collaborated with the Japanese occupation; the American policy, in contrast, was to draw a curtain over the activities of those difficult occupation days; that policy would permit former collaborators eventually to reassume positions of influence. For example, Manuel Roxas, born in 1892, had served in the pro-Japanese Laurel government during World War II but had been saved from prosecution by the intervention of Douglas MacArthur.[2] He then achieved election as the first president of the republic with the support of the venerable and dominant Nacionalista Party's liberal wing, which set itself up as the Liberal Party. When President Roxas ordered a crackdown on disorders in the countryside, the Huks entered into open armed rebellion.

The main island of the archipelago is Luzon, with an area of forty thousand square miles, the size of Kentucky. The focus of Huk activity was there. Central Luzon had long been an area of wide-spread absentee landlordism, one of the greatest curses that can be-fall an agricultural community. Violent agrarian unrest had been the main theme of the history of this part of the Philippines from time immemorial. Serious social ills went unheeded by a mainly Filipino administration out of touch with the common people and rife with corruption. Officials high and low exploited the peasantry in a variety of ways.

The widespread and sometimes quite open collaboration by Luzon landlords with the wartime Japanese occupation scandalized a growing number of peasants already exasperated with the diffi-culties of their lives. Luis Taruc, who emerged as the principal Huk military leader, wrote: "When we dealt with [the landlords] harshly, it was because they were betraying our country to the Japanese and oppressing the common people. This knowledge of the period is essential to an understanding of Huk activities." The Huk conflict with the Japanese had been partly a response to the oppressive na-ture of the occupation. It was also, however, an expression of the deep anxieties produced by the breakdown of traditional patron-client relationships in the countryside, a breakdown stimulated by overpopulation. Carlos P. Romulo noted that "the majority of Huk complaints came out of *injustices* concerning the land." Years after the rebellion was over, Taruc wrote: "It must be fully understood that one cannot separate the problem of rebellion from that of the peasantry. It is most important to recognize that this is an urgent problem—perhaps the most urgent of our day—in every one of the newly developed [sic] countries." Gen. Douglas MacArthur, whose name is inextricably linked with the history of the Philippines, once tartly observed, "If I worked in those sugarfields, I'd probably be a Huk myself."[3]

The Huks Gain Ground

The Huks employed against the Philippine republic the classic meth-ods of guerrilla warfare so familiar to the islands. They were espe-cially efficient at robbing payroll offices, trains, and cargo trucks in central Luzon.[4] Their success in such operations no doubt owed a great deal to the presence among their recruits of groups that can correctly be labeled common criminals.

The paramilitary Philippine Constabulary was the government's main instrument for dealing with this challenge. The constabulary was not well prepared for this sort of warfare, or for any other. The United States had handed over to the new Philippine republic surplus war equipment worth billions of dollars in the money of the early 2000s. Little found its way into the hands of the armed forces; much of it was simply stolen. The constabulary's tactical response to the Huks was unimaginative and largely useless. Edward Lansdale, the Air Force major general who served as an intimate security adviser to the presidents of both the Philippines and South Vietnam, wrote critically of the usually futile and often destructive encirclement tactics used by government forces.[5]

Inadequate equipment and poor tactics were not the total of the constabulary's shortcomings. The treatment of the peasants of Luzon at the hands of both the constabulary and civil officials fueled the Huk revolt. The propensity of soldiers to help themselves to the possessions of the peasants and to commit even worse offenses against these humble citizens of the republic whom they were supposed to be serving and protecting produced many recruits and supporters for the Huks, especially between 1948 and 1950. Soldiers led by good officers do not systematically abuse civilians, especially those of their own nationality. The oppressive behavior of Filipino troops reflected in large part the influence of political interference within the officer corps that corrupted the soul of the armed forces and reduced their antiguerrilla efforts to worse than nothing. Years later, Luis Taruc consistently maintained that the true regenerative source of the Huk rebellion was government provocation and terrorism against the hapless civilians.[6] Without abuses of this kind, the Huk rebellion might never have assumed the serious proportions it eventually attained.

On the death of President Manuel Roxas in 1948, Vice President Elpidio Quirino (born 1890) succeeded to the presidency. The Huks believed that Quirino's continuation in the Malacañan Palace would prolong and aggravate the corruption and inefficiency of the national government and thus smooth their path to power. They therefore cynically supported his reelection efforts as much as they could. But Quirino did not need the help of the Huks. He held onto the office by vote buying, vote stealing, and voter intimidation on a massive scale. The "dirty election of 1949" was a boon to the Huks:

by undermining the faith of both intellectuals and common citizens in the processes of democracy, it seemed to close off the path to peaceful change.[7] If there was no hope of removing an oppressive and corrupt government through the ballot box, then all disaffected elements of the population would eventually have to turn to armed rebellion under the leadership of the Huks. Taruc maintains that several members of the wartime Huk movement who had been elected to Congress in 1947 were illegally deprived of their seats and became convinced thereby that armed revolt was the only valid option. The perversion of the electoral process in the Philippines was thus worth thousands of fighters to the Huk cause.

Ramon Magsaysay Defeats the Huks

Less than four years after the end of World War II, while civil war continued in Greece, the long struggle in China neared its fateful climax, and Ho Chi Minh's forces struggled on in French Vietnam, the Communist-led rebellion in the Philippines increased in strength. The Huks had between 11,000 and 15,000 fighters. Opposing them were somewhere around 25,000 members of the constabulary. At the end of 1949, Mao proclaimed the establishment of the Chinese People's Republic; in imitation of their victorious ideological brothers in China, the Philippine Communists changed the name of their armed forces to the People's Liberation Army. By June 1950, when the North Koreans invaded the South, the Huks were able to deploy around 20,000 guerrillas. Although the guerrilla leader Luis Taruc wrote afterward that there was never any real danger that Manila would fall to the Huks, during 1950 the rebellion was obviously reaching a new and dangerous level. In March and again in August 1950, the Huks carried out some spectacular raids in the Manila area. The boldness and magnitude of these operations shocked the Quirino administration into realizing that the war was going badly: something drastically different had to be done. President Quirino called in the army to assist the out-classed constabulary. And in September 1950 he appointed as secretary of defense, to be directly in charge of fighting the Huks, Ramon Magsaysay.[8]

Of pure Malay stock, unlike much of the Philippine elite, Magsaysay had been born in 1907, the son of a high school carpentry teacher. He was a bus company manager before World War II and served as a Liberal Party congressman from 1946 to 1950, becoming chairman of the House National Defense Committee. But to the Quirino administration, Magsaysay's primary credential was that he had fought as a guerrilla against the Japanese occupation and therefore presumably would know how to fight the Huks. This expectation proved to be exceedingly well founded.

For Magsaysay the first order of business was clearly to improve relations between his troops and the peasantry; it is a sound principle that when "competing with a vigorous rebellion, a precarious authority should be concerned with respect for the people's dignity at least as much as with the level of their income." Ex-guerrilla Magsaysay knew from experience that big sweeps by government military units were hardly ever effective. Even if the rebels have not been previously tipped off by informants, guerrillas can hardly help but hear the movement of large numbers of troops from very far away.[9] But worse than that, sweeps provide too many occasions for the abuse of civilians: tired soldiers, unable to catch their ever-elusive enemies, will often vent their frustrations on the civilians at hand. Magsaysay therefore instructed his commanders that troops should never enter a village in an attitude of hostility unless they were sure it contained active guerrillas. Instead, soldiers should approach peasants as if they were, or were soon to become, allies. Remembering the American GIs of World War II, Magsaysay supplied candy for his soldiers to hand out to village children. He also saw to it that the army provided medical help to peasants who needed it. In a really brilliant move, Magsaysay had army lawyers represent poor peasants in land cases against wealthy landlords, and peasant litigants actually won many of these cases. Within a matter of months, Magsaysay's reforms began to improve the image of the armed forces and undermine the hopes of the Huks.[10]

As a cause of Huk success, the armed forces' poor military tactics had ranked second to their poor relations with villagers. (These two deficiencies—bad field tactics and bad civil relations—seem almost always to go together.) Demanding more aggressiveness from his soldiers, Magsaysay sent Battalion Combat Teams to enter areas where the armed forces had not gone before. Feeling safe in these unvisited areas, the Huks had been using them to improve their living standards by growing food in fields they had laboriously cleared.

The discovery of the food-growing areas by government forces meant serious hardships for many Huks. Interference with their food supplies can have an even more disruptive effect on guerrillas than interference with their weapons supplies. Eventually, the troops learned not to move in until just before the crops were ready for harvesting. Toward the end of 1951, aggressive tactics on the part of Magsaysay's troops forced the remaining Huks to retreat into swamps and other undesirable areas; there they were cut off from contact with civilians, unable to obtain sufficient food, and exposed to numerous illnesses.[11]

Magsaysay understood what happened to reforms when their instigator simply issues instructions and then sits in his office, expecting them to be carried out. To ensure compliance with his directives to military commanders concerning correct treatment of civilians and aggressive tactics against guerrillas, he made numerous unexpected visits, usually by plane, to military forces even in remote areas. Edward Lansdale, a close adviser to Magsaysay, has recorded how the defense secretary's unscheduled descents from on high to bestow medals and praise or to remove on the spot lazy and incompetent commanders electrified the military into conformity with his wishes.[12] Magsaysay introduced a special telegraph service to his headquarters; for a nominal fee, any citizen in the country could send the secretary of defense a message about abuses or problems. He also placed the constabulary under military (that is, under his) control. He fired all the incompetents and criminals he could find (alas, there were more than a few) and also those who had established comfortable or lucrative relationships with the guerrillas.

Magsaysay singled out the leaders of the insurgency for special attention. He offered what to ordinary Filipinos were fabulous rewards for the arrest of individual Huk leaders, identified by name—not as rebels but as felons, wanted for a particular criminal act, such as murder, rape, or arson, at a particular time and place. Magsaysay widely publicized the names of Huk leaders captured in this way. These procedures helped reduce the image of the Huks from Robin Hoods to common criminals. They also sowed dissension between Huk leaders and their followers: no insurgent commander could be sure whether or for how long his comrades would be able to resist the allure of sudden wealth. Another special weapon against the

Huks consisted of small ranger units whose unique function was to track down and kill notorious Huk leaders.[13] Predictably, leadership roles among the Huks rapidly lost their former attractiveness.

No weapon against guerrillas is more effective than a good intelligence organization. The intelligence available to the armed forces greatly improved under Magsaysay, partly because the image of the soldiers benefited from their new respect for civilian dignity, partly because Magsaysay offered big rewards for information leading to the capture of guerrillas or the discovery of arms caches, and partly because of the universal rule that intelligence flows more freely to the side that is perceived to be winning. Intercepted couriers often provided valuable information. As in other insurgencies, captured guerrillas, when treated well, often changed sides and offered their captors all kinds of interesting intelligence. Through such sources Magsaysay was able to bag most of the members of the politburo of the Philippine Communist Party, along with literally truckloads of documents that provided him and his military commanders with much fascinating reading.[14]

But the easiest and cheapest solution to guerrilla war is to overcome the guerrillas' will to fight and induce them to surrender. The increased pressure on the Huks was having that effect, but Magsaysay went further. He knew that many who fought with the Huks were neither convinced Communists nor hardened criminals; he could win them over with the right approach. So Magsaysay developed his amnesty policy. The announcements of amnesty carefully avoided the word "surrender," using in its place euphemisms such as "coming in." The amnesty policy also excluded real criminals, thus further sowing discord within rebel ranks.[15] (Government forces should take great care to rigidly segregate guerrillas who have surrendered from those who have been captured.)

Many of the Huks, however, could not simply "come in." Some Filipinos had joined the Huks when they were mere boys; for them and for others the movement had been home and family for a decade. If they left the guerrilla organization, they would have no place to go. It was therefore necessary to provide these unfortunates with a new life. Magsaysay's wise solution to this problem was to open up virgin lands on southern islands far from Luzon to provide a homestead to any surrendered guerrilla who wanted one. A former Huk normally received twenty acres; he also got help from the army to build a little house, a small loan to tide him over until the first crop, and maybe a work animal or two. Those who accepted this amnesty-with-a-farm changed overnight from threats to the constitutional order into productive and eventually taxpaying citizens. The final payoff, once the land-to-surrendered-Huks policy was seen to be working, was that popular opinion began to turn against those Huks who continued fighting: since the war was obviously lost, was it perhaps that these holdout guerrillas did not want to give up because they did not wish to work on the land like peasants?[16]

A house, some cash, and a little land: so simple a concept, so inexpensive a program, so effective a weapon against the guerrillas. Naturally, these methods did not work with the ideologically motivated intellectuals who composed the hard core of the insurgency, but Magsaysay's progressive isolation of those individuals from their peasant base reduced them to the status of fish out of water.

The 1951 congressional elections were approaching. Eager to avoid a repetition of the travesties of 1949, some members of the Commission on Elections requested the assistance of the secretary of defense. With the help of a civic action group called the National Movement for Free Elections (NAMFREL), which is still in existence today, Magsaysay deployed the army to ensure relatively peaceful balloting and an honest count. Compared to the 1949 presidential contest, the 1951 elections were a model of orderliness and probity; in fact, the opposition Nacionalista Party won every single senate seat up for election that year. By demonstrating that there was indeed a realistic alternative to violence for the adjustment of grievances, the elections dealt a major blow to the insurgency: "to all intents and purposes, the 1951 elections sounded the death knell of the Hukbalahap movement."[17]

Magsaysay Becomes President

Ramon Magsaysay improved military tactics against the Huks, cut down military abuse of the civilian population, and ensured clean congressional elections in 1951. He employed the same combination of tactics against the Huks that the Americans had used a half-century before against Aguinaldo's followers: unrelenting military pressure plus the mitigation of serious irritants. As a result thousands of Huks were captured or killed, gave themselves up, or just melted away from the movement. Yet as secretary of defense, subordinate to President Quirino, Magsaysay lacked the full power to uproot the political and economic abuses that contributed to the Huk rebellion. "Good troops employing proper tactics cannot make up for an unsound government and political base." Therefore, in March 1953 Magsaysay resigned his defense post to seek the presidential nomination of the opposition Nacionalista Party. As the Magsaysay campaign unfolded, Filipinos saw for the first time a major presidential candidate leave the comfortable and predictable route of the large cities to seek votes and speak to the people in the villages and the remote islands.[18] (In contrast, Quirino was recovering from serious surgery and took a relatively less visible part in the campaign.)

Another Quirino cabinet member was also seeking election to the highest office. Carlos P. Romulo, born in 1899 under the U.S. flag, had been Philippine ambassador to the United States and to the United Nations, president of the UN General Assembly, and secretary of foreign affairs under President Quirino. Like Magsaysay, Romulo had concluded that the Huks would never be thoroughly defeated while Quirino and men like him ruled the country.

A very great deal indeed was riding on this election. Luis Taruc urged his followers to support Quirino (as they had in 1949). In Washington, Secretary of State John Foster Dulles agreed with Edward Lansdale that the presidential contest had to be free and honest if the Huks were to be finally overcome. Besides issuing verbal warnings, the United States took several measures to prevent Quirino from using the tactics of 1949 against Magsaysay in 1953. The State Department made sure that numerous American reporters went to the Philippines to cover the election; U.S. government funds discreetly bolstered the Magsaysay campaign. Magsaysay had of course resigned as secretary of defense and thus no longer had control of the military, but U.S. army officers urged their friends in the Philippine Army to guard the honesty of the balloting. President Quirino, aware that he was in trouble, tried to stir up anti-Americanism over U.S. interference in the campaign but without success (having experienced the Japanese occupation, Filipinos found anti-Americanism to be very weak tea.) Magsaysay received the vital support of NAMFREL (whose establishment in 1951 had been facilitated by CIA funds), and the Filipino press was much more vigilant than in 1949. Impressed with the clear evidence of Magsaysay's popularity and fearful of splitting the anti-Quirino vote, Romulo withdrew from the race and asked his supporters to vote for Magsaysay. Finally, the leaders of the powerful Roman Catholic Church forcefully reminded their adherents of their duty not only to go to the polls but to vote to prevent the triumph of corrupt men.[19]

In the end it was an overwhelming victory for Magsaysay: 2.4 million votes for him, 1.15 million votes for Quirino.[20] (In 1949 the announced results gave 1.6 million votes to Quirino and 1.5 million to his opponents, principally José Laurel, who had served the Japanese occupation as "President of the Philippine Republic" from 1943 to 1945 and had been pardoned for that by Quirino in 1948.)

With the immensely popular Magsaysay in the Malacañan Palace, completely in control of the armed forces and fully in position to expand his land-to-surrendered-Huks program, the end of the struggle was clearly in sight. In May 1954 Luis Taruc himself came out of the jungle to surrender; that is the conventional date for the end of the Huk insurgency. When Taruc gave himself up (to receive a twelve-year prison sentence), some in the government said that he was merely a Trojan horse, that this move was just some Communist deception. They were wrong. A few Huk units went on fighting, but they were composed mainly of hard-core Communists or real criminals (or both), and they never posed a threat to Manila or any other sizable town. Perhaps 12,000 Huks lost their lives between 1946 and 1954; 4,000 were captured, and another 16,000 surrendered.[21]

A Closer Look at the Huks

In the early days of World War II, Communist leaders of the Huk guerrillas had no serious plans beyond resistance to the Japanese occupation; at least that was the view of Luis Taruc, and it may be accurate.[22] It was inevitable, however, that the Communists would soon turn their thoughts to postwar conditions and would consider the probabilities of a "proletarian" revolution led by the "vanguard" party. (We should try to keep in mind that in those days [1943–1946] the complete Maoist model of revolution that would so dominate global political thought during the 1960s and 1970s was not yet available.)

Although many Communists were sympathetic to the peasants, they did not share their goals nor really understand them. The leaders of the Philippine Communist Party were mostly urban, and many of them were well educated. Their chief was Vicente Lava, who had obtained a Ph.D. from Columbia University and was a professor of chemistry at the University of the Philippines. Luis Taruc, who would become the major hero of the Huk movement, was born not far from Manila in Pampanga province; he had studied medicine for years at the University of Manila but had had to withdraw in 1934 for lack of funds. Elected to Congress in 1946, he was not permitted to retain his seat because of accusations that he and others associated with him had used terrorism to gain election. By the spring of 1947, he had gone back to the mountains and to the guerrilla life. Of the peasants who bore arms as Huks, the majority apparently wanted merely the return of the system of stable tenant farming with its traditional patron-client relationships as it had existed before the 1930s. The Communists, in contrast, wanted a real social and political revolution, based on the urban masses, pursuing a Stalinist policy of forced industrialization and efforts to uproot the traditional family structure.[23]

As the tactics of the government forces under Magsaysay improved, the tactics of the Huks under their Communist leadership deteriorated. The Communists needed to expand their base from central Luzon, but they were reluctant to reach out to other opposition groups to form the classic Leninist broad front. Instead the Huks tried to spread their rebellion into adjacent areas by sending small detachments of guerrillas into them. Usually such efforts were not successful. Many Huk leaders wore better clothes and smoked better cigarettes than the peasants whose acceptance they sought as their liberators. Often the men sent into a new district to start up a rebel movement were criminals or men who acted like criminals. By 1951 the Huk rebellion was clearly sinking into an irreversible decline.[24]

Confronted with the mounting evidence of their inevitable defeat, the Communists began to turn their frustration and anger against members of the Huk movement. They executed young fighters and sympathizers for such infractions as sleeping while on duty or asking leave to go home, behaviors the Communists viewed as preludes to surrender. If a Huk's relatives asked him to give up, the Communists would tell him that the only way he could prove his continuing loyalty to the movement was to kill those relatives. Senseless acts of destruction and cruelty, such as the murder of the widow of President Manuel Quezon and her daughter in August 1949, hurt the Huk cause both inside and outside the movement. Taruc bitterly criticized the Communist Party leadership for insisting on prolonging the fighting after 1950, when it had become clear that the struggle was lost.[25]

The Question of American Troops

In 1950 the Philippine republic had been independent for less than five years. For fifty years before that, Americans in large numbers, civilian as well as military, were present in the islands and involved with Philippine affairs in the most intimate ways. In 1907, only a few years after the Aguinaldo insurgency had come to an end, the Americans set up the first popularly elected legislature in the history of Southeast Asia. By 1916 all literate Filipino males had the right of suffrage. The Americans fostered labor unions, pressed for the limitation of absentee landlordism, and constructed a well-paid civil service staffed more and more by Filipinos. American English was in wide use, and many Filipinos felt admiration, or at least amused affection, for Americans. All of this elicited one day an exasperated sigh from Nationalist Party leader Manuel Quezon: "Damn the Americans, why don't they tyrannize us more?" Entering the post–World War II period, Washington wanted the Philippines to become the showcase of democracy in East Asia. Thus, the United States had a tremendous emotional and ideological stake in the Philippines. President Quirino was eager to have American troops, in some capacity at least, in the Philippines.[26] The Truman administration had sent some U.S. military personnel to help train the Philippine armed forces. And of course in the Philippines there was no danger that American troops might have to confront Soviet satellite forces, or even the Soviet Army itself, as there had been in Greece, or Chinese troops, as in Korea. The introduction of U.S. ground combat forces into the struggle against the Huks was therefore not so unthinkable as a later generation of Americans (or Filipinos) might imagine.

No one in Washington seems to have given serious consideration to a possible large-scale commitment of U.S. troops at least until 1950, because until then American political and military leaders did not see a Huk victory as a real possibility. Besides that, the United States was preoccupied with the conflicts in China and Greece and the construction of the North Atlantic Treaty Organization. In

April 1950 the chargé d'affaires at the U.S. embassy in Manila, Vinton Chapin, cabled his superiors in Washington that the Philippine armed forces were not doing very well because of their passive tactics and their mistreatment of the peasantry. This latter failure was aggravated by the tendency of the Philippine troops to rely too much on artillery, a tool that obliterates the distinction between guerrillas and civilians. At that time the U.S. military mission to the Philippines consisted of officers who were unskilled in counterguerrilla operations. Moreover, the Huk rebellion, in Chapin's view, had grown out of the need for agrarian reform. In addition, the Huks were able to point to Quirino's fraudulent election and also liked to brand him a tool of "American imperialists." Thus, though sending American ground forces would shift the balance of power against the Huks, nevertheless Chapin recommended that "the employment of United States troops against Filipinos outside our bases should probably be considered only as a last resort. Such action would provide our enemies all over Asia with valuable propaganda and might be expected to cause many Filipinos to regard us as invaders and to join forces with the Huks." The Americans would probably be better off doing in the Philippines what they had done in Greece, sending better-prepared U.S. advisers in larger numbers.[27]

Nevertheless, in early 1950 the deteriorating Philippine situation alarmed the Truman administration. The president wrote to his secretary of state that "failure of the Philippines experiment which all Asia watches as evidence of American intentions and abilities could only have the most unfortunate repercussions for the United States both abroad and at home." Shortly after this presidential announcement, North Korean troops stormed across the thirty-eighth parallel; soon U.S. forces were in Korea literally fighting for their lives around Pusan. Later that year the Chinese Communists intervened massively in the conflict. At the same time, Washington was assuming a greater and greater responsibility for the supply of French and Vietnamese forces fighting the Vietminh in Indochina. Yet, even in those desperate circumstances, U.S. Ambassador to Manila Myron Cowen stated his belief (September 29, 1950) that the United States should at least consider sending a reinforced division to the Philippines. And a "top secret" draft paper by the deputy director of the Office of Philippine and Southeast Asian Affairs, dated January 19, 1951, reads in part as follows: "It is assumed that the United States is determined, regardless of the cost and despite any eventualities, as part of its Pacific policy to retain the Philippines within the orbit of the democratic powers and to deny it to the Soviet orbit. This is the irreducible minimum of American security and interests in the Pacific and the Far East." To achieve that minimum, the author of the secret document approved the idea of sending two American divisions to the Philippines.[28]

In contrast, a National Security Council Staff Study had concluded in November 1950 that at that time Philippine armed forces, if well trained and adequately equipped, ought to be able to defeat the Huks, provided that the Huks received no important outside aid.[29]

American analysis usually emphasized the dual need for good leadership and land reforms. A Department of State paper prepared in June 1950 for the staff of the National Security Council stated in part: "Since the tragic death of President Roxas in 1948, Philippine leadership has been discouragingly weak and short-sighted." A National Security Council Staff Study noted that "leadership of the Philippine Government has been largely in the hands of a small group of individuals representing the wealthy propertied classes who, except in isolated instances, have failed to appreciate the need for reform and the pressures generated among the less prosperous and more numerous groups of the population." Secretary of State Dean Acheson had a particularly unfavorable opinion of the ethics and abilities of President Quirino and was annoyed by the latter's "overweening vanity and arrogance."[30] Washington policymakers were also aware that the fraud and violence of the 1949 presidential election had seriously undermined public trust in the government, thereby playing into the hands of the Huks.[31]

In line with these views, on February 15, 1951, Ambassador Cowen advised the State Department that the Communists automatically placed outside the law any peasant to whom they gave land. The United States and the Philippines must therefore defeat the Huks by carrying out effective land reform programs, including resettlement of landless peasants on desirable lands. Cowen also reminded Washington that everyone who was killed by U.S.-supplied arms had relatives who might thereafter support the Communists, making necessary new expenditures for arms. The secretary of state reflected this general stance. "We strongly believe," he wrote, "that the only way to beat the Communists is to show our ability to carry out under democratic processes those reforms they advocate which are worthwhile. Land redistribution is one such reform."[32]

In another message to the president, Acheson said, "If there is one lesson to be learned from the China debacle it is that if we are confronted with an inadequate vehicle it should be discarded or immobilized in favor of a more propitious one." However, if the U.S. government encouraged the removal of President Quirino, it would become known and would resound all over Asia, presumably to the detriment of American foreign policy on that continent.[33] Gen. George Marshall told Romulo that he "did not wish to have the same experience that he had in China in supplying arms to an Army which was guided by political interests."[34]

In light of such advice, the Truman administration moved toward the position of making assistance to Manila contingent on internal political, military, and economic reforms. Unfortunately, however, the Philippine leaders felt that they could do whatever they wanted and ignore the need for reform, since they could in the last analysis count on the United States to save them.[35]

Of all the reasons why the Americans did not send combat units to the Philippines, one of the most decisive was that among the least eager to get involved in the fighting were the leaders of the U.S. armed forces. On September 6, 1950 (a few days after the appointment of Magsaysay as defense secretary and at a time when the Korean War was going very badly for the Americans), a memorandum from the Joint Chiefs of Staff to Secretary of Defense Louis A. Johnson noted that the possibility was definitely developing that a militant minority organized by the Huks would overthrow a corrupt and discredited regime. The United States had guaranteed the security of the Philippines by the agreement of March 14, 1947; but "such intervention would require, in light of the present world situation [the fighting in Korea and the building up of NATO] a considerable increase in the extent of mobilization currently envisaged." But it was above all the Joint Chiefs' belief that the roots of the Philippine rebellion were primarily political that caused them to have serious doubts about the advisability of widening American participation in the conflict. In the same memorandum, the Joint Chiefs said, "The basic problem [in the Philippines] is primarily political and economic. Military action should not be an alternative for a stable and efficient government based on sound economic and social foundations." It was inequities in land ownership that constituted the roots of the Huk rebellion, as well as the preference for guerrilla life that some men had acquired during the Japanese occupation. Therefore, "direct United States military intervention in the Philippines would be justifiable, from a strategic point of view, only if there remained no other means of preventing Communist seizure of the islands." The memorandum concluded that present conditions in the islands did not warrant the sending of U.S. combat forces. Instead the United States should increase shipments of military materiel to the Philippines, augment the number of security personnel on U.S. installations there, and raise the American military mission to Manila, the Joint U.S. Military Advisory Group (JUSMAG), to a strength of thirty-two officers and twenty-six enlisted persons. JUSMAG itself opposed the direct assignment of American officers to Philippine combat units.[36] Before the end of 1951, however, any prospects for a Huk victory had clearly evaporated; so had any prospect of deploying U.S. combat forces.

Reflection

A guerrilla insurgency has the best chance to succeed when it is directed against the occupation of a country by a foreign power. But the mere foreignness of the opponent is no magic formula for insurgents; the foreigners must cooperate by being hateful as well. More than forty years before the Huks, the efforts of the Aguinaldo forces to rally support by an appeal to anti-Yankeeism and national independence had crashed upon this rock. Rather than invading a previously independent country, the Americans were only superseding a Spanish colonial regime compared to which they were manifestly a great improvement. Moreover, they provided written promises of eventual independence.

The Huks were of course even less able to use national independence as an issue, fighting as they were against a republican government of their own people. Communist efforts to rally the nation against "American imperialism"—especially in the aftermath of the Japanese occupation—were simply not relevant or even credible to the peasantry or, ultimately, to most of those in the guerrilla bands. Unable to assume the mantle of outraged nationalism, the Huks found themselves increasingly deprived of domestic issues as well.

This had a profoundly important effect on the insurgents, because compared to their Communist leaders, most rank-and-file Huks were fighting for very limited goals. When Magsaysay restored elections as an alternative to the violent path to change and began making obvious efforts to mitigate the worst social irritations fueling the rebellion, the peasant foot soldiers of revolution abandoned the struggle in large numbers.[37]

Military pressure on the Huks increased at the same time. Magsaysay accomplished this without relying on the highly destructive weapons of jet aircraft and long-range artillery that aroused such controversy when used in Vietnam. He put more vigorous commanders in the field, who moved into those areas the guerrillas had come to rely on for rest and food. He sowed discord within the Huk ranks by offering rewards for the capture of specific individuals. He provided ordinary guerrillas with a way out through amnesty and resettlement.[38] But of all Magsaysay's military measures, the most important, the one that most effectively undercut the insurgency, was his successful insistence that military abuse of civilians come to a halt.

Two additional facts invite our consideration. From 1951 to 1954 the United States provided the Philippines with $95 million in nonmilitary economic aid, enabling Magsaysay to spend more money than he otherwise would have on social improvements. Simultaneously, the severe limitations on both the number of American military personnel in the Philippines and their activities there allowed—required—the Philippine armed forces to solve their own problems and develop their own methods.[39]

The Huks therefore found themselves confronting an indigenous reformist government defended by increasingly effective armed forces and backed by the resources of the United States. In such circumstances, the only hope of the insurgents would have been assistance from outside. Here the geography of the Philippines exerted its decisive influence: for the Huks, as for Aguinaldo, there could be no sanctuary, no possibility to obtain any systematic aid from outside. In this vital matter the contrast between the Philippine case on the one hand and those of South Vietnam and Afghanistan on the other is as broad as the South China Sea.

Like the American government in its fight against Aguinaldo, the Magsaysay administration in its fight against the Huks linked good military tactics and effective political programs that doomed the geographically isolated guerrillas. These two cases suggest that there may be something like a law of successful counterinsurgency, namely that governments enlightened enough to pursue a sound political strategy will also adopt sound military tactics. They further suggest that those who seek to defeat the insurgencies of tomorrow would do well to study the insurgencies of yesterday. Reflection on these Philippine experiences could yield generous rewards. Yet it is not clear that the U.S. Army or civilian policymakers learned very much from them.[40]

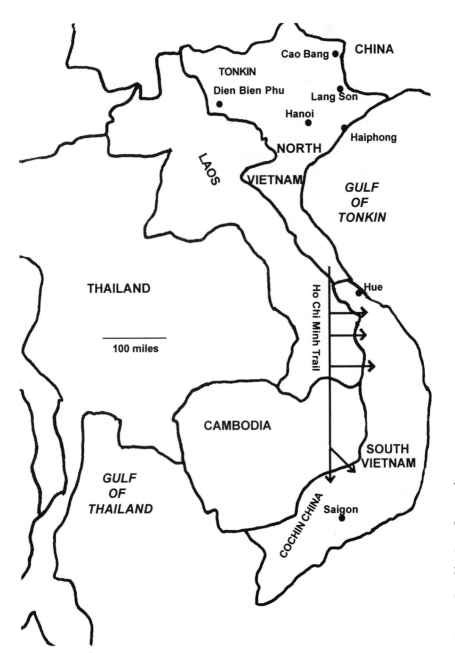

Indochina, post-1954.

7

Vietnam

A Case of Multiple Pathologies

Involvement in the Vietnam conflict divided American society more deeply than any other event since the Civil War. That Southeast Asian struggle ended decades ago but continues to affect U.S. society and foreign policy today.

Many helpful studies are available regarding the origins of U.S. involvement in Vietnam and precise aspects of U.S. military operations there.[1] I am therefore not concerned here with the continuing debate on the wisdom of U.S. entry into the struggle, nor with a detailed review of the combat record. Instead, I focus on certain aspects of the struggle that may help place the American experience in context, including the nature of the Communist enemy; the South Vietnamese allies, especially the regime of Ngo Dinh Diem, the armed forces of South Vietnam, and indigenous anticommunist elements; and some fundamental flaws in the American approach to the conflict. I also suggest an alternative strategy for preserving a South Vietnamese state.

The Enemy

In Vietnam the Americans encountered an enemy whom they called the Vietcong. Organized and directed by the Hanoi Politburo, the Vietcong would increasingly be superseded by the North Vietnamese Army. Their roots were located in the long struggle between French colonialism and Vietnamese Communism.

The French sought to justify their occupation of Vietnam by proclaiming their devotion to their *mission civilisatrice*, even though at the end of World War II 80 percent of the native population was illiterate.[2] Nevertheless, Vietnamese with modern education were not lacking. The French had created a native intelligentsia, produced by French schools in both Vietnam and France. But when members of this elite sought positions commensurate with their education, either in the government or in the private sector, they were often disappointed. Even when such persons obtained white-collar employment, they would likely find themselves subordinate to Frenchmen with educational attainments notably inferior to theirs. The thousands of Vietnamese who had served in Europe with the armies of France during World War I, and had learned much about the great world, returned to their native land to find conditions deeply disillusioning.

The French administration was completely unwilling to make any concessions even to moderate Vietnamese advocates of reform. Criticism of the colonial status of Vietnam was illegal. Vietnamese returning to their own country found that they had no political rights, in jarring contrast to the freedoms they had enjoyed in France. It is then no great mystery that French policies of race-based social exclusion eventually produced the conviction among many educated Vietnamese that they would never be able to achieve their aspirations unless French control of Vietnam came to an end. In other words, French policies in large part produced the modern nationalist movement in Vietnam. Because the contemporary era has been obsessed with economics and fixated on the class struggle, not a few have missed the extent to which political conflict in this century was fueled by the desire of the intelligentsia to get into positions of authority. Nevertheless, the underemployment and lack of status of educated Vietnamese, and the roadblocks to positions of power and dignity for them, are at the heart of the Vietnamese revolution.[3]

But even so, why and how did this emergent nationalist tendency among the educated native elite turn into a mass movement with wide peasant support? And why and how did this nationalist movement come to be dominated by Communists, in contrast to the nationalist movements in India, Burma, Indonesia, and Algeria? A satisfactory answer to these questions would have to include the following elements: mistakes and weaknesses of the noncommunist nationalists in Vietnam; vital outside assistance to the Communists; a Communist strategy well adapted to their circumstances; and the physical elimination by the Communists of their rivals.

The leaders and members of the various noncommunist nationalist parties, of which the most prominent was the VNQDD, came mainly from the educated urban elites; they tried without success to establish a constituency among the rural majority. In 1930 they launched an entirely premature and badly coordinated armed uprising against the French, as a result of which they were almost entirely eliminated from the scene. Later, their collaboration with the Japanese occupation discredited them.

The Communists were also hard hit by the suppression following the 1930 rising. But they received training and sustenance from the Soviet Union and were able slowly to rebuild and even expand their organization. When the Communist-supported Popular Front government came to power in France in 1936, Vietnamese Communists were released from prison. The illegality of political opposition to French rule within Vietnam, vigorously enforced by the secret police, severely hobbled the reappearance of the noncommunist nationalists. Repression was much less effective against the Communists, trained abroad in the arts of clandestine operations.

The Japanese Contribution

In June 1940 France fell before the Nazi blitzkrieg; two months later the Imperial Japanese Government forced the French authorities in Vietnam to grant them effective control of that country under a flimsy veil of continued French sovereignty. It would be impossible to overemphasize the effect the Japanese invasions had on the future of East, South, and Southeast Asia. Surrounded by an aura of omnicompetence and invincibility, for many decades the Europeans had been able to hold their vast imperial territories with remarkably small armed forces. Their defeat and humiliation at the hands of Asians stripped them of their prestige and signaled that they had at last lost the Mandate of Heaven. By breaking the mythic power of the Europeans, the Japanese paved the way for postwar revolution in the East and thus for Ho Chi Minh and his Communists.

During the Japanese occupation, almost all surviving Vietnamese nationalist leaders remained outside the country, mainly in Chiang's China. But the well-organized Communists for the most part stayed inside Tonkin (the northern part of Vietnam), in touch with local realities and possibilities. There they organized a front group called (in short form) the Vietminh, containing elements of several noncommunist parties but safely under Communist direction. Early in 1945 the Japanese dispensed with the last vestiges of French rule in Vietnam. Without an effective intelligence organization or sufficient numbers of troops, the Japanese occupation was neither able nor concerned to root out or even harass the Vietminh. So during the last months of World War II, the Vietminh were free to organize and expand almost at will. By the time of the Japanese surrender, the Vietminh had built up a sturdy little armed force of about five thousand, under the command of a former high school history teacher named Vo Nguyen Giap. They told the Allies that this was an anti-Japanese army and received advice and supplies from the OSS.[4] Yet in fact "the Viet Minh never dreamed of sacrificing its precious troops in the hopeless and ultimately unnecessary task of fighting the Japanese."[5]

Besides disrupting the anticommunist activities of the French, the Japanese made other contributions to Vietminh growth. During the war the Japanese shipped a lot of rice out of Vietnam; they also forced many peasants to abandon rice cultivation and grow jute instead. At the same time Allied bombings damaged transportation lines from the rice-rich South to Tonkin. Thus, in the winter of 1944–1945, a serious famine struck northern Vietnam; perhaps as many as two million people died. Seizing on a popular issue, the Communists led demonstrations demanding the opening of government granaries. This was "a key to the development of the movement in rural areas throughout the north."[6]

Suddenly and unexpectedly, in mid-August 1945 the empire of Japan surrendered to the Allies. With French forces either scattered or imprisoned and the thirty thousand Japanese troops in Vietnam interested only in returning home as soon as possible, there was no one to stop Giap's carefully husbanded little Vietminh army from marching out of the wilds of Tonkin into Hanoi. There Ho Chi Minh proclaimed the Democratic Republic of Vietnam, with himself as its head—these events being known thereafter as the "August Revolution." The fact that Ho was in control of the capital city, however briefly, with an armed force and a functioning administration, and apparently with the blessing of the United States, attracted to the Vietminh many noncommunists who in the last analysis preferred Ho to a return of the French. Thus Ho's regime was able to present itself to the outside world as a national coalition, rather than the Communist-dominated front that it was.[7]

It was the defeat of the Japanese, not the popularity of the Vietminh, that made possible the August Revolution. Without the acquiescence, indeed the benevolence, of the Japanese forces, the Vietminh could never have pulled off their spectacular coup of proclaiming independence from the center of Hanoi. More than that, elements in the Japanese army were determined that the defeat of their own country would not mean the end of resistance to the Western Allies: in the confused days after the surrender, the Japanese delivered money, tanks, artillery, and more than thirty-one thousand rifles to Giap's forces. Several hundred Japanese soldiers (at least) chose not to return home but to join the ranks of the Vietminh outright.[8]

Thus, by remaining inside Vietnam during the Japanese occupation and taking quick advantage of the chaos following Japan's surrender, the Communists established their superiority over the nationalists. The Communists had also been developing an effective political program based on an insightful analysis of conditions in Vietnam: they had always understood that there could be no Communist regime in Vietnam without national independence, but they now arrived at two additional and powerful truths: that there could be no national independence without peasant support for an anti-French struggle, and that there would be no peasant support without the promise of a social revolution, that is, a pledge to distribute among the peasantry the lands and possessions of the French and their Vietnamese followers. By presenting a program of land reform, the Communists were able to break out of the urban ghetto of modern Vietnamese nationalism and organize the mass base without which no revolution against the restored French would have been possible.

The Politics of Murder

Now comes perhaps the most important part of the answer to the question of how the Vietnamese Communists were able to dominate the nationalist movement. A crucial point is that the Communists did not want an independent Vietnam unless it was completely controlled by them. They did not want to be one element in a Vietnamese nationalist movement and government; they wanted total domination. "Indeed, the fight for independence was for them only a vehicle for the conquest of power." To attain that end they embarked on a vast campaign to assassinate their noncommunist rivals. "The elimination of their opponents was one of the most common means the Communists used to establish Vietminh control over the entire nationalist movement."[9]

The policy of dominance through murder was all too successful. "The Stalinists [Vietminh] saw to it that those whose brilliance might have dimmed their own luster were buried in good time." Not only were the Vietminh able thus to establish their control of the anti-French movement, but they also severely weakened the future state of South Vietnam. This "Communist policy of killing all true nationalist opponents of the Viet Minh" deprived that future state of the services of many who might have given it vigor and safety.[10] The Vietminh also sought through assassination to decapitate the indigenous religious sects, and for good measure they killed every Trotskyite they could locate.

After the North-South partition of Vietnam in 1954, the Communists continued to wield their very effective weapon of assassination. By 1960 Communist terrorists in South Vietnam had murdered 1,400 local officials, including about 20 percent of the village chiefs as well as many schoolteachers, who were a special target. By 1965 the Vietcong had killed or abducted about 25,000 civilians. The effects of this vast terror campaign, both on the morale of the civilian population and on the ability of the government in Saigon to administer the country, was quite devastating.[11]

The French War

Stretching north to south about a thousand miles, the distance from Rome to Copenhagen, Vietnam is roughly the size of Finland, or of Illinois and Missouri combined. In essence the country is made up of two great deltas, those of the Red River and the Mekong, linked by a narrow coastal plain that tapers down to fifty miles at the waist.

During the war between the French and the Vietminh (1946–1954)—the prelude to the U.S. involvement—most of the fighting took place in Tonkin, the area Americans would come to know as North Vietnam. A brief review of the most salient aspects of that conflict may illuminate the situation into which the Americans entered soon after.

France was the first of the Western powers to confront a Maoist people's war and also perhaps the least ready for such a confrontation. The defeat and occupation of France by the Nazis, followed by the Allied invasions and the consequent large-scale fighting across northern France, had deeply demoralized and exhausted the French. To these conditions one must add the stunning frivolity of the politicians of the post-1945 Fourth Republic. Not only did they forbid the use of draftees in Vietnam; in addition, during the eight-year conflict they threw up and pulled down no fewer than sixteen cabinets and sent seven different military commanders to Vietnam. And however many and serious were the shortcomings of the Vietminh, French forces in Vietnam were fighting an essentially anachronistic war to hold on to a nineteenth-century empire, an enterprise that to many Europeans no longer made any sense either economically or ethically. Nevertheless, the support of the French cause by Emperor Bao Dai's army and the powerful southern religious sects[12] made the conflict a true civil war; the involvement of the Soviet bloc and the Americans made it an international war as well.

By 1953 the Vietminh military leader, General Giap, had command of about 300,000 fighters of various grades. According to the standard ten-to-one formula for defeating guerrillas, the French would have needed 3 million troops in Vietnam. Such a number was out of the question. But what about at least three to one? That ratio would call for 900,000 troops on the French side. In fact, as the conflict entered its last and most desperate phases, the forces under the French flag totaled perhaps 265,000, including 50,000 French nationals in the army,[13] 30,000 colonial troops (mainly North African and Senegalese), 20,000 Foreign Legionnaires, and 150,000 Vietnamese, plus 15,000 in the French Far Eastern naval and air forces. To these one may add another 150,000 Vietnamese in Bao Dai's National Army and 30,000 armed members of the sects and the Catholic militias, for a grand total of (at most) 450,000, or just about half of what the French needed to achieve even the utterly inadequate ratio of three to one over the Vietminh. And despite more than seven decades of colonial contact and control, the French army was woefully short of officers who could speak Vietnamese, making the effective gathering of intelligence exceedingly difficult.[14]

Given the severe manpower constraints under which the French in Vietnam were operating, their manner of making war there was ill-advised. They certainly forgot, or ignored, the teachings of Gallieni and Lyautey about counterinsurgency. The behavior of the French reflected the soldier's original sin: underestimating the enemy. They liked to execute deep thrusts into enemy-held territory along known roads; later those thrusts had to be withdrawn in less than glorious circumstances. They also liked to drop airborne troops behind enemy lines, establishing strong points that had to be supplied by their inadequate airpower or by ground convoys lacking air cover. They would afterward abandon these strong points, suffering heavy losses in the process. At Cao Bang, on the mountainous Chinese border, the French possessed a good fort with impressive defenses both natural and manmade. In 1950 the High Command in Hanoi decided to abandon Cao Bang. Accordingly, 1,600 troops plus hundreds of civilians set out for the city of Lang Son, eighty-five miles to the south; at the same time 3,500 French Moroccan troops advanced north to meet and escort the party coming from Cao Bang. The two groups linked up, only to be finally cut to ribbons by the swarming Vietminh in "the greatest defeat in the history of French colonial warfare."[15]

The events at Cao Bang persuaded the French that they must abandon Lang Son, a city of one hundred thousand. To escape the Vietminh, the French withdrew from the city without first blowing up their munitions. Thus the Vietminh obtained a great windfall: ten thousand 75 mm shells, invaluable gasoline, clothing, medicine, and much else. It was "France's greatest colonial defeat since Montcalm had died at Quebec."[16]

With the fall of the French border strongholds at Cao Bang and Lang Son, the Vietminh had unrestricted access to supplies and advisers from newly Communist China. The French could not now hope to retain all, or even most, of Tonkin. The situation clearly called for the French to turn the Hanoi-Haiphong area into an enclave and to retrench into Cochin China, with its large population and small Communist presence.[17] But instead the French tried to fight on everywhere.

By 1954 the war had clearly become stalemated. Aside from a debilitating inadequacy of manpower, the French supposed that their principal problem arose from the fact that Giap had learned the hard way not to engage in pitched battles. As long as the war remained essentially guerrilla, the French would continue to be at a grave disadvantage. They must therefore entice Giap into accepting a major battle. Thus, the French High Command decided to build the fortress at Dien Bien Phu.[18] A French stronghold so far from the Red River Delta base would surely prove to be an irresistible temptation to Giap.

Indeed it did. Vietminh casualty rates had been very high, and the great powers were preparing to gather at Geneva to discuss the Vietnam situation. If all went well for the Communists at Dien Bien Phu, Giap would strike a decisive blow not at a fortress in Indochina but at opinion in metropolitan France and at the Geneva Conference. That is what the battle came to be about.

At Dien Bien Phu about 13,000 French, colonial, and Vietnamese soldiers fought 100,000 Vietminh and their Chinese advisers. The Communist attack began on March 13, and its outcome was evident from almost the first day. With the garrison cut off, the French tried to supply the fortress by air but did not have enough planes; furthermore, the antiaircraft fire (much of it Chinese) over Dien Bien Phu was thicker than that over Germany in World War II.[19] The whole world stopped to watch the last days of the drama, which ended on May 8, exactly nine years after the surrender of Nazi Germany.

Dien Bien Phu was a tactical disaster for the French but hardly a strategic one; after all, they had committed about one-twentieth of their Vietnam assets to the battle, whereas Giap had committed almost half of his. Nevertheless, for winning this one-sided, small-scale jungle battle, Giap achieved the reputation of a modern-day Napoleon. More importantly, as the Vietminh leaders had hoped, the fall of Dien Bien Phu had broken the will of the Paris politicians to continue the war. And so at Geneva the French military and the Vietminh signed an agreement (rejected by the legitimate government of Vietnam) to partition the country at the seventeenth parallel. That was the birth of North and South Vietnam.[20]

During the conflict, fatal casualties on the French side were approximately as follows: from metropolitan France, 21,000; from French Union forces, 55,000; of the Vietnamese in all allied forces, 18,000, with an additional 23,000 allied Vietnamese prisoners never accounted for. The cream of the French officer corps was destroyed, including 1,300 lieutenants; by 1953 more French officers were dying annually in Vietnam than were graduating from the national military academy at Saint Cyr. Two thousand women had served with the French ground forces, another 150 in the air and navy; almost 100 of these were killed in action. In proportion to population, the 21,000 soldiers from metropolitan France who lost their lives would be equivalent to more than 100,000 American deaths today, twice the number of American deaths that eventually occurred in Vietnam. "The numbers suggest that the French troops fought hard in Indochina."[21]

As for the Vietminh, nobody knows how many died, but estimates run to 400,000. Civilian deaths almost certainly exceeded 500,000. That was what Ho Chi Minh was willing to pay for a Vietnam under his control. And even at that price, he wound up with only half the country.

Perhaps the French could not have won in Vietnam under any circumstances, if winning is defined as reducing the Vietminh challenge to a nuisance level to be handled by police methods. But the French certainly could have avoided the actual outcome, and perhaps they could have held onto some very populous areas of Vietnam. To do that, they would have had to adopt at least two of the following courses of action: (1) send substantial reinforcements from metropolitan France; (2) create a true Vietnamese army, properly trained, equipped, and officered; (3) close the border with China, by military or diplomatic means; (4) address some of the main socio-economic grievances of the peasantry; and (5) employ a conservative military strategy, including retrenchment into Cochin China, while holding the Hanoi-Haiphong region as an enclave. As it happened, the French adopted none of these policies.[22]

A final observation on the Franco-Vietminh conflict: even if the sins of the French were as scarlet, that in itself would in no way disprove the proposition that years later large strata within the population of South Vietnam did not wish to be conquered by the Communists.

Ngo Dinh Diem

On June 18, 1954, at Paris, Pierre Mendès-France became prime minister of France and was eager to make the best deal with the Vietminh that he could. And on that same day, and in that same city, Ngo

Dinh Diem announced that Emperor Bao Dai had appointed him prime minister of Vietnam, with full emergency powers. The Eisenhower administration would call Diem the Churchill of Southeast Asia; the Kennedy administration would come to view him as the principal source of American frustrations in Vietnam.

Diem was born in 1901, in the city of Hue. The son of a mandarin, he was a Christian like Chiang Kai-shek and Syngman Rhee, a member of one of the oldest Catholic families in Vietnam. Diem attended the same secondary school as Ho Chi Minh, Vo Nguyen Giap, and Pham Van Dong, the three men who would become the principal leaders of Vietnamese Communism. Declining a scholarship to study in Paris, he instead attended the French-run School of Law in Hanoi, from which he graduated first in his class.[23] Before Diem was twenty-five, Emperor Bao Dai appointed him governor of Binh Thuan Province, and in 1933 he made him minister of the interior. Diem's nationalism antagonized the French so much that he had to resign. In 1944–1945, as the Pacific War blazed to its painful conclusion, the Japanese, then the French, and then Bao Dai offered Diem the premiership; in 1946 Ho Chi Minh wanted to make him minister of the interior of his new revolutionary regime. Perceiving each of these offers to be laden with strings, Diem turned them all down. By 1950, with the Vietcong seeking his death and the French unwilling to protect him, Diem left Vietnam and journeyed to Rome, the United States, and France. Three more times Bao Dai invited Diem to become prime minister. But Diem wanted to direct the war against the Vietminh, and the French would not permit that. By refusing time and again to accept high office at the price of becoming a puppet, Diem demonstrated his "perfect integrity, competence, and intelligence" to Vietnamese nationalists.[24]

In 1954 Diem at last became prime minister with the full powers he had so long demanded. But taking office amid the wreckage of the French empire in Indochina, Diem found that in fact he controlled hardly more than a few square blocks of downtown Saigon. The criminal Binh Xuyen gang ran the Saigon police; southern Communist cadres were busily laying their plans; religious sects with their private armies were entrenched not far from Saigon; a million refugees were about to flood into the country from the north; Bao Dai, the French, and Diem's own generals were conspiring against him; and the politburo in Hanoi, backed by the Soviet Union and

Maoist China, glared down upon him with undisguised malice. Even his private offices were defenseless against any group of assassins who might choose to burst in. In the midst of this chaos and hostility, Diem must try to establish his authority, eliminate the vestiges of French colonialism, control the centrifugal forces in Southern society, and devise a plausible plan to prevent Ho Chi Minh from swallowing up his state. Hardly anybody expected Diem to last very long.

The most pressing immediate need was to establish personal security for Diem. That was done with the help of the legendary Edward Lansdale (called "the Clausewitz of Counterinsurgency") and Philippine Army colonel Napoleon Valeriano, both fresh from the victorious struggle against the Huks. Then Diem secured the backing of President Eisenhower and support from such influential senators as Mike Mansfield, Hubert Humphrey, and John F. Kennedy. He imposed his authority on the army and the sects. He smashed the power of the piratical Binh Xuyen. He attacked malaria, extended education, and settled almost a million northern refugees.[25] He wrote a new republican constitution and got himself elected first president of the Republic of Vietnam. And he approved the Strategic Hamlet Program, a fundamentally sound plan for separating the peasants from the guerrillas. In his first two years in office, Diem had, apparently, thwarted all his enemies.

Understandably, the Hanoi Politburo concluded by 1959 at the latest that terrorism and assassination would not overthrow South Vietnam and decided on a full-scale insurgency.[26] Faced with this new challenge, desperate to find reliably anticommunist and personally loyal helpers, Diem surrounded himself with members of his family and filled public offices with those who shared his outlook. Thus, the Diem government became disproportionately Catholic, urban, northern, and European-educated, in a mainly Buddhist, peasant, and xenophobic south.[27] Nevertheless, the New York Times attributed Diem's 1961 reelection to rising prosperity and widespread anticommunism in South Vietnam. In December of that same year, President Kennedy assured Diem of American support and priority assistance.[28]

But in fact Washington was becoming disenchanted with Diem. Looking for a true nationalist to set up against Ho Chi Minh, the Americans had certainly found one in Diem. But they grew increasingly unhappy as he proved to be (predictably) a difficult ally, declining to accept automatically the advice the Americans lavished upon him. In holding onto and building his power, Diem had beaten incredible odds; this undeniable fact, along with his deep religious commitment, increased his self-confidence. Diem had not bent to the French or the Japanese, to Bao Dai or to Ho Chi Minh, and he "had considerable reason to doubt the superior judgment of transient Americans concerning the ability and reliability of men with whom he had spent most of his life." He resisted "the assumption that we Americans understood better than Diem the kinds of policies and programs he should be conducting in order to win the struggle against the Communists."[29] Above all, Diem would not permit his country to be taken over and torn up by what he saw as naive and technology-happy Americans. But in Washington this was the Camelot era (in more senses than one). To the Kennedy people, South Vietnam was the place where they were going to refute the theorists of People's Revolutionary War in Peking and at the same time show Nikita Khrushchev that Kennedy was indeed tough. Diem wanted to ultimately bring peace to his country; Washington wanted to whip the Vietcong. Those desires were quite incompatible.

The American press corps in Saigon openly loathed Diem. In their eyes everything wrong in South Vietnam was Diem's fault. Pierre Salinger has testified to the hostility American correspondents showed toward Diem, and Ambassador Maxwell Taylor wrote of their "full-scale vendetta" against him, "To me, it was a sobering spectacle of the power of a relatively few young and inexperienced newsmen who, openly committed to 'getting' Diem . . . were not satisfied to report the events of foreign policy but undertook to shape them."[30] The hostile American reporters got their chance in the summer of 1963 when a dispute arose between local officials in Hue and some Buddhist monks over who could fly what flags on Buddha's birthday. When several demonstrators were killed, Diem tried to soothe tempers, without success. Under the leadership of a group of highly politicized and ambitious Buddhist monks thoroughly infiltrated by Communist agents, the Hue affair turned into a full-scale attempt to overthrow Diem. Soon American newsmen were eagerly supplying the breakfast tables of Washington with photographs of monks immolating themselves. The American electorate could not put these events into the context either of traditional Buddhist practice and belief or of a country wracked by terrorism and insurgency.

Increasingly sensational reporting from Saigon shook President Kennedy's commitment to Diem.[31]

The Buddhist crisis also provided opportunity to Ambassador Henry Cabot Lodge in Saigon and Averell Harriman in Washington, who both thoroughly detested the insubordinate Diem.[32] Under their prodding, in September 1963 President Kennedy announced that aid to the South Vietnamese Army would be cut. Diem's generals interpreted this as a signal that Washington wanted him thrown out (yet Defense Secretary Robert McNamara, CIA director John McCone, Vice President Lyndon Johnson, and former ambassador to Saigon Frederick Nolting all opposed such a move). None of Diem's Washington enemies seem to have worried very much about who, or what, would follow him. On November 2, after an attack on the presidential palace, South Vietnamese generals captured Diem and his brother Ngo Dinh Nhu and murdered them both.[33]

To Hanoi and the Vietcong, these events were heaven-sent.[34] Diem's death threw the country into the hands of less than inspired generals whom the world viewed as completely dependent on the Americans. It also quite predictably opened the floodgates of instability: coup followed coup, purge followed purge, and the Strategic Hamlet Program fell by the wayside. Buddhist self-immolations, supposedly caused by Diem, did not stop but instead increased. Less than a year and a half after Diem's murder, with South Vietnam on the brink of Communist conquest, President Johnson decided that he must inundate the bleeding country with American troops.

President Kennedy had stated that the major purpose of his administration's involvement in South Vietnam was to reassure America's allies about the reliability of American guarantees. It is not clear how American complicity in the overthrow of Diem was supposed to advance this purpose. The Kennedy administration had connived at the killing of a legitimate and friendly head of state.[35] It had thereby saddled the United States with total responsibility for the fate of South Vietnam. Years later, CIA director William F. Colby identified the removal of Diem as America's first great mistake in Vietnam; many agree with him.[36]

The South Vietnamese Army

Not a few Americans have placed the blame for the debacle of the anticommunist cause in Vietnam directly on the shoulders of the South Vietnamese Army, the ARVN (Army of the Republic of Vietnam), an organization whose most distinguishing features are alleged to have been cowardice and desertion. From these premises many conclusions are drawn about the outcome of the war and about how the United States should deal with future insurgencies.

The foundations of the Army of the Republic of Vietnam were those Vietnamese who had fought against the Vietminh either in the French forces or in Bao Dai's Vietnamese National Army (400,000 by July 1954), plus a liberal admixture of former Vietcong who had grown disillusioned with the Communists. When the French Army left South Vietnam in 1956, American officers arrived to assist in training and expanding the ARVN.[37]

Rather than developing the type of armed forces that had proved so effective against subversion in Malaya and the Philippines, American advisers strove to build an ARVN capable of repelling the North Korean invasion of 1950. The ARVN became roadbound like the French army and overreliant on heavy firepower like the American army. Most U.S. advisers were competent, well-trained, and well-meaning, but they served only one-year tours, did not speak the language, and taught and learned disappointingly little. The United States also provided the ARVN with inferior equipment. For instance, the ARVN did not get the M-16 rifle until after the Tet Offensive of 1968; before then it was completely outclassed by the Communist forces, which were armed with excellent automatic weapons (and some veterans claim the M-16 was not as good as the Communists' AK-47). Even as late as the 1970s, the ARVN's American-made M-41 tank was inferior to the Soviet T-54.[38] Nobody paid much attention to the elements that are most crucial in the early stages of an insurgency, namely the police and village militia.

The Romans created armies that were small, well-trained, and well-equipped. The ARVN was just the opposite. Because the ARVN was always engaged in fighting and always short of good officers, an average unit received less than two hours' training a week and hardly any political education.[39]

There was a chronic shortage of officers, especially middle-grade ones. That was because one had to have a high school education to receive an officer's commission. This rule excluded the peasant class almost entirely. The ARVN had one of the world's best-educated officer corps: in the mid-1960s, 5 percent of the generals, 13 percent of colonels, and 15 percent of other officers held Ph.D.s. In 1967 one-fifth of ARVN officers were Catholics, twice the Catholic proportion of the general population, because Catholics were more likely to have attended European-type schools.[40] A quarter of the officers were northern-born. Politicization of the officer corps had gone far under Diem (and contributed to his death). Under President Nguyen Van Thieu, political considerations became even more central, because the ARVN had become the main institution holding the country together.[41] Political and personal connections were the key to advancement; good field commanders were left in the field.

In spite of these grave problems, the South Vietnamese Marine Division and the Airborne Division had no equals among the North Vietnamese Army (NVA).[42] In 1974 a noted British authority ranked the ARVN second only to the Israeli army among free-world land forces.[43] The ARVN would do its best fighting when its back was to the wall, in the disastrous spring of 1975. For example, the last bastion between Saigon and the conquering Communists was the town of Xuan Loc. The place was held by the Eighteenth ARVN Division, nobody's idea of a prize unit. Yet the Eighteenth put up ferocious resistance; to finally take Xuan Loc, the NVA had to commit four of its best divisions.

The Question of Desertion

Desertion rates in the ARVN were high. American journalists somehow perceived that as proof that the South Vietnamese people did not want to fight against the North, indeed that they wished for a Northern victory, just as if the connection between political conviction and military valor is always direct and obvious. The causes of ARVN desertion, however, were mainly sociological, not political. In rural South Vietnam, desertion carried no social stigma for the offender or his family, nor did the government search out and punish deserters with any vigor. Much more importantly, the ARVN assigned peasant draftees to units far from their home provinces. This practice was deeply at variance with the values of rural society (a consequence of having an officer corps drawn overwhelmingly from the educated urban sectors). "Few steps the [Communist] Party could have taken would have been so effective in crippling the morale and effectiveness of the government's military forces as was the government's own decision to adopt a policy of nonlocal service." This ill-considered sending of young peasant draftees far away from home accounts for the high desertion rates among first-year soldiers at harvest time and around the supremely important Tet holidays. ARVN soldiers served for an indefinite time period, unlike Americans, who had a one-year tour of duty; clearly it would have been much better to rotate ARVN soldiers, after a fixed tour, to militia battalions near their homes.[44]

These causes of desertion within ARVN hardly suggest eagerness for a Communist victory. The effects of desertion are also enlightening. Some who deserted ARVN later rejoined. Other deserters joined militia units close to home. In vivid contrast to both the ARVN and the Vietcong, among the militia, who were defending their native province or village, desertion rates were close to zero, in spite of the fact that their casualty rates were higher than the ARVN's. And here is another very crucial point: desertion from the ARVN hardly ever meant defection to the Communists. But for the Vietcong, not only were desertion rates as high as those in the ARVN, but also two hundred thousand Vietcong actually defected to the South Vietnamese forces.[45]

One last observation on this subject: one month before Gettysburg, the largest battle ever fought in North America, the Army of the Potomac, which was the principal force defending the Union, was down to half strength because of desertions. During the American Civil War, the general desertion rate in the Federal forces was 330 per 1,000 and among the Confederates 400 per 1,000.[46]

South Vietnamese Casualties

One of the more puzzling beliefs about the Vietnam conflict is that the South Vietnamese did not do very much fighting. But in fact, the ARVN paid a very high price in blood. During the entire Vietnam conflict from 1954 to 1975, 57,000 Americans lost their lives, a number almost exactly equaled by highway fatalities in the United States in the year 1970 alone. Between the beginning of the Kennedy buildup in 1961 and the fall of Saigon in 1975, the Americans incurred an average of 4,000 military deaths a year. The comparable figure for the Korean war is 18,000 U.S. military deaths per year and for World War II, 100,000 per year.

From 1954 to 1975, ARVN combat deaths were higher than those of the Americans every year. In all, about 200,000 ARVN personnel were killed; some authors give higher figures; and these numbers do not include the militia (nor civilians).[47] But to say that the South Vietnamese army took higher casualties than the Americans only touches the surface, because the population of South Vietnam was many times smaller than that of the United States. If American military fatalities had been in the same proportion to the population of the United States as the ARVN's were to the population of South Vietnam, they would have numbered not 57,000 but 2.6 million. How is one to comprehend this figure? What does "2.6 million American military deaths" mean? It means this: total American military fatalities in all the wars the Americans fought during two hundred years—from the American Revolution through Vietnam, including World War I and World War II and both sides in the Civil War—amount to less than 1 million. In the long struggle against an armed Communist takeover, the ARVN alone (excluding the militia, whose casualty rates were higher) suffered, relative to the South Vietnam population, more than forty times as many fatalities as the Americans.

The ARVN, with an inappropriate structure (established by Americans), second-rate weapons, and inadequate training, saddled not only with fighting a war of survival but also with running a country, and consequently riddled with political interference and financial corruption—with all these handicaps—nevertheless stood up to twenty years of warfare while suffering enormous casualties and in the end collapsed because it was short of ammunition, gasoline, even clean bandages. That is quite a record.

The Territorial Forces

Any plan to resist the Communist conquest of South Vietnam should have anchored itself on local militias—the Territorial forces—organized to protect their own homes from the guerrillas. But in the beginning, such forces received little official attention, no training, and few weapons, and the weapons they did receive were of poor quality. Reorganization in 1964 produced the Regional Forces and the Popular Forces (RF/PF—called "Ruff-Puffs" by Americans). The Popular Forces were organized in thirty-man platoons and served on the hamlet and village level, the Regional Forces in one hundred–man companies on the provincial level. The task of the PFs was to resist guerrillas trying to enter their village just long enough for RF units to come to their assistance. But in the Popular Forces there were no pay, no rank, and no system of recognition and reward.[48] Their weapons were castoffs; their training was sketchy. Even if the PFs in a certain village were lucky enough to possess a radio with which to call for help, the Regional Forces often lacked the mobility to respond in time.

All this changed radically with the 1968 Tet Offensive. Many Territorial units performed well during the crisis; Saigon responded by finally giving them good weapons, although they did not receive the M-16 until 1970. Gen. William C. Westmoreland observed that if the ARVN and the Territorials had received proper weapons, equivalent to the Communist standard AK-47 automatic rifle, at an earlier date, South Vietnam might have been ready to defend itself a full year earlier. At the end of 1968 there were approximately 392,000 Territorials; a year later there were 475,000. Between 1968 and 1972, the ARVN suffered 37,000 fatal casualties, the Territorials 69,000. During the 1972 Easter Offensive, RF units gave especially good accounts of themselves against NVA forces at the siege of Hue and elsewhere. By 1973, when the last U.S. ground combat units were long out of South Vietnam, Territorial forces numbered over half a million. The heavily populated Mekong Delta provinces were mostly under control of these "Ruff-Puffs." The Territorials received only between 2 and 4 percent of the war budget, but they accounted for 30 percent of VC and NVA combat deaths. They were "the most cost-efficient military forces employed on the allied side."[49]

Vietnamization

After the Tet Offensive (see the section titled "The Great Tet Offensive") came the "Vietnamization" program, an unfortunate name implying that the ARVN would henceforth do its proper share of the fighting, whereas of course the ARVN had been doing at least its share for years. Vietnamization had two major aspects: first, the long-overdue upgrading of American equipment delivered to the ARVN, and second, the reduction of U.S. combat troops in Vietnam—also overdue.

The 1972 Easter Offensive provided the great test of Vietnamization. In the spring of that year General Giap threw the entire NVA, the "most efficient fighting machine in all Asia,"[50] against the South. Nearly all American ground combat units had by then been evacuated. For practical purposes, on the ground the South Vietnamese stood alone. The Communist attack was four-pronged, blasting across the ludicrously named Demilitarized Zone and through "neutral" Laos and Cambodia. The offensive began on March 30; before mid-May it was clearly a failure. The ARVN had withstood the best efforts of the Vietcong in 1968; now it withstood the best efforts of the NVA in 1972. In the picturesque language of Gen. Creighton Abrams, "By God, the South Vietnamese can hack it!" The ARVN had demonstrated that if it could count on replacement parts for its U.S.-made equipment and if it had U.S. air support, especially the all-powerful B-52s so feared by the NVA, it could stand up to Hanoi indefinitely.[51]

And—once again—insistent Communist calls during the Easter Offensive for the southern urban population to rise up against their oppressors had fallen on ears quite deaf.

Third-Country Forces

In addition to South Vietnam and the United States, several "third countries" contributed troops to the struggle. In 1966 there were 53,000 of them, by 1969 70,000. Of the latter, the largest component was 50,000 South Koreans, all volunteers, mainly stationed in the dangerous Military Region I, just below the border with North Vietnam. Thailand sent another 12,000. The Australian government, very worried about a Communist takeover in the South, contributed 8,000 well-trained counterguerrilla troops. New Zealand also sent several companies. The Philippines dispatched mainly medical support groups. President Johnson declined the Taiwan government's offer of combat forces for political reasons. Of these third-country forces, 5,200 died in combat.[52]

The Great Tet Offensive

By the spring of 1967, two years of large-scale American presence in South Vietnam had resulted in enormous losses for the Communists. The Hanoi regime was in fact requiring its own people to suffer a casualty rate about twice as high as that suffered by the Japanese in World War II. In 1969 General Giap told a European interviewer that between 1965 and 1968 alone, Communist military losses totaled 600,000. By way of comparison, from 1960 to 1967, 13,000 Americans lost their lives in Vietnam, fewer than those who had died in the United States in that same period from falling off the roofs of their houses.[53]

In return for its egregious losses, Hanoi had little to show. The Thieu government had clearly stabilized itself; morale among the Vietcong was sinking. In response to those depressing conditions, Hanoi began to make plans for a great offensive, to coincide with the Tet holidays of 1968. In the Tet Offensive plans, the Communists appear to have had two main objectives: first, to disorganize the ARVN, and second, to provoke a great popular uprising in the cities, especially Saigon. "The primary objective of the Tet offensive was to win the war by instigating a general uprising"; indeed, this concept of the war ending in a general uprising "represents the major Vietnamese contribution to the theory of people's war." If all went according to plan, the Americans would find themselves in effect without a country to defend, and they would go home. The Tet Offensive was nothing less than Hanoi's acknowledgment that its guerrilla campaign against the South had failed. And it would become the central event of the Vietnam War.[54]

South Vietnam was no police state. Thus it was relatively easy for the VC/NVA to infiltrate numerous small groups into the cities. Allied commanders in Saigon were aware well before January 1968 that something big was brewing, but for the most part they refused to believe that the enemy would throw aside the guerrilla tactics that had served them well and instead suicidally rise to the surface and confront allied firepower.[55] This incredulity on the part of the Americans was a major element producing the surprise of Tet. Like the events immediately preceding the Japanese attack on Pearl Harbor, American skepticism about the likelihood of a major Vietcong offensive illustrates a severe weakness of even the best intelligence system: human beings are loath to believe any information that seems to contradict common sense, hesitant to conclude that the enemy is about to make a major mistake.

On January 30, with half of the ARVN on leave during the traditional holiday truce, which the Communists had pledged to respect, the offensive exploded. Vietcong units attacked cities and military installations all over South Vietnam. In Saigon they tried to storm the presidential palace, the ARVN headquarters, the airport, and the radio station. A suicide squad of fifteen managed to penetrate the outer grounds of the U.S. Embassy compound. The fate of South

Vietnam seemed to hang in the balance. But the ARVN held together.[56] The total lack of response to their calls for urban uprisings stunned the Vietcong. And they suffered devastating casualties.

Today there is no dispute that Tet was a calamity of unparalleled dimensions for the Communists. Of 84,000 Vietcong involved in the offensive, some 30,000 were killed. "In truth, the Tet Offensive for all practical purposes destroyed the Viet Cong."[57] This bloody debacle has prompted some, including former Vietcong, to suggest that the Tet Offensive was a plot by Hanoi not only to destabilize and discredit the ARVN but also to engineer a massacre of the Vietcong, "killing two birds with one stone" and thus removing all obstacles to Hanoi's eventual takeover of the South. Whatever the validity of these allegations, the guerrilla conflict would henceforth fade into the background. After Tet, the war openly became a conventional war of conquest by the NVA. It took four years for the Communist side to feel sufficiently recovered to launch another offensive.[58] In effect, Tet "was the end of People's War, and essentially, of any strategy built on guerrilla warfare and a politically inspired insurgency."[59]

Communists and their apologists tried to explain away the failure of the large and growing urban population of South Vietnam to rise up against the government; they said that the ARVN was too strong for the civilians to confront. But such an explanation will not do. Both Louis XVI and Nicholas II maintained large armed forces in their capital cities and nevertheless suffered dethronement and death. The Hungarian Army did not prevent the popular earthquake in Communist Budapest in 1956; the superbly equipped Iranian army did not save the Shah in 1978; nor did well-armed and thoroughly indoctrinated troops stop the revolutions in East Germany, Czechoslovakia, and Romania in 1989. Even in April 1975, during what were obviously the last days of the Saigon government, the South Vietnamese people did not rise. It is hard to avoid concluding that the inhabitants of the Southern cities never rose up in support of the Communists because they did not wish to do so.[60]

For the South Vietnamese, Tet transformed the war not only militarily but also politically. Wherever the Vietcong had achieved temporary control, they committed atrocities against civilians. The massacres at Hue were especially horrific: survivors and relatives in that city exhumed the bodies of thousands of students, priests, and government workers and their families, many of whom had been buried alive. These events alarmed the Southern population and steeled its determination to resist conquest by the North. The Thieu government distributed arms to hundreds of thousands of new militia members. In the words of a close student of the war, "Before the Tet Offensive, 18-year-old villagers would lie and say they were 13 to get out of the draft; after the Tet Offensive, 13- and 14-year-olds would lie and say they were 18 to get into the draft before the Communists got to them. The perception of the craziness of what the Communists were doing was increased, and the idea that they were inevitable winners was so deflated that people changed very much how they felt."[61]

In summary, the Communists had suffered an undeniable, devastating military reverse. Nevertheless, in one of history's most stupefying ironies, the Tet Offensive turned out to be the beginning of the end of both the Johnson administration and the American commitment to the South. That is, Tet turned from a military disaster into a political triumph for the Communists. How could this have happened?

The American News Media

Self-serving or ill-informed persons often criticize the news media. It does not follow, however, that one ought to dismiss all criticism of the news media as self-serving or ill-informed.

In 1994 Senate majority leader George Mitchell (D-Maine) said that the American news industry was "more destructive than constructive than ever." Representative Barney Frank (D-Mass.) opined, "You people [the media] celebrate failure and ignore success. *Nothing about government is done as incompetently as the reporting of it.*"[62] Supposing for the moment that these statements by two experienced political leaders are not totally without merit, what do they mean? Are they not obviously saying that American reporters, in the American capital, operating within the American culture, fluent in the American language, fail to inform the American public correctly about American political processes? But if such statements have merit, is it unreasonable to inquire whether reporting of events in Vietnam by American journalists who were familiar with neither Leninist political tactics nor guerrilla warfare nor Vietnamese culture, who spoke none of the local languages, or even French—is it unreasonable to ask whether such reporting might have sometimes been less than acute?

During and after Tet, neither *Newsweek* nor *Time* published one single article on the ARVN, and apparently no newspaper in the United States ever ran even one positive story on the fighting performance of a single ARVN unit. The unprecedented mass arming of the civilian population after Tet was a very big story indeed, but the news media never got it. The only Pulitzer Prize in the war went to photographer Eddie Adams, for his picture of Gen. Nguyen Ngoc Loan executing a Vietcong prisoner in the streets of Saigon at the height of the Tet Offensive. Quite understandably, this graphic illustration of the brutality of guerrilla war shocked millions of Americans. It was seldom explained to them that throughout Tet, especially in Saigon, VC terrorists deliberately attacked the wives and children of ARVN officers and that just before the picture was taken Loan had viewed the bodies of a family of six children whom that VC prisoner had massacred.[63]

Without doubt, some of the reporting of the war was of good quality; "those few TV newsmen who actually covered ARVN troops in combat were a good deal less disparaging in their broadcasts than their colleagues who did not." And the universally respected dean of American journalists, Walter Cronkite, reported to the American people from Vietnam that during Tet the ARVN had fought well, with no defections, and that the Vietcong had suffered "a military defeat."[64] But these instances were not typical. Television in particular presented the Tet Offensive as an unprecedented catastrophe for U.S. forces, a totally unexpected, nearly complete, and probably irredeemable breakdown of security all over South Vietnam. Few viewers of the nightly network news could escape the suggestion that the United States was bogged down in a dirty war against invincible enemies for the sake of feckless allies.

The failure of the enormously expensive and prestigious (in those days) U.S. news media to get the real story to the American people had some of its roots in the very nature of the television news industry, which "increased the power and velocity of fragments of experience, with no increase in the power and velocity of reasoned judgment." Regular viewers of the Cronkite or Huntley-Brinkley newscasts saw more infantry combat during Tet than did most U.S.

troops in Vietnam at the time.[65] This "nightly portrayal of violence and gore and of American soldiers seemingly on the brink of disaster contributed significantly to disillusionment with the war."[66]

Another major problem with the reporting on Vietnam was the nature of the situation being reported. Some journalists perhaps consciously allowed their political preferences to override their professional responsibilities. Others were no doubt simply naive. But above all, American journalism, even more than the American academic, intelligence, and military communities, was woefully short of people knowledgeable about Southeast Asia, and especially about the complexities of the struggle in Vietnam. Armed with the sketchiest ideas of the country's recent history and sometimes none at all of its more distant past, unfamiliar with guerrilla warfare, dependent on English-speaking informants, picking up rumors from one another in the bars of Saigon, pressured increasingly by editors to supply stories that would "grab attention," many reporters drew false conclusions from false premises. More and more newsmen portrayed South Vietnam as a land of corruption, crime, cowardice, and cruelty. All these elements were indeed easy to find in a war-torn South Vietnam open to minute scrutiny from the press. North Vietnam was not subjected to such scrutiny, but few journalists seemed to appreciate the consequences of that profound asymmetry; at any rate the closed nature of the North meant that the scars and blemishes of the South were magnified. Sometimes reporters saved themselves the discomfort of gathering news on their own by purchasing stories from helpful Vietnamese, who after the war turned out to be agents of Hanoi. The influential Harrison Salisbury of the *New York Times* sent from Hanoi searing reports of supposed American bombing atrocities supplied to him by the North Vietnamese government.[67]

Few reporters in Saigon during the Tet Offensive had seen the terrific destruction of cities in World War II or Korea. Many of them were therefore profoundly shocked and frightened at the violence they saw or heard around them, especially in the formerly pleasant Saigon. The isolation and inexperience of many reporters stimulated "the media's penchant for self-projection and instant analysis" so that major network "specials" on Tet "assumed average South Vietnamese reactions [to Tet] were those of American commentators"[68] and thus that everybody in Saigon was as overwhelmed and terrified by the offensive as the newsmen themselves were.

These alarming flaws in journalistic coverage later provoked devastating criticism, not only from experts on Vietnam but also from within the ranks of professional journalists. One veteran newsman has written that "drama was perpetuated at the expense of information." Another journalist wrote that "the *New York Times* and many others had succeeded in creating an image of South Vietnam that was so distant from the truth as not even to be good caricature." Robert Elegant, former editor of *Newsweek* and winner of three Overseas Press Club Awards, charges that the "press consistently magnified the allies' deficiencies, and displayed almost saintly tolerance of those misdeeds of Hanoi it could neither disregard nor deny."[69] The *Economist* noted that many journalists believed everything claimed by the National Liberation Front (the Vietcong) or Hanoi. North Vietnamese propaganda had "turned skeptical newsmen credulous, careful scholars indifferent to data, honorable men blind to immorality."[70] To say the very least, the coverage of Vietnam, and especially of the crucial Tet Offensive, "cannot be treated as a triumph for American journalism."[71] A most effective and authoritative dissection of the failings of the American news industry during the Vietnamese conflict is found in "Viet Nam: How to Lose a War," by Robert Elegant, in the August 1981 issue of *Encounter.*

The Vietnam conflict revealed profound weaknesses in the American news industry. More than three decades afterward, it is not in the least clear that these flaws have been corrected, or even admitted. Most regrettably, many accounts of the war by journalists were no worse than some produced by academicians, at the time and for long thereafter.

American Mistakes

In the last analysis, one must concede that although reporters sensationalized and obfuscated the most distressing aspects of the war, they did not create them. The errors of the news media were grave, but they would not have had so great an impact on the American public and on Congress if there had not been in fact another set of grave errors, perpetrated not by journalists but by politicians and soldiers in Washington and Saigon. No single one of those errors lost the war for the United States and its allies, but their cumulative effect was decisive. Among the errors were the Americanization of the war, the bombing of North Vietnam, the strategy of attrition, and the acceptance of the permanent invasion of the South through the Ho Chi Minh Trail.

Americanizing the War

The murder of President Diem unraveled the frail fabric of the South Vietnamese state. By 1965 the Communists appeared to be on the brink of victory. In response, the Johnson administration completely broke with the policy of President Eisenhower and began sending a huge army to Vietnam. This fateful decision occurred in a remarkably offhand manner and against the advice of CIA director John McCone. Just as they had decided to jettison Diem without any clear idea of what was to follow, so in 1965 the Americans decided to take over the war.[72]

Washington was undaunted, even unimpressed, by the failure of the French in Vietnam. After all, the French had been fighting to hold onto a colonial position: in contrast, the Americans would be fighting not for the domination of South Vietnam but for its independence, stability, and prosperity. Moreover, the United States was incomparably richer, stronger, and more united than the Fourth Republic had ever been. Clad in these comforting and self-evident truths, the Johnson administration plunged ahead. In January 1961, when President Eisenhower left office, 875 U.S. military personnel were in Vietnam. In November 1963, when President Kennedy died, that number had multiplied nearly twenty times, to more than 16,000. Two years after Lyndon Johnson became president, there were 187,000, and in two more years there were half a million. These troops arrived in South Vietnam knowing little about Vietnamese society or about the French experience there. More ominously, they knew little about guerrilla warfare, and the army's policy of one-year tours of duty ensured that lessons learned at great cost had to be learned again and again.[73] Many officers served a mere six-month tour, a practice that led to serious problems and abuses. Even if the Americans achieved success (however defined), how long could such a huge force remain in Southeast Asia? Meanwhile, the presence of so many foreign, unattached, and (by Vietnamese standards) rich young males contributed greatly to the disruption and corruption of Vietnamese society.

Even half a million U.S. troops did not provide the numerical preponderance that successful counterguerrilla warfare requires. When the Americans increased their forces in South Vietnam by any given number, Hanoi countered the move by increasing its own forces there by merely a fourth or even a tenth of the American number. In fact, the numerical superiority enjoyed by the allies over the Communists existed on paper, not in the field. The American forces, and the ARVN whom they had trained, had a very big "tail": by the end of 1968, a mere 80,000 out of 536,000 American servicemen in Vietnam were combat infantry.[74] The rest mainly provided support for the combat troops. Thus, most of the time the allies had a very small advantage or no advantage at all where it counted: the number of fighting men prepared to contest control of the countryside. That is not the way to defeat guerrillas, or anybody. By sending these forces to the other side of the Pacific Ocean, the Johnson administration prevented an immediate victory of the Communists, but it also opened up a fissure in American society that it did not know how to close or even contain.

Bombing the North

Arguably, the French effort in Vietnam had come to grief because of grotesquely inadequate airpower. In contrast, American airpower was to be the big ace in the Johnson administration's hand. Specifically, bombing the North would serve as a substitute for stopping the invasion of the South. Quite probably, air interdiction alone would not have succeeded in persuading Hanoi to stop flooding South Vietnam with troops and munitions. But the Johnson administration conceived and executed the air campaign so badly that the bombing not only failed to accomplish its purpose but also became a weapon in the hands of opponents of both the war and the United States, at home and abroad.

The United States dropped several times more bombs in Vietnam than it had in all theaters during World War II; the majority of them fell on South Vietnam, which the Americans were "defending." But the Americans never bombed North Vietnam the way they had bombed Germany and Japan; that is, they did not use bombing to break North Vietnamese civilian morale. On the contrary, the Johnson administration took great pains to avoid unnecessary damage to civilian areas in Hanoi and to the dikes that were essential to food production. The crucial port of Haiphong, through which poured Soviet supplies, also remained untouched. The bombing campaign aimed only at an incredibly restricted number of targets, often selected only hours previously by civilians in the White House thousands of miles away, and usually anticipated by North Vietnamese air defenses. The administration punctuated the air war with pauses—sixteen of them—that were somehow supposed to convince Hanoi of American "goodwill"; the North used the pauses to repair damage, improve defenses, and increase infiltration of the South. Johnson told his successor that "all the bombing pauses were a mistake."[75]

Despite all this restraint, critics of American involvement at home and overseas leveled charges of barbarism against the United States. They even used the term genocide, as if they actually lacked the wit to distinguish between Lyndon Johnson and Adolf Hitler. A U.S. senator from Massachusetts dismayed many Americans and delighted their enemies with his patently false charges that the U.S. Air Force was deliberately bombing dikes.[76]

However hobbled and inefficient, the air war against the North Vietnamese damaged Northern morale and interfered with their war effort. But the bombing did not prevent them from obtaining more than enough replacement equipment from the Soviets and the Chinese, and thus it did not decisively impair the North's warmaking capabilities. At the same time, approximately one out of twenty American bombs dropped in Vietnam were duds, whose high-quality metal the enterprising NVA recovered to make ammunition and booby traps with which to kill more Americans.[77] The Johnson administration's haphazard, ineffective use of American airpower against North Vietnam prolonged the war, increased American casualties, contributed to growing disunity in American society, and provided valuable ammunition to foes of democracy all over the globe. Conventional wisdom identifies the middle course as the right one. But in the on-again off-again, self-restrained bombing of North Vietnam, as in the entire war, President Johnson chose the middle course and was destroyed.

The Attrition "Strategy"

Sending an overly large American army to Vietnam and waging an ineffective bombing campaign against the North would not in themselves have ruined American aims, if American forces in the South had pursued an effective strategy. But they did not. First, the Americans took on major responsibility for fighting the guerrillas; that was a profound error. Then they compounded the error by choosing to fight the guerrillas the wrong way.

To provide security to the peasantry by separating the guerrillas from the civilians among whom they operate and from whom they draw sustenance—that is the core concept of classic (and successful) counterguerrilla warfare. General Westmoreland rejected such a strategy because it was defensive, and thus would negate the advantages possessed by the American fighting forces. He wished to emphasize U.S. superiority in mobility and firepower by pursuing aggressive tactics against the enemy. Therein lies the germ of what is usually called the strategy of attrition. The essence of the strategy was to employ superior technology to kill the enemy in numbers greater than could be replaced. Then the war eventually would simply peter out.

Attrition was not concerned with holding territory or increasing the number of peasants living in secure villages. Hence, there was no way to measure its progress but by the notorious "body count": adding up the number of Vietnamese corpses remaining after an encounter and then announcing that number to the world. That method of measuring progress may have been the biggest public relations disaster in American history. And nobody seemed to remember Clausewitz's dictum: "Casualty reports on either side are never accurate, seldom truthful, and in most cases deliberately falsified"; "that is why guns and prisoners have always counted as the real trophies of victory."[78]

For several reasons, key groups in the United States began to run out of patience with the war before attrition had achieved its objectives. First, for attrition to work, the enemy must fight. But in Vietnam the tempo of fighting was controlled by the Communists, who could fight or not as they chose. And when they did fight, they often "hugged" American units so closely that they rendered American artillery and airpower ineffective. It is true that with their superior firepower the allies were able to break the back of the Vietcong for good during the Tet Offensive. But here again it was the insurgents who chose the confrontation, even though their choice violated the most elementary principles of sound guerrilla tactics. That is, Tet was a great victory for the allies, but it was handed to them on a platter.

Second, attrition ignored the brutal fact that the Hanoi party-state was willing and able to impose enormous sacrifices on its own people. Years before, Ho Chi Minh had declared that the Vietminh would suffer ten times as many deaths as the French and still win. And General Giap revealingly observed that "every minute, hundreds of thousands of people die all over the world. The life or death of a hundred, a thousand or tens of thousands of human beings, even if they are our compatriots, represents really very little."[79]

Third, although the intent of the Johnson-McNamara policy of gradualism was to force Hanoi to abandon the struggle by slowly increasing the military pressure on it, in fact the policy provided Hanoi with time to absorb each blow before the next was delivered. Moreover, the administration's gradualism included repeated public and private assurances to Hanoi that the United States would not attack North Vietnam on the ground. That is, the Johnson-McNamara administration never threatened the existence of the North Vietnamese party-state. Consequently, Hanoi was free to employ every ounce of its strength against the attrition strategy in the South. Gradualism worked against attrition: in the end it exhausted not the North Vietnamese but the Americans.

In Vietnam the Americans expended bullets, bombs, rockets, and shells sufficient to destroy all the soldiers in all the armies that ever existed in the history of the world. At certain points in the war, it cost the United States four hundred thousand dollars to kill one enemy soldier. That unprecedented, absurd use of American military technology indeed killed many of the enemy; it also killed many neutral and friendly civilians. The American way of combat was exceedingly destructive; no American would wish his home or neighborhood to be "liberated" in the style of the American forces in the Vietnam War. The side effects of American combat tactics made many converts to the Vietcong.[80] If the Americans had not been able to be so prodigal with money and equipment, they might have been forced to come up with a real strategy.

The Communist enemy suffered severely from attrition; that was a main reason for the launching of the disastrous Tet Offensive. And throughout the long conflict, U.S. forces never lost a significant battle, a military record probably unparalleled in history. Yet the combination of growing American casualty lists, an increasingly negative presentation of the war by the American news media, and the seemingly endless nature of the struggle caused Americans at home to question the value of the war; for all this, nothing was more responsible than the strategy of attrition.[81]

Permanent Invasion: Laos

Almost all the problems American forces encountered in the struggle to save South Vietnam had their roots, to one degree or another, in the failure to stop Hanoi's invasion of the South. The principal route of invasion—the famous Ho Chi Minh Trail—went through Laos. President Eisenhower had warned President Kennedy that Laos was the key to South Vietnam, and General Taylor told Kennedy as early as 1961 that the insurgents could not be beaten as long as infiltration via their Laotian sanctuary went unchecked.[82]

The "trail" was begun in 1959 and had a decade later become a network of roads down which poured thousands of troops and trucks every month. The construction of the Trail was in itself an epic. Built at the cost of vast sacrifice of human life, through some of the most inhospitable territory to human beings in the world, the Trail was a victory over forbidding terrain, debilitating climate, physical exhaustion, and omnipresent insects, snakes, fungus, and infection. This logistical triumph would cost many Americans their lives and the South Vietnamese their freedom, and needlessly so.

If the troops from North Vietnam who had infiltrated the South in small batches between 1959 and 1965 had all come in at the same time, it would have looked like a Korea-style invasion. Instead, the Trail confronted American and ARVN troops with a sort of slow-motion Schlieffen Plan, by which they were constantly being outflanked.[83]

General Westmoreland and others wanted to cut the Trail on the ground by sending three divisions across Laos to the border of Thailand, a distance comparable to that between Washington and Philadelphia. (The South Korea Demarcation [Truce] Line is almost 150 miles long; the French built the impressive and successful Morice Line running almost 600 miles along the Algerian-Tunisian border; in the 1980s, the Moroccans built the Hassan line, a ten- to twelve-foot-high rock-and-sand antiguerrilla wall with sensors and radar running hundreds of miles.) Gen. Bruce Palmer advocated extending the Demilitarized Zone (DMZ) across to Thailand; three U.S. divisions would hold this line, supported by intensive airpower. The U.S. Navy would blockade North Vietnamese ports and threaten the coast with invasion; there would be no "strategic bombing" of the North. Thus the United States would execute a double mission: (1) block the infiltration and invasion into South Vietnam, and (2) train and equip a first-class ARVN. Cut off from replacements and heavy equipment, the Vietcong would eventually wither. Most of all, "in defending well-prepared positions U.S. troops would suffer fewer casualties."[84]

The Johnson administration, however, forbade any attempt to use ground forces to block the Trail across Laos; it intended to stem the tide of men and supplies by airpower alone. Accordingly, the Americans carried out the most intensive bombing campaign in the history of warfare. It was to no avail. Traffic down the Trail was slowed but not stopped. President Johnson later wrote that of course he was aware that "North Vietnamese and Viet Cong forces were enjoying almost complete sanctuary in Laos and Cambodia." But then why not put a stop to this? Because in 1962 President Kennedy had agreed to the "neutralization" of Laos, and, in President Johnson's exact words, in May 1967 "we were all concerned that entering Laos with ground forces would *end all hope of reviving the 1962 Laos agreement, fragile though it was, and would greatly increase the forces needed in Southeast Asia*."[85]

Leaving open the Ho Chi Minh Trail seemed to allow no alternative to massive bombing of North Vietnam. Why and how bombing would have a greater effect on the North Vietnamese than it did on the British or the Germans in World War II was never made clear. In any event, North Vietnamese officials told Robert Shaplen that they shot down twenty-five hundred U.S. aircraft engaged in bombing the Trail.[86]

The failure both to close the Trail and to adopt an alternative strategy that would have neutralized its effects also meant that Hanoi could fight on interior lines, a tremendous advantage. It meant that the enemy was free to invade South Vietnam continuously: the NVA's colossal 1972 Easter Offensive would have been quite impossible without the Laotian springboard. It meant that when hard pressed by allied forces, the enemy could simply retreat into Laos or Cambodia. Thus the policies of the Johnson administration made a lasting, or even a temporary, American military victory impossible. And that fact, in turn, meant that attrition—killing large numbers of North Vietnamese who came down the Trail into South Vietnam—would take longer than key segments of the American public would accept. Indeed, like the bombing of the North, attrition itself was a substitute strategy forced on the Americans through their failure to interrupt the Ho Chi Minh Trail. But "it was impossible to defeat North Vietnam decisively in South Vietnam without stopping the invasion" via that Trail.[87]

Since the fall of Saigon, many in Hanoi have expressed the conviction that the Trail was the key to their success. They are not alone in that opinion. Sir Robert Thompson has written that "if they [the North Vietnamese] had not had this unmolested avenue through Laos, the insurgency in Vietnam could have been stopped at any time in the early 1960s." Several prominent Johnson administration figures concur. "Surely," wrote William P. Bundy, "we could have held a line across Laos and South Vietnam with significantly fewer men than we eventually employed within South Vietnam, far less American casualties, and in the end much greater effect and less bloodshed in the South itself." "In retrospect," stated Ambassador Bunker, "I am more certain than I was in 1967 that our failure to cut the Ho Chi Minh Trail was a strategic mistake of the first order." And Walt Rostow declared that the failure to act against the Ho Chi Minh Trail in 1962 "may have been the single greatest mistake in United States foreign policy in the 1960s."[88]

Popular Opposition to Communist Conquest

Long before partition in 1954, the southern provinces of Vietnam were different in crucial ways from those to the north. For centuries before the arrival of the French, Vietnam had usually been divided between a northern and a southern kingdom, the border generally in the area of the seventeenth parallel. The indigenous Cao Dai and Hoa Hao sects had their strongholds in the southern provinces. French political and social presence was much more firmly planted in Cochin China (Saigon and the Mekong Delta) than in the rest of the country. During World War II the Japanese occupation treated Cochin China as a distinct area. At that time, the Vietminh sought refuge near or across the China border, thus necessarily establishing their base in northern Tonkin. After the Japanese surrender, elements of Chiang Kai-shek's army occupied the northern provinces, while British forces entered the southern ones, and the returning French first reestablished their control in the Saigon area.

The Vietcong were never able to develop much support in the large and constantly growing cities of South Vietnam, and the grisly massacres of civilians in Hue during the Tet Offensive helped solidify the urban rejection of the Communist side. A source very friendly to the Communists estimates that in 1974 there were about 5,400 activists in Saigon, a city of 2.5 million people. That is why the constant, ardent exhortations by the Communists for the urban population to stage a general uprising produced such little effect during both the Tet and the Easter Offensives. In the countryside Communist support, although much stronger than in the cities, had been declining for a long time. That was occurring in part because the Communists had to employ draconian compulsion to replace their growing combat losses and in part because in the early 1970s the South Vietnamese government had carried out "the most extensive land reform program yet undertaken in any non-Communist country in Asia." In the mid-1970s, estimates of support for the Communist side put it at less than one-third of the South Vietnamese population. Catholics, Northern refugees, members of the powerful Southern religious sects, army officers and their families, the urban middle class—all were militantly hostile to a Northern conquest. Some of those groups overlapped, but taken together they were very numerous; the ARVN and the Territorials together numbered over a million men. Notably, the Territorial forces (RF/PF), suffering the highest casualty rates, also had the lowest desertion rates. Above all, the ARVN had stood up both in 1968 and in 1972 against the very best the Communists could throw at it. The ARVN as a fighting force could bear comparison to the Israeli army. And in 1975 Northern premier Pham Van Dong conceded that from 50 to 70 percent of the Southern population would need to be persuaded of the benefits of "reunification."[89] That an incredibly large percentage of the Southern population became "boat people" suggests that he knew what he was talking about.

Yet, despite the obvious fact that broad strata of the South Vietnamese population opposed a Communist takeover, and despite the obvious fact that the ARVN and the Territorials had stood up to the maximum Communist military pressure—despite all this, powerful forces were converging not only to take all American forces out of the war but also to leave the South Vietnamese friendless and weaponless.

The United States Abandons Its Allies

On January 27, 1973, after four years of negotiations, Washington and Hanoi signed the Paris Agreements. The principal effect of those accords was that all remaining U.S. fighting forces withdrew from South Vietnam and all U.S. air attacks on the North ceased. But North Vietnam continued to keep almost a quarter of a million troops in South Vietnam and another fifty thousand in Laos. This stunning, deadly asymmetry—the Americans leave, the North Vietnamese stay—caused President Thieu to refuse his assent. President Nixon threatened Thieu with a unilateral American signature but also assured him in writing that if Hanoi resumed its effort to conquer the South, it would call down upon itself U.S. airpower. In fact, however, the cessation of American air strikes allowed the North, in complete violation of the accords, to greatly increase the number of its troops inside the South.[90]

After the peace accords, President Thieu refused to yield another province, village, or ARVN strong point to the Communists, no matter how exposed and vulnerable to attack such places might be. This policy of holding everywhere was extremely unwise, allowing the Communists to pursue their familiar tactic of amassing great numerical superiority at the point of attack. The ARVN was stretched so thin that it possessed neither a strategic reserve to rush to the point of danger nor troops to interdict Communist movements in Laos and Cambodia.

Precisely in these circumstances of great peril, South Vietnam's American ally began to openly turn against it. On July 1, 1973, Congress forbade any combat in or over Vietnam after August 15, 1973. This repudiation of President Nixon's promises to President Thieu gave Hanoi an unmistakable green light for invasion. Congress also slashed assistance to Saigon; after 1973, the South Vietnamese were receiving less than one-third the dollar amount of aid they had obtained in 1972, in inflated dollars. By 1974 the United States had spent $150 billion (perhaps $400 billion in 2001 values) on the war. The Saigon government was asking for only 1 percent of that total. But Congress cut aid to South Vietnam to only $700 million, not nearly enough for the ARVN to keep its American equipment in working order. (Yet from 1976 to 1980, Congress would pour out $15 billion to Israel and Egypt.)

These Congressional measures "seriously undermined South Vietnamese combat power." The ARVN had to cut its radio communications by 50 percent. Many Saigon fighter aircraft ceased to fly for lack of replacement parts. Artillery batteries in the Central Highlands could fire only four shells per day. By the summer of 1974, each ARVN soldier was allotted eighty-five cartridges a month. Bandages removed from soldiers who had died were washed and used again. During this time the Soviets were supplying Hanoi with great quantities of oil, ammunition, and heavy weapons.[91]

The halting of American air strikes had been an incalculable gift to the North, because NVA divisions, with their great numbers and their tanks, were infinitely more vulnerable to air attack than VC units had ever been (as the Easter Offensive had shown). And then, the drastic reductions in American aid to the South convinced Hanoi that "a fundamental turning point" had been reached in the conflict.[92] Accordingly, in December 1974 North Vietnamese Army units overran Phuoc Long Province. To this dramatic, undeniable repudiation of the peace agreements, the United States made no response. In fact, in his first State of the Union address, President Ford mentioned Vietnam not even once. The Hanoi Politburo now had absolute assurance that it could do as it wished.

The Fall

On March 11, 1975, NVA units seized Ban Me Thuot. Hanoi had publicly ripped up the Paris peace accords and defied the United States. By way of response, the Democratic Caucus of the House of Representatives rejected President Ford's plea for emergency aid for South Vietnam. (Even the Soviets, when they pulled their troops out of Afghanistan, did not abandon their allies so utterly, although they might have done so with much justification.) Thereupon, President Thieu revealed to his generals a plan for strategic retrenchment: except for enclaves at Hue and Da Nang, the ARVN would withdraw from Military Regions I and II (the northern and central parts of South Vietnam) and fall back to consolidated positions in Military Region III (which included Saigon) and Military Region IV (the Mekong Delta.)

Retrenchment was in fact long overdue. Most of the ARVN's thirteen divisions were in MRs I and II, which contained only 20

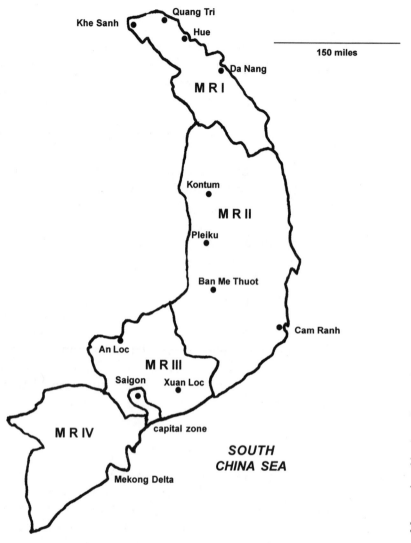

Quang Tri

Khe Sanh

Hue

150 miles

Da Nang

M R I

Kontum

M R II

Pleiku

Ban Me Thuot

Cam Ranh

An Loc

M R III

Saigon   Xuan Loc

M R IV   capital zone

SOUTH
CHINA SEA

Mekong Delta

South Vietnam Military Regions, 1972.

percent of the South's population. Thieu had not previously carried out a consolidation of ARVN forces toward the densely populated southern provinces because he had always believed that the United States would not desert South Vietnam. When Thieu at last decided on a pullback, the South was without American advisers, without fuel and replacement parts, without even the goodwill of its mighty onetime ally across the Pacific. And Thieu and his staff had done little serious preparation for such a massive operation. Many key ARVN officers and civil officials did not know what was happening. Often the roads and bridges designated for retreat to the South were impassable.

When the civilian population in the northern provinces realized that the ARVN was retreating, memories of the Communist massacres of civilians in Hue in 1968 provoked a torrent of refugees who clogged the roads to Hue and Da Nang, making both movement and defense almost impossible. North Vietnamese aircraft constantly strafed and bombed the helpless civilians thronging the roads. The numerous Hanoi agents inside the Saigon civil service and army spread rumors and panic. Many soldiers added to the chaos by leaving their units to search for their families and ensure their escape toward the south; here was the disastrous payoff of the ARVN's policy of assigning draftees far from their home villages.

Almost overnight, retrenchment turned into collapse. Most of the ARVN forces that had been holding MRs I and II simply disintegrated. On March 24, the North Vietnamese captured the ancient capital of Hue. Six days later Da Nang, where the U.S. Marines had landed ten years before, in the first days of President Johnson's Americanization of the war, fell to the invader amid scenes of indescribable suffering. Yet the Southern government still held Saigon; it still held the Mekong Delta: every single one of the Delta's sixteen provincial capitals and scores of district capitals were in Saigon hands. Between Saigon and the Cambodian border, many ARVN units were fiercely resisting the NVA. Some ARVN units had broken out of the encirclement at Xuan Loc and were headed for Saigon. Thirty miles north of Saigon, the Fifth ARVN Division was fighting to get to the city. There was no uprising or disturbance inside the capital. Plans were afoot to turn Saigon into a second Stalingrad.[93] And with the whole NVA beginning to concentrate around Saigon, the ever-expected B-52s could smash Northern military power for a decade. Furthermore, the rains were coming, the tropical inundations that would halt the NVA's tanks in a sea of mud and give beleaguered Saigon the chance to repair its position.

But on April 30 the new president, Gen. Duong Van Minh, assassin of Diem, announced the surrender. Halfway through his speech, the heavens opened and the rains poured down, the rains that would have mired the Northern offensive. Twenty-five years to the day after President Truman first authorized assistance to the French war effort in Vietnam, Saigon fell.[94]

To Lose a War

In the Vietnamese conflict, the Americans confronted an experienced Communist regime that had been able, through a successful struggle against an important European power, to establish a near-monopolistic claim on the cause of national independence. To say the least, this capture of the nationalist banner by Leninists has been a rare phenomenon in world politics.[95] The Americans vastly escalated their ground commitment to the war without the assistance or even the approval of their principal European allies. They permitted the country that they were pledged to defend to be subjected to continuous invasion through the territory of two officially neutral neighboring states, an invasion that the Americans could have prevented. During the conflict the White House patched together a program of Americanization and attrition almost perfectly guaranteed to arouse that impatience for which the American electorate is notorious. Countries avowedly hostile to the United States openly sent its adversaries great quantities of essential munitions. It may be very difficult to imagine a future American administration allowing itself to stumble and sink into a similar strategic swamp; nevertheless, careful reflection on the Vietnam wars will surely yield up some insights, although they may turn out to be unpalatable.

Because of the debacle in 1975, one of the most important "lessons" of the Vietnam conflict is also the most overlooked: people's revolutionary war—that invincible Maoist weapon of the 1960s—failed. The United States, of all the industrialized democracies, is probably the most culturally alien to underdeveloped countries; nevertheless, however expensively and destructively, the Americans and their allies beat the Vietcong guerrillas, despite the fact that the latter possessed sanctuaries and received outside help. Any list of the causes of the defeat of the Vietcong would include irresistible American firepower, sweeping land reform, determined South Vietnamese resistance, and the Communists' fatal abandonment of classical guerrilla tactics in the Tet Offensive.

But why then did South Vietnam fall? One sometimes hears the observation that the United States should never again become involved in a war on behalf of a government that does not enjoy the support of its own people. This is another way of saying that the fall of South Vietnam was the fault of the South Vietnamese: the final and total defeat of the Saigon government is taken as proof that the South Vietnamese people did not truly desire (and probably were not really worthy of) independence. Hence, there was nothing that the Americans could have done to save them.

It certainly is not hard to understand that many Americans should wish to shift the blame for the outcome of the war primarily or solely onto the South Vietnamese. But the conquest of South Vietnam by the NVA in 1975 does not prove that its people desired the Communist victory any more than the conquest of South Korea by the North Korean Army in 1950 or the defeat of the Spanish Republic by Franco's forces or the subjugation of the Confederate States by the Union armies proves that any of those populations desired those outcomes.

Recall that in Communist Hungary in 1956, in Fulgencio Batista's Cuba in 1958, in PDPA Afghanistan in 1980, in Nicolae Ceausescu's Romania in 1989, the armed forces of those tightly controlled police states broke apart under remarkably little pressure.[96] But even under the ferocious blows of Tet and the Easter Offensive, the South Vietnamese army did not break up. On the contrary, the ARVN, along with the Territorials, sustained huge casualties year after year after year. The steadfastness of the fighting forces, the wide distribution of arms to the population by the Saigon government after Tet, the unwillingness of the inhabitants of Saigon to rise up against their government in 1968 or in 1972 or even in 1975, the consequent necessity for the whole North Vietnamese Army to fight its way through to Saigon, the constant flow of refugees southward even in the weeks of collapse in 1975, the tragic epilogue of the Boat People—surely none of these things indicates that a majority of the people of South Vietnam desired conquest by Hanoi.

No, it was not the desire of the South Vietnamese for Communism that caused the fall of South Vietnam. The truth is much more embarrassing than that. By 1973 South Vietnam was becoming what the Americans always said they wanted it to be, a country with a stable government and at least some of the external trappings of democracy. The war also had become what the Americans always said they wanted it to be, not a guerrilla conflict but a clear-cut conventional campaign of conquest by Hanoi. In such a war the ARVN needed only American supplies and air support to stand up to the best efforts of the NVA, as the 1972 Easter Offensive had demonstrated. And precisely at the conjunction of all these favorable developments, precisely when South Vietnam was in the best shape it ever had been, the U.S. Congress decided to repudiate and abandon its ally. The Americans slashed their aid to the South while the Soviets continued theirs to the North. The South Vietnamese were not only cut off from supplies; they were psychologically isolated as well: surrounded by enemies, they could look to no other country for assistance or even sympathy. It was in these devastating circumstances that President Thieu attempted the retrenchment that turned into disaster.

Then the Americans watched as North Vietnam, trampling on a peace agreement that the United States had signed a scant two years before, launched perhaps the largest conventional invasion Asia had witnessed in thirty years. In the face of this invasion, South Vietnam's American-trained and American-equipped armed forces ground to a halt for lack of supplies. In Hanoi's 1972 Easter Offensive, the South Vietnamese, bolstered by U.S. airpower and supplies, repulsed General Giap's best efforts. In Hanoi's 1975 offensive, the South Vietnamese, deprived of promised U.S. support, came apart.

Cutting off its allies from their only source of supplies and replacement parts was but part of the picture. All through the war, what passed for American strategy had permitted Hanoi to construct across so-called neutral neighboring states a complex of major military highways, like a noose around South Vietnam. Thus, when the Americans abandoned their allies, the outflanked South Vietnamese fell victim to the geography of Indochina that enabled Hanoi to substitute invasion for subversion.

True, the South Vietnamese could not have preserved their independence without long-term American assistance, but the same was once true of the West Europeans and the Israelis. The South Koreans, under U.S. protection for decades, today live in independence and prosperity. And since the American impact was much greater on South Vietnamese society than on that of South Korea (it was, in fact, far more comparable to the U.S. impact on Japan by 1951), the people of South Vietnam, whatever their political frailties, would by now quite possibly have made significant advances toward some recognizable kind of democracy. But they never got the chance.

It is at the very least unbecoming for Americans to heap all or most of the blame for their unhappy experience in Vietnam on the heads of the South Vietnamese, since it was the United States that permitted the murder of President Diem, insisted on pursuing an inappropriate military strategy, allowed the Ho Chi Minh Trail to function, imposed a disastrously one-sided treaty on Saigon, and finally declined to supply the South Vietnamese even with replacement parts—all this done to an ally that had suffered a notably higher rate of military fatalities than the Americans.

One sometimes hears that the lost struggle to preserve South Vietnam was not totally in vain, because it provided other countries in Southeast Asia with sobering evidence of what Communism really meant, and time—two decades—to get their economic and political houses in order. Probably this is of little consolation to the South Vietnamese people, who after an incalculable effusion of blood and an unimaginable destruction of the environment were forced to dwell in Asia's most efficient police state and most mismanaged economy. Their fate has been inexpressibly sad.

A Different Strategy

The Hanoi regime was tightly in control of its population, determined to have its will at any cost, and thus impervious to considerations of loss of life. To *defeat* that adversary would have required the United States and South Vietnam to carry the land war to the North. But Washington deemed such a strategy impossible for both political and military reasons. Consequently, the so-called attrition strategy was an effort to defeat North Vietnam primarily through actions inside the South, which was probably not possible, and certainly not possible within a time frame that the misinformed American electorate would tolerate. And even if attrition had worked, it would have saved South Vietnam only *for the time being;* there could be no guarantee that the Americans would support an attrition-based war in the future. Hence, the survival of South Vietnam required another—an altogether different—strategy, a strategy to permit the Americans to assist in the defense of South Vietnam at a reasonable cost in lives, money, and damage to the human and natural environment.

Certainly there is no easy way to defeat a well-organized guerrilla insurgency receiving massive outside help; that is what the allies were facing up to at least 1967. But the Johnson-McNamara policy in Vietnam stands out as a model of what not to do. Sending a huge American army to Vietnam for active campaigning ignored the essence of counterguerrilla war: it sought to kill rather than isolate the guerrillas. It neutralized American technological advantages, caused needless American casualties, inflicted tremendous hurt on friendly civilians, alarmed our friends, gratified our enemies, and exhausted the American public.

Americans were in fact doing some effective thinking about how to fight guerrillas in the context of Vietnam, but sadly, their efforts and warnings went unheeded. A significant indicator of American ability to formulate effective plans for counterinsurgency is the Army study called PROVN, "A Program for the Pacification and Long-term Development of South Viet Nam." Commissioned by the army chief of staff in July 1965, PROVN was finished in March 1966, a nine hundred–page document earmarked for internal army circulation only. Having questioned numerous army officers about their experiences in Vietnam and studied the history of that country, PROVN's youngish officer-authors declared that "without question, village and hamlet security must be achieved throughout Viet Nam." Attaining that primary objective required "effective area saturation tactics in and around populated areas"—the first essential step in a serious clear-and-hold strategy.[97] PROVN also advocated cutting the Ho Chi Minh Trail, increasing direct U.S. supervision of South Vietnamese government activities, and placing all U.S. personnel and programs in the South under a single head, the U.S. ambassador. Partly because of PROVN's direct criticisms of the search-and-destroy methods then in place, it received polite inattention until General Abrams took command in 1969, by which time the war had become largely a conventional one.

One approach to the fundamental problem of civilian security, perhaps "the most imaginative strategy to emerge from the Viet Nam conflict," was the CAP program, the Combined Action Platoons, begun in August 1965. A Marine rifle squad of 14 men, all volunteers, would receive permanent assignment to a particular village, to work with and train a Popular Forces platoon of 38 men. (In practice most CAPs had fewer than 14 Marines, and in later years not all were volunteers.) Typically a village included five hamlets over an area of about four square kilometers, with a population of perhaps 3,500 persons. By the end of 1967 there were 79 CAPs, and 114 by early 1970, all in the exceedingly dangerous MR I, just below the border with North Vietnam. At the height of the program, 42 Marine officers, 2 Navy officers, 2,050 enlisted Marines, and 126 Navy hospital corpsmen were involved. "The Combined Action Program's basic concept was to bring peace to the Vietnamese villages by uniting the local knowledge of the Popular Forces with the professional skill and superior equipment of the Marines." The permanent presence of Marines protected the villagers from excessive American firepower, but most of all it signaled to the villagers that they would not be abandoned.[98]

General Westmoreland did not like the CAPs. In his memoirs he devotes exactly one paragraph to the program, saying: "I simply had not enough numbers to put a squad of Americans in every village and hamlet."[99] It is not easy to understand exactly what the general meant: to place a rifle squad of Marines into, say, two thousand villages would have required 28,000 troops, about one-twentieth of the total American military personnel in Vietnam in 1968; but this small fraction of U.S. troops would have provided physical and psychological security to—and deprived the enemy of—over seven million peasants.

To be worthwhile, any alternative strategy would have had to separate the bulk of the Southern population from the VC and the NVA, keep the number of American troops within reasonable limits, optimize American firepower, minimize American and friendly civilian casualties, neutralize the effects of the Ho Chi Minh Trail, and place the main responsibility for coping with guerrillas where it belonged—on the Vietnamese.

Analysts of the conflict have forcefully argued that the fundament of a proper strategy for the United States was to halt the continuous invasion of South Vietnam by blocking the Ho Chi Minh Trail. In their scenario, American and ARVN forces would have deployed along a roughly east-west axis across Laos to the border of Thailand. I suggest here a different alternative strategy, based on several important assumptions. The first is that the Johnson administration would have continued to veto a move into Laos, on the grounds that it would widen the conflict, invite an NVA attack through northeastern Thailand, put too many Americans on the ground too far from blue water, and so on. The second assumption is that President Johnson would have continued to forbid an invasion even of the southern provinces of North Vietnam because he and his advisers feared a Chinese intervention on the Korean model. That was not an unreasonable fear, given the experiences of the decision makers in Washington. In fact, by the end of the Johnson administration, nearly a third of a million Chinese military personnel served in the Vietnam conflict as engineers and antiaircraft troops. The third assumption concerns clear-and-hold counterinsurgency operations of the type so ably advocated by Sir Robert Thompson.[100] Clear-and-hold means patiently, systematically, and permanently driving the guerrillas out of first one area, then another, then another. That strategy produced excellent results in Malaya and is probably the best response to insurgency in any country where the guerrillas are essentially lacking a true sanctuary. In South Vietnam, however, clear-and-hold tactics would not in themselves have been sufficient because the insurgency was only one arm of the campaign to destroy the Saigon government, the other being a slow-motion invasion (fast-motion in 1972) from the North via Laos. Any successful strategy needed to be based on clear thinking about South Vietnam's geography.

A New Geography

Geography was destiny for South Vietnam. If that state had been a peninsula, like South Korea or Malaya, or an archipelago, like the Philippines, its defense would have been incomparably easier. But it was neither of those things. Instead, the country was too big, too poorly shaped, too exposed to flanking attacks from Laos and Cambodia to defend in its entirety. The allies would neither invade the enemy's base (North Vietnam) nor prevent him from coming at them as he chose (down the Ho Chi Minh Trail). Thus, in order to succeed they would have had to remake the geography of South Vietnam to their own advantage: *to redefine the shape of political South Vietnam.* That is the essence of the strategy proposed here: a demographic frontier combined with the techniques of counterinsurgency.

A map of South Vietnam emphasizing demography circa 1970 would have shown the overwhelming majority of the population living in greater Saigon and the Mekong Delta (Military Regions III and IV), plus a few urban centers along the coast. Defending these areas is the heart of the alternative strategy proposed here. The northern boundary of Military Region III (approximately twelve degrees north latitude) constituted a rough "demographic frontier" dividing the heavily populated from the sparsely populated provinces. In this alternative strategy, most U.S. and some ARVN forces would deploy along that line and along the border between MR III and Cambodia, supported by mobile reserves. Behind the allied troops holding the demographic frontier, ARVN units and the Territorial forces would deal with remaining Vietcong elements. (With far fewer U.S. troops in country, the ARVN and the Territorials could have received weapons whose quality equaled those of the Communists much sooner.) Units modeled on the Combined Action Platoons (CAPs) would operate in highly exposed districts.[101] All civilians living above the demographic front line but wishing to come into allied territory would be welcomed. Hovering above this deployment of forces would be the awesome airpower of the allied states.

Some carefully selected and highly trained South Vietnamese guerrilla units might remain behind (on the north side of the demographic frontier) in the highlands. In MR I, allied forces would hold Hue and Da Nang, supported by the U.S. Navy. Hue was a tremendously important symbol to all Vietnamese, and both places would serve as potential launching areas for seaborne flanking attacks (Da Nang would be the Inchon of South Vietnam, except that the Americans would already be there). The refugees who would surely inundate those two coastal cities could be sea-lifted south, behind the demographic frontier.

If there had been a true front line, with the enemy on one side and the civilians on the other, superior American firepower could have had free play. The United States could have deployed in Vietnam not a partly conscripted army of half a million but a much smaller professional, even perhaps volunteer, force that by pursuing conservative tactics would have incurred far fewer losses: no more chasing the enemy, no more search and destroy, no more body counts, no more booby-trap casualties—and no more one-year tours, either. The bombing of North Vietnam would have been unnecessary, the Ho Chi Minh Trail irrelevant.

Confronting such a front line, Hanoi would have had two choices:

either to abandon the struggle by accepting this de facto new partition, which was much more advantageous militarily to the South, or else to seek a decisive confrontation in the teeth of overwhelming allied fire superiority. In addition to greatly decreasing the size of the American forces in Vietnam and directing their firepower toward the enemy and away from civilians, this strategy, by creating a true rear area, would have made possible a thorough clear-and-hold cleanup in the regions of dense population, and it would also have allowed time for serious social and economic improvements to take hold in those same areas.

The supreme advantage of the demographic strategy—next to reducing American and South Vietnamese casualties—would have been that the debacle of 1975 could not have occurred. In January 1975 most of the ARVN was in the sparsely populated Central Highlands and the dangerously exposed Military Region I below the seventeenth parallel. President Thieu's decision to remove the bulk of these forces to positions closer to Saigon was a very good one and should have been carried out years earlier. But the 1975 retrenchment turned into a catastrophe for two main reasons. One was hasty planning; the other was the presence of the families of ARVN soldiers in the Central Highlands and other exposed areas. The perfectly understandable desire of ARVN soldiers to see to it that their relatives did not fall into Communist hands resulted in disintegration of many ARVN units and the conquest of the South.

Instead of stationing soldiers far from their home areas and letting their families follow them, the government, under the demographic strategy, would have let the families stay put in their true homes and deployed the soldiers to defend them. If the ARVN had been previously (before 1975) concentrated farther south, in an orderly manner, with their families on one side of them and the Communists on the other, not only would a retrenchment have been unnecessary, but retreat or desertion also would have become hardly thinkable. No one ever thought the Eighteenth ARVN Division was worth much, but in the last days of the war, after its dependents had been evacuated southward, it put up a truly ferocious defense of Xuan Loc.[102]

Some Objections

Of course, objections to this strategy come immediately to mind. In the first place, a demographic strategy is defensive, giving the initiative to the enemy. But so what? The Ho Chi Minh Trail put General Westmoreland's forces on the defensive anyway (and on exterior lines), but they refused to acknowledge this and thus could not take advantage of it. The pace of the fighting was dictated by the NVA and the VC, not by the United States. The Communists could control the level and locus of fighting mainly because of their sanctuaries in Cambodia and especially in Laos. How to eliminate or nullify those sanctuaries—that is the question. Clausewitz wrote that "it is easier to hold ground than to take it" and that "the defensive form of warfare is intrinsically stronger than the offensive."[103] Under this demographic strategy, if the enemy "took the initiative," so much the better for the allies: NVA forces mounting major attacks against one or more points on the frontier would pull down on top of themselves everything from B-52s to the sixteen-inch shells of the USS *New Jersey*, while confronting highly mobile allied forces operating from behind prepared positions on interior lines. One should never forget what happened to Giap's forces during the Easter Offensive, when they were attacking under the most favorable conditions. (In what was perhaps his biggest victory, the battle of Fredericksburg, Robert E. Lee was fighting from a prepared defensive position that his enemies obligingly attacked.)

A second objection might ask how one could induce the South Vietnamese government to abandon large sections of its territory. But they did it anyway in 1975, only in the worst possible circumstances. There was nothing sacred about the seventeenth parallel; the French had made it a border, not the South Vietnamese. South Vietnam had no obligation to defend indefensible territory—and neither did the United States. Allied strategy should have focused on preserving a viable South Vietnamese state, not this or that arbitrary line on a map. Moreover, trading territory for survival is a venerable stratagem: the Russians retreated before Napoleon and Hitler; the Chinese retreated before the Japanese; Lee defended Virginia, not Arkansas. Most of the South Vietnamese and almost all of the Americans who were killed during the war met their fate in the territory between the thirteenth and the seventeenth parallels—for what? And it was precisely there that the ARVN collapsed into chaos. By trying to hold everything, the South Vietnamese lost everything.

Perhaps another objection would be that a demographic strategy would require the commitment of American forces for too long. But how long is that? American troops have stood guard in Germany, Japan, and Korea for more than two generations. Besides that, assume that *attrition* had worked the way it was hoped, that Hanoi concluded that conquest of South Vietnam was too costly in the face of serious American commitment. Would not the attempt to conquer be renewed as soon as American commitment ceased? Thus, the independence of South Vietnam, like that of West Germany, would require an indefinite and credible American involvement. The real question concerning the demographic strategy is not "how many years?" but "how many U.S. casualties?" which such a strategy, properly executed, could have dramatically decreased.

8

El Salvador

A Long War in a Small Country

The only Central American republic without an Atlantic coastline, El Salvador is the smallest Spanish-speaking state in Latin America, the size of Massachusetts. In 1980, when the insurgency broke out, its population was about 3.9 million. El Salvador is the very stereotype of a Central American society: for generations it has been a commodity-export economy, with grave maldistribution of land and wealth and a dreary history of oligarchical control and military dictatorship.[1] The country has the highest population density in Latin America; the living conditions of the lowest strata were for decades the worst of all Latin American countries except perhaps Haiti. Certainly no other Central American society had a greater potential for class conflict.

In 1932 the Communist Party of El Salvador launched an armed revolt, which the army brutally and effectively suppressed. Out of those events the army emerged as and remained the dominant institution in the country's political life. This army consisted of an officer elite presiding over peasant conscripts; the common soldiers did not receive decent training or care, and the unprofessional officer corps had no real mechanism for rewarding competence or weeding out incompetence. In close alliance with the oligarchy, the army compiled a notable record of human rights abuses, including massacres of restless peasants.

The example and rhetoric of the Castro regime galvanized the Left all over Latin America. Accordingly, in 1961 the Salvadoran Communist Party again organized an armed uprising, which the army quickly defeated. The Communists then decided to turn away

Central America, 1984.

from violence: aside from the painful lesson of the 1961 failure, the party decided that some scope existed for legal opposition, and eventually it tended to condemn all guerrilla uprisings as "focoism" in the style of the disastrous Guevara expedition in Bolivia. The Salvadoran Communists would not again embrace armed struggle until 1980.[2]

Another profoundly destabilizing factor was at work in the 1960s: the Catholic Church first began to engage in rural organization, founding cooperatives and similar groups with a pronounced religious emphasis. Out of these efforts grew independent local peasant organizations, which were not revolutionary or even overtly political in themselves, but the revolutionary Left sought to infiltrate and manipulate them. The backwardness of the society, the deteriorating standards of life in the countryside, and the unresponsiveness of the government, combined with church activism and the spread of so-called liberation theology, began to produce demands for serious change by certain middle-class elements, including some army officers. In the presidential elections of 1972 and 1977, massive government fraud against reformist candidates effectively closed off the electoral road to change.[3] Then in October 1979 a military coup installed a predominantly civilian junta that pledged to carry out reforms but proved unable to pursue coherent policies or to prevent the escalation of violence. Thus, the stage was set for an insurgency.

The FMLN

In December 1979 several Salvadoran revolutionary groups gathered in Castro's Havana to organize the Farabundo Marti National Liberation Front (FMLN). The name derived from a Salvadoran Communist contemporary of the Nicaraguan Augusto Sandino (who himself was never a Communist). The bold leadership and effective tactics of the FMLN, augmented by the ineptitude of the army, soon presented a serious challenge, approximating a conventional war. The insurgents operated in battalion-sized units and cleared the Salvadoran Army out of whole regions. For their part, elements of the oligarchy, the army, and the police sanctioned the activities of "death squads," which sought to achieve the elimination of anyone identified as dangerous to the regime. Oscar Romero, the archbishop of San Salvador, shot in March 1980, was almost certainly one of their victims. And in its efforts to get at guerrillas, the army killed many civilians who found themselves in the way.

The conflict in El Salvador emerged during a very anxious period for the United States. Saigon had finally fallen to the North Vietnamese army in 1975, mobs in Tehran had taken the American embassy staff hostage in 1979, Pol Pot was devastating Cambodia, the Soviets had invaded Afghanistan, and Cuban troops were fighting in Angola. The presence of thousands of Cuban soldiers and schoolteachers in neighboring Nicaragua also alarmed Washington. The Salvadoran Left was going to pay a very high price indeed for the close ties that the Nicaraguan Sandinistas had established with Havana and Moscow.[4]

According to the teachings of Mao Tse-tung, the small size of El Salvador should have been a serious disadvantage to the guerrillas. The border with Honduras, however, had never been well defined; both governments had no-entry zones for their troops, and these areas (bolsones) provided the insurgents with convenient sanctuaries. In addition, the rebels received priceless assistance, including military training, from neighboring Nicaragua and from the USSR, Cuba, Bulgaria, East Germany, and Vietnam.[5]

In these difficult circumstances, the Carter administration, although preoccupied with many other foreign crises, decided in the spring of 1980 that the United States must help the Salvadoran government overcome the challenge from an insurgency that was clearly Communist-controlled. U.S. assistance to the government of El Salvador was probably not the decisive factor, and certainly not the only factor, in the defeat of the insurgency. Nevertheless, President Carter's decision was one of the most important events of the entire conflict. Because analyses of U.S. involvement in El Salvador tend to become enmeshed in and reflect the analyst's attitudes toward President Reagan, it is worth noting that it was President Carter who committed the United States against the FMLN and that this commitment had the open support of Honduras, Guatemala, and Venezuela, among others.[6]

Despite the Carter administration's resolve, the Salvadoran government and army seemed to be on the verge of collapse. The economy was badly deteriorating. The insurgents were able to mobilize between ten and twelve thousand fighters, a formidable array indeed and one far greater than either the Cuban Fidelista or the Nicaraguan Sandinista insurgencies had commanded. In January 1981 the FMLN launched its "final offensive." Scoring some impressive gains at first, by the end of the month it was receding. Thus, before any appreciable American aid had reached El Salvador, it was clear that the government was not going to fall.[7] Most notably, the popular uprising that the FMLN called for in conjunction with the January offensive was a resounding failure. This was the first major indication that support for the insurgents was not as widespread as many outside El Salvador liked to claim, a point to receive more attention later.

Succeeding Jimmy Carter in January 1981, President Reagan believed like his predecessor that the victory of the FMLN would be interpreted as a triumph for the Sandinistas and Castro and, behind them, the Soviet Union.[8] Determined to prevent that, Reagan dispatched a small number of U.S. military advisers to El Salvador, and in January 1982 army officers from that country began training in counterinsurgency techniques at Fort Bragg, North Carolina. Out of those efforts would eventually arise a better-equipped and more competent Salvadoran army. Such training was sorely needed in light of that army's peculiar shortcomings, notable among which were (1) the "tanda" system, whereby an entire class of officers received promotion at the same time, negating any concept of merit, (2) structural corruption, whereby officers profited from government payments for nonexistent soldiers and sold goods at inflated prices to their troops, and (3) a reluctance on the part of many officers to see the war end, because U.S. aid would then also end. And so bitter fighting raged across the little country during the early 1980s.

At the same time, the Americans were trying to promote political and social reforms. Vice President George Bush visited the capital, San Salvador, in December 1983 to deliver a tart message: if human rights abuses by government forces did not visibly decrease, then American assistance would. Bush told his audience, "Your cause is being undermined by the murderous violence of reactionary minorities." He especially insisted on the necessity for the army not to interfere with the approaching elections.

A month after Bush's visit, the prestigious Bipartisan Commission on Central America, the so-called Kissinger Commission, appointed by President Reagan, delivered its long-awaited report on the subject of the strategic and ideological interests of the United States in Central America.[9] This document requires attention.

The Kissinger Commission Report

The Kissinger Commission identified the armed struggle in El Salvador as in large part the result of foreign Communist interference. Certainly, conditions in El Salvador were wretched for many, but "if wretched conditions were themselves enough to create such insurgencies, we would see them in many more countries of the world." "We have stressed before, and we repeat here: indigenous reform movements, even indigenous revolutions, are not themselves a security concern of the United States."[10] But in El Salvador, "the roots of the crisis are both indigenous and foreign. Discontents are real, and for much of the population conditions of life are miserable; just as Nicaragua was ripe for revolution, so the conditions that invite revolution are present elsewhere in the region as well. But these conditions have been exploited by hostile outside forces—specifically by Cuba, backed by the Soviet Union and now operating through Nicaragua—which will turn any revolution they capture into a totalitarian state . . . in the image of their sponsors' ideology and their own."[11]

The conflict in El Salvador thus had strategic implications of the first order. "Cuban and now Nicaraguan support was subsequently critical in building the fighting forces of the Farabundo Marti Liberation Front in El Salvador, in maintaining them in the field, and in forcing them to unite in a combined effort in spite of the deep-seated distrust among the guerrilla factions. Indeed, it was a meeting hosted by Castro in December 1979 that had produced agreement among the Salvadoran insurgent factions to form a coordinating committee, as was publicly announced the following month." And "by 1979, in terms of modern military capabilities Cuba had become perhaps the strongest power in the Western Hemisphere south of the United States." "As a mainland platform, therefore, Nicaragua is a crucial stepping stone for Cuban and Soviet efforts to promote armed insurgency in Central America." "The use of Nicaragua as a base for Soviet and Cuban efforts to penetrate the rest of the Central American isthmus, with El Salvador as the target of first opportunity, gives the conflict there a major strategic dimension." "Therefore, curbing the insurgents' violence in El Salvador requires in part cutting them off from their sources of foreign support."[12]

The commission rejected the concept of power-sharing between the government and the insurgents, because "to install a mixed provisional government by fiat would scarcely be consistent with the notion that the popular will is the foundation of true government." Instead, the goals of U.S. policy must be the creation of a functioning democratic state that could and would carry out long-overdue social reforms. "The essence of our effort together must be the legitimation of governments by free consent—the rejection of violence and murder as political instruments, of the imposition of authority from above, the use of the power of the state to suppress opposition and dissent." "A major goal of US policy in Central America should be to give democratic forces there the time and the opportunity to carry out the structural reforms essential for that country's security and well-being"; in short, "to promote peaceful change in Central America while resisting the violation of democracy by force and terrorism [sic]."[13] "Experience has destroyed the argument of the old dictators that a strong hand is essential to avoid anarchy and communism. . . . The modern experience of Latin America suggests that order is more often threatened when people have no voice in their own destinies. Social peace is more likely in societies where political justice is founded on self-determination and protected by formal guarantee."[14] Therefore, said the members of the commission, "We believe that a true political solution in El Salvador can be reached only through free elections in which all significant groups have a right to participate." To that end, "in March 1984 [El Salvador] will elect a president under a permanent constitution," in preparation for which "a system of international observation should be established to enhance the faith and confidence of all parties in the probity and equity of arrangements for elections."[15]

Democratic forces faced a serious threat, however, from the insurgents and their foreign backers: "Although their absolute numbers have not increased over the past three years, and although they have not attracted the broad popular support they hoped for, the guerrillas after four years of experience in the field demonstrate an increasing capacity to maneuver, concentrate their forces and attack selected targets."[16]

In the short term, therefore, the United States must help the gov-

ernment of El Salvador avoid violent overthrow: "A successful counterinsurgency effort is not a substitute for negotiations. But such an
effort—the more rapid the better—is a necessary condition for a
political solution." The El Salvador government would not have carte
blanche, however: "military aid should, through legislation requiring periodic reports, be made contingent upon demonstrated
progress toward free elections; freedom of association; the establishment of the rule of law and an effective judicial system; and the
termination of the activities of the so-called death squads, as well as
vigorous action against those guilty of crimes and the prosecution
to the extent possible of past offenders. These conditions should be
seriously enforced."[17]

Many grave obstacles lay ahead. Said the commission's report:
"The dilemma in El Salvador is clear. With all its shortcomings, the
existing government has conducted free elections. But it is weak.
The judiciary is ineffective. The military is divided in its concerns,
and in the degree of its respect for human rights. Privileged Salva-
dorans want to preserve both their political and economic power."
The activities of the "death squads" are, like those of the insurgents,
"morally and politically repugnant to this Commission, which
strongly supports the consolidation and defense of democratic institutions in El Salvador."[18]

The release of the Kissinger Commission Report, following
closely upon Vice President Bush's remarks in San Salvador, improved the climate for congressional support of the Salvadoran government. Between 1979 and 1987 the United States provided $2 billion
in economic and $700 million in military assistance. During the same
period Salvadoran security forces increased from ten thousand to
fifty-six thousand.[19] In 1980 the ratio of security forces to insurgents
was only 1.5 to 1; by 1987 it was nearly 8 to 1. Certainly one must be
cautious about such figures, because they can be used to gloss over
important qualitative questions. But clearly, if the ratio is changing
over time in favor of the guerrillas, the government is losing the
war; that was the opposite of the situation in El Salvador.

Slowly Creating a Democracy

In the spring of 1982, elections for a new Legislative Assembly took
place. In spite of FMLN threats and acts of terrorism to keep Salva-

dorans from voting, the turnout was high. Foreign observers concluded that, in the Central American context, these were fair elections. The governing Christian Democrats did much less well than predicted, receiving 41 percent of the votes, whereas ARENA, the National Republican Alliance, obtained 29 percent. The Assembly chose Alvaro Magana, holder of a master's degree in economics from the University of Chicago, as its provisional presiding officer.

ARENA was the first serious and open political vehicle of the upper classes since the early 1930s. Hitherto they had been content to let the army run the country. Roberto D'Aubuisson, who founded the party in September 1981, was born in 1944 in modest family circumstances. A former army officer, he was associated with the notorious "death squads" that meted out execution to proven and suspected insurgents; some linked him with the death of Archbishop Romero. D'Aubuisson himself was a frequent target of assassination attempts and terrorist acts. Called by the *Washington Post* "the most charismatic politician in El Salvador," he would run unsuccessfully for president in 1984.

Meanwhile, President Reagan found a reformist center that he could persuade the U.S. Congress to support. The embodiment of that center was José Napoleon Duarte (1925–1991), elected president of El Salvador in May 1984. Duarte, the illegitimate son of a tailor, had been able to attend and graduate from Notre Dame University because his father had won a lottery. A civic activist and critic of the status quo, he was one of the founders of the Christian Democrats, a party that for years was the principal opponent of the Salvadoran establishment. In his memoirs he summed up Salvadoran politics in this way: "For forty years, a military dictatorship had protected the interest of a few wealthy families." Duarte took office as mayor of the capital city, San Salvador, in 1964 and served three terms. Most observers believe that he had won the presidential elections of 1972 but had been counted out; this closing off of the route of peaceful change was a major contribution to the outbreak of massive insurgency a few years later. In the 1984 presidential contest, Duarte defeated Roberto D'Aubuisson 54 percent to 46 percent. His inauguration was the first time in the history of El Salvador that an opposition candidate had peacefully attained the presidency.[20]

In the Legislative Assembly elections of March 1985, President Duarte's Christian Democrats won a majority of seats: the returns showed them with 505,000 votes and 33 seats, ARENA and other rightist parties with 367,000 votes and 25 seats, and minor parties with 222,000 votes and 2 seats. Before the voting, army leaders had made clear their intention to uphold the results of the elections.[21] Thus, as the military situation stabilized in favor of the government, electoral democracy was slowly establishing itself in the society.

By this time it was obvious that the insurgency would not triumph and that, although the war had become a stalemate, the scales were increasingly tipping toward the government side. Under these circumstances, the FMLN's internal fissures began to widen. The FMLN had never been one homogeneous organization; on the contrary, it was an alliance (organized in Havana) of five different guerrilla groups, suspicious of and even hostile toward each other. In 1985, with the war not going well and regular elections taking place, the most hard-line of the guerrilla organizations, the ERP, began to radicalize the FMLN's tactics. The guerrillas made the destruction of the economic life of the country their central goal. They continued to force peasant youths into their armed units. Government officials and their relatives became the target of a systematic program of assassination; the rebels chose for their victims not the worst but the most popular and honest officers, politicians, and administrators (recalling the Vietcong assassination program in South Vietnam). By thus downgrading its actions from guerrilla war to terrorism ("urban guerrilla warfare") the FMLN began to suffer a serious loss of prestige and popular support and to alienate the less intransigent elements of its own membership.[22]

Although the violence continued inconclusively, growing disputes within the FMLN over the strategy of terror eventually produced a major breakthrough: in 1989 several leading figures in the FMLN publicly renounced guerrilla revolution in favor of political participation. Most notable among those disillusioned FMLN supporters was Ruben Zamora. A one-time student for the priesthood, ex–Christian Democrat, former university professor, and prominent figure of what was called the democratic Left, Zamora returned to El Salvador in 1987 after eight years in exile. And in the March presidential election of that same year, Alfredo Cristiani, a Georgetown University graduate who had ousted D'Aubuisson as head of ARENA, won an easy victory, witnessed by the international press. In a large voter turnout, Cristiani received 53.8 percent against 36.6

percent for the candidate of President Duarte's Christian Democrats. The inauguration of Cristiani represented the country's first handover of power by a civilian president to the civilian leader of the opposition. Shortly thereafter most of the FMLN leadership decided to enter into negotiations with its former archenemies of ARENA. Following the collapse of these talks, in November 1989 the FMLN launched another major offensive. This was their most ambitious military effort ever, but it failed nonetheless.[23] The FMLN's revolutionary strategy was bankrupt.

This final, public bankruptcy coincided with the ending of the Cold War. For many Americans, one of the most disheartening aspects of Salvadoran society during the eighties had been what appeared to be the erosion of moderate political elements and the strengthening of the extremes. But both sides soon felt the pressures generated by the ending of the Cold War. Support for the FMLN from Communist countries was drying up. At the same time, leaders of the army and ARENA realized that with the Soviet Union imploding, Washington found the specter of a Communist regime in El Salvador considerably less menacing than before, to say the least. Hence, the United States now felt itself in a position actually to be able to cut off aid. Furthermore, the 1989 offensive, although a failure, seemed to suggest that the Salvadoran Army would be unable to achieve outright military victory for the foreseeable future. It was time to make a peace. Accordingly, in January 1992, with UN Secretary-General Boutros Ghali and U.S. Secretary of State James Baker in attendance, the administration of President Cristiani and the FMLN signed peace accords in Mexico City. The FMLN undertook to disarm under UN supervision and to transform itself from a guerrilla army into a political party; some of its members were to be permitted to enroll in a new national police force. The UN pledged to send up to one thousand military and civilian supervisors into the country. The treaty marked the end of a twelve-year insurgency that had taken an estimated seventy-five thousand lives.[24]

The next presidential election, in March 1994, took place peacefully in the presence of 3,000 international observers, 900 of them from the United Nations. ARENA nominee Armando Calderon received 49 percent of the vote; Ruben Zamora, as the candidate of a Marxist coalition based on the former insurgents, obtained 26 percent (the candidate of the Christian Democrats had only 15 percent).

The April runoff election (necessary since no candidate had received the required majority of the vote) gave Calderon 68 percent, Zamora 32 percent. ARENA did less well in the Legislative Assembly elections, winning 39 of the 84 seats in that body, while the FMLN and two leftist allies took 22 and the Christian Democrats 18. Calderon was the third freely elected civilian president in succession.

Neither Vietnam nor Cuba

In spite of this apparently benign denouement, U.S. counter-insurgency efforts in El Salvador have been the object of searching criticism. Among their most notable critics has been Benjamin Schwarz. The essence of his argument is that the counterinsurgency strategy of the U.S. government did not defeat the FMLN and must therefore be considered a failure. Although the war in El Salvador eventually ended in a way that Washington found acceptable, that result derived mainly from changes in the international environment, especially the end of the Cold War and the unexpected electoral defeat of the Sandinista regime in Nicaragua, not from the application of the principles of American counterinsurgency. The long American involvement in the conflict from 1980 to 1990 had achieved, at the cost of much bloodshed and destruction, only a stalemate, not a victory. "If the conflict in El Salvador presents the ideal for implementing counterinsurgency doctrine, but after 11 years of effort that doctrine has not achieved its goals, then perhaps the doctrine is flawed."[25]

For Schwarz, the heart of U.S. strategy in El Salvador consisted of three objectives: (1) improve the performance of the Salvadoran armed forces, (2) encourage the distribution of land to landless peasants, and (3) institute democratic elections.

The United States did indeed, to a notable degree, help to increase the size and efficiency of the Salvadoran Army; it also succeeded in reducing the number of major human rights abuses. American assistance, however, could not change the whole culture of the army, which was after all rooted in the culture of El Salvador itself. Schwarz points out that according to the Kissinger Commission, the training of the Salvadoran Army by American instructors would curtail abuses, but the slaying of six Jesuits in the capital city in 1989 showed that such training was by no means an infallible formula. Moreover, the Kissinger Commission had stressed the importance of building local civil defense forces, but the Salvadoran Army resisted giving weapons to local groups. In part this reflected the army's desire to save weapons against the day when the United States might abandon El Salvador, as it had abandoned South Vietnam a few years before.[26]

In addition, the Americans found it very hard to force El Salvador's establishment to carry out political and economic reforms. U.S. political leaders of both parties made it clear that they would not in the end suffer El Salvador to fall under FMLN control; hence, threats by the Americans to wash their hands of El Salvador if that country's government did not do what was required were not credible. The Salvadoran establishment usually (and correctly) saw the reforms demanded by the United States not as a means of extending its control but of destroying it. Land distribution was a centerpiece of the Kissinger Commission recommendations, but Salvadoran landowners and their army allies sabotaged land reform in several ways, including violence against peasants. President Cristiani vigorously criticized land reform on classical economic grounds; furthermore, even the most extensive and sincere program of land redistribution could not solve El Salvador's basic problem of overpopulation.[27]

Finally, according to Schwarz's critique, American policymakers consistently confuse democracy with democratic institutions such as orderly elections. But in a country like El Salvador, torn by years of internecine war, democratic elections are problematical because, among other problems, they presuppose a willingness on the part of the losers to accept defeat and allow the winners to govern until the next elections.[28] In El Salvador, moreover, the United States intervened noticeably to prevent the electoral victory of intransigent rightists and bolster the fortunes of the favored Christian Democrats, and that intervention achieved only limited success.[29]

A Different Perspective

These are serious indictments of the general American approach to the conflict in El Salvador. But even if one grants that Schwarz's analysis has merit (as it does), one can arrive at a drastically different evaluation by approaching the question of the success or failure of American policy in El Salvador from a different perspective. If success for U.S. policy is defined as the decisive military defeat of the FLMN in a relatively short time,[30] then clearly U.S. efforts were quite disappointing. But such a definition of success in guerrilla warfare would be unrealistic and ahistorical. The aims of the United States under Presidents Carter, Reagan, and Bush were to prevent the imposition of a pro-Soviet dictatorship on another Latin American state, while avoiding a massive deployment of U.S. armed forces on the order of the Dominican intervention of 1965. Those aims were fulfilled; it is therefore not clear why the outcome should not be seen as constituting a success for U.S. policy.[31]

That outcome, moreover, was achieved in some remarkably unfavorable circumstances. Recall that (1) in the early years a military victory by the FMLN appeared imminent to many observers, because (2) El Salvador exhibited multiple, severe, and obvious social pathologies, (3) the numerous organized and dedicated insurgents were receiving assistance from the Soviet bloc and especially from neighboring Nicaragua, and (4) the principal anti-FMLN groups—the army, the elite, and the Christian Democrats—had incompatible aims. In addition (5), left-wing opinion all over the world, including within the United States, vitriolically and ceaselessly opposed U.S. involvement, especially during the Reagan presidency, (6) the recipients of American assistance hardly qualified as poster persons for enlightened government, (7) the conflict went on for many years, a circumstance that is supposed (with some validity) to cause democratic polities to lose interest, and (8) the United States never had as many as two hundred military personnel in El Salvador.[32] Yet in the end, armed conflict ceased in El Salvador as pro-U.S. administrations succeeded each other through effective elections.

Thus, contrary to fashionable predictions (and perhaps hopes), El Salvador never turned into "another Vietnam." And why should it have? The differences between the wars in El Salvador and Vietnam were, or ought to have been, much more impressive than the similarities. Consider simply the basic dimensions of the struggle: El Salvador had one-eighth the area and one-fifth the population of South Vietnam alone. Another contrast is in the locus of the struggle: Washington is nearer to the South Pole than to Saigon, but San Salvador is closer to Houston and San Diego than either of those cities is to New York. And there is no Communist China in Central America.

In addition to these fundamental conditions of demography and geography, the determination of three U.S. presidents to prevent an FMLN takeover in El Salvador powerfully affected the outcome. Acutely aware that committing substantial U.S. ground combat forces in El Salvador was politically impossible, Presidents Carter, Reagan, and Bush had no choice but to work to strengthen the Salvadoran armed forces. American aid and pressure resulted in significant upgrading of the Salvadoran Army's military capabilities.[33] And despite continuing serious shortcomings, that army's treatment of civilians indisputably improved. Thus, if the United States had not intervened, the El Salvador conflict would almost certainly have been much more ferocious.

Consistent U.S. pressure also hastened the coming of honest elections, which quickly clothed the Salvadoran government with much legitimacy at home and abroad. The return of free elections to El Salvador in 1984, as to the Philippines in 1951 (see chapter 6), deprived the insurgents of their most powerful argument in favor of violent revolution, that there was no peaceful way to change an intolerable situation. Repeated dire threats by the FMLN against those who participated in the elections only served to underline and increase its isolation. The commonsense thesis popularized by Che Guevara, that one cannot successfully make violent revolution against a democratic government (or even a pseudodemocratic one), received new confirmation. In El Salvador as elsewhere, "the ballot box . . . has proven to be the coffin of revolutionary movements."[34]

But if the elections were free and honest, why did the FMLN candidates not win them? Here we arrive at the very important[35] question of how much popular support the FMLN really had.

Insurgent Weaknesses

There are at least two good reasons to strongly suspect that outside estimates of FMLN support were often exaggerated. First, the Salvadoran population failed repeatedly to heed FMLN calls for a massive popular uprising. One might explain, or explain away,[36] such repeated failure except for the complicating presence of the second reason to question FMLN popular support, namely the generally poor showing its candidates have made in internationally supervised elections since the end of the war. The FMLN's unimpressive vote totals, especially in 1994 (only two years after the fighting ended), inescapably suggest that its authoritarian Marxism and its increasingly terrorist tactics in the late 1980s had made it more and more unattractive to broad strata of the Salvadoran society.

Such a position seems to contradict a widely held conception about Third World revolutionary movements. Some commentators easily assume that glaring socioeconomic disparities produce popular (especially peasant) protest, which the regime meets with savage repression, which in turn triggers a revolutionary struggle. But poverty, even of the most indefensible sort, is not enough to generate revolution, as societies from India and Bangladesh to Haiti and Honduras suggest, and as Lenin, Trotsky, and Guevara have taught. To the contrary, Blanquists, Bolsheviks, and Focoists have all believed, or at least claimed, that a small dedicated group of revolutionaries can, and sometimes must, substitute for objective revolutionary conditions. Hannah Arendt has shown that this approach to revolution has been the dominant one in the twentieth century.[37] Furthermore, if socioeconomic factors determined the outbreak of the FMLN insurgency, why did the war come to an end with the socioeconomic system still fundamentally intact?[38]

To put it all another way: why did the outcome in El Salvador differ so dramatically from that in Cuba and in Nicaragua? The fundamental explanation for the FMLN failure, first on the battlefield and then at the ballot box, lies in the inability (and unwillingness) of its leaders to imitate the Cuban and Nicaraguan models by forging a broad coalition behind a program of democratic revolution, thereby isolating the regime and avoiding or negating American intervention.

Let us cut through the clouds of romanticization and propaganda and recall the actual circumstances in which the Castro brothers came to power in 1959. The widely disseminated myth of a massive peasant uprising that destroyed an American-equipped army is a perfect example of what Chalmers Johnson meant by "getting the paradigm wrong." The truth is that the coming to power of the Castros was the result of a collapse, not of a revolution, and certainly not a peasant revolution under the banner of Marxism. Fulgencio Batista (who had first been elected president of Cuba back in 1940 with Communist support) established a dictatorship in 1952 that became increasingly repressive, corrupt, personalistic, and thus narrowly based. That extortionist regime alienated decisive elements of the population, including businessmen and church leaders. Like the regime, the army was corrupt and confused.[39] Campaigning in the Sierra Maestra at the head of a few hundred guerrillas, Fidel Castro told the Cubans (and the *New York Times*) that he would restore the constitution of 1940, and perhaps at the time he meant it. Thus the building blocks were available for a broad coalition under a middle-class revolutionary banner that promised the swift return of electoral democracy, *not* the imposition of a Leninist dictatorship. (With some important changes in detail, much of this description would apply to the Somoza regime toppled by the Sandinistas in July 1979.)

To forge in El Salvador an interclass coalition along the lines of the Fidelistas and the Sandinistas was essential because the core of the FMLN was not extensive. Very nearly all revolutions in Latin America since World War II, successful or not, have been organized by elements of the urban middle class, with university personnel being especially prominent. "With some notable exceptions, the literature that emphasizes the role of peasants in revolution tends to ignore the role of professional revolutionary organizations, groups that tend to be disproportionately middle class in social composition." This has been true in the Castro, Sandinista, and Sendero Luminoso conflicts, and for El Salvador as well. The hard core of the FMLN—middle class, university associated—never had much organized support in urban areas to begin with. By the late 1980s the terrorist activities of some FMLN elements (kidnappings, assassinations, forcible recruitment, laying mines near populated areas, bombing cafés) had alienated large elements of the war-weary population.[40]

Resistance to Revolution

On the other side, the Salvadoran upper and upper-middle classes were nearly unanimous in their backing for the army. That unity was rooted in the defeat of the peasant-based Communist uprising of 1932, which had solidified "the strongest anticommunist sentiment in Latin America."[41] Besides that, the fate of the Cuban middle class under Castro was a grim lesson duly noted throughout Latin

America. Conservative forces, moreover, were able to attract or purchase considerable support among workers and peasants: thus the
rightist ARENA Party won the internationally supervised presidential elections in both 1989 and 1994 and obtained 44 percent of the
vote in the 1991 Legislative Assembly elections.

And certainly not least, no stretch of imagination could make
President Duarte into either a Batista or a Somoza. The El Salvador
of 1989, in which for the second time in a row a freely elected civilian leader of the opposition was inaugurated as president, was clearly
not the El Salvador of 1979, to say nothing of the Cuba of 1959. During Duarte's administration international support had increased for
the government and decreased for the guerrillas.

Thus, the grim solidarity of the upper strata and their dependents, the open authoritarianism (at least) of the FMLN, and the
increasing democratization under Duarte prevented El Salvador from
following the scenario of Cuba and Nicaragua, in which isolated
regimes with many enemies and few supporters eventually collapsed. In contrast, the struggle in El Salvador was a civil war, with
the FMLN facing a broad interclass phalanx of enemies whom it
could not divide and thus failed to defeat.[42]

Because the FMLN could not mobilize a sufficient mass in Salvadoran society, it had no alternative to taking power by force. But
American aid and tutelage was increasing the size and competence
of the Salvadoran Army to the point where the prospects for rebel
military victory became ever dimmer. Simultaneously, help for the
FMLN from foreign states began to diminish. It is no denigration of
the personal bravery of many of the FMLN guerrillas to recognize
that both materially and psychologically they were dependent on
outside assistance. But as the Cold War entered its final phase, the
Soviets rapidly lost interest in the Salvadoran contest; there was of
course no way to involve China in the struggle; and the unexpected
electoral debacle of the neighboring Sandinista regime in February
1990 gave the coup de grace to whatever vision of military victory
the guerrillas may have still entertained. Thus, the course of the Salvadoran insurgency was intimately sensitive to developments in the
international environment.[43]

And not incidentally, if the analysis presented here is generally valid, then U.S. efforts in El Salvador were worthwhile because they protected that country from the bloody imposition of

an economically devastating police state on the Cuban and East European models.

In summary, El Salvador's government, legitimating itself and undermining its enemies through democratic elections, retained the support of most of the country's middle classes, along with substantial segments of the peasantry and the town workers, and also of the U.S. government. In these ways the Salvadoran case contrasts fundamentally and decisively with the Cuban and Nicaraguan experiences. From the point of view of the United States, instead of "another Vietnam," El Salvador was more like a return to the Greek model. That is, the United States provided economic aid and military equipment to the Salvadoran government, along with a limited number of military advisers to tone up the local armed forces, providing time for its ally to deal with its more egregious shortcomings. Again, in El Salvador as in Greece, the insurgents had already clearly failed even before they lost their sanctuary, Yugoslavia in the one case and Nicaragua in the other (see chapter 5).

Like the American campaign against Aguinaldo, the conflict in El Salvador deserves a great deal more close and dispassionate scrutiny than it is likely to receive.[44]

Afghanistan, 1980.

9

Afghanistan

Cracking the Red Empire

To describe the guerrilla insurgency in Afghanistan during the 1980s requires a whole string of superlatives. The revolt of the Afghan people against Soviet occupation was "the largest single national rising in the twentieth century."[1] It was the longest military struggle the Soviets ever experienced; their direct involvement in the war extended from December 1979 to mid-1988. In the course of that war, Soviet troops reached Qandahar, the southernmost expansion of Russian power since the days of Peter the Great. The Soviets pursued one of the most destructive counterinsurgency policies ever seen, and also one of the most unsuccessful. The war inflicted the clearest reversal on Soviet military power since the fall of Berlin. It provided the stage for the biggest clandestine CIA operation in history. It was perhaps the most satisfying experience the Americans ever had with guerrilla warfare. The Afghan insurgents received assistance from a most diverse coalition of states. All of this, along with the proclamation of the Carter Doctrine, helped set in motion forces that would soon exert the profoundest effects on the entire global situation.

The Far Country

Arnold Toynbee called Afghanistan, situated at the intersection of the Middle East and East Asia, one of the two great crossroads of cultural dispersion before the Renaissance. The country is approximately equal in size to France, Belgium, the Netherlands, and Switzerland combined, or to Illinois, Indiana, Michigan, Ohio, and

Wisconsin combined. Afghanistan is five times the size of Greece or British Malaya, and thirty-one times the size of El Salvador. During the nineteenth century, Afghanistan served as a buffer between the czarist and the British empires. The modern world burst in upon the country with the First Afghan War, 1839–1842.[2] The British found it much easier to overrun Afghanistan than to control it; they would not be the last to make this distressing discovery. The war ended with the annihilation of the British garrison at Kabul, the greatest British defeat in modern history up to the fall of Singapore. After World War II the British left India, and the Americans were far away and uninterested. Hence, there was no longer any counterweight to Soviet pressure.

Of the preinvasion population of about 16 million, 600,000 lived in Kabul, the capital and only really large city. The population displays much ethnic and linguistic diversity; in terms of numbers and geographical position, the most important ethnic component is the Pushtuns. The population was overwhelmingly rural, large landholdings were rare, the literacy rate was 10 percent, and nine out of ten Afghans adhered to Sunni Islam.[3]

The Communist Regime

On July 17, 1973, after a bloodless coup in Kabul against King Zahir, former prime minister Mohammed Daoud proclaimed himself president. Full of grandiose ideas about economic development, Daoud asked the Americans for aid, which they refused. He then approached the more receptive USSR. But Daoud soon turned against the Soviets, and in April 1978 leftist army officers murdered him along with all the members of his family. Afterward, the Afghan Communists called this coup by a handful of army officers the Great Saur [April] Revolution. The installation of a Communist cabinet followed the coup; exactly how or why is not clear. Direct Soviet participation in the Saur coup seems to have been minimal.[4]

The Communist party—the PDPA, the People's Democratic Party of Afghanistan—had existed only since January 1965. Its founders were all from the country's social elite; there were no worker or peasant activists, and in the 1969 parliamentary elections (in which women voted, not for the first time) the PDPA won only two seats out of more than two hundred. Yet this minuscule party contained two irreconcilable factions: the Khalq (the masses) and Parcham (banner). In general, Parchamis were relatively sophisticated Kabulis; the Khalqis were provincial, Pushtun, and military.[5] The regime turned against the Parcham faction, with the result that young and inexperienced Khalqis found themselves in high positions in which they soon made a disaster of government programs. The noncommunist intelligentsia and the religious leadership also became a target of the regime, which admitted killing twelve thousand political prisoners in 1978–1979.

Social progress at full speed became the watchword. Women must become literate: police and young PDPA activists therefore dragged village women from their homes and forced them to sit in classes and hear attacks on their religion. Islamic religious teachers (mullahs) who opposed this practice were shot out of hand, without trial. With 320,000 mullahs in the country, the regime's attitude was decidedly ill advised. Afghans came to view the policies of the Kabul clique as "repulsively anti-Islamic." The regime also believed in land redistribution, a prelude to collectivization. In the villages land was taken from "rich landlords" and handed over to "poor peasants" on the Leninist model. Such actions cut tenant farmers off from the age-old village social security system provided by patronage from larger landholders and also offended traditional Islamic concepts of legality.[6]

Launching headlong attacks on the whole Afghan way of life, treating all who resisted such attacks (which eventually included the large majority of Afghans) as enemies to be crushed, the PDPA approach suggests not naive sympathy but profound hostility toward the common people. The PDPA intended to impose not liberation but modernization, whatever the cost, however destructive: a true Central Asian Stalinism. "It was the attempt by a minority regime to drastically alter the existing Afghan value system and social structure, and the brutality associated with this attempt, that finally provoked large-scale resistance." This tiny PDPA minority, urban-oriented, foreign-educated, religion-hating, peasant-despising, teacher-killing (reminiscent of the Greek Communists) kindled the wrath of the people against it. In March 1979, nearly a year before the Soviet invasion, furious crowds killed hundreds of Afghan Communists and scores of Soviet personnel in the streets of Herat. The regime restored control in the city at the cost of perhaps five thousand civilian deaths. By the eve of the Soviet invasion, as many as twenty-three out of twenty-eight Afghan provinces were under guerrilla control.[7]

The Invasion

Signs that the Kremlin had decided it might be necessary to invade Afghanistan were visible as early as the spring of 1979. Among those signs were visits to Kabul by high-ranking Soviet officers, including Gen. Ivan Pavlovskii, commander of the invasion of Czechoslovakia in 1968. The invasion of Afghanistan was in fact modeled on the Czechoslovakian scenario: subversion of an unreliable Communist regime and its replacement, after Soviet troops had taken control of the capital city in a lightning move, by pliant stooges.

In preparation for the coming invasion, Soviet advisers began removing the batteries from Afghan army tanks during the last weeks of December for "winterization" and gathering up antitank ammunition for "inventory." Afghan army officers invited to a Soviet reception got drunk and found themselves locked up. On December 24 flight after flight of Soviet airborne troops began to descend upon Kabul, seizing key positions and buildings. Simultaneously, ground troops poured across the border, heading for Kabul and Herat. On December 27 special Soviet units attacked the palace where President Hafizullah Amin was living. They sustained many casualties in the fierce fight during which they killed Amin and members of his family.[8] Moscow brazenly told the world that the Afghan government had requested Soviet aid. A request for assistance—that is, for invasion—was in fact made, but by Babrak Karmal, an Afghan puppet of Moscow, from a radio station inside the Soviet border, after twenty thousand Soviet troops had already crossed the frontier.[9] In return for his services, the Soviets installed Babrak as president. They also proclaimed that Amin had all along been a CIA agent.[10]

A masterpiece of its kind, the takeover had been better planned and executed than even the Czech invasion; practice makes perfect. Amin might have organized resistance around Kabul, called for a popular rising, or requested foreign assistance. "But Amin could do [none of these things] because the first move of the Soviet invasion was an airborne coup de main which suppressed any attempt at resistance."[11] The timing seemed good, too: the Carter administration was reeling from both foreign and domestic setbacks, the American polity was still punch-drunk from Vietnam and Watergate and distracted by the upcoming presidential election and the Iranian hostage crisis. But the invasion, technically a success, did not work out as intended. Instead of quenching popular resistance to the Communist regime in Kabul, it inflamed it. Seizing Kabul was the easy part; enforcing the authority of a Russian puppet regime over the rest of the country would prove a greater challenge. Indeed, the Soviets would soon embark upon what can only be described as a textbook case of how not to wage war against guerrillas.

Why the Soviets Invaded

At the time many observers expressed the belief that the main reason for the Soviet invasion of Afghanistan was to prevent the overthrow of a Communist regime; that is, to enforce the Brezhnev Doctrine. But that explanation is problematical. From an ideological standpoint, the Afghanistan that the Soviets invaded in 1979 was not a Communist or even a socialist state, but merely a state ruled by persons calling themselves Communists. Moreover, there are other, much more historically rooted, explanations. Afghanistan's geography, notably its thousand-mile border with the USSR, made it inescapably interesting to its northern neighbor. Czarist Russia had long cherished ambitions to move toward the shores of the Indian Ocean. Leon Trotsky said in 1919 that "the road to Paris and London lies through the towns of Afghanistan, the Punjab, and Bengal." (Trotsky was of course wrong about this, as about so many other things—dead wrong, so to speak—but that is irrelevant: he and other Communist leaders probably believed it.) The infamous Hitler-Stalin Pact of 1939 identified the future area of Soviet territorial expansion as being "south of the Soviet Union in the direction of the Indian Ocean" and "in the general direction of the Persian Gulf."[12]

After World War II Stalin displayed little interest in what came to be called the Third World, occupied as he was with digesting and imposing socialism on his new subjects in Eastern Europe. But when Khrushchev emerged as supreme leader by 1957 at the latest, he displayed a neo-Trotskyite interest in the underdeveloped world as the weak link in the defenses against Soviet expansionism. Accordingly, he paid a lot of attention to neighboring Afghanistan. There was much ethnic overlap between Soviet Central Asia and Afghanistan's northern, Soviet-contiguous provinces, which also contain most of its natural resources. Impressive mountain chains divide these northern provinces from the rest of the country, and for decades there had been sentiment in favor of at least regional autonomy in the area.[13] In addition, a pro-Soviet Afghanistan would have made a perfect base from which to propagate the independence of "Baluchistan" and "Pushtunistan." The success of this maneuver would achieve the dismemberment of Pakistan, ally of the United States and China, and the establishment of a group of Soviet protectorates stretching all the way from the USSR border to the Arabian Sea.

Under Khrushchev, therefore, the Soviets gave Afghanistan loans, delivered MiG-15 fighters, and built three air bases in the country. Many Afghan army and air force officers and cadets went to the Soviet Union for training.[14] Most of the officers who had been exposed to the Soviet Union came back to Afghanistan profoundly impressed with the military might of their northern neighbor. The king, suspicious of these returnees, would not let them rise to the highest ranks; here was one of the roots that destroyed the monarchy and eventually brought the country to its subsequent catastrophe. Another was that the educational reforms of the 1950s began to produce an element in the population cut off from both the traditional power wielders and the conservative masses. Embarrassed by their country's position in the world and their own position within their country, these new would-be elites looked to the Soviet Union for inspiration.

Thus, quite aside from the Brezhnev Doctrine, "the invasion appears as the logical culmination of decades of Soviet [and czarist] policies aimed at achieving ever-greater control of Afghanistan." Concerns for stability along the southern border also figured prominently in the Kremlin decision to invade. If the Soviets had not invaded in 1979 and the friendly regime in Kabul had been replaced by a militantly anticommunist and Islamic one, the effects on the millions of Muslims living in Soviet Central Asia could have been cataclysmic. Lastly, the context in which the invasion took place was one of increasingly bold international behavior on the USSR's part. Article 28 of the Brezhnev constitution of 1976 proclaimed, "The foreign policy of the USSR shall aim at . . . supporting the struggle of peoples for national liberation." Soviet submarines were making repeated incursions into Swedish waters, Soviet aircraft wantonly downed a Korean airliner in 1983, and so on. The invasion of Afghanistan merely underlined in red that the world was "confronted by clear evidence of an utterly novel boldness on the part of the Soviet military leaders, and of an equally new confidence on the part of the Kremlin in the professional competence of their military colleagues."[15]

A People in Arms

Armed risings occurred in several provinces shortly after the Saur coup. These were revolts against government policies, not necessarily intended to precipitate or end in the fall of the government itself; armed resistance to unpopular Kabul actions was a venerable exercise. But the PDPA in Kabul responded with such violence that it drove the resisters to real civil war.[16] Then came the Soviet invasion, the first true foreign occupation of Afghanistan in modern times. Now opposition to government policies would be overshadowed by the explosive, elemental power of outraged religion.

Truly tremendous odds confronted the Afghan freedom fighters (as President Reagan called them), including the enormous disparity in size, wealth, population, and technological capacity between Afghanistan and the Soviet Union; the proximity of the invading power; the geographical and political isolation of Afghanistan; a widespread tendency in world capitals to write the country off as being "within the Soviet sphere of influence"; and internal disunity—approaching fragmentation—within the insurgent ranks. As one keen observer put it, "the Afghan Resistance is not an army but rather a people in arms; its strengths and weaknesses are those of Afghan society."[17]

Local leadership had traditionally been independent of national or even provincial control; in this conflict the first loyalty of the guerrilla was usually to his commander, often a tribal or provincial figure of importance. The localism, individualism, and readiness to defend one's honor so characteristic of the Afghan people made them excellent prospects for guerrilla war; but these admirable traits worked against them as well because individualism and localism hindered resistance unity. Indeed, within the insurgency were many potentially explosive rivalries: among the various religious, regional, and tribal groups inside Afghanistan; among the exiled party politicians in Pakistan; between those politicians and the guerrilla commanders inside Afghanistan; and among the guerrilla commanders themselves. Ethnic divisions made it possible for the Kabul regime here and there to recruit local militias, composed of tribes or clans different from those in the area that supported the resistance. "The majority of them [members of these militias] are simply mercenaries attracted by the substantial pay (about £30 per month)"; "throughout the war, the militia's willingness to take Communist money has far exceeded their willingness to fight."[18]

Entering Afghanistan in 1980, Gerard Chaliand noted that the resistance was vastly popular but politically weak. Unlike many other post–World War II guerrilla movements, the Afghan resistance was overwhelmingly conservative in its political orientation (resembling the Spanish guerrillas that fought Napoleon's occupation). But the old precoup establishment—especially army officers and professional politicians—was largely absent from the leadership of the resistance. The pre-Saur political structure seemed completely shattered. In its place was rising a new leadership group, including many non-Pushtun elements. But the lack of unity (and worse) within this group presented an unattractive picture to the outside world. The resistance movement divided into many different parties, each with its headquarters in Pakistan, which funneled supplies to particular guerrilla bands associated with them inside Afghanistan. They also sought to represent the resistance to the outside world. Lacking central coordination, the insurgents never developed an overall strategy. Thus the Soviets could operate against one group at a time.[19]

Disarray inside the resistance ranks lessened to some degree after 1984. Significant moves toward at least formal unity among most of the groups resulted in a unified delegation being sent to the Fortieth Anniversary celebration at the United Nations. In January 1987 leaders of the resistance parties in Peshawar proclaimed a united program consisting mainly of two points: (1) the Soviets must withdraw completely from Afghanistan and (2) the resistance mujahideen (meaning "warriors of God") would govern the country until free nationwide elections were held. Early in 1988 resistance leaders established a provisional government that included the heads of the principal parties.[20]

The mujahideen lacked weapons as well as unity. For years they were poorly equipped, much more so than their contemporaries in

El Salvador or Angola. Most guerrilla units captured their guns from Soviet and Kabul forces. Defectors from the Kabul army and from ostensibly pro-Kabul local militias were another source of weapons and ammunition. Foreign arms shipments did not assume any importance until well after the Soviet invasion.[21] Pakistan, Egypt, Saudi Arabia, China, and Kuwait sent arms; particular types of modern weapons supplied by the United States became especially crucial in the mid-1980s.

At first everything seemed stacked against the resistance. The dominant theory of guerrilla warfare holds that as the fish move in the water, so the guerrillas move among the civilian population, receiving life-giving sustenance and life-saving intelligence from it. But by 1984, because of the dreadful depredations of the Soviet invaders and their murderous marionettes in Kabul, the impoverished civilians in many areas were not able to provide the guerrillas with food, so that the freedom fighters had to carry their own. In fact, the guerrillas themselves often had to provide food for starving villagers.[22]

Both the KGB and KhAD, Kabul's East German–trained intelligence/secret police, penetrated the various resistance groups inside Afghanistan, in Pakistan, and in Europe. That some KGB agents were from Soviet Central Asia facilitated the infiltration. This is one area where the fragmentation within the resistance did not have entirely negative consequences, because it limited what the KGB and KhAD could discover. KhAD operated with some effect in the refugee camps in Pakistan, spreading rumors and dissension and occasionally killing a resistance leader. These two intelligence agencies also took Afghan children to the Soviet Union, where they were trained in the use of explosives and sabotage and then sent back to infiltrate resistance units.[23]

Assets of the Resistance

But of course the resistance picture was not all bleak, or the war would have soon ended with a Soviet victory. The fragmented nature of Afghan society made resistance unity impossible, especially since no truly charismatic leader appeared who could transcend the tribal, regional, and religious differences among the freedom fighters. But it also deprived the Soviets of a target against which to launch a major decisive attack. The resistance was amorphous and there-

fore almost impossible to destroy. Recall that it was a loosely organized, multilingual Afghan commonwealth that inflicted a humiliating defeat upon the mighty British Empire in the First Afghan War.
The years of combat against the Soviets also helped forge at least to
some degree a new sense of Afghan nationality.[24]

Covered with rugged mountains, Afghanistan is well suited to
guerrilla warfare. Most of the mujahideen came equipped with strong
bodies and stoic souls, the products of many centuries of spartan
living. The resistance also had the truly priceless asset of a sanctuary in Pakistan. That country served not only as a place where guerrillas could leave their families in relative safety but also as an
irreplaceable conduit for outside assistance. But above all, the fundament and strength of the resistance was Islam. Western analysts
are often uncomfortable with the subject of religion and tend to ignore the essential place of Islam in the resistance movement. From
the first days of the Soviet invasion, however, the guerrillas were
fighting not only for national (or more accurately, provincial) freedom, most especially they were fighting for the true religion. The
one weapon that the resistance never lacked, therefore, that most
important weapon for any army, was high morale; after all, as the
freedom fighters would ask, If God is with us, who shall prevail
against us?[25]

Exactly how many guerrillas were active at any one time cannot
be known. Estimates vary from 80,000 to 150,000, with the latter figure probably too high. Arrayed against the insurgents by 1985 were
115,000 Soviet troops, along with 30,000 regular Afghan army troops
(down from a preinvasion force of 100,000), and perhaps 50,000 in
other Kabul units. The Communist forces controlled the cities and
large towns, and the resistance controlled the countryside.

The mujahideen supply effort often consisted of men carrying
backpacks over little-known but dangerous trails. Medical care was
almost totally lacking. The mujahideen were most active at night,
attacking small fortified posts, blowing up bridges, launching rocket
attacks. "Sniper fire from the insurgents was a particular headache
for the Soviets."[26] They also relied heavily on the classic guerrilla
tactics of mining roads and ambushing convoys. The paucity of good
roads magnified the effects of those tactics, so that the tasks of sending supplies to and maintaining communications between regime-
held urban centers became especially difficult and dangerous. Here

and there the mujahideen would literally isolate a city or fortress, requiring the Soviets to supply the place by aircraft, sometimes for years. And assassinations of government figures, notorious collaborators, and even Soviet officials, increased yearly.

In the early years, Soviet and Kabul forces emerged from the cities to carry out large "sweeps" of the surrounding guerrilla-infested territory. The usual response of the mujahideen to these major efforts was simply to fade into the hills. Villagers would also disappear, abandoning their homes and their scanty possessions. The troops would arrive in a designated area and find no one to kill, little to loot, and nothing to eat. Unable to live off the land, they would have to bring in supplies by truck convoy—always very risky—or retreat to their strongholds. When the troops went away, the villagers would return. This was the general pattern of repeated Soviet-Kabul campaigns in the strategic Panjshir Valley. Sometimes, however, the insurgents would not retreat in the face of enemy forces. The typical attack would place Kabul troops in the lead, with Soviet soldiers behind them. The mujahideen knowledge of the terrain allowed them to set up ambushes in places through which they knew the enemy troops would be channeled. Usually the insurgents would let the Kabul forces pass and then concentrate fire on the Russians. In the meantime, many of the Kabul soldiers would have run away or defected to the mujahideen. Sometimes a freedom fighter would strap a homemade gasoline bomb to his body and leap onto a Russian tank.[27] Neither side took many prisoners.

The resistance did not have a strategy for the defeat of the Soviets, whose superior firepower and discipline made that impossible. Instead, the insurgents sought to make the war so expensive for the invaders that they would eventually negotiate or just get out altogether. The objective of the resistance was stalemate, and it achieved that before the end of 1985.

None of this would have been possible except for the truly incredible incompetence and self-destructive tendencies of the regime in Kabul.

The PDPA Regime

The leaders and activists of the PDPA were urban or urban-oriented, and they admired all aspects of Soviet society, as they imagined it.

Consequently, they seethed with impatient and embarrassed contempt for traditional Afghanistan. In no area did these characteristics show so clearly, or with such disastrous consequences, as in regime policies toward the peasantry, the overwhelming majority of the population. No doubt many small farmers and landless peasants were quite poor and could have benefited from land reform, a principal PDPA program. But many country people were reluctant to participate in land reform activities that seemed unnecessarily punitive, confiscatory, and repugnant to local custom and Islamic law. PDPA activists sent to stir up class feelings in the rural areas made the peasants march in formation through the streets of their villages, shouting strange slogans and denouncing unknown enemies ("American imperialists"). Rural people considered such behavior to be immodest and demeaning. Apparently no opportunity was lost to annoy, offend, or shock the peasants: PDPA activists even forbade dancing at weddings and set very low maximums for how much food could be served at these celebrations. All this deeply affronted concepts of propriety and hospitality among the peasantry.

Now, a proper Marxist-Leninist revolution of course requires a proletariat. Because such a class was hardly visible in Afghanistan, PDPA activists decided to create a "Proletariat of Women," who presumably would be glad to support radical social change. As anybody but PDPA zealots could have predicted, village women were not interested in fulfilling the role of historic substitute for the Petrograd proletariat; besides that, the government made few efforts to follow up on this idea (it faced more explosive problems). The whole project collapsed, but not before additional strata of the Afghan rural population had been further alienated. And things were not much better in Kabul itself. Many reports described government or party agents entering a private house on the pretext of searching for rebels and weapons and then simply looting the place. Even before the Soviet invasion, Afghan civil society had begun to crumble, and the process accelerated over the years. Early in the occupation, many members of the Afghan elite either defected to the resistance or escaped to foreign countries: diplomats, athletes, airline crews, almost everybody who was in a position to get out of the country. The educational system suffered mortal wounds. The PDPA put intense pressure on schoolteachers to join the party; those who refused lost their jobs, often their freedom, and sometimes their lives. Higher education was totally disrupted: almost the entire preinvasion faculty of Kabul University had been purged or had fled by the end of 1981. Their posts were filled by Russians or by unqualified PDPA members. By 1985 perhaps 50 to 75 percent of the preinvasion university faculties had been thrown into prison, driven into exile, or killed.[28]

Aware that it was attracting few supporters, the PDPA resorted to the time-tested Leninist expedient of the front organization. The National Fatherland Front was supposed to provide an umbrella group for people who would not join the PDPA but might be induced to support the government because they disliked the resistance. Like all the other PDPA programs, the Front came to nothing.

Yet within the PDPA, hostility between Parcham and Khalq continued and even intensified, in spite of the fact that the party-regime was fighting for its very survival. After the overthrow and murder of Amin, President Babrak Karmal freed his fellow Parchamis from prison; they immediately turned on their Khalqi persecutors, humiliating and even killing many.

The fissure within the party was taking on aspects of a traditional Afghan blood feud. It nevertheless reflected some serious policy differences. The Parcham side was totally pro-Soviet and favored "softening" the PDPA revolutionary program in order to attract more support or at least calm some of its opponents. The Khalqis, however, grew ever more bitter and intransigent toward the resistance, indeed toward the whole population; they wanted a total, immediate revolutionary assault on the entire fabric of Afghan society. Correctly perceiving the Kremlin as being in favor of "softening," many Khalqis displayed increasing suspicion and hostility toward their Russian mentors.

For their part, the Soviets despaired of finding real support for Communism in a country like Afghanistan; accordingly, they sent ten thousand Afghan children to the Soviet Union to mold them into the nucleus of a new Communist society. In November 1984 alone, nearly nine hundred Afghan children under ten years old were sent to the USSR for ten years of schooling.[29]

But the most dreadful result of the PDPA's war against Afghan civil society and the Soviet invasion and subsequent campaign to destroy the resistance was depopulation. Out of a preinvasion population of 16 million, more than 1 million civilians lost their lives; additional millions fled across provincial or national borders, so that whole areas of the country became uninhabited. These disasters, this massive killing and destruction, did not trouble PDPA activists; on the contrary, one official stated that even if in the end only a million Afghans were left alive, that number would be sufficient to build the new socialist society.[30]

The PDPA Army

While the actual Soviet invasion was occurring, most Afghan troops allowed themselves to be disarmed by Russian advisers and soldiers. There were exceptions: the Afghan Eighth Division put up very stiff resistance and suffered heavy casualties. Predictably, the subsequent military performance of regime troops was so miserable that the Soviets found themselves, to their dismay, assuming an ever-greater share of the fighting. Contributing to the poor performance of the puppet army was the condition of the officer corps. Almost all the postinvasion officers were new men. What had become of the eight thousand officers of the pre-1978 army? The PDPA regime had killed great numbers of experienced officers because they were not Communists or because they belonged to the wrong PDPA faction. (As late as September 1982, General Wodud, commander of the Central Corps, was found shot dead in his office.) Many of the rest had gone into exile, accepted jobs in other government agencies, or joined the resistance.[31] Political interference with promotions and assignments also weakened and demoralized the officer corps. Of the officers who belonged to the PDPA, most were Khalqis; the Babrak Karmal regime, as well as the Russians, distrusted them and therefore took care to give them less critical assignments.

As the war raged on, the training period for officers was cut from three years to two. Some officers who deserted to the resistance claimed that they had had only three months of training. The conditions among enlisted men were comparably bad. In addition to poor preparation and humiliating subservience to the Russians, the Kabul troops were often improperly used. For example, the 444th Commando Brigade was perhaps the best of the regime units; parachuted into the Panjshir Valley in the summer of 1985, in one of the many efforts to sweep the area, it was decimated.[32]

But the Kabul army was being destroyed most of all by the unwillingness of its members to serve. Most of those who deserted just went home, but significant numbers wound up with the resistance, often bringing their invaluable weapons with them. Of the eighty thousand men in the Afghan army on the eve of the invasion, over half either deserted or defected to the resistance.[33] Even before the Soviet occupation, the unreliability of the Kabul forces had assumed alarming proportions. In May 1979, for example, on the road between Gardez and Khost, the motorized brigade of the Afghan Seventh Division—the entire unit, two thousand officers and men, with armored vehicles, heavy weapons, everything—surrendered to the guerrillas without a fight. Mutinies, including the killing of officers, were common. During most of the war, regime troops outside the defense perimeter of the capital city were completely unreliable.

Consequently, Soviet officers planned most of the Kabul forces' operations. The Soviets suspected, with reason, that officers even of the highest ranks of the Kabul army were collaborating with the insurgents; so they forced any Afghan, even a general officer, who entered the precincts of the Ministry of Defense to submit to a personal search. Rightly fearing infiltration of the Kabul army by mujahideen, Soviet commanders never informed their Afghan allies of operations until the very last moment. They eventually deprived their allies of what tanks and heavy weapons the resistance had not destroyed, for fear that those also would eventually fall into insurgent hands. So great became the Russian distrust for the Kabul forces that the latter were not allowed to have on hand at any one time more than a week's supply of materiel. Conditions eventually sank to such depths that Kabul soldiers were required to turn in their weapons when not fighting. The Russians tried to increase the reliability of the Afghan army by training officers in the Soviet Union, but many of them also deserted or defected.[34] Resistance fighters naturally targeted Kabul officers, so that they became even more reluctant to lead their men into combat.

The PDPA regime tried desperately to induce men to join its forces and not to desert or defect. It sent conscripts to duty away from their home areas. The minefields that surrounded regime garrisons and forts served both to keep the mujahideen out and the troops in. Another method was accelerated promotion: one defecting officer told the mujahideen that of four hundred men in his unit, no less than twenty were brigadier generals. The salaries of officers were much higher than for comparable civilian jobs, and young men who joined the Kabul paramilitary forces were paid more than what a deputy minister received before the 1978 coup. Any tenth grader who volunteered for the army would receive a twelfth-grade diploma after completion of his military service. Any eleventh grader who volunteered would be guaranteed admission to any institution of higher education without having to take entrance examinations. All these inducements proved inadequate. Hence, in 1984 the draft age was lowered to sixteen, and eventually the government declared all males between fourteen and fifty liable to conscription (PDPA members were exempt). These moves, plus an increase in conscripted service from three years to four, contributed to mutinies and defections even in the Kabul area.[35] When the mujahideen captured young regime conscripts, they usually either paroled them to their homes or incorporated them into the ranks of the resistance.

As 1987 dawned, the regime had about 30,000 regular troops, with 10,000 in the air force and perhaps another 40,000 in paramilitary units, secret police, and militia organizations. Relatively few new officers joined the PDPA, and some who did were acting on the request of the resistance to infiltrate the party. And in the midst of these dangers and calamities, violence between the Khalq and Parcham factions raged without letup.[36]

The Background of the Soviet Strategy

The Afghanistan invasion was of course not the first time Russian troops faced Muslim guerrillas in mountainous terrain. During their conquest of the Caucasus, from 1820 to 1860, the Russians developed their basic strategy for dealing with situations of this type. That strategy included the following components: (1) isolate the insurgent region, (2) destroy the insurgent leadership, and (3) devastate the local economy so that it cannot sustain the guerrillas. To these ends, the Russians advanced slowly into the Caucasus, building roads and bridges as they went, constructing lines of forts, laying waste to settlements, driving off and killing cattle, and—most important of all—bringing in enough troops to make these activities effective. Even so, from time to time forts in the Russian line would be overrun with heavy losses; for example, in 1845, near Dargo, insurgents killed or captured four thousand Russian soldiers, including three generals. The Russians were able to take advantage of internal cleavages among their opponents: in later phases of the Caucasus conflict, Christian populations in Georgia and Armenia supported the Russians against the Muslim guerrillas. The resistance received encouragement and sometimes weapons from the Turks and the British.[37]

The inhabitants of Russia's Central Asian provinces (the ones bordering or close to Afghanistan) were considered so politically unreliable that the czarist army would normally not accept recruits from those areas. But the huge losses suffered by the Russian Army in World War I led to the imposition of the draft in Central Asia, a move that provoked massive and persistent riots. During the 1920s and 1930s the Soviet regime faced a serious rising in the same territories, which it called the Basmachi Revolt, in essence an outright struggle between Leninism and Islam. Predictably, tribal rivalries weakened the Basmachi insurgents,[38] but their revolt lasted a long time, in part because the kingdom of Afghanistan allowed them to cross the border at will. Soviet troops also crossed into Afghanistan several times. The Kremlin never resolved these deep-rooted conflicts, and during World War II the Germans found many willing recruits among the ranks of captured soldiers from Soviet Asia.

When the Afghanistan war broke out, most of the USSR's Central Asian subjects had inferior educations and were found in the lower ranks of the Soviet Army and in the less technical and non-combat branches of the service. Consequently, many ethnic Russians came to believe that an unfairly large share of the blood cost of the war in Afghanistan was being borne by young Russians. But some evidence suggests that the Kremlin wished to preserve its Russian units and therefore sent to Afghanistan troops drawn disproportionately from other ethnic groups.[39]

The Soviet War

Considered in itself, the Soviet invasion of Afghanistan was a great success, a model operation. Yet, as the fighting developed, "the overall counterinsurgency capabilities of the average Soviet conscript [were] unimpressive."[40] And so they remained. It is not hard to account for this.

The Soviet Army had long enjoyed a formidable reputation as a fighting force. This was mainly due to its great size, but also to its achievements against Germany in World War II. But between the surrender of Nazi Germany in May 1945 and the invasion of Afghanistan in December 1979, the Soviet Army had had less real combat experience than the armies of Britain, China, Colombia, Egypt, France, India, Israel, Pakistan, Portugal, South Korea, Syria, Turkey, the United States, or Vietnam. Probably for that reason the Soviet Army sought to give as many of its officers as possible a "turn" at the Afghanistan fighting, a policy similar to that pursued by the U.S. Army in Vietnam, and probably with the same negative effects on the progress of the war. An "Afghan Brotherhood" grew inside the Soviet Army and might eventually have replaced the dominance of those who served in "the West" (World War II) with those who served in "the South" (Afghanistan).[41]

Not only had the Soviet Army been untested in extended combat for decades, much like the U.S. Army, it had been built to fight World War III, to fight NATO forces in Europe, not Central Asian mountaineers armed with antique rifles and homemade gasoline bombs (called, ironically, "Molotov cocktails"). True, in the 1940s and early 1950s elements of the Soviet Army had waged a fierce campaign to exterminate guerrillas in the Ukraine, but since that struggle was "secret," even a nonevent, there were no serious studies on the topic for wide use within the Soviet Army. Modern Soviet counterinsurgency doctrine was thus woefully underdeveloped.[42]

Another major factor affecting the Soviet performance was that the number of Soviet troops committed to the conflict was inadequate. The Soviets had expected that Kabul forces would do most of what fighting needed to be done. By January 1980 there were only about 50,000 Soviet troops in Afghanistan, many of them Central Asian reservists recently mobilized; the invasion of Czechoslovakia a decade earlier had been on a much larger scale. But the intensity of popular resistance, as well as the reluctance to fight and the tendency to desert shown by the Kabul troops, made it clear that the Soviets were going to have to carry a much bigger share of the fighting than originally planned. They were never able to do that effectively because Moscow never committed enough troops to Afghanistan. Five years after the initial invasion, the Soviets had 115,000 military personnel inside Afghanistan, raised to 120,000 by 1987. Fully 22,000 of those were needed just to hold down Kabul. The total number amounted to less than 4 percent of all Soviet ground forces; only perhaps 6 of 194 Soviet combat divisions were in Afghanistan on a full-time basis. Admittedly, over 50 percent of those forces were combat troops, a much higher ratio than the Americans ever reached in Vietnam. But after subtracting garrison security forces, the Soviets were left with only about one battalion in each province for offensive operations.[43] Even with their Kabul allies, the Soviets never remotely approached the ten-to-one ratio of government troops to insurgents that many students of guerrilla warfare have believed necessary for victory.

Soviet forces in Afghanistan lacked not only numbers and experience but also training. Many Soviet privates arrived in Afghanistan after having been trained for a mere month.[44] Even noncommissioned officers (NCOs) often knew little about tactics or leadership. The Soviet Army threw into mountain warfare youths who had never even seen a real mountain.

Serious morale problems plagued the Soviets almost from the beginning of the war and eventually reached crisis proportions. Those conscripts who were sent to Afghanistan were often ones who had been unable to pay the proper bribes to avoid such service. Brutality by older soldiers against younger ones, even against NCOs, was common and not infrequently resulted in death. Health services for the troops were substandard; alcoholism and drug abuse were common. Increased combat activity after 1982 meant increased casualties. Many of the soldiers had been told that they were in Afghanistan to save the people; what they encountered must have severely shaken them, accounting to a large degree for the increasing incidents of theft and sale of weapons to the resistance, in return for drugs, including heroin. Naturally, the Soviet Army reflected in many ways the larger society from which it was drawn: centralization, rigid discipline, and punishment for failure discouraged initiative among junior officers. All of these conditions combined constituted a very severe handicap in fighting guerrillas, where so much depends on small-unit action under vigorous officers.[45]

Strategy and Reality

All these insufficiencies, especially in numbers and training, dictated the strategy eventually adopted by the Soviets, a modified enclave strategy. In essence it had five elements: (1) hold Kabul and the other main cities with enough forces to prevent expulsion, (2) protect communications between those cities (Soviet supply lines were long: Kabul is well over 400 km from the Soviet border and Qandahar is 600 km from Herat; control of the roads was so tenuous that Soviet bases and even the garrisons in big towns had to be supplied mainly and sometimes exclusively by aircraft), (3) clear guerrillas out of the northern Afghan provinces in order to safeguard supply routes to Soviet forces in Kabul and to prevent any spillover of fighting from northern Afghanistan into the Muslim provinces of the USSR, (4) launch periodic sweeps to break up mujahideen concentrations or seize their strongholds, and (5) interdict infiltration from Pakistan and Iran. As the conflict dragged on and the frustration of the Soviets increased, they also sought to build up a Sovietized Afghan elite that would one day take over the war and run the country; in addition, they attempted to systematically destroy the economy of those provinces that were outside Soviet control.[46]

The mounting Soviet difficulties in Afghanistan need not have come as a total surprise. The USSR had been extending help to Third World regimes fighting against guerrillas for a long time. Almost everywhere—not only in Afghanistan but also in Angola, Cambodia, Ethiopia, and Mozambique—Soviet assistance had produced disappointing results. The unimpressive Soviet record of counterinsurgency in the Third World had several causes. First, and most obvious, was the absence of good counterinsurgency doctrine. Second, the Soviets were generally unsuccessful in denying the guerrillas outside assistance and sanctuaries. Third, they tried to get the army of the host regime to do most if not all of the real fighting; in itself this was a sound idea, but Soviet efforts to build up forces capable of carrying out such a responsibility were disappointing at best (Afghanistan merely being a most egregious case). Fourth, the Soviets, and the regimes they controlled or influenced, would not address the root causes of the local insurgency: disastrous government policies.[47] The Soviet method, the "socialist" prescription, for dealing with Third World societies (or any society in their grip) was centralized political control, a bureaucratized, collectivized economy (including agriculture), and brutal repression of any who dared protest. Of course such policies aggravated rather than alleviated the conditions that had produced the insurgency.

All of this helps explain how the Soviet Army performed so well in the invasion but not well at all in the long struggle to subdue the rebellious rural population.

Nevertheless, Soviet forces in Afghanistan learned. They eventually placed less emphasis on ineffective and dangerous big-sweep operations. They began to rediscover some classic counterinsurgency tactics, including airlifting small, well-trained detachments of Special Purpose Forces (Spetsnaz), of which perhaps five thousand were in Afghanistan in 1986. Still, at the end of the fighting, as at the beginning, most Soviet forces consisted of road-bound motorized rifle units. But at least they had begun placing at the head of convoys turretless tanks with mine-detecting rollers mounted on the front.[48]

A major innovation was the introduction of the helicopter gunship as the mainstay of the Soviet effort. In February 1980 and again in April, when antiregime and anti-Soviet riots gripped Kabul, the Soviets strafed the crowds with these heavy-gunned helicopters, killing hundreds. But it was against guerrillas, not civilian rioters, that the Soviets found the best use for these machines, and they turned out to be their most effective weapon. The Soviets had sixty helicopters in Afghanistan in mid-1980; by the end of 1981 they had more than three hundred. The helicopters provided the Russians with the kind of firepower normally obtainable only from tanks, but the helicopters could be used in the mountains, where tanks cannot operate. Gunships escorted convoys passing along especially vulnerable sections of mountain roads. But helicopters are relatively slow and can be easily hurt, especially their rotor blades, as the Americans had learned to their great cost in Vietnam. In January 1982 freedom fighters in Paktia Province were able to down a helicopter transporting a Soviet lieutenant general.[49] Nevertheless, until the resistance obtained heavy machine guns in 1983, there was little defense against the gunships. In 1986 the Russians introduced helicopters with armored bottoms that were almost totally immune to machine-gun fire.

But the days of nearly complete domination of the battlefield by Soviet helicopters were drawing to a close. In 1983, using surface-to-air missiles (SAMs), resistance fighters shot down several helicopters near Khost. The introduction of SAMs sent waves of panic throughout the Soviet establishment in Afghanistan. Nobody knew how many SAMs the freedom fighters had, but the knowledge that they had any at all forced helicopter pilots to fly higher than was effective. And in the latter half of 1986 the United States at last began providing the resistance with the excellent Stinger missile, which was lightweight and easy to use. This weapon obliterated the dominance of the helicopter gunship: "the Stinger missile . . . robbed the Soviet forces of their command of the air." Beginning in 1987, Soviet helicopter and fighter aircraft losses reached 1.2 to 1.4 a day, or 420 to 500 a year. Consequently, the Soviets sharply cut back their air operations. Indeed, "the [mujahideen's] acquisition of surface-to-air missiles was critical to their ability to counter . . . Soviet tactics. Since late 1986, when SAMs were used in significant numbers, the mujahideen were able to move without constant fear of helicopter attacks."[50]

Actually, the Soviets had already lost about one thousand aircraft before December 1986, when large numbers of Stingers first reached the battlefield. Thus, "it is important to stress that the Stinger alone scarcely forced the USSR to withdraw from Afghanistan. The sheer dedication and persistence of the Mujahideen did that."[51]

The Destruction of Afghan Society

When Western governments have found themselves trying to suppress an insurgency, they have typically tried to separate the guerrillas from the civilian population and win the goodwill of the latter. That was not the Soviet way. In Afghanistan they made some efforts at winning over the religious leaders by suggesting the compatibility of Leninism and Islam, by helping to repair mosques, and so forth. But the Soviets did not seek to "win the hearts and minds" of the peasantry; rather, their method was to drain the water in which the guerrillas swam: to destroy any civilian population friendly to, or even proximate to, the guerrillas.[52] The Soviets sought, by forced migration, to empty the provinces along both the Soviet and the Pakistan borders. But since virtually the whole country rose against the Soviets and their Kabul puppets, the policy of devastation was eventually unleashed against nearly every province.

The insufficiency of the Soviet and Kabul troop numbers, the low level of their training and morale, and the tenacity of the resistance led inexorably to the most appalling aspect of the entire war: the Soviet policy of depopulating the main resistance areas. The distinguished anthropologist Louis Dupree called this policy "migratory genocide." Helsinki Watch and other human rights organizations reported that the Soviets were waging a campaign of deliberate terror against the civilian population. They systematically bombed villages, attacked columns of refugees, killed or maimed animals, and chopped down orchards.[53] In October 1981, when the resistance captured a noted Soviet geologist and offered him in exchange for fifty Afghan hostages, the Soviets replied by killing all the hostages. A report issued by the United Nations in the autumn of 1982 suggested that the Soviets had used chemical weapons, and they apparently employed poison gas campaigning in the Panjshir Valley in the spring of 1984. They trained children to act as saboteurs and even assassins. Responsible observers have accused them of the deliberate and repeated bombing of hospitals.[54] Numerous witnesses have testified that Soviet aircraft often dropped explosive devices in the shape of toys and pens; "their main targets are children, whose hands and arms are blown off."[55]

During the first year of Soviet occupation, these policies turned 1.5 million Afghans into refugees. Within a few more years, over 4 million Afghan men, women, and children had become refugees; no one knows how many were killed. In 1985 perhaps one Afghan in three was an internal or external refugee. Soviet claims that this disaster, this "migratory genocide," resulted from the machinations of native reactionaries and CIA troublemakers were embarrassing in their pedestrian mendacity. The world, for the most part, including notably the Western media, pretended to be ignorant of this crime. But truth, an elementary respect for truth, forces one to recognize that the refugee status of so many people, inside Afghanistan, in Pakistan, and in Iran, was not an accidental or unavoidable consequence of war; it was an intended, engineered result, a "part of Soviet warfare strategy."[56]

The War Rages On

Risings against the PDPA regime had begun in October 1978, more than a year before the Soviet invasion. In March 1979 in Herat, the country's third-largest city, serious fighting took the lives of hundreds of Afghan Communists and Soviet personnel. Thousands of civilians were killed as the regime restored control.[57] By November 1979, a month before the invasion, insurgent forces dominated

Badakhshan Province (the link to China) and most of the Hazarajat, the center of the country. During 1980 strikes and demonstrations rocked Kabul. Because Afghan soldiers often refused to fire on student demonstrators, Soviet troops had to do much of the killing.

After their invasion, the Soviets pursued a very conservative strategy, limited mainly to holding key cities and the roads between them. Because of that policy and because they lacked confidence in the Kabul army, there were few sizable operations during the first year of Soviet occupation and for much of 1981. The road-bound, mountain-hating Soviet Army thus failed to take advantage of mujahideen disunity, lack of equipment, and inexperience with modern guerrilla techniques. More than half of the country was under insurgent control by the end of 1980.[58] In April 1981 mujahideen killed the deputy head of KhAD in Kabul. That same month and again in September insurgents briefly overran Qandahar, the country's second-largest city. By the end of 1981 every single Afghan province was experiencing some form of armed resistance.

Much more elaborate "pacification" efforts dominated 1982. The Panjshir Valley lies about sixty miles northeast of Kabul; resistance control of the valley threatened the capital, the vital Bagram Airbase, and road communication between Kabul and the Soviet Union. About 14,000 Soviet and Kabul troops attacked the 5,000 insurgents in the Panjshir, whose leader was Ahmed Shah Massoud. After campaigning hard for six weeks and suffering 3,000 casualties and 2,000 defections, the Soviet-Kabul forces withdrew. During the following year the insurgents extended their control to about two-thirds of the country's territory and three-quarters of its population. The Soviets again bombed Herat, killing thousands of civilians. The insurgents in turn carried out increasingly frequent and deadly attacks inside Kabul, hitting the Soviet Embassy and assassinating numerous Kabul regime officials and collaborators. As the fourth year of the Soviet occupation drew to a close, resistance casualties totaled between 50,000 and 100,000, Soviet and regime casualties between 50,000 and 60,000.[59]

The Soviets increased the tempo of the fighting during 1984. For big offensive movements they no longer relied on conscript units but on trained mountain fighters. They again attacked the Panjshir, this time with 20,000 Soviet troops, five hundred armored vehicles, and thousands of Kabul soldiers—and again they failed. In June the Soviets launched a massive effort around Herat, forcing some insurgent groups to retreat into Iran. High-altitude saturation bombing was a common feature of these campaigns, and in October Soviet forces also looted the city of Qandahar twice.[60] Concerted efforts were made to assassinate key insurgent leaders. Radio Kabul announced the death of Ahmed Shah Massoud, the "Lion of the Panjshir," a onetime engineering student who had become the most famous of the resistance chiefs. The announcement turned out to be quite premature. Many of the assassination attempts, especially by KhAD, failed because the intended victims were tipped off in time. Massoud and his followers would survive no less than nine Soviet-directed offensives against them.

As the sixth year of occupation opened, close to ten thousand Soviets and their wives (no children) lived in a special ghetto in Kabul, surrounded by barbed wire, armed guards, and great danger. Life in Kabul had never been secure, but during 1984 conditions deteriorated. In March alone, fifteen PDPA officials were killed by the resistance in just one area of the city. On August 31 a bomb went off at Kabul International Airport; less than a month later, another action inside the city destroyed a dozen Soviet armored vehicles and killed numerous regime troops.[61]

The year 1985 saw another major (and unsuccessful) Soviet offensive in the Panjshir. The insurgents were now acquiring heavy weapons, and above all they had improved their air defenses. By reducing Soviet airpower, the resistance was able to increase the number and effectiveness of their ambushes along roads, thus defeating the basic Soviet strategy of maintaining communications between major cities.[62] Life in the capital became even more perilous, while Ahmed Shah Massoud led a spectacular raid on the five hundred–man fort at Pechgur, capturing almost all the troops and many weapons. Clearly, at the end of the sixth year of Soviet occupation, the war had become stalemated.

In early 1986 the PDPA declared a six-month cease-fire, but neither their troops nor the Soviets reduced operations against the resistance under this or subsequent so-called cease-fires. The Soviets dumped Babrak Karmal and replaced him with the head of the secret police, one Najib. Mujahideen often succumbed to the temptation to kill Kabul army prisoners, and consequently mass defections by Kabul troops had practically ceased; sometimes they would actually stand and fight. The insurgents had never yet held a provincial capital for any extended period, and KhAD agents had penetrated their organizations. But the guerrillas had even more thoroughly penetrated the regime: it was very difficult for Kabul or the Soviets to mount surprise operations because of the omnipresence of resistance agents and sympathizers. Security in Kabul became ever more inadequate. In September the resistance overran the fort at Ferkhar, killing or capturing three hundred Kabul soldiers.[63] Significantly, Massoud was now deploying units of men who were willing to fight not only in their own province but anywhere in the whole northern region.

During 1987 the war discernibly worsened for the Soviet-Kabul side. The insurgents by then had permanent bases in strongly defended mountain areas, their leaders were cooperating more closely, and they were getting better equipment from outside. In Paktia Province, on the Pakistan border, a major Soviet-Kabul operation including Spetsnaz commandos was repulsed with heavy losses. A sizable Soviet effort to open the road between Gardez and Khost, closed by the guerrillas for years, failed as well. Mortar shells continued to hit the Soviet Embassy in Kabul, and to the north of the capital rockets fell on Bagram Airbase, the most important Soviet installation in the country. Because the resistance was increasingly using fairly long-range artillery, the Soviets had to expand their security perimeter around Kabul. During the summer the Soviets abandoned several outlying posts, leaving most of the country without any Soviet presence at all. The resistance showed growing willingness to target Soviet forces and operate in Soviet-controlled areas. In July insurgents stormed Kalafgan, only fifty miles from the Soviet border, and seized priceless artillery. The Soviets acknowledged that the resistance had actually raided into the territory of the USSR itself (reports of such forays had appeared in the Western press years earlier). *Izvestia* illustrated the growing desperation of the Kremlin when it charged that the mujahideen were being trained by instructors from Pakistan, France, Saudi Arabia, the United States, China, Egypt, Iran, Britain, and even Japan.[64]

But the most important new aspect of the conflict was the increasing availability of the American Stinger. The first of these one-man surface-to-air missile launchers had been delivered to the insurgents in the autumn of 1986. Hitherto, it had always been very dangerous for the resistance to stand and fight against Soviet and

Kabul forces because of the probability of air attacks. The Soviets relied more and more on their total control of the air to surprise resistance forces and devastate rural society. Now painfully aware that the resistance possessed Stingers, Soviet and Kabul pilots began to fly at inefficiently high altitudes, and daylight airlifts of supplies and troops became rare. This diminishing of their airpower was thus the latest in a series of devastating blows suffered by the Soviets.[65]

The Outside World

International relief workers and diplomatic agencies estimated that by the end of 1988 1.3 million Afghan men, women, and children had died as a direct result of the war. Additional tens of thousands had been maimed for life. One-third of the prewar population of 16 million had fled across one or another border, producing the planet's largest refugee mass. Three-quarters of Afghanistan's villages had been destroyed or abandoned. "Moscow," said the *Washington Post,* "[was] committing one of the world's great crimes." Nevertheless, the international response was astonishingly subdued. "The discrepancy between the magnitude of the tragedy and the international attention it receive[d] work[ed] very much to Moscow's advantage." The Soviets counted on being able to carry out this genocide in relative secrecy, with the world simply pretending to forget about Afghanistan. The Soviets from time to time issued threats about what might happen to foreign journalists captured in the company of mujahideen, but the undeniable lack of concern of the world's press was of enormous help to Moscow.[66]

Pakistan provided the most essential foreign support of the freedom fighters. It gave shelter to millions of Afghan victims of war, and all of the important Afghan political parties made their headquarters in Peshawar. Most crucial of all, Pakistan allowed its territory to be used for transshipment of aid from other countries into Afghanistan. With its scores of mountain passes, the fourteen hundred-mile-long Afghanistan-Pakistan border was the lifeline of the resistance. Helping the Afghan resistance posed many risks to Pakistan. Major ethnic groups overlap the border between Pakistan and Afghanistan, and the Soviets promised to punish Pakistan by stirring up Baluchi and Pushtun nationalism, a menace to the country's very existence. If the Soviets had decided to make an all-out effort against the huge mujahideen infrastructure that lay over the eastern border, Pakistan would have been in mortal peril. But the Soviets held back from a major blow, no doubt influenced by the hostility toward its Afghanistan aggression of all the world's other great powers, from the United States to China, from West Germany to Japan. In June 1981 the Chinese premier significantly made a visit to a refugee camp near Peshawar; two years later the U.S. secretary of state, George Shultz, told refugees in Pakistan, "We are with you." Even so, many Pakistanis paid with their lives for the policy of assisting the insurgency: in 1984 alone, Soviet air and artillery "errors" killed two hundred Pakistanis. It is true that corrupt Pakistani officials siphoned off some of the aid flowing through that country from the outside world; sometimes old weapons replaced new ones. Yet without the support of the Pakistani government, it is hard to see how the Afghan resistance would have survived.[67]

The resistance received help from other Islamic states as well. Aside from Pakistan, Saudi Arabia was the first and for a while the only country to give tangible aid to the mujahideen. But then President Anwar Sadat of Egypt began supplying weapons he had received from the Soviets before his 1972 break with them.[68] In January and May 1980, conferences of foreign ministers of Muslim countries condemned the Soviet invasion. Various Islamic conferences issued invitations to resistance leaders.

In that most self-consciously militant of Muslim states, Iran, the leadership was at least as embittered against the Americans as against the Russians. As the Soviet genocide in Afghanistan became well known, and Soviet units in pursuit of fleeing insurgents crossed into Iran on several occasions,[69] the Iranians after September 1980 had to devote most of their attention to their bloody and protracted conflict with their Muslim neighbor to the west, Iraq. Nevertheless, Teheran included mujahideen leaders in its own delegation to the May 1980 Islamic Conference (from which Kabul's representatives were banned) and supplied arms to particular Afghan resistance groups, almost exclusively those drawn from the Shia minority.

Soviet clients and semiclients in the Islamic world, such as Syria, South Yemen, and the PLO, gave at least verbal support to the Kabul regime. In 1987 Saddam Hussein received the Kabul prime minister in Baghdad, the highest-level reception any member of the puppet government had enjoyed outside the Soviet bloc up to that time.[70]

In Beijing the leadership viewed the Soviet occupation of Afghanistan as another move in a gigantic Soviet encirclement of China, a strategy including Vietnam, India, and Mongolia. Accordingly, China repeatedly declared that the withdrawal of all Soviet forces from Afghanistan was a precondition for improved relations between the two Communist behemoths.[71] The Chinese backed Pakistan, their only friend in the region. They also sent rocket launchers, heavy artillery, and assault rifles into Afghanistan, but in what quantities no one outside the Chinese government seemed to know.

In Europe, governments, political parties, and private groups reacted with hostility to the invasion. The Italian Communist Party was so bitter about Afghanistan that its leaders were refused permission to address the Twenty-sixth Soviet Party Congress in Moscow in 1981. But perhaps the most active sympathy for the Afghan resistance arose in France. French medical personnel provided significant help to refugees, often at the peril of their lives. French citizens helped found Radio Free Kabul in 1981, identified by the Kabul regime as "a Jewish radio station."[72] And in 1987 the French foreign minister met with resistance leaders in Pakistan.

At the United Nations, large majorities voted annually that "all foreign troops" should leave Afghanistan. In 1986 the vote was 122 to 20. It is not clear exactly how these votes assisted the Afghan people, whose villages and society were being destroyed. As late as September 1986, when the facts about Afghanistan were undeniable, UNICEF actually presented an award to the puppet regime in Kabul for its literacy campaign, a campaign whose brutality had in part sparked the insurgency in the first place.[73] And here the role of India deserves attention. At the Emergency Session of the United Nations General Assembly in January 1980, the Indian representative criticized the General Assembly for presuming even to discuss the Soviet invasion of Afghanistan. Consistently refusing to condemn the Russian occupation, India recognized the Kabul regime and extended aid to it. In 1987, when the United Nations voted that "foreign troops" should leave Afghanistan by a vote to 123 to 19, India abstained. On May 3, 1988, the chief of the Kabul regime visited New Delhi, the only noncommunist capital to accord him full honors as a head of state. Meanwhile, the vaunted and misnamed Non-Aligned Movement accomplished absolutely nothing for the suffering millions of Afghanistan.

And what was the United States doing?

The Americans and the War

The nature of the Soviet intervention and of the Afghan response to it, as well as internal political problems facing the Carter administration, helped shape U.S. involvement in the conflict. The number of active-duty U.S. military personnel in direct contact with the war in Afghanistan was quite limited; at the same time the unfolding and outcome of the struggle provided much profound satisfaction to many Americans.

The traditional American approach to Afghanistan received succinct expression in 1953, in a message from the Joint Chiefs of Staff to President Eisenhower: "Afghanistan is of little or no strategic importance to the United States." Presidents Truman and Eisenhower each denied requests from Afghanistan for military assistance. Soviet moves to increase their influence in Kabul did not cause alarm in Washington; no one believed there was much the United States could do about it in any case. Americans viewed Afghanistan as within the "Soviet sphere of influence" and believed that the country would never be able to move out of the Soviet orbit, no matter how much assistance the United States might send. The National Security Council informed President Eisenhower in 1956 that providing arms to Afghanistan might well provoke strong Soviet countermeasures. In addition, Pakistan, Washington's faithful ally in the ill-fated Baghdad Pact, had age-old border disputes with Afghanistan; hence, any American plans to assist the Afghans would have aroused strong protests from Karachi. Rarely was there anybody in the U.S. Embassy in Kabul who could speak adequate Dari. Thus, it may be no surprise to find that the name Afghanistan does not appear even once in the index of volume one of Eisenhower's presidential memoirs. It does not appear at all in the memoirs of President Truman, Secretary of State Dean Acheson, or the theorist of containment George F. Kennan.[74]

Pakistan had the support of Secretary of State Dulles in its border disputes with Afghanistan. President Daoud therefore turned to the Soviets, who constructed the Bagram airport north of Kabul and the Salang Pass through the mountains near the Afghan-Soviet border. The Soviets found both very useful in the 1979 invasion.

Moscow anticipated no real trouble with the United States over the invasion of Afghanistan. The Americans, after all, had done little about the Soviet invasions of Hungary in 1956 and of Czechoslovakia in 1968. Agonizing in its "Vietnam Syndrome," the United States ignored Soviet activities in Ethiopia and Angola. By 1979 the Carter administration was clearly foundering. Another reason the Kremlin expected no effective response from the Americans was that it expected no effective response from the Afghans.[75]

But the invasion thoroughly alarmed the Carter White House. In a historic hyperbole, the excited U.S. president called the Soviet move into Afghanistan "the greatest threat to world peace since the Second World War."[76] Washington viewed the invasion as extremely ominous. It was not only the first-ever Soviet military move outside the boundaries of the Soviet bloc, but it also brought the Red Army perilously close to the source of major Western and Japanese oil supplies. "If the Soviets could consolidate their hold on Afghanistan," Carter later wrote, "the balance of power in the entire region would be drastically modified in their favor, and they might be tempted toward further aggression."[77]

President Carter's response to the invasion was truly multifaceted. He postponed consideration of the Salt II treaty by the Senate (where in light of the invasion it was dead anyway). He proclaimed an American boycott of the 1980 Moscow Olympics, in which he was joined by West Germany, China, Japan, and fifty other countries. He canceled wheat sales to the Soviets, asked the United Nations to condemn the invasion, and initiated legislation aiming at a reintroduction of the military draft. Perhaps most importantly in Moscow's view, Carter called for greatly augmented help for Pakistan, sent Defense Secretary Brown to Beijing, and began the flow of military and financial assistance to the mujahideen. And just in case the Kremlin entertained ideas about further advances toward the Persian Gulf, the president issued this warning in his State of the Union message on January 23, 1980: "Let our position be absolutely clear: An attempt by any outside force to gain control of the Persian

Gulf region will be regarded as an assault on the vital interests of the United States of America, and such an assault will be repelled by any means necessary, including military force."[78]

During the Greek Civil War, President Truman had announced that it would be the policy of the United States to aid free peoples resisting subjugation or subversion by Communist forces. This position, the essence of the Cold War Containment policy, became known as the Truman Doctrine. During the Afghan conflict, President Reagan proclaimed that U.S. assistance would go not only to free peoples resisting the imposition of Communism but also to subjugated peoples seeking to escape from it, a position soon called the Reagan Doctrine.[79] This doctrine was rightly seen as a challenge to, indeed a repudiation of, the so-called Brezhnev Doctrine, which held that once Communists had acquired control of a country, by whatever means, the Soviet Union and other fraternal socialist states would never allow that country to have any other kind of government—ever. The Brezhnev Doctrine had been the basis for the invasion of Czechoslovakia by the Warsaw Pact.

In spite of all this, during the early years of the conflict the flow of American military assistance to the mujahideen was not very great. There was no sizable Afghan ethnic element within American society to put pressure on Congress; U.S. news media coverage of the fighting and destruction inside Afghanistan was scanty. One observer wrote that only about 20 percent of resistance weapons came from foreign sources. By the end of 1984 the United States was providing only perhaps $80 million a year in aid to the Afghan resistance.[80]

As both Soviet brutality and mujahideen determination became ever clearer, American commitment to the resistance deepened, in the White House and in Congress. U.S. aid increased to $470 million a year by 1986 and $700 million by 1988 (figures vary). A significant proportion of that aid never made it out of Pakistan into Afghanistan, something American policymakers will have to take into consideration in similar future conflicts. The Central Intelligence Agency received overall charge of assistance to the insurgents. This became the largest "covert" CIA operation since Vietnam. The CIA often provided the insurgents with Soviet-made weapons, fearing that a too-blatant U.S. assistance program would provide the Soviets with a good excuse to retaliate against Pakistan.[81]

The Soviet Departure

After more than seven years of occupation and combat, the military situation from the Soviet point of view was at best an embarrassing stalemate. The mujahideen could not capture the big cities because they could not overcome the combination of Soviet airpower and firepower, fortifications, and land mines that defended them (the Soviets laid down tens of millions of mines in Afghanistan; most mujahideen casualties were caused by them).[82] The Soviets and their Kabul allies had lost their complete domination of the air; they controlled little of the countryside, holding only the largest cities, the key airports, and the north-south highway to Kabul, and all of this tenuously. By 1987 the insurgents were better armed and more determined than ever before.

In eight years of war the Soviets had suffered between 48,000 and 52,000 casualties, including at least 13,000 to 15,000 deaths. If one accepts the latter figure (which is probably too low), it amounts to 35 Soviet deaths per week between December 1979 and December 1987. In view of the fact that the Soviets were combating a resistance force of between 100,000 and 200,000, this was hardly an oppressive number of fatalities. But the point is that such a figure was far more than anybody in the Kremlin would have predicted in January 1980. The divergence between Soviet expectations and actual losses is even greater for the number of aircraft, including helicopters, downed by the resistance, perhaps 500 lost in 1987 alone (the Stinger effect). The mujahideen had also destroyed about 600 tanks, 800 armored personnel carriers, and several thousand other military vehicles; Western correspondents sometimes reported seeing dozens of Soviet and Kabul army vehicles destroyed in a single engagement.[83] And there was no end in sight.

The war was costing the Soviets about $3 billion annually by 1984. A lot of the expense was being recovered through Russian exploitation of Afghanistan's mineral resources. Had the Soviets won the war, Afghanistan's economic future would have been grim indeed.[84]

Brezhnev's war was imposing many other costs on Gorbachev's Russia. By dissipating the mystique of the invincible Soviet Army, by bringing Washington and Beijing closer together, by creating profound hostility among Islamic states, by providing one of the levers

President Reagan used to pry big defense budgets out of his Congresses—in all these ways the occupation of Afghanistan was not enhancing Soviet security but undermining it.

But of all the war's effects on the Soviet Union, perhaps the most menacing was a peculiar Soviet variation of the venerable Domino Principle: the long-term consequences of the endless Afghanistan fighting for the Soviet Union's Muslim population, fifty million strong and rapidly increasing. These peoples lived in territories (Soviet Central Asia) conquered by the Russians relatively recently. They were held inside the Soviet Union not by the appeal of Marxism— "perceived not as an international philosophy but as a technique devised by the Russians to protect their colonial rule"—but by the power of the Soviet Army and the secret police. There was practically no intermarriage at all with ethnic Russians. The Central Asians were truly subject peoples. Now, the subject peoples of the British and French empires had shown relatively little inclination to challenge their imperial overlords—until they saw them defeated at the hands of an Asian people in World War II. What conclusions, then, might Russia's Central Asian Muslim subjects draw from the events in Afghanistan, where the Invincible Red Army had for years been hard pressed by the warriors of God, the Red Star eclipsed by the Crescent, Leninism tamed by Islam, an Islam resurgent all over the world and nowhere more vigorous than on the southern borders of the Soviet empire? What if the international response to the war in Afghanistan taught the Central Asians that there was indeed a Muslim world community that stretched far beyond the borders of their less-than-invincible utopia?[85] No one could provide certain answers to these questions. But at a minimum, in the words of a U.S. State Department report, "by 1987 the mujahideen had fought the Soviet and regime [Kabul] forces to a stalemate: Moscow's Afghan policy had alienated it from the Islamic, Western and non-aligned countries; and the Soviets failed to find a client leader in Kabul who could capture the loyalty of the Afghan people."[86] How had the Soviets become entangled in this predicament?

The Elements of Stalemate

What happened to the Soviets in Afghanistan can perhaps best be understood as the mutually aggravating effects of four basic circumstances. First, the invading Russians found themselves confronted with a forbidding terrain inhabited by hardy and high-spirited people who saw themselves as intolerably provoked into a defense of both their liberties and their religion. In a word, Afghanistan was no Czechoslovakia. (Did no one in the entire USSR power structure foresee this?)

Second, right from the start the Soviets greatly overestimated the ability of their modern weapons technology to cut off supplies to the guerrillas. Weapons got in from Pakistan, from America, from Iran and China and Egypt and Saudi Arabia—surely one of the most heterogeneous coalitions ever seen, and daunting indeed in its implications for Moscow. The Soviets thus came to understand how very difficult it is to defeat a popular insurgency possessing secure sources of outside aid. (Indeed, they had encountered great difficulty in suppressing insurgency in the Ukraine after World War II, even though outbreaks there were totally isolated from the world.) And late in the war, but not too late, foreign supporters of the mujahideen provided them with weapons that came close to driving the vaunted Red Air Force from the daytime skies. In analyzing this war, it would be impossible to overestimate the importance either of the willingness of foreign powers to supply the insurgents with modern weapons or the failure of the Soviets to isolate the country from that assistance.[87]

Third, the various political formulas advanced by Moscow to mitigate the Afghanistan problem had all failed miserably. From the beginning the Soviets and their mannequins in Kabul had responded to Afghan armed resistance in ways that only made their opponents more determined. Subsequent attempts to reverse those blunders, such as engineering major leadership changes and launching a "national conciliation government," achieved nothing. Efforts to establish a pro-Soviet government in Kabul that would be popular and legitimate, or a least tolerated by the Afghan people, failed utterly. The Soviet political failure produced the military failure.[88] Is it not astonishing, truly, that in a country like Afghanistan, with so many and such profound racial, religious, linguistic, ethnic, and tribal fissures—is it not astonishing that the Soviets proved so incapable of developing effective divide-and-rule policies?

Fourth, the Soviets never came close to committing troops in numbers sufficient to subjugate the country or even to possess major parts of it securely. The numerical inadequacy was the root of the Soviet terror campaign against the civilian population: lacking the manpower for pacification, they turned to depopulation. But the tremendous firepower of the Soviet armed forces, with apparently no limitations whatsoever on its use, enhanced by incursions into Pakistan and assassinations of resistance leaders in Peshawar, did not intimidate the insurgents. On the contrary, the Soviet terror policy actually constructed a vast support system and recruiting ground for the resistance among the millions of Afghans who fled across the borders into Pakistan and Iran. Thus, depopulation fatally backfired. The Soviets paid a very high price indeed for their systematic inhumanity.

One way to respond to all this would have been to decide finally to win the war. But "the Soviet leadership recognized that there could be no military solution in Afghanistan without a massive increase in their military commitment."[89] There were approximately 200,000 mujahideen in 1987, and perhaps 100,000 of them were active fighters. To reach the standard ten-to-one ratio of soldiers to insurgents widely believed necessary to wage conclusive counterguerrilla warfare, and assuming that the ineffective Kabul forces remained at around 80,000 (an optimistic assumption indeed), the Soviets would have had to put at the minimum more than 900,000 troops into Afghanistan—eight times their actual commitment. The logistical challenges of supplying such a force in the Afghan terrain were staggering. And by the middle of the 1980s the Soviet leadership had ceased trying to hide the fact that the Soviet Union was facing a systemic economic crisis with the most profound and alarming implications.

Yet, even if the Kremlin had bitten the bullet and decided on a massive increase of its troop levels in Afghanistan, that alone would not have guaranteed either quick or complete success. The Americans had sent to South Vietnam, a territory one-quarter the size of Afghanistan, an army five times the size of the Soviet force there. Assisting the Americans in South Vietnam was an indigenous allied force eventually numbering 1 million out of a population of about 17 million, compared to the 80,000 men and boys the Kabul regime was able to scrape together out of a population of 15 million.

So, although the Soviets had not suffered actual defeat in Afghanistan, they faced either continuous conflict or unacceptable escalation. Why was Gorbachev obligated to pursue and perhaps massively escalate this depressing war—against precisely what danger, for precisely what gain, and at precisely what internal and international costs? This Afghanistan mess was not even his creation; it was Brezhnev's. By 1988 Brezhnev was dead, and most of the members of the Politburo who had supported his invasion were also dead or retired. "In the final analysis, Moscow deemed the overall costs of pursuing a military solution to be too high." And so the Kremlin chose to withdraw from Afghanistan.[90]

On April 14, 1988, Pakistan and the PDPA regime signed accords at Geneva; the United States and the Soviet Union were guarantors of the pact. And "on May 15 [1988], in compliance with the Geneva agreement, the Soviets began to withdraw their troops from Afghanistan," monitored by the United Nations Good Offices Mission to Afghanistan and Pakistan. By February 1989 all or almost all Soviet troops had left Afghanistan, but substantial numbers of advisers and KGB personnel remained. Those advisers, along with Soviet-supplied aircraft, would play a crucial role in the defense of Kabul, and Moscow continued to supply the Kabul regime to the tune of $250 million per month.[91]

What the War Meant

References to Afghanistan as "Russia's Vietnam" were very common in the 1980s and to some degree thereafter. Such a comparison has some validity: "The Soviet forces in Afghanistan repeated the U.S. experience in Vietnam, in that they did not lose but could not win at a politically acceptable cost."[92] Nevertheless, though no two wars can ever be exactly the same, the contrasts between the American and the Soviet conflicts in Asia are so arresting that one should be especially skeptical of facile comparisons between them.

Three fundamental differences between the Vietnamese and the Afghan conflicts, quite aside from the size of the Soviet and American troop commitment, come quickly into view. First, Afghanistan was just over the Soviet border. In contrast, Washington is 9,000 miles from Saigon. It would therefore be less misleading to compare the Soviet withdrawal from Afghanistan to an American withdrawal not from Vietnam but from northern Mexico.

Second, the proportion of the South Vietnamese population willing to associate itself publicly with the Americans was much higher than the proportion of the Afghan population openly supporting the Soviets.[93] (The final conquest of Saigon by a massive North Vietnamese Army invasion does not disprove this statement but confirms it.)

The third and perhaps most decisive contrast was the nature of the opponents the Americans and the Soviets each faced. American casualties in Vietnam were a great deal higher than Soviet casualties in Afghanistan, but that disparity was by no means due solely to the much smaller Soviet troop commitment. The mujahideen were brave and resilient, but in Vietnam the Americans faced an enemy much better trained, organized, and equipped than the Soviets ever dreamed of in Afghanistan. The Hanoi Politburo had developed its military and political techniques during long years of struggle against the French. It gave the Communist-led insurgency in the South unity, direction, and discipline. It sent southward a constant and increasing flow of well-trained combatants with effective weapons. It eventually committed quite substantial military formations. And it learned how to manipulate public opinion in the United States. The mujahideen had nothing like all that.

No, the meaning of the Afghan insurgency must be sought beyond sweeping and misleading comparisons to Vietnam.

For nearly a decade the Soviets poured out upon the poor and simple people of Afghanistan the full horror of a deliberate campaign of annihilation. By 1988 roughly 1.25 million Afghans "had died as a result of aerial bombing raids, shootings, artillery shelling, antipersonnel mines, exhaustion and other war-related conditions."[94] Wielded with utter indifference to questions of legality or humanity, the fearsome technology of the Soviet armed forces nevertheless proved insufficient for victory. At a truly frightful price, and with good help from their well-wishers in the outside world, the Afghan people fought to a stalemate the forces of a totalitarian superpower on their very border. And Afghanistan provides an exceedingly rare example of guerrillas prevailing without the support of conventional armed forces.

The Afghan struggle was indeed a mortifying colonial reverse for the world's last multinational empire. But it was so much more than that: by successfully refusing to be made into a Central Asian imitation of Ceausescu's Romania, the Afghan freedom fighters inflicted the first (but not the last) indisputable reverse on the "historical inevitability of Marxism-Leninism" of which Brezhnev had so confidently boasted. This double defeat helped stimulate the gathering forces of change inside the Soviet empire, hastening the process of its decomposition. Thus, the brave, sad, martyred people of Afghanistan helped in no small measure to alter the entire course of world politics.[95] In a most ironic, fitting, and devastating way, Trotsky turned out to be right after all about the connection between revolution in Asia and Europe: the cries of battle in the Afghan mountains had their echo in the cries of freedom on the Berlin Wall.

10

Implications and Provocations

Let us now briefly review the most salient aspects of the conflicts examined in this volume and see whether they yield up any generally useful conclusions.

The American Revolution

The southern colonies that the British tried to subdue were vast in terms of eighteenth-century communications. Direct and indirect foreign assistance to the American side drew off British forces to other pressing areas and played a major role in the bagging of Cornwallis's army. In the Carolinas the British found themselves confronted by one of history's great guerrilla chiefs, Francis Marion, the Swamp Fox. The guerrillas effectively disrupted British lines of communications and harassed small parties of troops. The guerrillas' impact was the greater because for much of the time they were operating symbiotically with regular American forces under the very capable Gen. Nathanael Greene. (Nearly two hundred years later, the United States found itself confronting the same sort of powerful guerrilla-regular symbiosis in Vietnam.)

The situation brings into clear focus the inadequacy of British numbers, in North America as a whole and in the Carolinas in particular. That numerical insufficiency made irresistible the loyalist mirage that enticed the British to mount a major effort in the southern colonies in the first place. It also accounted for the failure of Cornwallis's strategy of strong points. And it was linked to the self-defeating punishment of the civil population (the burning of churches and plantations, the destruction of Georgetown, South Carolina).[1] For Cornwallis to suppress the Carolina guerrillas with the forces available to him was almost certainly impossible.

The American Civil War

In Virginia the dash and courage of Mosby and his followers showed to great advantage because, even though they were operating in the presence of large numbers of Federal troops, the attention of those forces was riveted on Richmond.

In Missouri, in contrast, there were never enough Union soldiers and militia to maintain order. Thus, some of the worst aspects and consequences of guerrilla warfare were obvious for all who wished to see. In many ways Missouri, a Union state, suffered more than secessionist Georgia or South Carolina.

Nevertheless, after Appomattox some Confederates wished to carry on a guerrilla struggle. Union leaders had no plans for dealing with such a challenge. But the dread specter never materialized. The Confederacy was thoroughly exhausted by clear defeat in a devastating war few had expected and further demoralized by years of bitter political infighting, as well as profound unease regarding slavery. A guerrilla movement would have had no conventional forces to support it, because the major Southern military leaders refused to countenance a continuation of the fighting. Finally, advocacy of continued struggle collapsed under Lincoln's easy peace terms, the absence of an alien enemy, and the knowledge that no outside assistance would be forthcoming.

The Philippines: 1898

There was nothing foreordained about the American victory against the Philippine insurrection. On the contrary, the situation confronted the Americans with potential disaster. U.S. forces were totally alien to the Filipinos, far from home, and few in number.[2] They had no experience as colonial administrators. They possessed no air support, no medevac, no AWACs, not even telephones. At home, the Philippines conflict was arousing great political controversy.

Certain objective factors, however, favored the Americans. The geographical isolation of the islands meant that the insurgents could count on no outside aid, and numerous ethnic rivalries within the native population inhibited the growth of nationalistic sentiment. The Americans capitalized on these objective factors by employing tactics that hurt the guerrillas without spilling blood. They provided written promises of eventual independence to the Filipinos. They practiced a policy of attraction: building schools, fighting disease, improving the courts, cleaning the streets. They recruited many indigenous personnel as scouts and auxiliaries. They bought up guns and disrupted the insurgents' food supplies. This general approach provided scope for the complex ethnic and class divisions of Philippine society to work against the insurgents.

Accordingly, the symbol of the American presence became not the helicopter gunship but the schoolhouse. Herein lay the foundations of that peace and friendship which characterized Philippine-U.S. relations for the rest of the 1900s.

With regard to the campaigns against the Moros, American soldiers found those opponents to be personally courageous but strategically and tactically primitive. Both the culture and the geography of the Moros severely limited their efforts. Besides that, the Americans generally displayed a willingness to respect Islam, which did a good deal to calm the situation. In the end the Moros decided that they hated the Americans much less than they hated the Spanish and the Christian Filipinos, and eventually they settled down to a grudging but serviceable peace.

Nicaragua

In Nicaragua during the 1920s and 1930s, the United States was not pursuing an imperialist adventure. On the contrary, the small numbers of American military personnel in that country were a response to the repeated requests of the constitutional authorities there and the leaders of both major Nicaraguan political parties for help in restoring order in the face of chronic minoritarian rebellions, in an area the U.S. government considered highly strategic.

With specific regard to the Sandino uprising, important political factors severely limited its appeal. One factor was partisanship:

Sandino was the leader of one faction of the Liberal Party, automatically making him unacceptable to the Conservatives. Another factor was the government's electoral legitimacy; the Liberals (Sandino's own party) were in power in Nicaragua most of the time, as a result of relatively free and honest elections supervised by U.S. forces. Thus, Sandino's insurgency had no chance of mobilizing anything like a majority of the Nicaraguan people.

But the guerrillas did enjoy some key advantages. Unsupervised international borders were close at hand. In addition, the number of American military personnel in the country was too small to effectively hold posts, protect communications, patrol borders, and chase guerrillas all at the same time. The numerical insufficiency was the result of widespread opposition within the United States to any Central American intervention, which was in any case always viewed in Washington as short-term.

Nevertheless, when the American forces left Nicaragua, the affairs of that country were in the hands of duly elected civilians. And the U.S. Marines learned some valuable lessons from their Nicaraguan experiences, especially regarding the treatment of civilians, the control of firepower in settled areas, and the value of local recruits.

Greece

As World War II ended, Greece—poor, mountainous, on the periphery of Europe, devastated by war, and bordered by new Stalinist states—might well have seemed the ideal European setting for a Communist insurgency. But the Communists suffered a defeat as thorough as it was unpredicted.

Many have identified Tito's closing of the Yugoslav border against the guerrillas as the key factor in their defeat. It was undeniably a grave blow to the insurgent cause. But before the border closing, the guerrillas were already strategically defeated. U.S. aid and advice to the Greek government helped create a larger, more vigorous, better-commanded army. The guerrillas threw away their tactical advantages against that ever-improving army by adopting conventional tactics. Most of all, they polluted the water in which they had to swim by grossly and systematically mistreating the peasant population.

The Philippines: The Huk War

The Huk rebellion fed on government corruption and incompetence in the wake of the devastation of World War II. The arrival on the scene of Ramon Magsaysay severely reduced the appeal of the insurgents. He greatly improved the military's treatment of the civil population and restored elections as a peaceful path to change. He supplemented those effective measures with easy amnesty for guerrillas who would give themselves up and fabulous rewards for the capture of those who would not.

Other factors weighed heavily against the Huks: in the independent Philippine republic there was no foreign oppressor to rise against, and geography ruled out any effective help for the guerrillas from abroad. Therefore, the insurgency, which reached its peak by mid-1950, had ceased to be a menace by mid-1952. The United States was greatly interested and deeply involved in the struggle, but not a single U.S. combat unit was deployed against the Huks.

El Salvador

The Salvadoran guerrillas, the FMLN, had an excellent hand to play: the country suffered from many obvious problems, the electoral path to change had been crudely blocked, the army was brutal and inept, and outside aid flowed to the insurgents across borders that were near at hand. But consistent U.S. aid and pressure improved the army's tactics and its treatment of the civil population. The United States also insisted on free elections, which divided the insurgents and showed how limited their support was. The report of the bipartisan Kissinger Commission placed the struggle in El Salvador in a larger context, much as the Truman Doctrine had done for the Greek conflict. The end of the Cold War convinced almost everybody that the time to make peace had arrived. Thus, order returned to El Salvador under pro-U.S. administrations, with no U.S. combat units having been sent there and with very few American casualties.

Afghanistan

The Afghan mujahideen enjoyed those advantages most prized by guerrillas: popular support, high morale, favorable terrain, foreign sanctuary, and copious assistance from the outside.

Nonetheless, the counterinsurgency waged by the Soviet Union was incredibly poor. Consider that the Soviets, allegedly the world's greatest military power, were fighting in an undeveloped and remote country just across their border. The Afghan guerrillas fought without the support of conventional units. Above all, the racial, ethnic, linguistic, and religious diversity of Afghanistan provided the Soviets with unparalleled opportunities to divide their opponents. The Soviet inability to take advantage of fissures in Afghan society is simply stunning. Nor were the Soviets able to prevent help for the mujahideen from pouring across the Pakistan and Iran borders. Communist political failure was even more decisive in Afghanistan than in Greece thirty-five years before.

The Soviets completed this political failure with disastrous military tactics. Their brutally destructive assault on the civil population only deepened the determination of the resistance. Soviet tactics derived in part from an inadequate commitment of troops, a situation reminiscent of the Napoleonic failure in Spain. The Americans, perceiving an opportunity, exploited it at little cost to themselves but with incalculable cost to the Soviet empire. As it turned out, the failure in Afghanistan was not some peculiarity of time and place but instead foreshadowed the Russian debacle in Chechnya in the mid-1990s.[3]

The guerrilla war in Afghanistan deserves much study by Americans, not least because in years to come the U.S. government may well find itself supporting another popular uprising in the same general area of the Asian continent. And Americans might further wish to ponder the great strength the Afghan resistance derived from the lively religious faith of most of its members. What might happen if American forces ever find themselves confronting that kind of strength?

Vietnam: The Great Exception

In 1963 the Communist rulers in Hanoi were orchestrating a guerrilla insurgency in South Vietnam. Reacting with excited incomprehension to sensational and obscene images of Buddhist self-immolations avidly furnished by the news media, high U.S. officials gave their approval to a coup against President Diem, which predictably ended in his murder. Punishment for this unconscionable act was not long in coming: the chaos following the killing of Diem led directly to the dramatic escalation of the U.S. presence in Vietnam. That depressing episode provides the clearest possible warning of how dangerous it is when Washington decision makers try to micromanage political affairs in a cultural context of which they know little.

Sending so many Americans to a guerrilla war in a far-away country of questionable strategic importance to the United States was a formula for disaster. The mistakes and crimes inevitable in such a conflict, along with the wastefulness and destructiveness of the American way of war, blazed nightly on American television screens. The culmination of the process was the mishandling by the news media of the Tet Offensive of 1968, the turning point of the war. The president and his advisers, huddled in the lower depths of the White House, busied themselves with selecting targets for the U.S. Air Force in Vietnam; they also repeatedly halted the bombing to prove American "goodwill." Both of these activities cost American and allied lives. Confronted by the Tet crisis, the administration could not explain its purposes to the American electorate and thus mercifully disappeared from the stage, leaving the dreadful mess in Vietnam for its successors to clean up as best they could.

For nearly twenty years, the Americans failed to deal effectively with South Vietnam's most serious vulnerability and North Vietnam's most effective weapon: the Ho Chi Minh Trail. Nevertheless, the Americans and their allies defeated the guerrillas. The cost in American lives was equivalent to the number of fatalities on U.S. roadways in 1970 alone. Not only had the Vietcong suffered defeat, but also South Vietnamese opposition to conquest by Hanoi was wide and deep.[4] That is why the destruction of South Vietnam required a massive invasion by the North Vietnamese Army, an invasion that developed because the South Vietnamese were abandoned, even repudiated, by their self-anointed American protectors.

However regrettable the initial U.S. commitment to Vietnam or the subsequent escalation of that commitment may have been, surely very few today can contemplate the final American desertion of the South Vietnamese without deep disquiet.

And what, in the end, did the conquest of South Vietnam prove? A leading British authority on insurgency offered this troubling answer: "Perhaps the major lesson of the Viet Nam war is: do not rely on the United States as an ally."[5]

The Past and the Future

What are some general conclusions or inferences to be derived from the comparison of these conflicts? Here is one: during the American Revolution and the U.S. Civil War, Americans demonstrated great prowess as guerrillas. Analysis of their campaigns ought to be incorporated into the conscious view of those who will command U.S. forces against guerrillas in the future: to understand why Marion, Sumter, Mosby, and others were successful is to begin (at least) to understand how to defeat guerrillas.

And, perhaps even more importantly, in the opening years of the twentieth century American armed forces achieved a clear and lasting victory over insurgents in the Philippines. In fact, of the seven instances examined in this book in which the United States intervened abroad in a guerrilla struggle, important American objectives were achieved in six: the Philippines (twice), Nicaragua, Greece, Afghanistan, and El Salvador. The great exception was South Vietnam, where the United States defeated the insurgency and then abandoned the country and its people to blatant invasion.

The deplorable experience in Vietnam overshadows American thinking about guerrilla insurgency. This is understandable but unfortunate. The conflict in the Philippines, and in Nicaragua as well, demonstrated that U.S. forces could operate effectively against guerrillas under adverse circumstances. Notably, they carried out their mission with what would today be considered remarkably low levels of technology. The absence of advanced weaponry was an advantage, actually, because it restricted the ability of the Americans to inflict damage on civilian areas and forced them to work out a sound strategy.

Nevertheless, given certain features of contemporary American society, it would be better, with few if any exceptions, for the United States not to take on the burden of direct confrontation with insurgents. Whatever the particular circumstances, U.S. troops would be by definition foreigners, and there is but a bayonet's breadth between "foreigners" and "invaders." In addition, insurgencies based on ethnic or religious differences, or both, tend to be extremely bitter and hence protracted. The type of effort the United States pursued against the Greek Communists, the Philippine Huks, and the Salvadoran FMLN, however—assistance to the incumbent government without actual commitment to combat—both minimizes American vulnerabilities and emphasizes American strengths.[6] Those strengths include providing financial help to the local government while dissuading other governments from aiding the guerrillas, and assisting the local armed forces with intelligence, mobility, and operational advice. The United States would also be in a position to pressure the assisted government, if necessary, to limit the abuse of civilians and to provide a peaceful alternative to insurgency. If, despite that assistance, the local government appears too weak to stave off a guerrilla challenge, then the United States could invite the military participation of friendly regional states or, where politically appropriate, of the former colonial power.[7]

Table 1 summarizes the argument so far. Clearly, the table does not *prove* that U.S. indirect aid was the determining factor in the cases in which the United States achieved its major aims. All of those conflicts might conceivably have turned out more or less the same without U.S. involvement. But the summary provided in the table certainly illustrates that from the 1940s through the 1980s, outcomes greatly desired by the United States have not required the participation of American combat forces. It further suggests that the outcome in South Vietnam might have been profoundly different had the United States employed a more conservative strategy there.

If what has been said so far is true, or mainly true, then it is reasonable to conclude that when top U.S. government and military decision makers consider possible U.S. involvement in a future guerrilla insurgency, the presumption should be against committing U.S. ground forces: the burden of proof must be on the advocates of such a course of action. Serious answers need to be provided to very basic questions. First, major guerrilla insurgencies do not usually arise in countries with reasonably efficient, reasonably decent governments. Is that why the local government cannot handle the guerrillas without U.S. troops? Second, what, precisely, is the U.S. national interest in the conflict? Can the supposed U.S. national interest be convincingly presented to the American electorate, especially given

Table 1. Relationship of U.S. Combat Role to U.S. Policy Attainment

	Primary U.S. Combat Role	*No Primary U.S. Combat Role*
U.S. Achieves Major Objectives	Philippines (post-1898) Nicaragua	Greece Philippines (Huks) El Salvador Afghanistan
U.S. Does Not Achieve Major Objectives	Vietnam	

Note: There is no instance in which the U.S. played a supportive noncombat role in an insurgency and failed to attain major objectives.

the disappearance of the Soviet Union? And not least, what evidence is there that U.S. combat intervention will solve or even alleviate the problem?

If, nonetheless, an American administration casts the die and commits U.S. combat forces against a foreign insurgency, the most important battle becomes the battle for American opinion. Most guerrilla conflicts in the Third World (but not only there) will exhibit extreme political and moral ambiguities that will disturb the U.S. electorate; even the very low-key, low-casualty Nicaraguan episode aroused much controversy in the United States, before the television age. Guerrillas can protract the conflict, furthermore, by avoiding contact with U.S. and local forces, and the guerrillas can then choose to make contact in spectacular ways. The U.S. polity remains vulnerable to the "Tet Offensive effect," as in Vietnam in 1968 and El Salvador in 1989. In the terminology of Clausewitz, the U.S. foreign policy "center of gravity" lies in a usually inchoate public opinion bombarded by sensational television images. For its own protection, and perhaps survival—not to speak of the national interest—any U.S. administration making a commitment to combat in a guerrilla war will have to insist that U.S. foreign policy, especially military intervention, is not conducted to provide the news media with pictures. That caution should be in place even if the agents of the media were familiar with guerrilla tactics and the culture of the country at risk. Hence, a first order of business should be to establish firm control of any large cities, and especially the capital, as soon as possible, with painstaking attention to security in those places and complete determination to prevent a "Tet." In that way the U.S.

government will have more influence over the kind of news stories reaching Americans at home.[8]

Real Victory

Even where it is attainable, military victory is ephemeral. That is especially true for counterinsurgency. A guerrilla war is not over merely because the guerrillas disappear. Disappearance is a basic tactic of those who wage guerrilla war effectively. Real victory means an enduring peace. Such a peace cannot derive from the mere physical cowing of the enemy. If a government, even one apparently successful in its counterinsurgency, does not eventually achieve a measure of conciliation with important strata (at least) among those elements of society that supported the insurgency, then the insurgency can recur and require that the government undertake another costly struggle, perhaps unsuccessfully. "If historical experience teaches us anything about revolutionary guerrilla war," wrote Samuel Griffith, "it is that military measures alone will not suffice."[9] An enduring victory, an enduring peace in a guerrilla insurgency, requires a political settlement resting on broad foundations.

The possibility of a lasting settlement will be deeply affected by the way counterinsurgent forces approach the question of how to combat the guerrillas. With an eye on the peace to follow, the counterinsurgent forces need to limit to the greatest degree possible the amount of blood that is spilled.

Limiting Bloodshed

Historically proven methods exist for seriously weakening a guerrilla movement without creating great numbers of casualties on either side. To begin, if the guerrillas can be pushed into undesirable areas of a country and confined there, then even without one single shot being fired, they have been strategically defeated. One of the best-known methods of forcing guerrillas to abandon a given area without fighting is to saturate it with troops and police (this is the initial phase of the "clearing and holding" strategy). Lines of fences or chains of blockhouses, or both, can reduce the insurgents' access to the more desirable or strategic regions of the country; they can also serve to disrupt the flow of outside assistance.[10] Diplomatic pressure can further prevent or at least limit help to the insurgents from foreign countries. Once significant areas of the country have been cleared of guerrillas, responsible authorities can address civilian grievances.[11] Intelligence activities should focus on the arrest of guerrilla leaders. Providing large cash rewards for help in capturing guerrilla leaders sows distrust among the insurgents. Well-timed amnesties decrease the numbers and the morale of the guerrillas. Trading cash or, where appropriate, the release of a prisoner, for handed-in weapons, no questions asked, can denude whole areas of firearms, especially if the guerrillas are not receiving significant outside help. Another tactic, potentially quite effective, is to deprive the guerrillas of sufficient food by controlling sales from civilian sources and by hunting out the guerrillas' food-growing areas.

But of all the options in a low-casualty strategy for defeating guerrillas, the two most fundamental are undoubtedly (1) the provision of a peaceful alternative to insurgency and (2) the display of rectitude.

A Peaceful Road to Change

A peaceful alternative to violence means peaceful methods of effecting or pursuing change. That means methods for resolving clashes of interest, methods that are widely viewed as legitimate, often but not necessarily including free elections. They might also involve incorporating or reincorporating estranged elements of the population into the political process. It is important to understand the people at whom the peaceful alternative is directed. That is, one should not expect the availability of a peaceful alternative to dampen the ardor of ideological fanatics, religious zealots, or those whose main interest in insurgency is to taste the delights of power. Such persons, however, are relatively rare. A peaceful alternative has time and again satisfied those who supported insurgency because they perceived no other path to the redress of grievances. Examples of peaceful alternatives helping to end internal conflict are easy to find: Lincoln's generous reconstruction plan; the American policy of attraction in the Philippines; the continuous functioning of Parliament in wartorn Greece; and the restoration of free elections in Nicaragua in the 1920s, in the Philippines in the 1950s, and in El Salvador in the 1980s.

The Centrality of Rectitude

Finally, lasting victory based on conciliation requires the counter-insurgent forces to display rectitude: that is, right conduct toward the civilian population. In the words of the distinguished British theorist of counterinsurgency Sir Robert Thompson, that means acting "in accordance with the law of the land, and in accordance with the highest civilized standards."[12]

There is impressive testimony to the importance of rectitude for those who would defeat guerrilla insurgency. Clausewitz observed that "war is an act of force to compel the enemy to do our will": that is, "war is merely the continuation of policy by other means." Surely it cannot be "our will," our "policy," to galvanize the opponent's population into outraged resistance, but that is the predictable result of violating rectitude. The British Royal Commission investigating the 1919 massacre of Indian civilians at Amritsar expressed this idea succinctly: "The employment of excessive measures is as likely as not to produce the opposite result to that desired." The Philippine insurgent leader Luis Taruc wrote that the principal force generating the Huk rebellion was government provocations and outrages against hapless civilians. In his study of contemporary French counterinsurgency, Pierre Boyer de Latour insisted that "the army exists to protect the safety and the possessions of civilians." During the height of the American effort in Vietnam, Nathan Leites wrote that when "competing with a vigorous rebellion, a precarious authority should be . . . concerned with respect for the people's dignity at least as much as with [raising] the level of their income." Certainly the destructiveness of the U.S. effort in Vietnam—the sufferings inflicted upon civilians and the natural environment, intended or not—troubled the consciences of many Americans. The Salvadoran Army's reputation for systematic human rights abuses became a serious issue in the United States. And in the 1980s the Soviet experience in Afghanistan shows clearly what can happen to an army when it tramples down the basic tenets of civilization.[13] Habitual or systematic abuse of civilians has been the Achilles' heel of more than one counterinsurgency effort.

Rectitude of course does not mean that the guilty are not punished. On the contrary, rectitude requires that the guilty be distinguished from the innocent and pay an exemplary penalty.

To behave correctly toward civilians is not usually the overriding disposition of armed young soldiers who find themselves in a strange country filled with people who want to kill them; this is especially so because by definition guerrillas seek to look like and hide among the civilian population. But however difficult and against the grain, right conduct is essential to the maintenance of good morale and good discipline. Furthermore, unchecked cruelty and injustice create recruits and sympathizers for the guerrillas and thus increase casualties among the counterinsurgent forces. A sustained display of rectitude, in contrast, will make it incomparably easier to gather intelligence from civilians. And certainly, all lapses from good conduct by American or U.S.-backed forces will be splashed again and again across every television screen in the world, undermining support for involvement within the American electorate.

One needs to display rectitude not only toward the civilians but toward the enemy as well. In contrast to the obvious costs entailed by a neglect or repudiation of rectitude, government forces that gain a reputation for right conduct can take advantage of a very important but sometimes overlooked fact about guerrillas: some find themselves among the ranks of the guerrillas through outright coercion, and others who joined voluntarily come to repent of it. If guerrillas like those understand that upon capture or acceptance of amnesty, they will be dealt with decently, they will have all the more reason to abandon the struggle and no reason at all to fight to the death when trapped. Captured or surrendered guerrillas who receive decent treatment often provide a gold mine of information to their captors. And soldiers who display rectitude toward the enemy will find it all the easier to do the same toward civilians.[14]

To those ends, one of the best methods is to deploy counterinsurgent troops in their home areas—yet another serious argument against the use of U.S. troops in overseas insurgencies. If U.S. combat forces are nevertheless to confront guerrillas, it is essential to indoctrinate junior officers with the overwhelming importance of right conduct. At least some officers need training not only in the language but also in the culture—most especially including the religious sensibilities and sexual mores—of the civilians among whom they will be operating. Individual U.S. units should also remain in the same place for an extended period, so that they become familiar with and to the inhabitants.

Ensuring proper physical care of the troops is essential. And clearly, the forces committed against the guerrillas must be numerically sufficient for accomplishing their assigned mission; from the Carolinas to Afghanistan, there is an unmistakable link between inadequate numbers and bad behavior. Counterinsurgency on the cheap is a delusion heading for disaster.[15] Finally, but assuredly not least, there must be absolute prohibition against the setting of minimum quotas for dead guerrillas—no "body counts"!

The road of guerrilla war is littered with the wreckage of those who forgot about or sneered at rectitude, from the comparatively limited failings of the British in the Carolinas to the egregious and self-destructive tactics of the Soviets in Afghanistan and including the French in Spain, the Spanish in Cuba, the Japanese in China, and the Germans in Yugoslavia (as well as the Greek and the Philippine Communists).[16] In the end, right conduct is right strategy. Rectitude is worth many battalions.

Notes

Note: Complete publication information for abbreviated citations may be found in the bibliography.

Introduction: The Americans and Guerrilla Insurgency

1. The term *guerrilla insurgency* refers to that form of conflict in which opponents of a regime seek its overthrow or modification by pursuing classical guerrilla tactics. Guerrillas generally avoid confrontation with government armed forces except in limited planned encounters such as ambushes and attacks on isolated outposts. Emphasizing speed and deception, guerrillas seek to win small victories through numerical superiority at particular points of encounter. Guerrilla warfare is the kind of war the weak seek to wage against the strong. It is about tactics, not about ideology: not only Communists but also monarchists, nationalists, religious groups, and others have engaged in guerrilla insurgency.

2. And then the Vietnamese themselves in Cambodia.

3. Years ago, a special project to investigate American readiness to confront guerrillas stated baldly, "The United States does not understand low-intensity conflict nor does it display the capability to adequately defend against it." "Report of the Joint Low-Intensity Conflict Project," Fort Monroe, Va., Aug. 1, 1986. To say the least, it is not clear that many fundamental improvements have occurred since those lines were written. See Daalder, "United States and Military Intervention." And see Downie, *Learning from Conflict*. On the religious nature of guerrilla wars, see, inter alia, Hoffman, *'Holy Terror'*; and Martin Van Creveld, *The Transformation of War* (New York: Free Press, 1991).

4. Consider the continuing controversy over the effects of the Unconditional Surrender policy of the Allies during World War II. And see Ernest R. May, *"Lessons" of the Past: The Use and Misuse of History in American Foreign Policy* (New York: Oxford Univ. Press, 1973), esp. chap. 4.

5. On the importance of the international environment to the appearance and the success of revolutionary movements, see Theda Skocpol, *States and Social Revolutions* (New York: Cambridge Univ. Press, 1979); Jack A. Goldstone,

Revolution and Rebellion in the Early Modern World (Berkeley, Calif.: Univ. of California Press, 1991); McClintock, *Revolutionary Movements in Latin America.*

6. This work is not intended to be an exhaustive compendium of conflicts but rather an examination of representative or illustrative cases. It therefore does not seek to include every single instance in which the United States played some role in a guerrilla struggle. Of the conflicts not included here, some might consider the most notable to be the one in Haiti and the *Contras* affair in Nicaragua. The *Contras* episode is, unfortunately, still thoroughly steeped in domestic partisan controversy (as well as in arguments over the basic facts of the case), whereas the Haitian case, similar in crucial aspects to that of 1920s Nicaragua, would not affect the conclusions reached here. For U.S. actions in Haiti, see Langley, *Banana Wars;* James H. McCrocklin, *Garde D'Haiti, 1915–1934* (Annapolis, Md.: U.S. Naval Institute Press, 1956); Hans Schmidt, *The United States Occupation of Haiti 1915–1934* (New Brunswick, N.J.: Rutgers Univ. Press, 1971); Millett, *Semper Fidelis.* During the Cold War the United States assisted guerrilla movements from Central America to Central Asia, including (besides the notable case of Afghanistan) those in Angola, Cambodia, Nicaragua, and Tibet.

1. American Guerrillas: The War of Independence

1. Americans of today know hardly anything of these ferocious clashes between Indians and colonists. For the spectacular raid on Deerfield, Massachusetts, see Francis Parkman, *A Half-Century of Conflict* (Boston: Little, Brown, 1910), vol. 1, chap. 4. For a literary presentation, see the works of James Fenimore Cooper, especially *The Last of the Mohicans.*

2. On these much-neglected wars, see Parkman, *Half-Century of Conflict;* and Francis Parkman, *Montcalm and Wolfe,* 2 vols. (Boston: Little, Brown, 1910). A much shorter treatment is George M. Wrong, *The Conquest of New France* (New Haven, Conn.: Yale Univ. Press, 1918).

3. Samuel Eliot Morison, *The Oxford History of the American People* (New York: Oxford Univ. Press, 1965), p. 172. On the development of an American political self-consciousness and philosophy, see Page Smith, *John Adams* (Garden City, N.Y.: Doubleday, 1962), vol. 1; Dumas Malone, *Jefferson and His Time,* vol. 1, *Jefferson the Virginian* (Boston: Little, Brown, 1948).

4. See Bernard Bailyn, *The Ideological Origins of the American Revolution* (Cambridge, Mass.: Harvard Univ. Press, 1967), esp. chap. 1, "The Literature of Revolution," and chap. 4, "The Logic of Rebellion."

5. Royster, *Revolutionary People at War,* p. 5. Bailyn, *Ideological Origins of the American Revolution,* p. vi.

6. Quoted in Bailyn, *Ideological Origins of the American Revolution,* pp. 158–59.

7. James Thomas Flexner, *George Washington: The Forge of Experience* (Boston: Little, Brown, 1965), p. 339.

8. Mackesy, *War for America,* p. 62 n.

9. Anderson, *Command of the Howe Brothers.* Chatham is quoted in Morison, *Oxford History*, p. 216. John W. Derry, *Charles James Fox* (New York: St. Martin's, 1972), pp. 71, 73. Mackesy, *War for America*, p. 5, passim.

10. Derry, *Charles James Fox*, p. 65.

11. See the very good strategic survey in Weigley, *American Way of War*, chap. 2.

12. Pancake, *This Destructive War*, p. 241.

13. Mackesy, *War for America*, p. 166.

14. Ibid., p. 176. See Anderson, *Command of the Howe Brothers.* In 1778 the Spanish had 20 ships of the line in European waters and another 20 in the West Indies, compared to 54 in the entire British home fleet, and the Dutch navy was small but tough. See Mackesy, *War for America*, pp. 174–75, 395. See Dull, *French Navy and American Independence;* and Higginbotham, *War of American Independence*, pp. 243–44.

15. The quotations are in Curtis, *Organization of the British Army*, pp. 55, 56. On regimental composition, see also Bowler, *Failure of the British Army*, p. 12.

16. Not many years after these events, the Duke of Wellington (no less) observed, "We have in the service the scum of the earth"; he also said, "None but the worst description of men enter the regular service." Elizabeth Longford, *Wellington: The Years of the Sword* (New York: Harper and Row, 1969), pp. 321, 245. Pancake, *This Destructive War*, p. 37. It was against a bunch of drunken Hessians that Washington was to achieve his first notable victory. Curtis, *Organization of the British Army*, p. 52. The 1781 British army figures have been computed from tables in Mackesy, *War for America*, pp. 524–25; and Curtis, *Organization of the British Army*, p. 51.

17. Shy, *People Numerous and Armed*, chap. 9, "The Military Conflict."

18. Mackesy, *War for America*, p. 66. Bowler, *Failure of the British Army*, p. 9. Carp, *To Starve the Army*, p. 55.

19. Bowler, *Failure of the British Army.* p. 241.

20. Ibid., pp. 6–7.

21. Ibid., chap. 5.

22. Ibid., pp. 239, 53, quotation on p. 239. Owing to American provincialism and distrust of central authority, the supply problems of the Continental armies were in some ways worse than those facing the British. See Carp, *To Starve the Army.*

23. These were in 1776 "largely untrained, undisciplined, untried amateur soldiers, poorly armed, meagerly equipped and supplied, led by an amateur commander in chief, who was supported by amateur officers." Ward, *War of the Revolution*, p. 209.

24. Ward, ibid., p. 209. Mackesy says 25,000. *War for America*, p. 86.

25. Mackesy, *War for America*, p. 408.

26. Pancake, *This Destructive War*, p. 149. George Otto Trevelyan, *The American Revolution*, ed. Richard B. Morris (New York: David McKay, 1964), p. 300. Wallace, *Appeal to Arms*, p. 11.

27. See Mackesy, *War for America,* pp. 115–17.

28. Ward, *War of the Revolution,* vol. 1, p. 400 ff. Mackesy, *War for America,* pp. 58–60.

29. Howe had a "fleet of more than 260 warships and transports, laden with fifteen to eighteen thousand soldiers, innumerable horses, fieldpieces and small arms, quantities of ammunition, provisions and military equipment of every sort." Ward, *War of the Revolution,* vol. 1, p. 329. Nickerson, *Turning Point,* vol. 1, chap. 3. Anderson argues that the so-called missing instruction from Germaine is irrelevant, because nobody expected that Burgoyne would need Howe to move in force before Burgoyne reached Albany. See *Command of the Howe Brothers,* chap. 14.

30. Ward, *War of the Revolution,* vol. 2, p. 490.

31. Fuller, *Military History,* pp. 284, 308. Pancake, *This Destructive War,* p. 42. How many men actually surrendered to the Americans is a disputed question. On the difficulty of determining the exact number of Burgoyne's troops toward the end of the campaign, see Nickerson, *Turning Point,* vol. 2, pp. 435–52. The real victor at Saratoga was Benedict Arnold, but the incompetent Gates got most of the credit. That was a grave injustice and would bear much bitter fruit, eventually including Arnold's tragic defection from the American cause and the disastrous defeat of the American army under Gates at Camden, South Carolina. On the Saratoga Campaign, see Mackesy, *War for America,* chaps. 5–7; Ward, *War of the Revolution,* vols. 1 and 2, chaps. 36–43; Fuller, *Military History,* vol. 2, chap. 9.

32. Nickerson, *Turning Point,* vol. 1.

33. Mackesy says the British offer was made in order to free British forces to fight the French peril. *War for America,* pp. 185–89, 219–21. Samuel Flagg Bemis, *The Diplomacy of the American Revolution* (Bloomington: Indiana Univ. Press, 1935), chap. 5; Perkins, *France in the American Revolution,* p. 240.

34. Vergennes (1717–1787) would be the chief French negotiator of the treaty that ended the war. French help to the Americans had not been insignificant even before Saratoga. See Orlando W. Stephenson, "The Supply of Gunpowder in 1776," *American Historical Review* 30 (Jan. 1925); Claude H. Van Tyne, "French Aid before the Alliance of 1778," *American Historical Review* 39 (Oct. 1925); see also CIA, *Intelligence in the War of Independence.* The quotation is in Mackesy, *War for America,* p. 141.

35. Nickerson, *Turning Point,* p. 404. Mackesy, *War for America,* p. 147.

36. Alfred Cobban, *A History of Modern France* (Baltimore: Penguin, 1957), vol. 1, p. 122. "In the achievement of his foreign policy goals, Vergennes unintentionally helped to destroy the society and monarchy he wished to preserve." Orville Murphy, *Charles Gravier, Comte de Vergennes: French Diplomacy in the Age of Revolution, 1717–1787* (Albany: State Univ. of New York Press, 1982), p. 398.

37. Murphy, *Charles Gravier,* pp. 251, 250.

38. The quotation is in Mackesy, *War for America,* p. 159. This is an infelicitous phrase, recalling Churchill's sponsorship of the disastrous Italian cam-

paign that began in 1943 and was still going furiously when Berlin surrendered two years later. Gruber, "Britain's Southern Strategy," p. 238. Clinton, born in Newfoundland, son of the colonial governor of New York, was thirty-eight years old at the time of the Declaration of Independence and had made a distinguished record in the French and Indian War.

39. The relatively large number of loyalists who settled in eastern Canada after the revolution, and their descendants, laid the foundation for a distinctly cool attitude in English-speaking Canada toward the United States, lasting for generations afterward. DeMond, *Loyalists in North Carolina*, p. 200. The quotation is in Nelson, *General Horatio Gates*, pp. v.

40. Smith, *Loyalists and Redcoats*, pp. 165, ix, 169.

41. On this point, if on no other, the British strategists resemble the Communist leaders in Hanoi, always predicting but never seeing a major popular uprising against the government of South Vietnam.

42. Nelson, *American Tory*, p. 92; see the discussion of figures in Lambert, *South Carolina Loyalists*, pp. 320–21.

43. DeMond, *Loyalists in North Carolina*, p. 50.

44. Many Scots had supported the unsuccessful uprisings of 1715 and 1745 (the latter under Bonny Prince Charlie) aimed at restoring the House of Stuart to the throne whence it had been evicted by the "Glorious Revolution" of 1688. Ibid., pp. 51–52. The House of Hanover had acceded to the English throne in 1714, with George I. His great-grandson, George III of England, was also King of Hanover. The quotation is in Lambert, *South Carolina Loyalists*, p. 306.

45. Pancake, *This Destructive War*, p. 42. Bowler explains, regarding the British and German troops' search for provisions for themselves and their horses, "The foraging operations were never gentle affairs. Although most senior officers recognized the need to carry out these operations with a minimum of disruption and distress to the civil population, the plundering tendencies of the British and German regulars were almost impossible to restrain, as the repeated injunctions against that practice in army orders testify. The number of Americans, in the South and elsewhere, who were driven from loyalty to neutrality, or neutrality to opposition, can never be known, but it was surely large. And their numbers were swelled by those who were victims of corrupt practices of commissaries, quartermasters and barrackmasters." *Failure of the British Army*, pp. 242–43. Mackesy, *War for America*, p. 112. Lambert, *South Carolina Loyalists*, p. 203.

46. Smith, *Loyalists and Redcoats*, p. 141.

47. At Inchon, MacArthur had had 70,000 troops. The quotation is in Fuller, *Military History*, vol. 2, p. 312; see also Ward, *War of the Revolution*, vol. 2, p. 703. Clinton, *American Rebellion*, p. 171.

48. Ward, *War of the Revolution*, vol. 2, p. 706.

49. Lambert, *South Carolina Loyalists*, p. 18. Greene, *Life of Nathanael Greene*, vol. 3, p. 10. The quotation is in Ward, *War of the Revolution*, vol. 2, p. 704.

50. The quotation is in Ward, *War of the Revolution*, vol. 2, pp. 731–32. For

an attempt to defend Gates's conduct both before and after the Camden debacle, see Nelson, *General Horatio Gates.*

51. Ward, *War of the Revolution,* vol. 2, p. 737. Gruber, "Britain's Southern Strategy," p. 229. Wickwire and Wickwire, *Cornwallis,* pp. 192–93. The quotation is in Alden, *South in the Revolution,* p. 249. One distinguished student of these affairs, William B. Willcox, writes that Cornwallis never understood the role of sea power in the struggle. *Portrait of a General,* pp. 442–43.

52. Pancake, *This Destructive War,* p. 139. Ward, *War of the Revolution,* vol. 2, p. 745. Fuller, *Military History,* p. 313.

53. Clinton, *American Rebellion,* p. 228, my emphasis.

54. Ward, *War of the Revolution,* vol. 2, pp. 753, 762. Cornwallis is quoted in Wickwire and Wickwire, *Cornwallis,* p. 269. For a good description of the battle of Cowpens, see Ward, *War of the Revolution,* vol. 2, chap. 69; for King's Mountain, see chap. 67 in the same work. Weigley, *American Way of War,* p. 31.

55. Ward, *War of the Revolution,* vol. 2, p. 748.

56. Alden, *South in the Revolution,* p. 259. Mackesy, *War for America,* p. 407. Sir John Fortescue, quoted in Ward, *War of the Revolution,* vol. 2, p. 844. Weigley, *American Way of War,* p. 36. see also Thayer, *Nathanael Greene;* Thane, *Fighting Quaker.*

57. Wallace, *Appeal to Arms,* p. 245.

58. Niccolo Machiavelli, *The Art of War* (New York: Da Capo, 1965), originally published in 1521, book six. *Henry V* 3.6.116–17.

59. Royster, *Revolutionary People at War,* p. 278.

60. Ibid., p. 321. But he adds, "The Americans most often mistaken for neutrals were probably revolutionaries who wanted the fruits of independence without the violence of war" (p. 281).

61. Bass, *Swamp Fox,* p. 112.

62. Ward, *War of the Revolution,* vol. 2, chap. 62; John Shy, "American Society and Its War for Independence," in Higginbotham, *Military Analysis.* Weigley, *American Way of War,* p. 26.

63. Ward, *War of the Revolution,* vol. 2, pp. 661, 660. Pancake, *This Destructive War,* p. 83.

64. Bass, *Swamp Fox,* p. 57.

65. For examples of the murders, see ibid., p. 90; for the surrender after Fort Balfour, p. 176; the quotation is on p. 183.

66. Ward, *War of the Revolution,* vol. 2, p. 706, passim. Gregorie, *Thomas Sumter,* p. 148 n. Bass, *Gamecock,* p. 100, Greene quoted on p. 151. The revolutionary civil government of South Carolina in 1781 and after allowed loyalists to win readmission into the community by serving in the militia for six months.

67. McCrady, *South Carolina in the Revolution,* p. 139. Gregorie, *Thomas Sumter,* p. 147.

68. Pancake, *This Destructive War,* p. 244.

69. Bass, *Gamecock,* pp. 90, 106, passim, quotation on p. 90.

70. Gregorie, *Thomas Sumter*, pp. 111, 172. Ward, *War of the Revolution*, vol. 2, p. 662.

71. Bass, *Swamp Fox*, p. 59.

72. McCrady, *South Carolina in the Revolution*, p. 137. The quotations are in Gregorie, *Thomas Sumter*, p. 198; and Alden, *South in the Revolution*, p. 242.

73. The first quotation is in Ward, *War of the Revolution*, vol. 2, p. 661. Weigley, *American Way of War*, p. 27. Bass, *Swamp Fox*, pp. 66–76. Lee, *Memoirs of the War*, p. 174.

74. Bass, *Swamp Fox*, pp. 68, 70. Rankin, *Francis Marion*, p. 131. The quotation is in Bass, *Swamp Fox*, p. 91.

75. Bass, *Swamp Fox*, p. 126. Pancake, *This Destructive War*, p. 110. Bass, *Swamp Fox*, p. 22; see also Gerson, *Swamp Fox*. Greene, *Life of Nathanael Greene*, vol. 2, p. 167.

76. Rankin, *Francis Marion*, p. 123.

77. Ibid., p. 298. Clinton, *American Rebellion*, p. 501.

78. Lee, *Memoirs of the War*, p. 203. Bowler, *Failure of the British Army*, p. 91. Clinton, *The American Rebellion*, pp. 476–77.

79. Bass, *Swamp Fox*, pp. 189–96. The quotation is in Bass, *Gamecock*, p. 156.

80. Bass, *Gamecock*, p. 217.

81. Gregorie, *Thomas Sumter*, p. 80, quotation on p. 95.

82. Bass, *Gamecock*, pp. 84–85.

83. Gregorie, *Thomas Sumter*, pp. 137, 89. Bass, *Gamecock*, p. 57.

84. Gregorie, *Thomas Sumter*, pp. 156, 191, 103.

85. Bass, *Gamecock*, pp. 177, 144, 3, quotations on pp. 177, 3.

86. Bass, *Swamp Fox*, pp. 207–8. Lighthorse Harry Lee is quoted in Lee, *Memoirs of the War*, pp. 174–75; and in Bass, *Swamp Fox*, p. 210.

87. The prisoner is quoted in Gregorie, *Thomas Sumter*, p. 123. Bass, *Swamp Fox*, p. 74.

88. Greene is quoted in Bass, *Gamecock*, p. 120, my emphasis. Mackesy, *War for America*, pp. 404–5. Rankin, *Francis Marion*, p. 299.

89. Alden, *South in the Revolution*, p. 267. Bowler, *Failure of the British Army*, p. 240.

90. Ward, *War of the Revolution*, vol. 2, p. 706; Fuller accepts the figure of 8,300 in his *Military History*, vol. 2, p. 312; but Mackesy says Clinton left Cornwallis with only 4,000. *War for America*, p. 342. At any rate, Cornwallis did receive reinforcements from Clinton after the latter had arrived in New York (p. 406).

91. Cornwallis to Clinton, Apr. 23, 1781, in Clinton, *American Rebellion*, p. 512. Mackesy, *War for America*, p. 408; see also Ward, *War of the Revolution*, vol. 2, pp. 796–97. Johnston, *Yorktown Campaign*, p. 26. The second quotation is in Wickwire and Wickwire, *Cornwallis*, p. 321.

92. Weigley, *American Way of War*, p. 36. The quotation is in Mackesy, *War for America*, p. 408. In the New Jersey campaign of 1776–1777—the prelude to

Saratoga—General Howe established numerous posts across that province, but Washington showed that even the still-maturing Continental army could easily destroy such strong points.

93. Mackesy, *War for America*, p. 461.

94. Ibid., p. 434.

95. "The blunders of British generals have frequently been stressed, but the negligence, corruption and inefficiency which pervaded the administration of the army, and the manifold natural obstacles that stood in the way of an attempt to suppress rebellion in America have been rarely accorded adequate recognition." Curtis, *Organization of the British Army*, p. 148. Among the voluminous writings on Washington's importance in the war, see James Thomas Flexner, *George Washington in the American Revolution* (Boston: Little, Brown, 1968), chap. 58, "Cincinnatus Assayed."

96. Ironically, in 1782 a British fleet decisively defeated de Grasse in the West Indies. Weigley, in Higginbotham, *Military Analysis*. Mackesy, *War for America*, p. 395.

97. "The first, the supreme, the most-far-reaching act of judgment that the statesman and commander have to make is to establish the kind of war on which they are embarking. . . . This is the first of all strategic questions and the most comprehensive." Clausewitz, *On War*, book 1, chap. 1.

98. Pancake, *This Destructive War*, p. 220; out of a total engaged for both sides of 4,400, there were nearly 1,400 casualties. Ward, *War of the Revolution*, vol. 1, chap. 78.

99. Wickwire and Wickwire, *Cornwallis*, pp. 192–93.

100. McCrady, *South Carolina in the Revolution*, p. 138.

2. Confederate Guerrillas: The War of Secession

1. Basler, *Works of Lincoln*, vol. 5, p. 49.

2. Weigley, *American Way of War*, p. 131; Hattaway and Jones, *How the North Won*, pp. 217, 233, 336.

3. Basler, *Works of Lincoln*, vol. 6, p. 108. Hattaway and Jones, *How the North Won*, p. 250.

4. Hattaway and Jones, *How the North Won*, p. 491. Brownlee, *Gray Ghosts*, p. 108.

5. Mosby, *Memoirs*, p. 5.

6. Ibid., pp. 12; quotation on p. 16.

7. Ibid., p. 147.

8. Wert, *Mosby's Rangers*, pp. 293, 75.

9. Ibid., p. 34.

10. Brownlee, *Gray Ghosts*, p. ix. The quotation is in Mosby, *Memoirs*, pp. 149–50. Wert, *Mosby's Rangers*, pp. 63–64, 111.

11. Wert, *Mosby's Rangers*, pp. 98, 92, 192, quotation on p. 83.

12. Ibid., p. 81, passim. The quotation is in Mosby, *Memoirs*, p. 284.

13. Wert, *Mosby's Rangers,* pp. 132–33, 271–72.

14. Ibid., p. 122.

15. Siepel, *Rebel,* p. 133. Wert, *Mosby's Rangers,* pp. 260, 196, 115, Augur quoted on p. 199.

16. Wert, *Mosby's Rangers,* pp. 197, 248–49, quotation on p. 197.

17. Ibid., pp. 69–70, passim; for the importance of plunder, see p. 84. For an example of Mosby's signature, see *Mosby, Memoirs,* p. 199. Beringer et al., *Why the South Lost,* p. 345.

18. Wert, *Mosby's Rangers,* pp. 138–39, 142, 266–67, 251–52. "Although for the most part good fighting men, his rangers were, in some ways, the 'feather-bed soldiers' they were accused of being. They were strangers to camp routine. They slept not outdoors but in comfortable quarters provided by a sympathetic populace. They seldom if ever made coffee for themselves, let alone fried bacon, soaked hardtack, or washed a shirt. Most couldn't pitch a tent and didn't know the first thing about cavalry drill." Siepel, *Rebel,* p. 101.

19. Wert, *Mosby's Rangers,* pp. 157, 140, quotation on p. 157.

20. Bruce Catton, foreword to Brownlee, *Gray Ghosts,* p. viii. James Ramage does not believe that Mosby's activities extended the war; see his excellent *Gray Ghost: The Life of Col. John Singleton Mosby* (Lexington, Ky.: Univ. Press of Kentucky, 1999), p. 345.

21. Mosby maintained "that his men tied up so many troops and caused so much uncertainty in the [Shenandoah] Valley that Grant was unable to marshal sufficient force to crush Petersburg before spring. With some justification [Mosby] made the claim that his men had provided Richmond and the Confederacy with six extra months of life." Siepel, *Rebel,* p. 127. Wert, in *Mosby's Rangers,* did not agree. The quotation in the text is in Wert, *Mosby's Rangers,* p. 292.

22. Stuart is quoted in Wert, *Mosby's Rangers,* p. 138. Ulysses S. Grant, *The Personal Memoirs of U. S. Grant,* ed. E.B. Long (New York: Grosset and Dunlap, 1962), p. 372.

23. Mosby, *Memoirs,* chap. 20.

24. Castel, *William Clarke Quantrill,* p. 23, quotation on p. 43.

25. Ibid., pp. 64–65. The quotation is in Carl W. Breihan, *Quantrill and His Civil War Guerrillas* (New York: Promontory, 1959), p. 52.

26. Brownlee, *Gray Ghosts,* p. 104, quotation on p. 60. Castel, *William Clarke Quantrill,* pp. 77–80.

27. Monaghan, *Civil War on the Western Border,* p. 279. Proslavery hoodlums raided the town in 1856. Connelley, *Quantrill and the Border Wars,* p. 308.

28. McPherson, *Battle Cry of Freedom,* p. 786. Fellman, *Inside War,* p. 25. For vivid descriptions of the raid, see Castel, *William Clarke Quantrill,* pp. 122–41; and Connelley, *Quantrill and the Border Wars,* pp. 335–96.

29. Brownlee, *Gray Ghosts,* p. 124.

30. Fellman, *Inside War,* p. 201.

31. Ibid., p. 206; but see also Schultz, *Quantrill's War.*

32. Castel, *William Clarke Quantrill*, p. 141. Brownlee, *Gray Ghosts*, pp. 124, 125.

33. Brownlee, *Gray Ghosts*, p. 126. Fellman, *Inside War*, p. 95.

34. Connelley, *Quantrill and the Border Wars*, pp. 278–80. The quotations are in Fellman, *Inside War*, pp. 259, 106.

35. Brownlee, *Gray Ghosts*, p. 133. The quotation is in Castel, *William Clarke Quantrill*, p. 156.

36. Castel, *William Clarke Quantrill*, pp. 151–52, 213. Connelley, *Quantrill and the Border Wars*, pp. 383, 455, 456. Monaghan, *Civil War on the Western Border*, p. 345. Brownlee, *Gray Ghosts*, p. 231.

37. Fellman, *Inside War*, p. 5.

38. Ibid., p. xvii, quotations on pp. 51, xvi. Governor Claiborne Fox Jackson and some members of the legislature met in the town of Neosho and declared Missouri's secession in November 1861, but Federal troops and loyal civilians held the state in the Union. Of Missouri whites who fought in the Civil War, three-quarters fought for the Union. McPherson, *Battle Cry of Freedom*, p. 293.

39. Fellman, *Inside War*, pp. 24, 251, xix. Basler, *Works of Lincoln*, vol. 6, p. 500.

40. A "territory" was not (yet) a state.

41. Nevins explores many of the issues and events of the Kansas troubles in his *Ordeal of the Union*.

42. Brownlee, *Gray Ghosts*, p. 31.

43. Ibid., p. 26; see also Fellman, *Inside War*.

44. Brownlee, *Gray Ghosts*, pp. 32, 35, quotation on p. 32, my emphasis.

45. Ibid., pp. 10, 39, quotations on pp. 43, 47, 50. This was the same Lane who barely escaped with his life from the slaughter at Lawrence in 1863. Fellman, *Inside War*, p. 164, passim.

46. Brownlee, *Gray Ghosts*, pp. 190, 196, quotation on p. 190.

47. Written in March 1864; see Castel, *William Clarke Quantrill*, p. 174.

48. Fellman, *Inside War*, p. 188.

49. Ibid., pp. 216, 93, 112 n, 172, 53, 175. Brownlee, *Gray Ghosts*, pp. 85–86.

50. Fellman, *Inside War*, p. 87.

51. Ibid., pp. 117, 128.

52. Ibid., p. 170, quotation on p. 166.

53. Ibid., pp. 38, 49, my emphasis.

54. Monaghan, *Civil War on the Western Border*, p. 316. Fellman, *Inside War*, pp. 108–10.

55. Brownlee, *Gray Ghosts*, pp. 185–86. The quotation is in Fellman, *Inside War*, p. 94.

56. Fellman, *Inside War*, pp. 167, 137 ff., quotation on p. 142.

57. Robert L. Kerby, "Why the Confederacy Lost," *Review of Politics* 35 (July 1973). "The Confederates' refusal to consider the guerrilla alternative may be a major reason why the South lost the Civil War." Beringer et al., *Why the South*

Lost, p. 342. See the discussion in Gary W. Gallagher, *The Confederate War* (Cambridge, Mass.: Harvard Univ. Press, 1997).

58. Beringer et al., *Why the South Lost,* p. 436. Grant quoted in Hattaway and Jones, *How the North Won,* p. 701.

59. Quoted in Morison, *Oxford History,* p. 698.

60. Escott, *After Secession,* p. 26, passim.

61. Ibid., chap. 2. Dowdey, *Lee,* pp. 121, 126, Lee quoted on p. 679; see also Nevins, *War for the Union: The Improvised War, 1861-1862* (New York: Scribner's, 1959), pp. 110–11.

62. For the origins of the state of West Virginia, see Nevins, *War for the Union,* vol. 1, pp. 139–44, 106. Richard Nelson Current, *Lincoln's Loyalists: Union Soldiers from the Confederacy* (New York: Oxford Univ. Press, 1992), p. 18. Humes, *Loyal Mountaineers of Tennessee,* p. 9. Current thinks the number is closer to 40,000. *Lincoln's Loyalists,* p. 60, passim.

63. Escott, *After Secession,* p. 171. Wiley, *Road to Appomattox,* pp. 43, 47 ff., quotation on p. 43.

64. Austin and Tallahassee were the only Confederate state capitals to remain unoccupied by the end of the war. Wiley, *Road to Appomattox,* chap. 2.

65. The Union states in 1861 were California, Connecticut, Delaware, Illinois, Indiana, Iowa, Kentucky, Maine, Maryland, Massachusetts, Michigan, Minnesota, Missouri, New Hampshire, New Jersey, New York, Ohio, Oregon, Pennsylvania, Rhode Island, Vermont, and Wisconsin; during the war Kansas, Nevada, and West Virginia achieved statehood. The Confederate States were Alabama, Arkansas, Florida, Georgia, Louisiana, Mississippi, North Carolina, South Carolina, Tennessee, Texas, and Virginia.

66. Allan Nevins, *The Emergence of Lincoln,* vol. 1, *Douglas, Buchanan and Party Chaos 1857–1859* (New York: Scribner's, 1950), p. 19.

67. Weigley, *American Way of War,* p. 130.

68. Allan Nevins, *War for the Union: The Organized War, 1863–1864* (New York: Scribner's, 1971), p. 7.

69. Weigley, *American Way of War,* pp. 128–29.

70. Hattaway and Jones, *How the North Won,* pp. 684, 726.

71. The longer a war lasts, the more likely it is to attract new participants. See Geoffrey Blainey, *The Causes of War,* 3d ed. (New York: Free Press, 1988), chap. 15.

72. Besides that, Confederate territorial ambitions dictated an offensive strategy. The Confederacy claimed or coveted not only the seceded states but also Missouri, Kentucky, Maryland, and the Indian and New Mexico Territories. The Confederate flag had not eleven stars, but thirteen: the last two represented Missouri and Kentucky.

73. Lee's vision had the full support of President Davis. Richard M. McMurry, *Two Great Rebel Armies: An Essay in Confederate Military History* (Chapel Hill: Univ. of North Carolina Press, 1989); Russell F. Weigley, "Napoleonic Strategy: R. E. Lee and the Confederacy," in Weigley, *American Way of War,* pp. 92–

128. Lee continues to fascinate students of the secession conflict. Recent works on the subject include Joseph L. Harsh, *Confederate Tide Rising: Robert E. Lee and the Making of Southern Strategy* (Kent, Ohio: Kent State Univ. Press, 1998); Gary W. Gallagher, *Lee: The Soldier* (Lincoln: Univ. of Nebraska Press, 1996); James A. Kegel, *North and South with Lee and Jackson: The Lost Story of Gettysburg* (Mechanicsburg, Pa.: Stackpole, 1996); John D. McKenzie, *Uncertain Glory: Lee's Generalship Reexamined* (New York: Hippocrene, 1997); Charles P. Roland, *Reflections on Lee* (Mechanicsburg, Pa.: Stackpole, 1995); Emory M. Thomas, *Robert E. Lee* (New York: Norton, 1995).

74. Hattaway and Jones, *How the North Won*, p. 687. Antoine Jomini (1779–1869) was a Swiss general in the service of Napoleon and later the military mentor to the future Czar Alexander II; he wrote *Precis de l'art de la guerre* (1836), a work that shaped military thinking for decades, nowhere perhaps more than in the United States. On the strategy of Northern generals, see Donald, *Why the North Won*; T. Harry Williams, *Lincoln and His Generals* (New York: Dorset, 1952).

75. Murdock, *One Million Men*.

76. Moore, *Conscription and Conflict*, p. 11.

77. Ibid., chap. 4 and esp. pp. 56–57. Escott, *After Secession*; Wiley, *Road to Appomattox*, chap. 2. McPherson, *Battle Cry of Freedom*, pp. 611–12. The quotation is in Nevins, *War for the Union*, vol. 3, p. 13. Wiley, *Life of Johnny Reb*, pp. 337–39, 344.

78. Moore, *Conscription and Conflict*, pp. 279 ff. The quotation is in McPherson, *Battle Cry of Freedom*, p. 432.

79. Charles W. Ramsdell, *Behind the Lines in the Southern Confederacy* (Baton Rouge: Louisiana State Univ. Press, 1944), p. 117. Escott, *After Secession*, p. 111; see similar events in Wiley, *Life of Johnny Reb*, pp. 43–47; Nevins, *War for the Union*, vol. 4, pp. 235–41.

80. Nevins, *War for the Union*, vol. 4, pp. 239, 237.

81. Anderson, *By Sea and River*, p. 15. Nevins, *War for the Union*, vol. 3, pp. 338–39. Much of the information for this section on the blockade has come from Anderson, *By Sea and River*.

82. Nevins, *War for the Union*, vol. 3, p. 384.

83. Escott, *After Secession*, chap. 4. Morison, *Oxford History*, p. 698. Wiley, *Road to Appomattox*, chap. 2. Thomas B. Alexander and Richard E. Beringer, *The Anatomy of the Confederate Congress* (Nashville, Tenn.: Vanderbilt Univ. Press, 1972). McPherson, *Battle Cry of Freedom*, pp. 689–92.

84. Wiley, *Road to Appomattox*, p. 70.

85. Ibid., p. 65. Allan Nevins, *The War for the Union*, vol. 4, *The Organized War to Victory, 1864–1865* (New York: Scribner's, 1971), p. 248.

86. Barrett, *Civil War in North Carolina*, p. 29. Paludan, *Victims*, p. 69. Nevins, *War for the Union*, vol. 3, p. 13.

87. Lonn, *Desertion during the Civil War*, p. 231. Barrett, *Civil War in North Carolina*, pp. 190, 239. The quotation is from Tatum, *Disloyalty in the Confederacy*, quoted in Commager, *Defeat of the Confederacy*, p. 125. Paludan, *Victims*.

88. Catton, *The Army of the Potomac*, vol. 2, *Glory Road*, pp. 102, 255.

89. Escott, *After Secession*, chap. 6, p. 179. In 1789 the larger American community had, largely under Southern leadership, discarded confederation for a more effective, more national constitution. The embodiments of "federalism" were two Virginians—George Washington and John Marshall.

90. Perhaps the best evidence that there was no Confederate nationalism, at least in the same sense that there was and is a Polish or an Irish nationalism, is the disappearance of Southern secessionist politics after 1865.

91. Wiley, *Road to Appomattox*, p. 82. "Confederate ideology was defeated in large measure by the internal contradictions that wartime circumstances brought so prominently to the fore." Faust, *Creation of Confederate Nationalism*, p. 84.

92. Eaton, *Southern Confederacy*, p. 256.

93. After the war Davis refused to appear on the same platform with either Beauregard or Johnston, even at the dedication of Confederate war memorials. And see Steven E. Woodworth, *Jefferson Davis and His Generals: The Failure of Confederate Command in the West* (Lawrence: Univ. of Kansas Press, 1990), p. 277. Nevins, *War for the Union*, vol. 3, pp. 38–39. See William C. Davis, *Jefferson Davis: The Man and His Hour* (New York: HarperCollins, 1991); Steven E. Woodworth, *Davis and Lee at War* (Lawrence: Univ. of Kansas Press, 1995). And consult Jefferson Davis, *The Rise and Fall of the Confederate Government*, 2 vols. (New York: Appleton, 1881).

94. Eaton, *Jefferson Davis*, p. 272. Nevins, *War for the Union*, vol. 3, p. 37. Boyce is quoted in Beringer et al., *Why the South Lost*, p. 290. Eaton, *Southern Confederacy*, p. 259.

95. Wiley, *Road to Appomattox*, p. 78.

96. The quotation is in Nevins, *War for the Union*, vol. 3, p. 45. Davis, *Government of Our Own*, pp. 406–7.

97. The Confederate Congress actually declared war on the United States (May 1861)! And Confederate forces had been seizing dozens of Federal installations and vessels, and even firing on the flag of the United States, for many weeks before Sumter; see Harsh, *Confederate Tide Rising*, p. 8.

98. The "one great commanding figure is Lincoln, who grows in stature from crisis to crisis." Allan Nevins, *The War for the Union*, vol. 2, *War Becomes Revolution* (New York: Scribner's, 1960), p. ix.

99. Morison, *Oxford History*, p. 608. Basler, *Works of Lincoln*, vol. 8, p. 332. Nevins, *Statesmanship of the Civil War*, p. 51. And see Faust, *The Creation of Confederate Nationalism*, chap. 4.

100. Eaton, *Southern Confederacy*, p. 30. See an extended discussion on the fear of the eventual demise of slavery in Don E. Fehrenbacher, *The Dred Scott Case* (New York: Oxford Univ. Press, 1978), pp. 541 ff.

101. McPherson, *Battle Cry of Freedom*, pp. 549, 550, 311. See also Henry Adams, *The Education of Henry Adams* (New York: Modern Library, 1946), chaps. 8–14.

102. Nevins, *Statesmanship of the Civil War*, p. 53. Jefferson Davis immediately recognized how damaging this statement would be to the image of the Confederacy abroad.

103. Dumas Malone, *Jefferson and His Time*, vol. 6, *The Sage of Monticello* (Boston: Little, Brown, 1981). Irving Brant, *James Madison: Father of the Constitution, 1787–1800* (Indianapolis: Bobbs Merrill, 1950), p. 250. James Thomas Flexner, *George Washington: Anguish and Farewell 1793–1799* (Boston: Little, Brown, 1972), pp. 114–15, 485.

104. Bruce Catton, *The Coming Fury* (Garden City, N.Y.: Doubleday, 1961), p. 335. Long, *Robert E. Lee*, p. 83, my emphasis. Wiley, *Road to Appomattox*, chap. 3.

105. For extended discussion of these ideas, see Kenneth Stampp, "The Southern Road to Appomattox," in Kenneth Stampp, ed., *The Imperilled Union: Essays on the Background of the Civil War* (New York: Oxford Univ. Press, 1980).

106. Glatthaar, *Forged in Battle*, p. 122.

107. Ibid., p. 201. On blacks in the Union Army, see Cornish, *Sable Arm*; Nevins, *War for the Union*, vol. 2, chap. 20.

108. Wesley, *Collapse of the Confederacy*, chap. 5, pp. 140, 137. Wiley, *Life of Johnny Reb*, p. 329.

109. Wesley, *Collapse of the Confederacy*, p. 154.

110. Hunter is quoted in Bruce Catton, *Never Call Retreat* (Garden City, N.Y.: Doubleday, 1965), pp. 426–27. Cobb is quoted in Wesley, *Collapse of the Confederacy*, p. 160, my emphasis. And see Beringer et al., *Why the South Lost*, chap. 15, "Coming to Terms with Slavery."

111. Wesley, *Collapse of the Confederacy*, pp. 161, 162. Lee, letter dated January 11, 1865, in Catton, *Never Call Retreat*, p. 428. Escott, *After Secession*, chap. 8.

112. Escott, *After Secession*, p. 252.

113. Nevins, *War for the Union*, vol. 4, pp. 260–61; "Sherman himself did not order Columbia burned." Catton, *Never Call Retreat*, p. 434. Sherman himself worked throughout the night to see the fires put out. McPherson, *Battle Cry of Freedom*, p. 829; see also Barrett, *Sherman's March*, esp. chaps. 6, 17; and Lucas, *Sherman and the Burning of Columbia*. See Sherman's own brief treatment of this episode in his *Memoirs* (New York: Appleton, 1875), vol. 2, pp. 286–88.

114. Hattaway and Jones, *How the North Won*, p. 492. Numbers of these deserters joined the Union armies; Lonn, *Desertion during the Civil War*, p. 4. The quotation is in Dowdey, *Lee*, p. 519. See Barrett, *Sherman's March*, pp. 280–81.

115. Michael Fellman, *Citizen Sherman* (New York: Random House, 1995), pp. 226–27; John F. Marszalek, *Sherman: A Soldier's Passion for Order* (New York: Free Press, 1993). See Anthony James Joes, *Guerrilla Insurgency before the Cold War* (Westport, Conn.: Praeger, 1996), chap. 2, "Genocide in La Vendée," and chap. 3, "Guerrillas against Napoleon." Catton, *Never Call Retreat*, p. 467. Davis refused the offer of a ship. Fellman, *Citizen Sherman*, p. 240.

116. The quotation is in Eric Foner, *Reconstruction: America's Unfinished Revolution* (New York: Harper and Row, 1989), p. 36. Lincoln's purpose was "to weaken the confederacy by establishing state governments that could attract

the broadest possible support, and for that purpose he defined as a unionist virtually every white Southerner who took an oath pledging to uphold the Union and the abolition of slavery" (p. 62). See the text of the Proclamation in Basler, *Works of Lincoln*, vol. 7, pp. 53–56. Some representatives were also seated from Tennessee and Virginia.

117. Hattaway and Jones, *How the North Won*, p. 676. The quotation is in Brownlee, *Gray Ghosts*, p. 240.

118. Future guerrilla conflicts in Yugoslavia, in Vietnam, in Afghanistan, and in many other places would only confirm this principle.

119. Sadly, slave women did not escape the harshness of guerrilla war as lightly as white women did. Barrett, *Sherman's March*, p. 85, passim.

120. Beringer et al., *Why the South Lost*, p. 343. On April 4, 1865, the day after the fall of Richmond, President Davis issued a proclamation that in effect called for guerrilla resistance. Lee is quoted in Dowdey, *Lee*, p. 592, my emphasis. See Lee's advice, just before Appomattox, to younger officers against turning to guerrilla war in Gallagher, *Fighting for the Confederacy*, pp. 531–33.

121. Nevins, *War for the Union*, vol. 4, pp. 224 ff. Beringer et al., *Why the South Lost*, p. 438.

122. Beringer et al., *Why the South Lost*, p. 342; Brownlee, *Gray Ghosts*, p. 369. See Gallagher, *Confederate War*, esp. chap. 4, "Defeat." For a somewhat different view of this question, see Frederickson, *Why the Confederacy Did Not Fight*. Frederickson offers reasons why the planter aristocracy was reluctant to wage guerrilla war, but he does not address the failure of nonslaveholding whites to do so, on the Missouri model.

123. Gen. Edmund Kirby Smith surrendered the last important Confederate military force on June 2, 1865, in Texas.

3. The Philippine War: Forgotten Victory

1. In like manner, the territorial conceptions of Indonesian nationalists—which islands should be included in Indonesia and which should not—were created by their Dutch imperial rulers. See Rupert Emerson, *From Empire to Nation* (Cambridge, Mass.: Harvard Univ. Press, 1960), p. 125.

2. The quotations are in Phelan, *Hispanization*, pp. 6, 4, ix, 159. See also p. 131.

3. Ibid., p. 161.

4. Spaniards who came from Spain were *peninsulares*; those who were born in the colony were *creoles*. Wildman, *Aguinaldo*.

5. See French E. Chadwick, *The Relations of the United States and Spain: The Spanish American War*, 2 vols. (New York: Scribner's, 1911); Freidel, *Splendid Little War*; Bradford, *Crucible of Empire*. On the American army and the war, see Graham A. Cosmas, *An Army for Empire: The United States Army in the Spanish-American War* (Columbia: Univ. of Missouri Press, 1971).

6. In Manila Bay Dewey said "You may fire when you are ready, Gridley,"

a remark that became famous, for some unfathomable reason. Gates, *Schoolbooks*, chap. 1. For deep background, consult Taylor, *Philippine Insurrection*.

7. Sexton, *Soldiers in the Sun*, p. 248.

8. Imperial German possessions in the area included Kiaochow and Samoa.

9. Gates, *Schoolbooks*, chap. 1; Leech, *Days of McKinley*.

10. Otis was among other things a graduate of Harvard Law School and the main founder of the U.S. Army school at Fort Leavenworth. The exact number of troops is disputed. Linn, *U.S. Army*, p. 12.

11. Schurman (1854–1942) later served as ambassador to Greece and to Germany; Worcester (1866–1924) wrote *The Philippine Islands and Their People*. The quotations are in Gates, *Schoolbooks*, pp. 92–93.

12. Sexton, *Soldiers in the Sun*, p. 239.

13. Linn, *U.S. Army*, p. 169.

14. Gates, *Schoolbooks*, p. 186. The snows in the Greek mountains likewise seem to have interfered with guerrilla movements more than with those of the national Greek army.

15. Linn, *U.S. Army*, p. 43.

16. One wonders how many times a mother turned in her son's rifle in order to force him to quit the insurgency. Gates, *Schoolbooks*, p. 218.

17. See especially Linn, *U.S. Army*, pp. 154–55. The British concentrated the Boer population in large camps for several reasons: to cut off the Boer guerrillas from food and intelligence, to provide shelter for civilians whose houses had been burned, and to protect from reprisals Boer civilians and native Africans who had declared either neutrality or allegiance to the British. The unhealthful conditions in those camps were the result of incompetence, not malice.

18. Linn, *U.S. Army*, p. 27.

19. Gates, *Schoolbooks*, p. 168.

20. Linn, *U.S. Army*, pp. 110, 145. Gates, *Schoolbooks*, p. 175.

21. Linn, *U.S. Army*, p. 22. May, *Battle for Batangas*, pp. 138, 158.

22. Linn, *U.S. Army*, pp. 13, 19, 74, 164.

23. Gates, *Schoolbooks*, p. 164. Linn, *U.S. Army*, p. 158.

24. Aguinaldo, *Second Look*, p. 66.

25. Gates, *Schoolbooks*, pp. 215, 278.

26. Linn, *U.S. Army*, p. 16. The quotation is in Sexton, *Soldiers in the Sun*, p. 239.

27. Sexton, *Soldiers in the Sun*, pp. 255 ff. General Pershing, among others, blamed the Bryanites for prolonging the conflict. Vandiver, *Black Jack*, p. 254.

28. Aguinaldo, *Second Look*, p. 87. Leech, *Days of McKinley*, p. 350; Louis W. Koenig, *Bryan: A Political Biography of William Jennings Bryan* (New York: Putnam's, 1971), p. 292.

29. May, *Battle for Batangas*, p. 183, passim. Gates, *Schoolbooks*, p. 220.

30. See interesting details of this and other events in chap. 7 of Funston, *Memories of Two Wars*.

31. The Magdudukuts ("Secret Avengers") carried out Aguinaldo's promise to "exterminate all traitors." H.W. Brands, *Bound to Empire: The United States and the Philippines* (New York: Oxford Univ. Press, 1992), p. 55.

32. Linn, *U.S. Army*, pp. 129–30.

33. From May 1900 to June 1901, U.S. forces suffered 245 fatalities, 490 wounded, and 118 captured. Sexton, *Soldiers in the Sun*, p. 251.

34. For these Samar events, including the indescribable mutilations of the corpses of U.S. soldiers, see Schott, *The Ordeal of Samar*. The whole situation would almost certainly not have occurred if the number of U.S. forces on Samar, and for that matter in the Philippines as a whole, had been adequate. See Brian M. Linn, "The Struggle for Samar," in Bradford, *Crucible of Empire*. The quotation is in Gates, *Schoolbooks*, p. 254.

35. Sexton, *Soldiers in the Sun*, pp. 238, 283; Linn, *U.S. Army*, p. 25.

36. Henry F. Graff, ed., *American Imperialism and the Philippine Insurrection* (Boston: Little, Brown, 1969), p. xiv; Garel A. Grunder and William E. Livezey, *The Philippines and the United States* (Norman: Univ. of Oklahoma Press, 1951), p. 55.

37. Gates, *Schoolbooks*, p. 101.

38. May, *Battle for Batangas*, pp. 178, 193, passim.

39. Aguinaldo, *Second Look*, p. 83, quotation on p. 116.

40. Linn, *U.S. Army*, p. 60.

41. On Lyautey (1854–1934), see Andre Maurois, *Lyautey* (New York: Appleton, 1931); Sonia Howe, *Lyautey of Morocco* (London: Hodder and Stoughton, 1931); Douglas Porch, *The Conquest of Morocco* (New York: Knopf, 1982); Jean Gottmann, "Bugeaud, Gallieni, Lyautey: The Development of French Colonial Warfare," in Edward Mead Earle, ed., *Makers of Modern Strategy* (Princeton, N.J.: Princeton Univ. Press, 1941). The quotation is in Gates, *Schoolbooks*, p. 271.

42. Linn, *U.S. Army*, p. 170.

43. The quotation is in Jornacion, "Time of The Eagles," p. 252. Hurley, *Swish of the Kris*, pp. 87, 241.

44. Phelan, *Hispanization*, p. 4.

45. As the Spanish in the Philippines, the British in India, the French in Vietnam, and the Dutch in Indonesia always found it easy to raise relatively loyal native armies from among religious or ethnic minorities, or both.

46. Vandiver, *Black Jack*, p. 251. See also Smythe, *Guerrilla Warrior*. General Bates, son of Edward Bates, the prominent Whig politician and Lincoln's attorney general, had as a young officer fought in many of the great battles of the Civil War. See the text of the agreement between General Bates and the sultan of Sulu in Jornacion, "Time of the Eagles," appendix 1.

47. T.J. George, *Revolt on Mindanao: The Rise of Islam in Philippine Politics* (Kuala Lumpur, Malaysia: Oxford Univ. Press, 1980), p. 49. Jornacion, "Time of the Eagles," pp. 58 ff.

48. General Wood would be a principal although unsuccessful candidate

for the 1920 Republican presidential nomination. See Herman Hagedorn, *Leonard Wood*, 2 vols. (New York: Harper, 1931). The Moro Province was renamed the Department of Mindanao and Sulu in December 1913. Jornacion, "Time of the Eagles," pp. 199 ff.

49. Jornacion, "Time of the Eagles," p. 162. See also Andrew J. Bacevich, "Disagreeable Work: Pacifying the Moros 1903–1906," *Military Review* 62 (June 1982): pp. 49–62.

50. Vandiver, *Black Jack*, p. 266, passim.

51. George, *Revolt on Mindanao*, chap. 14.

52. Even if the Moros could do this, it would by no means guarantee victory, as the Huks discovered in the 1940s.

4. Nicaragua: A Training Ground

1. Karnes, *Failure of Union*. See also Woodward, *Central America*.

2. Walker (1824–1860) had an M.D. degree from the University of Pennsylvania; he was also an attorney and a newspaper editor in New Orleans. In 1853 he landed in Baja California and proclaimed it an independent republic with himself as president. His expedition to Nicaragua resulted in his receiving recognition as president of that country by the Pierce administration. Overthrown by a coalition of the other Central American states and the agents of Cornelius Vanderbilt, Walker twice tried to regain his position and later ended his short life before a Honduran firing squad. His memoir, *The War in Nicaragua*, is interesting.

3. See the discussion of U.S. Navy and Marine personnel going to Managua in U.S. Department of State, *Foreign Relations of the United States 1912* (Washington, D.C.: U.S. Government Printing Office, 1919), pp. 1037 ff. (hereafter designated *FRUS* with the appropriate year). The American minister to Managua had foreseen that the "withdrawal of all marines [from Nicaragua] would be construed as the tacit consent of the United States to renew hostilities." Dec. 14, 1912, *FRUS 1912*, p. 1069. The quotations in the text are in Macauley, *Sandino Affair*, pp. 76, 24; and Julius W. Pratt, *A History of United States Foreign Policy* (Englewood Cliffs, N.J.: Prentice-Hall, 1955), p. 606.

4. Langley, *Banana Wars*, p. 186. Pratt, *U.S. Foreign Policy*, p. 606; see also Pratt, *Colonial Experiment*, chap. 8. The quotation is in Perkins, *Constraint of Empire*, p. 148. Stimson served as secretary of war (1911–1913), secretary of state (1929–1933), and again as secretary of war (1940–1945); see Stimson, *American Policy*.

5. Perkins, *Constraint of Empire*, pp. 21, 23. Walker, "Nicaragua," p. 321.

6. See the May 1927 agreement on establishing the Guardia Nacional (at a strength of 93 officers and 1,064 enlisted) in *FRUS 1927* (Washington, D.C.: U.S. Government Printing Office, 1942), vol. 3, pp. 435–39. See also earlier plans in *FRUS 1925* (Washington, D.C.: U.S. Government Printing Office, 1940), vol. 2, pp. 624–27.

7. Millett, *Guardians*, p. 70.

8. Ibid., p. 77.

9. Ibid., p. 71.

10. Millett, *Semper Fidelis*, pp. 253, 106. For President Diaz's May 15, 1927, request to President Coolidge for help in supervising the elections of October 1928, see *FRUS 1927*, vol. 3, p. 350. See the reports on the 1928 elections by the American minister to Nicaragua to the secretary of state in *FRUS 1928* (Washington, D.C.: U.S. Government Printing Office, 1943), vol. 3, pp. 517–19.

11. Millett, *Guardians*, pp. 63–64. Macauley, *Sandino Affair*, pp. 65–66.

12. Millett, *Semper Fidelis*, p. 247; Megee, "Air Support in Guerrilla Operations," pp. 49–57.

13. Macauley, *Sandino Affair*, pp. 9, 226, 211.

14. Millett, *Semper Fidelis*, p. 254.

15. Macauley, *Sandino Affair*, pp. 285–86.

16. See explicit descriptions of these executions in ibid., pp. 212–13. For the Sandino seal, see p. 147.

17. Macauley, *Sandino Affair*, p. 166. Millett, *Guardians*, p. 94.

18. Perkins, *Constraint of Empire*, p. 152.

19. The quotation is in Langley, *Banana Wars*, p. 190. Macauley, *Sandino Affair*, pp. 234, 183–84. Henry L. Stimson, *On Active Service in Peace and War* (New York: Harper, 1948), p. 182, passim. Perkins, *Constraint of Empire*, p. 151.

20. Millett, *Semper Fidelis*, p. 262. On the activities of the Marines in Haiti, see Millett, *Semper Fidelis*; Langley, *Banana Wars*; McCrocklin, *Garde d'Haiti*; Schmidt, *Occupation of Haiti*.

21. Langley, *Banana Wars*, p. 206; this remains true even after adding the 1,800 Guardia Nacional members.

22. Quotation in Macauley, *Sandino Affair*, p. 269; Langley, *Banana Wars*, p. 212.

23. Macauley, *Sandino Affair*, p. 175.

24. Langley, *Banana Wars*, p. 212. The quotations are in Millett, *Semper Fidelis*, p. 252; and Macauley, *Sandino Affair*, p. 174; see also Megee, "Air Support in Guerrilla Operations."

25. U.S. Marine Corps, *Small Wars Manual*, p. 1-9d.

26. Ibid., p. 1-14j.

27. Ibid., p. 1-16c.

28. Ibid., p. 1-31d.

29. Ibid., p. 1-16d.

30. In addition, the historic hostility between Conservatives and Liberals soon made bipartisanship within the Guardia an impossibility. Nevertheless, the United States sanctioned the fifty-fifty division of officerships in the Guardia between the Liberals and the Conservatives, confusing bipartisanship with nonpartisanship. See *FRUS 1932* (Washington, D.C.: U.S. Government Printing Office, 1948), vol. 5, pp. 884, 900 ff.

31. Millett, *Guardians*, pp. 147–48.

32. Ibid., pp. 158–59, quotation on p. 160.

33. Perkins, *Constraint of Empire*, p. 158. Other useful studies of various aspects of American involvement in Nicaragua include Kammann, *Search for Stability*; Blasier, *Hovering Giant*; Goldwert, *Constabulary*; Munro, *Intervention and Dollar Diplomacy*; Perkins, *U.S. and the Caribbean*.

5. Greece: Civil War into Cold War

1. Greece would be "the first showcase of the American Will." Jones, *"New Kind of War."*

2. Burks, "The Greek Communist." Woodhouse, *Struggle for Greece*, p. 226.

3. Until fairly recent times, many Greeks still looked toward "Constantinople" rather than Athens as the true capital of Greek civilization.

4. Douglas Dakin, *The Greek Struggle for Independence 1821–1833* (Berkeley: Univ. of California Press, 1973).

5. Venizelos had been born a Turkish subject in Crete in 1864. A staunch antimonarchist, he headed the Liberal party for many years, served as prime minister several times between 1910 and 1933, and led Greece into the Balkan and the World Wars. Frequently an exile, often by choice, he died in Paris in 1936.

6. Kousoulas, *Revolution and Defeat*, chap. 4, p. 41, passim.

7. Ibid., chap. 10.

8. Condit, *Case Study*, p. 213.

9. Iatrides, *Revolt in Athens*, p. 277.

10. Woodhouse, *Struggle for Greece*, p. 25. See Serafis, *Greek Resistance Army*.

11. O'Ballance, *Greek Civil War*, p. 88.

12. Edward R. Wainhouse, "Guerrilla War in Greece, 1946–1949," in Osanka, *Modern Guerrilla Warfare*, p. 18.

13. The quotation is in Woodhouse, *Struggle for Greece*, pp. 77, 106. O'Ballance, *Greek Civil War*, pp. 81–82; Papagos, "Guerrilla Warfare," in Osanka, *Modern Guerrilla Warfare*, p. 230. Condit, *Case Study*, pp. 244 ff.

14. Condit, *Case Study*, p. 8, chap. 19. Kousoulas, *Revolution and Defeat*, p. 15, passim; O'Ballance, *Greek Civil War*, pp. 80–81. For a treatment more sympathetic to ELAS, see Mazower, *Inside Hitler's Greece*. Woodhouse, *Struggle for Greece*.

15. Kousoulas, *Revolution and Defeat*, pp. 175 ff; Iatrides, *Revolt in Athens*, pp. 26–27.

16. O'Ballance, *Greek Civil War*, p. 73. Condit, *Case Study*, pp. 235 ff.

17. Woodhouse, *Struggle for Greece*, p. 101; O'Ballance, *Greek Civil War*, pp. 92, 93.

18. The quotation is in Kousoulas, *Revolution and Defeat*, p. 187. Woodhouse, *Struggle for Greece*, pp. 112, 114. O'Ballance, *Greek Civil War*, p. 97.

19. O'Ballance, *Greek Civil War*, p. 96; Iatrides, *Revolt in Athens*, pp. 160–61.

20. Iatrides, *Revolt in Athens*, p. 226.

21. Churchill, *Triumph and Tragedy*, chap. 19. See also Richter, *British Intervention*. O'Ballance, *Greek Civil War*, pp. 98, 105.

22. Woodhouse, *Struggle for Greece*, pp. 133, 266; Condit, *Case Study*, pp. 85 ff. "More than any other action, the abduction and killing of these hostages—often selected for no better reason than that their relatively prosperous homes had aroused the envy or suspicion of some class-conscious [insurgent]—destroyed much of the moral credibility which EAM/ELAS had enjoyed in the eyes of the world until then." Mazower, *Inside Hitler's Greece*, p. 372. Kousoulas, *Revolution and Defeat*, p. 215; O'Ballance, *Greek Civil War*, pp. 111–12; but see also Iatrides, *Revolt in Athens*.

23. O'Ballance, *Greek Civil War*, p. 78. The Soviet military mission was headed by Col. Grigori Popov. See Churchill's notorious account of this agreement with Stalin over division of the Balkans in *Triumph and Tragedy*, pp. 226–27. See Iatrides, "Soviet Involvement"; Richard V. Burks, *The Dynamics of Communism in Eastern Europe* (Princeton, N.J.: Princeton Univ. Press, 1961).

24. See, for example, Kousoulas, *Revolution and Defeat*, pp. 232–33. For results and discussion of the 1946 elections, see Averoff-Tossizza, *By Fire and Axe*, pp. 165–68.

25. Griswold is quoted in *FRUS 1948*, vol. 4, *Eastern Europe and the Soviet Union* (Washington, D.C.: U.S. Government Printing Office, 1974), p. 113.

26. The quotation is from U.S. ambassador Lincoln MacVeagh and appears in *FRUS 1947*, vol. 5, *The Near East and Africa* (Washington, D.C.: U.S. Government Printing Office, 1971), p. 252. See Iatrides, *Greece in the 1940s*.

27. Averoff-Tossizza, *By Fire and Axe*, p. 203.

28. Woodhouse, *Struggle for Greece*, pp. 186, 205–6, 145. Averoff-Tossizza says the Democratic Army peaked at 30,000 active members. *By Fire and Axe*, p. 358.

29. McNeill, *Greece*, chap. 1. And consult Bickham Sweet-Escott, *Greece: A Political and Economic Survey 1939–1953* (London: Royal Institute of International Affairs, 1954).

30. See Robert L. Wolff, *The Balkans in Our Times* (Cambridge, Mass.: Harvard Univ. Press, 1956). There is a good discussion of Macedonian separatist terrorism in Hugh Seton-Watson, *Eastern Europe between the Wars, 1918–1941* (New York: Harper, 1967). A small classic is Barker, *Macedonia*.

31. According to Averoff-Tossizza, most KKE cadres did not actually serve in the guerrilla ranks, and that was one main reason for the reliance on forced recruitment. *By Fire and Axe*, p. 359. Woodhouse, *Struggle for Greece*, pp. 212, 254; Kousoulas, *Revolution and Defeat*, p. 252. Condit, *Case Study*, p. 18.

32. Murray, "Anti-Bandit War," p. 87.

33. McNeill, *Greece*, chap. 1.

34. Ibid., p. 27. Papagos, "Guerrilla Warfare," in Osanka, *Modern Guerrilla Warfare*, p. 234. Communist moles in the civil service and the GNA sabotaged communications; Jones, *"New Kind of War,"* pp. 152–53.

35. Papagos, "Guerrilla Warfare," in Osanka, *Modern Guerrilla Warfare*, p.

237. Vladimir Dedijir claimed that Yugoslavia gave the Greek rebels 35,000 rifles, 3,500 machine guns, 10,000 land mines, and 7,000 German antitank weapons. See Barker, "Yugoslavs and the Greek Civil War," p. 303. O'Ballance, *Greek Civil War*, p. 143. Woodhouse, *Struggle for Greece*, p. 185. But see the views of Stavrakis in *Moscow and Greek Communism*.

36. Woodhouse, *Struggle for Greece*, p. 173.

37. Ibid., pp. 205, 187, 183; Murray, "Anti-Bandit War," p. 94.

38. Murray, "Anti-Bandit War," pp. 95–96. Woodhouse, *Struggle for Greece*, p. 246.

39. Woodhouse, *Struggle for Greece*, p. 187.

40. Kousoulas, *Revolution and Defeat*, p. 241.

41. See Jones, "New Kind of War," chap. 8, "The Greek Children"; Lars Baerentzen, "The 'Paidomazoma' and the Queen's Camps," in Lars Baerentzen et al., eds., *Studies in the History of the Greek Civil War 1945–1949* (Copenhagen: Museum Tusculanum, 1987).

42. In summer 1947 the government began distributing arms to home guard units ("Country Self-Security Units"); many villagers, feeling more secure, then began providing information to the government. Jones, "New Kind of War," pp. 71–72. Woodhouse, *Struggle for Greece*, p. 213.

43. Kousoulas, *Revolution and Defeat*, p. 229. *FRUS 1947*, p. 268; Wittner, *American Intervention in Greece*, p. 228. John Lewis Gaddis, *The United States and the Origins of the Cold War* (New York: Columbia Univ. Press, 1975); John Spanier, *American Foreign Policy since World War II* (New York: Praeger, 1971); James F. Byrnes, *Speaking Frankly* (New York: Harper, 1947); Kennan, *Memoirs*, vol. 2, chaps. 8–12; Acheson, *Present at the Creation*, chap. 22. Iatrides, *Revolt in Athens*, pp. 282–87. But consult also Bruce Kuniholm, *The Origins of the Cold War in the Near East: Great Power Conflict and Diplomacy in Iran, Turkey and Greece* (Princeton, N.J.: Princeton University Press, 1980).

44. *FRUS 1947*, pp. 61, 30. Kennan, *Memoirs*, vol. 1, p. 318.

45. Jones, in "New Kind of War," puts it this way: "Without Soviet and East European documents, who can today determine the extent of Soviet involvement in Greece? In truth, the question is academic: the Truman administration *believed* that the Soviets were at least indirectly involved in that nation's affairs. American documents reveal considerable insight into Soviet behavior during the period, some of which was substantiated years after the civil war" (pp. ix-x).

Furthermore, as Jones (p. 6) correctly observes, whatever the extent of Soviet involvement, the fall of Greece to Communist insurgents would have been everywhere viewed as a significant defeat for the West at the hands of the Kremlin.

46. Spanier, *American Foreign Policy*, pp. 39–40.

47. Jones, "New Kind of War," p. 42.

48. X [George F. Kennan], "The Sources of Soviet Conduct," *Foreign Affairs*, July 1947, pp. 575, 581, 582.

49. *FRUS 1947*, pp. 220, 222.

50. *FRUS 1948*, pp. 3, 5.

51. Loy Henderson in *FRUS 1948*, p. 13; on the concept of the Soviets seeking to outlast the United States in Greece, see the draft report of the Department of State to the National Security Council of November 30, 1948, in *FRUS 1948*, p. 207.

52. *FRUS 1948*, p. 135.

53. Woodhouse, *Struggle for Greece*, p. 248. O'Ballance, *Greek Civil War*. Wittner, *American Intervention in Greece*, p. 234.

54. *FRUS 1947*, p. 221.

55. Wittner, *American Intervention in Greece*, chap. 4. *FRUS 1947*, p. 20.

56. *FRUS 1948*, p. 203. *FRUS 1947*, p. 442. Two decades later, similar arguments would rage around the issue of helping the South Vietnamese. The rough edges of the electoral processes in that country—with no democratic tradition and torn by civil war, invasion, and subversion—and the widespread corruption there, in a poor country inundated by American troops with plenty of cash, received extensive attention from the news media, which had the run of the South and no access at all to the North.

57. The quotation is in Kousoulas, *Revolution and Defeat*, p. 254. In July 1947 Sopholis rejected feelers from the EAM to include them in a coalition cabinet of "peace and reconciliation."

58. Wittner, *American Intervention in Greece*, p. 223. The quotation is in *FRUS 1948*, p. 57. *FRUS 1947*, p. 469.

59. *FRUS 1947*, pp. 460, 466–69.

60. Wittner, *American Intervention in Greece*, pp. 236, 247. MacVeagh is described by Acheson, *Present at the Creation*, p. 199. *FRUS 1947*, p. 273, Griswold quoted on pp. 361, 363. *FRUS 1948*, p. 208.

61. Jones, "New Kind of War," pp. 94–99, 132–33, chap. 5, passim. *FRUS 1947*, pp. 335, 383, Royall quoted on p. 335. Wittner, *American Intervention in Greece*, p. 239. Harper is quoted in *FRUS 1948*, p. 65. Gaddis, *Strategies of Containment*, pp. 22, 62.

62. Souers is quoted in *FRUS 1948*, p. 95. Wittner, *American Intervention in Greece*, p. 242; see the brief discussion in Jones, "New Kind of War," pp. 90–94. By August 31, 1949, the U.S. military mission in Greece consisted of 191 officers and men (p. 221).

63. The quotation is in Papagos, "Guerrilla Warfare," in Osanka, *Modern Guerrilla Warfare*, p. 238; see also Woodhouse, *Struggle for Greece*, p. 237. *FRUS 1948*, pp. 163, 198–99, 201.

64. Grady is quoted in Wittner, *American Intervention in Greece*, p. 246. Averoff-Tossizza maintains that the Democratic Army had no air force because its foreign backers did not want to give that unmistakable proof of their help for fear of U.S. retaliation. *By Fire and Axe*, p. 361. *FRUS 1948*, pp. 189–91, 211–12. O'Ballance, *Greek Civil War*, p. 216.

65. Kousoulas, *Revolution and Defeat*, pp. 258–59.

66. Ibid., pp. 258–59, 257. O'Ballance, *Greek Civil War*, p. 214.

67. Woodhouse, *Struggle for Greece,* pp. 238, 246, quotation on p. 258.

68. See Grady's report on Papagos of March 30, 1949 in *FRUS 1949* (Washington, D.C.: U.S. Government Printing Office, 1977); British foreign secretary Ernest Bevin wrote favorably of Papagos to Acheson on March 31, 1949. *FRUS 1949,* vol. 6 (1977), p. 286. See also the laudatory estimate by Averoff-Tossizza, *By Fire and Axe,* p. 366.

69. Murray, "Anti-Bandit War," p. 98.

70. In fact, a State Department internal memorandum of January 1949 began: "The Greek situation during the past year or more has degenerated. We have hardly held the line. A continuation of the present trend may bring defeat." *FRUS 1949,* p. 242.

71. Burks, "The Greek Communist." Wainhouse, "Guerrilla War in Greece"; O'Ballance, *Greek Civil War,* p. 134. Woodhouse, *Struggle for Greece,* pp. 209, 274, 187.

72. Wainhouse, "Guerrilla War in Greece," p. 25, passim; U.S. assistance to Greece during the conflict amounted to $353 million.

73. Woodhouse, *Struggle for Greece,* pp. 220–21.

74. Kousoulas, *Revolution and Defeat.*

75. Jones, *"New Kind of War,"* p. 190.

76. Averoff-Tossizza is sympathetic to Zachariades's decision, because guerrilla warfare had clearly failed. Mobile warfare was the Democratic Army's last card; Zachariades played it and lost. *By Fire and Axe,* pp. 363–64. Woodhouse, *Struggle for Greece,* p. 45.

77. Jones, *"New Kind of War,"* p. 200.

78. Woodhouse, *Struggle for Greece,* pp. 263, 267, 257, 262.

79. Some good commentaries on the Tito-Stalin split and its effects on Greece are Adam B. Ulam, *Titoism and the Cominform* (Cambridge, Mass.: Harvard Univ. Press, 1952); Wayne S. Vucinich, ed., *At the Brink of War and Peace: The Tito-Stalin Split in a Historic Perspective* (New York: Columbia Univ. Press, 1982); Joze Pirjevec, "The Tito-Stalin Split and the End of the Civil War in Greece" in Baerentzen, *Studies;* Elisabeth Barker, "Yugoslav Policy toward Greece" in Baerentzen, *Studies;* Elisabeth Barker, "Yugoslavs and the Greek Civil War" in Baerentzen, *Studies.* See also D. George Kousoulas, "The Truman Doctrine and the Stalin-Tito Rift: A Reappraisal," *South Atlantic Quarterly* 72 (summer 1973).

80. Murray, "Anti-Bandit War," p. 74.

81. Averoff-Tossizza, *By Fire and Axe,* pp. 357, 362.

82. But O'Ballance rejects this view in *Greek Civil War,* pp. 219–20.

83. Jones, *"New Kind of War,"* p. 219.

84. Kousoulas, *Revolution and Defeat.*

85. Ibid., p. 270. See somewhat different figures in Jones, *"New Kind of War,"* pp. 309 n. 20, 220; and see Averoff-Tossizza, *By Fire and Axe,* p. 355.

86. Galula, *Counter-insurgency Warfare,* p. 18.

87. Jones, *"New Kind of War,"* p. 224. Barker, "Yougoslavs and the Greek Civil War," in Baerentzen, *Studies,* p. 306.

88. Jones, *"New Kind of War,"* p. 197. According to Shafer, "American involvement in Greece should be read not as a success story but as a cautionary tale. True, the Greek government defeated the guerrillas, and the United States benefitted by their success. But contrary to the supposed lessons of Greece, the United States contributed little to the victory. American policymakers misperceived the crisis and prescribed irrelevant and even harmful solutions to it." In Shafer's analysis, the Greek Communists owed their defeat to their own mistakes, the Macedonian question, and the Tito border closing. *Deadly Paradigms*, p. 166.

89. Averoff-Tossizza, *By Fire and Axe*. The quotation is in Robert E. Osgood, *Limited War: The Challenge to American Strategy* (Chicago: University of Chicago Press, 1957), pp. 143–44.

90. Jones, *"New Kind of War,"* p. 4. Averoff-Tossizza, *By Fire and Axe*, p. 366.

91. See Johnson's little classic, *Autopsy on People's War.*

92. The Vietnamese Communists kept calling for and planning for the Great Uprising in Saigon, which never materialized either—not even after it had become clear that the North Vietnamese Army would enter the city. For democracies versus insurgents, see the report of the Policy Planning Staff, November 1948, *FRUS 1948*, pp. 199–200. Guevara, *Guerrilla Warfare.*

93. Woodhouse, *Struggle for Greece*, p. 233. Averoff-Tossizza writes, "The main reason for the defeat of the [Democratic Army] was the firm determination of the majority of Greeks to fight against it until the bitter end." *By Fire and Axe*, p. 357. See also O'Ballance, *Greek Civil War*, p. 210.

94. The quotation is in Woodhouse, *Struggle for Greece*, p. 267. Murray, "Anti-Bandit War," p. 70.

95. The quotation is in Iatrides, *Revolt in Athens*, p. 288. "The major cause [of Communist defeat] was the failure to win over the minds of the people—or at least a sizeable slice of them. In China Mao Tse-tung was most careful on this pont, and it was always the most important factor in all his calculations and plans. . . . The KKE never appreciated the importance of this, and thought that terror would be a sufficiently powerful substitute." O'Ballance, *Greek Civil War*, p. 210.

6. Back to the Philippines: The Huks

1. Romulo, *Crusade in Asia*, p. 63. See also the illuminating study by John W. Dower, *War without Mercy: Race and Power in the Pacific War* (New York: Pantheon, 1986).

2. For Huk activities regarding the Japanese, see Greenberg, *Hukbalahap Insurrection*. William Manchester, *American Caesar: Douglas MacArthur 1880–1964* (Boston: Little, Brown, 1978), pp. 421–22, 525–26.

3. Taruc, *He Who Rides the Tiger*, pp. 145–46. Romulo, *Crusade in Asia*, p. 148, my emphasis. Taruc, *He Who Rides the Tiger*, p. 188. See also William Pomeroy, *The Forest* (New York: International Publishers, 1963). Manchester, *American Caesar*, p. 420.

4. Kerkvliet, *Huk Rebellion*, p. 215.

5. Lansdale, *In the Midst of Wars*, pp. 20–21. And see Cecil B. Currey, *Edward Lansdale: The Unquiet American* (Boston: Houghton Mifflin, 1988).

6. Taruc, *He Who Rides the Tiger*, pp. 38, 144.

7. Romulo, *Crusade in Asia*, p. 88. Romulo says that "hundreds who had the courage to go to the polls were shot down and killed" by Liberal Party "goons." Carlos P. Romulo and Marvin M. Gray, *The Magsaysay Story* (New York: John Day, 1956), p. 97. Che Guevara maintained that a democratic government, or one with at least democratic trappings, could not be overthrown by armed force, because there appeared to be an alternative road to change; see his *Guerrilla Warfare;* Lansdale agrees that the electoral corruption helped the Huks.

8. Kerkvliet, *Huk Rebellion*, p. 210. Hammer, "Huks in the Philippines," p. 181. Taruc, *He Who Rides the Tiger*, pp. 88–89. According to Romulo, a Magsaysay admirer, "Quirino had the vision and the courage to support Magsaysay," and "Quirino had no evil in him." Romulo and Gray, *Magsaysay Story*, pp. 146, 97. For details on the appointment, see pp. 100–109 in the same work.

9. The quotation is in Leites, *Viet Cong Style*, p. 17. "[To fight guerrillas effectively, we should] organize our combat forces into small highly mobile forces armed with light automatic weapons." Baclagon, *Lessons from the Huk Campaign*, p. 172.

10. Valeriano and Bohannan, *Counter-Guerrilla Operations*, p. 206. Kerkvliet, *Huk Rebellion*, p. 208.

11. Kerkvliet, *Huk Rebellion*, pp. 208, 242.

12. Lansdale, *In the Midst of Wars*, pp. 42–44, passim.

13. Valeriano and Bohannan, *Counter-Guerrilla Operations*, pp. 97–98; this controversial practice antedated Magsaysay's secretaryship.

14. Luis Taruc, *He Who Rides the Tiger*, p. 97; Fairbairn, *Revolutionary Guerrilla Warfare.* Lucian Pye, *Guerrilla Communism in Malaya* (Princeton, N.J.: Princeton Univ. Press, 1956). Romulo, *Crusade in Asia*, p. 135. For a description of this great catch of Huk documents, see Romulo and Gray, *Magsaysay Story*, pp. 113–19.

15. Thompson, *Defeating Communist Insurgency*, chap. 8.

16. The resettlement program involved something like 5,000 persons, of whom 1,000 were former active Huk guerrillas. Blaufarb, *Counterinsurgency Era*, p. 33.

17. Valeriano and Bohannan, *Counter-Guerrilla Operations;* Kerkvliet, *Huk Rebellion*, p. 238; Romulo and Gray, *Magsaysay Story*, pp. 150–52; see also Lansdale, *In the Midst of Wars.*

18. The quotation is in Paret and Shy, *Guerrillas in the 1960s*, p. 45. For Magsaysay's efforts to secure the Nacionalista nomination, see Romulo and Gray, *Magsaysay Story*, pp. 183–215. Romulo, *Crusade in Asia*, p. 200, passim.

19. Taruc, *He Who Rides the Tiger*, p. 130. The Communist Party leadership was openly and bitterly divided by the question of support for Quirino, among

other matters. Lansdale, *In the Midst of Wars*, p. 106. Romulo makes the sensational assertion that before the election, Magsaysay and his supporters in the army and the Nacionalista Party made plans, in the event that massive fraud took place, to overthrow the Quirino administration by force. Romulo and Gray, *Magsaysay Story*, pp. 231–32. Currey, *Edward Lansdale*, chap. 6.

20. For an interesting analysis of the 1953 campaign and election results, see Starner, *Magsaysay and the Philippine Peasantry*, chaps. 3, 4, appendix 1.

21. For some details on the Taruc surrender, see Romulo and Gray, *Magsaysay Story*, pp. 279–81. Taruc, *He Who Rides the Tiger*, p. 138. Bashore, "Dual Strategy." Regrettably, President Magsaysay himself, while campaigning for reelection in March 1957, died in a plane crash not far from the spot where in 1521 Magellan the circumnavigator had lost his life.

22. Taruc, *He Who Rides the Tiger*, p. 24.

23. Ibid., pp. 12, 26. Kerkvliet, *Huk Rebellion*, chap. 7.

24. Taruc, *He Who Rides the Tiger*, p. 161. Kerkvliet, *Huk Rebellion*, pp. 217, 229, 233.

25. Taruc, *He Who Rides the Tiger*, p. 149. Kerkvliet, *Huk Rebellion*, p. 217. For further discussion of the relationship between Communist Party leadership and the Huk movement, see Pomeroy, "Philippine Peasantry and the Huk Revolt"; Richardson, "Huk Rebellion."

26. James C. Thompson Jr., Peter W. Stanley, and John Curtis Perry, *Sentimental Imperialists: The American Experience in East Asia* (New York: Harper and Row, 1981), p. 120. *FRUS 1951*, vol. 6, *Asia and the Pacific* (Washington, D.C.: U.S. Government Printing Office, 1977), p. 1536.

27. Greenberg, *Hukbalahap Insurrection*, pp. 99 ff. *FRUS 1950*, vol. 6, *East Asia and the Pacific* (Washington, D.C.: U.S. Government Printing Office, 1976), pp. 1433, 1435–38.

28. *FRUS 1950*, pp. 1443, 1495, Truman quoted on p. 1443. *FRUS 1951*, pp. 1498, 1501–1502, quotation on p. 1498.

29. *FRUS 1950*, p. 1517.

30. Ibid., pp. 1462, 1403, 1442. Acheson is notably reticent on this matter in his memoirs, *Present at the Creation*.

31. *FRUS 1950*, p. 1441.

32. *FRUS 1951*, p. 1507, quotation on p. 1537.

33. *FRUS 1950*, pp. 1442–43. As in the case of Ngo Dinh Diem in 1963.

34. *FRUS 1951*, p. 1504. All armies are of course "guided by political interests"; Marshall meant an army in which promotion and command were dictated by political influences in the worst sense.

35. See "The Position of the United States with Respect to the Philippines," National Security Council Statement NSC 84/2, November 9, 1950, Washington, D.C., *FRUS 1950*, p. 1408.

36. *FRUS 1950*, pp. 1485–89; *FRUS 1951*, p. 1549. In the fall of 1951, JUSMAG trained one company of Philippine airborne infantry; see Greenberg, *Hukbalahap Insurrection*.

37. Kerkvliet, *The Huk Rebellion,* pp. 207–8.

38. Magsaysay's resettlement involved perhaps 5,000 people, including about 1,000 former active Huks. Douglas Blaufarb, *Counterinsurgency Era,* p. 33.

39. Greenberg, *Hukbalahap Insurrection,* pp. 111, 149–54.

40. Cable, *Conflict of Myths,* chap. 4. But see also Robert A. Smith, *Philippine Freedom, 1946–1958* (New York: Columbia Univ. Press, 1958).

7. Vietnam: A Case of Multiple Pathologies

1. On the origins of U.S. involvement in Viet Nam, the beginning of wisdom is found in the *Pentagon Papers,* vol. 1; see also David L. Anderson, *Trapped by Success: The Eisenhower Administration and Viet Nam* (New York: Columbia Univ. Press, 1991); Billings-Yun, *Decision against War;* Berman, *Planning a Tragedy;* Hammer, *Death in November;* Lewy, *America in Viet Nam;* Logevall, *Choosing War;* McMaster, *Dereliction of Duty;* R.B. Smith, *An International History of the Viet Nam War,* vol. 1, *Revolution vs. Containment, 1955–1961* (New York: St. Martin's, 1983), and vol. 2, *The Kennedy Strategy* (New York: St. Martin's 1985).

For the military side, the reader may wish to consult Bergerud, *Dynamics of Defeat;* Davidson, *Viet Nam at War;* Hennessy, *Strategy in Viet Nam;* Hunt, *Pacification;* Andrew F. Krepinevich, *Army and Viet Nam;* Palmer, *Twenty-Five-Year War;* Sharp, *Strategy for Defeat;* Summers, *On Strategy;* Thayer, *War without Fronts;* West, *Small Unit Action;* Westmoreland, *Soldier Reports.*

2. Buttinger, *Dragon Embattled,* vol. 1, p. 173.

3. See Fall, *Two Viet Nams,* p. 35; Duncanson, *Government and Revolution,* p. 103; Hammer, *Struggle for Indochina,* p. 73; McAlister, *Viet Nam,* pp. 74, 300–301.

4. The Office of Strategic Services, a forerunner of the Central Intelligence Agency.

5. Buttinger, *Dragon Embattled,* p. 299.

6. Duiker, *Communist Road,* p. 103.

7. Ho Chi Minh was one of the man's many pseudonyms. The appearance of U.S. approval was due to the remarkable naïveté of several OSS personnel in the Hanoi area. See Buttinger, *Dragon Embattled,* vol. 1, pp. 292–300.

8. "It was the acquiescence of the Japanese rather than Viet Min strength which ensured Communist predominance over the disoriented Vietnamese caretaker government." McAlister, *Viet Nam,* p. 149; see also Duiker, *Communist Road,* p. 107; Hammer, *Struggle for Indochina,* p. 101; Fall, *Two Viet Nams,* p. 65; Huynh, *Vietnamese Communism,* p. 335; Truong Chinh, *Primer for Revolt,* p. 37 n; Fall says some Nazis stranded in Hanoi when the Japanese surrendered also decided to stay and fight on Ho's side. *Street without Joy* (Harrisburg, Penn.: Stackpole, 1964), p. 29.

9. Buttinger, *Dragon Embattled,* p. 399, 408. Of those who joined the Communist front in what became South Vietnam, Eric Bergerud writes: "Front Leaders in general greatly surpassed their GVN counterparts in terms of commitment, determination, and morale" because "the revolution also offered

an avenue of social advancement more exciting than anything the government [in Saigon] could propose. The insurgents would after all become the leaders of the new Viet Nam. The Party offered young men and women a powerful vision of the future. In return, it asked absolute political dedication, obedience, and a willingness to face the very real prospect of death." *Dynamics of Defeat,* pp. 4, 23.

10. Buttinger, *Dragon Embattled,* pp. 409, 412. On this whole issue, see also Truong Chinh, *Primer for Revolt,* p. 24; Fall, *Two Viet Nams,* p. 101; McAlister, *Viet Nam,* pp. 190–92; Bodard, *Quicksand War,* pp. 208–9; Hammer, *Struggle for Indochina,* pp. 158, 176.

11. Fall, *Two Viet Nams,* p. 281; Race, *War Comes to Long An,* p. 83; Duiker, *Communist Road,* p. 180; Scigliano, *South Viet Nam,* p. 140. Thompson, *Defeating Communist Insurgency,* p. 27; see also Herrington, *Silence Was a Weapon,* p. 137; and Robert Shaplen, quoted in *Pentagon Papers,* vol. 1, p. 334. It deserves notice that after the 1954 partition, the Communist leaders in Hanoi unleashed a bloody campaign of "land reform" that took an unknown number of lives; estimates run from 50,000 to 150,000. See Fall, *Two Viet Nams,* pp. 155–56; Honey, *North Viet Nam Today,* p. 8; Hoang Van Chi, *Colonialism to Communism,* p. 189.

12. On June 5, 1948, France recognized the independence of Viet Nam under Emperor Bao Dai. This was confirmed by the Elysée Agreement of March 1949. The Cao Dai and the Hoa Hao sects between them had several million members in the southern provinces. Assassinations of their leaders by the Vietminh had turned them bitterly against the Communists.

13. Out of a metropolitan population of over 40,000,000.

14. Estimates of the number of French and allied forces in Vietnam vary. I have derived these figures mainly from O'Ballance, *Indo-China War;* and Navarre, *Agonie de l'Indochine,* p. 46.

15. On Gallieni and Lyautey, giants of the French school of colonial warfare, see Maurois, *Lyautey;* Howe, *Lyautey of Morocco;* Porch, *Conquest of Morocco;* Douglas Porch, "Bugeaud, Gallieni, Lyautey: The Development of French Colonial Warfare," in Peter Paret, ed., *Makers of Modern Strategy: Machiavelli to the Nuclear Age* (Princeton, N.J.: Princeton Univ. Press, 1986). The French had no helicopters at all in Vietnam until 1950, when they acquired two; by 1954 they had ten in all Indochina. The quotation is in Lancaster, *Emancipation of French Indochina,* p. 218.

16. Fall, *Street without Joy,* p. 30.

17. Hanoi was the French capital and Haiphong was its seaport.

18. The strategic place to fight a knock-down battle with Giap would have been Cao Bang.

19. Fall, *Hell in a Very Small Place,* p. 337.

20. On what the Geneva conference did and did not do, see the *Pentagon Papers,* vol. 1, pp. 145–79; Robert E. Randle, *Geneva 1954* (Princeton, N.J.: Princeton Univ. Press, 1969); Smith, *History of the Viet Nam War,* vol. 1, chap. 2.

21. Naturally, casualty figures vary. These are derived from Fall, *Street with-*

out Joy; and O'Ballance, *Indochina War.* The quotation is in Thayer, *War without Fronts,* p. 9.

22. Readers of French may wish to consult some of the following: Pierre Boyer de Latour, *Le martyre de l'Armée française: De l'Indochine a l'Algérie* (Paris: Presses du Mail, 1962); Devillers, *Histoire du Viet-Nam;* Paul Ely, *L'Indochine dans la tourmente* (Paris: Plon, 1964); Henri Marc and Pierre Cony, *Indochine française* (Paris: Editions France-Empire, 1946); Jean Marchand, *L'Indochine en guerre* (Paris: Pouzet, 1955); Navarre, *Agonie de l'Indochine.*

23. See details on Diem in Buttinger, *Dragon Embattled,* pp. 1253–56. One of Diem's brothers later became an archbishop.

24. Fall, *Two Viet Nams,* p. 240. The quotation is in Devillers, *Histoire du Viet-Nam,* p. 63.

25. The 1 million refugees who poured into South Viet Nam were the proportional equivalent of 16 million refugees entering the United States in the year 2000.

26. See the previous discussion of Vietminh/Vietcong terrorism in the subsection "The Politics of Murder."

27. In this, Diem's government was certainly not unique in the Third World.

28. *New York Times,* Apr. 10, 1961. For sympathetic portraits of Diem, see Marguerite Higgins, *Our Viet Nam Nightmare* (New York: Harper and Row, 1965); Hammer, *Death in November;* Collins, *South Vietnamese Army,* pp. 23–24.

29. Taylor, *Swords and Plowshares,* p. 235. Colby, *Lost Victory,* p. 146. Kennedy administration demands that Diem institute instant "democracy" in war-torn, newly independent South Vietnam are laughable (or mortifying).

30. Certainly Diem was no Jeffersonian democrat, but what contemporary Asian leader was? Sukarno? Ho Chi Minh? Mao Tse-tung? Kim Il Sung? Pol Pot? Hammer, *Death in November,* p. 45; Taylor, *Swords and Plowshares,* p. 300. On the politicization of the American correspondents in Saigon, see William Prochnau, *Once upon a Distant War: Young War Correspondents and the Early Viet Nam Battles* (New York; Times Books, 1995).

31. See Duncanson, *Government and Revolution,* pp. 327–41; Scigliano, *South Viet Nam,* and Hammer, *Death in November,* are also revealing.

32. Colby writes of Lodge's "lone-wolf vendetta against the Diem regime." *Lost Victory,* p. 146. France's ambassador to Saigon, Roger Lalouette, warned Lodge against getting rid of Diem; moreover, "in the days of the French administration suicides of buddhists were very common and had no effect whatever on the population. They create much more excitement abroad than in Viet Nam" (see Lodge's message to President Kennedy, Aug. 30, 1963, *FRUS 1961–1963,* vol. 4, p. 58). See the work by Lodge's predecessor, Frederick Nolting, *From Trust to Tragedy.* Winters, *Year of the Hare,* is informative, as is Anne Blair, *Lodge in Viet Nam* (New Haven, Conn.: Yale Univ. Press, 1995).

33. Colby, *Lost Victory,* p. 147. See the reference to the U.S. "correspondents' hostility to the [Diem] government" in Assistant Secretary of State Manning to Kennedy, July 1963, *FRUS 1961–63,* vol. 3, p. 531. Ambassador Nolting

opposed the coup as bad policy and bad faith. Conference with President Kennedy, Aug 28, 1963, *FRUS 1961–63*, vol. 4, p. 3. The week before the coup, McGeorge Bundy asked the president, "Should we not cool off the whole enterprise?" (p. 465 n. 1). And as late as October 29, 1963, the president's brother, Attorney General Robert Kennedy, said that "to support a coup would be putting the future of Viet Nam and in fact all of Southeast Asia in the hands of one man not now known to us." At that same meeting, Gen. Maxwell Taylor and CIA director John McCone also expressed opposition to the coup (p. 470). On December 23, 1963, a few weeks after the murder of President Diem, McCone informed President Johnson, "There is no organized government in South Viet Nam at this time," because among other things the new military regime had fired 70 percent of the forty-two province chiefs (p. 736).

34. See for example Hammer, *Death in November*, p. 309; Colby, *Lost Victory*, p. 158.

35. Duncanson, *Government and Revolution*, pp. 339–41; Tran Van Don, *Our Endless War*, pp. 107, 112; Hammer, *Death in November*, pp. 293, 299; *Pentagon Papers*, vol. 2, p. 269; Warner, *Certain Victory*, p. 129. Read the squalid story of the conniving in the *Pentagon Papers*, vol. 1, pp. 232–70.

36. Colby, *Lost Victory*. General Westmoreland later wrote that "Diem's downfall was a major factor in prolonging the war." *Soldier Reports*, p. 62. For Lyndon Johnson, "the worst mistake we ever made was getting rid of Diem." Quoted in Henry F. Graff, *The Tuesday Cabinet: Deliberation and Decision on Peace and War under Lyndon B. Johnson* (Englewood Cliffs, N.J.: Prentice-Hall, 1970). Hammer concurs. See *Death in November*, esp. pp. 308–10. Duncanson wrote that Diem was "the embodiment of his country's soul, for good no less than for ill." *Government and Revolution*, p. xi.

37. Spector, *Advice and Support*, p. 131 and passim; Hammer, *Struggle for Indochina*, p. 287; Navarre, *Agonie de l'Indochine*, p. 46; Pike, *PAVN*, p. 5.

38. Well into the 1960s, the U.S. Army selected advisors on the basis of their ability to speak *French*, not Vietnamese. American officers tended to shun assignment as advisers to the ARVN because such service did not count for promotion, despite official assurances. Hunt, *Pacification*. The number of U.S. advisers peaked at around sixteen thousand, with many of them in administrative, not combat, roles. Robert W. Komer, *Bureaucracy at War: U.S. Performance in the Viet Nam Conflict* (Boulder, Colo.: Westview, 1986), p. 128. And see Robert D. Parrish, *Combat Recon: My Year with the ARVN* (New York: St. Martin's, 1991). Davidson, *Viet Nam at War*, p. 660; Collins, *South Vietnamese Army*, pp. 47, 101. See Westmoreland, *Soldier Reports*, p. 159. Every upgrade of weapons sent to the ARVN was in response to a previous superiority on the side of the enemy; hence the ARVN was almost always outclassed in equipment; Davidson, *Viet Nam at War*, p. 660. "On the military side we simply did not do the job with the South Vietnamese that we did with the South Koreans because we had always assumed that we would win the war for them." Thayer, *War without Fronts*, 257.

39. Thayer, *War without Fronts*, p. 71.

40. Goodman, *Institutional Profile*. Nevertheless, Buddhists, who comprised 59 percent of the general population, made up 62 percent of the ARVN officer corps (p. 9).

41. "ARVN at the same time held a politically troubled country together in the face of ever-increasing enemy strength. Few organizations in the world could have done so well." Westmoreland, *Soldier Reports*, p. 250.

42. Todd, *Cruel April*, p. 438.

43. Thompson, *Peace Is Not at Hand*, p. 169.

44. The quotation is in Race, *War Comes to Long An*, p. 164 n. Thayer, *War without Fronts*, p. 171.

45. Thayer, *War without Fronts*, pp. 163, 202; Pike, *PAVN*, p. 244; Westmoreland, *Soldier Reports*, p. 252.

46. Bruce Catton, *Glory Road* (Garden, City, N.J.: Doubleday, 1952), pp. 102, 255; Nevins, *War for the Union*, vol. 3, p. 131.

47. Thayer, *War without Fronts*, p. 106. Todd, in *Cruel April*, says that 250,000 ARVN were killed from 1960 to 1974 (p. 234). Of allied (American, South Vietnamese, and other countries') combat deaths from 1965 to 1972, 77 percent were South Vietnamese from all branches. Thayer, *War without Fronts*, p. 105.

48. An average province covered twelve hundred square miles, equivalent to a circle with a radius of twenty miles. Cao and Dong, *Reflections*, p. 42.

49. Hoang Ngoc Lung, *General Offensives*, p. 150. Westmoreland, *Soldier Reports*, p. 159. Hunt, *Pacification*, 214. The Territorials peaked at around 525,000 in 1973. Thompson and Frizzell, *Lessons of Viet Nam*, pp. 256–61; Ngo Quang Truong, *Territorial Forces*, p. 77. More than 170,000 members of all South Vietnamese forces had been killed by the end of 1972. It was always more dangerous to serve in the Territorial forces than in the ARVN. Le Gro, *Viet Nam from Ceasefire*, p. 330; Collins, *South Vietnamese Army*, p. 151. The quotation is in Thomas C. Thayer, "Territorial Forces," in Thompson and Frizzell, *Lessons of Viet Nam*, p. 258. Also see Thayer, *War without Fronts*, p. 166.

50. After the Tet Offensive, South Vietnamese armed forces won back most of the population and territory they had lost. One of Hanoi's principal reasons for the Easter Offensive was to force Saigon to redeploy its troops out of the countryside, thereby undoing the pacification gains since 1969. See Hunt, *Pacification*, p. 255. And see the excellent study by Chester Cooper et al., *The American Experience with Pacification in Viet Nam*, vol. 1, *An Overview of Pacification* (Arlington, Va.: Institute for Defense Analysis, 1972). The quotation is in *Economist*, Apr. 15, 1972, p. 15.

51. Abrams is quoted in Palmer, *Twenty-Five-Year War*, p. 122. See also Sorley, *Thunderbolt*, pp. 317–28. See Dong Van Khuyen, *RVNAF*; Goodman, *Institutional Profile*; Cantwell, *Army of South Viet Nam*.

52. Thayer, *War without Fronts*, pp. 34, 104. See Peter King, ed., *Australia's Viet Nam* (Sydney: Allen and Unwin, 1983).

53. *Washington Post,* Apr. 6, 1969. Oberdorfer, *Tet!* p. 81.

54. Wirtz, *Tet Offensive,* pp. 60, 23, passim. The real aims of the Tet Offensive remain controversial even today. In addition, General Giap may have been opposed to the whole idea.

55. "For the allies to predict the Tet offensive they would have had to overcome probably the toughest problem that can confront intelligence analysts; they would have to recognize that the plan for the Tet offensive rested on a communist mistake." Wirtz, *Tet Offensive,* p. 84. But see also Ford, *Tet 1968.*

56. The ARVN units, mostly half-strength for the holidays, did not crumble but did well. Wirtz, *Tet Offensive,* p. 224. General Westmoreland wrote, "The South Vietnamese had fully vindicated my trust." *Soldier Reports,* p. 332.

57. Taylor, *Swords and Plowshares,* p. 383. Other estimates of Vietcong casualties are much higher: Robert S. Shaplen, in *The Road from War: Viet Nam 1965– 1971* (New York: Harper and Row, 1971), suggests ninety-two thousand (p. 219). And see Tran Van Tra, *Concluding the 30–Years War.* The quotation is in Davidson, *Viet Nam at War,* p. 475. And see Palmer, *Summons of the Trumpet:* "The Tet Offensive was the most disastrous defeat North Viet Nam suffered in the long war" (p. 201).

58. See, among others, Truong Nhu Tang, *Viet Cong Memoir;* A. Charles Parker, *Viet Nam: Strategy for a Stalemate* (New York: Paragon, 1989). For the magnitude of the Communist disaster, see Tran Van Tra, *Concluding the 30– Years War,* p. 35; Duiker, *Communist Road,* p. 269; Lewy, *America in Viet Nam,* p. 76; Thayer, *War without Fronts,* p. 92; Shaplen, *Bitter Victory,* pp. 188–89; Blaufarb, *Counterinsurgency Era,* pp. 261–62.

59. Lomperis, *People's War to People's Rule,* p. 341; "People's War, as a banner that had led the Party through a generation of trials, was finished." "Never again was the Tet 1968 strategy repeated." Kolko, *Anatomy of a War,* p. 334. And see Johnson, *Autopsy on People's War.*

60. Apparently, lower-level VC cadres hid from their superiors their conviction that a popular uprising in their particular districts was most unlikely. Wirtz, *Tet Offensive,* pp. 82, 245. Timothy Lomperis, among others, is deeply impressed by the total absence of massive pro-Hanoi uprisings, not only in 1968 but in 1972 and 1975 as well. *War Everyone Lost,* p. 169.

61. Oberdorfer, *Tet!* p. 201; Dawson, *55 Days,* p. 92. Some estimate that after the conquest, the Communists killed at least another sixty-five thousand South Vietnamese. Todd, *Cruel April,* p. 427. The quotation is in Samuel Popkin, "The Village War," in *Vietnam as History,* ed. Peter Braestrup, p. 102. After Tet, "the population had substantially abandoned the VC cause," though not necessarily embracing that of Saigon; Blaufarb, *Counterinsurgency Era,* p. 271. To make up their heavy losses, the VC drastically increased their forcible recruitment of peasants; at the same time, increased mobilization by Saigon decreased the numbers available for this forcible Communist recruitment.

62. See the *New York Times,* Oct. 1, 1994, my emphasis.

63. Braestrup, *Big Story*, vol. 1, pp. 450, 461; Allan E. Goodman in Peter Braestrup, *Vietnam as History* (Washington, D.C.: Univ. Press of America, 1984), p. 90.

64. Braestrup, *Big Story*, vol. 1, p. 475. Cronkite on CBS-TV, Feb. 14, 1968. See Braestrup, *Big Story*, vol. 1, pp. 468, 175.

65. Oberdorfer, *Tet!* pp. 332, 242, quotation on p. 332.

66. Lewy, *America in Viet Nam*, p. 434.

67. Braestrup, *Big Story*, esp. vol. 1, p. 495. Pike, *PAVN*, p. 242. The principal supplier of war news and analysis to *Time* magazine was an officer of the NVA. See, among others, Todd, *Cruel April*. See the disedifying account of the Salisbury reports in Lewy, *America in Viet Nam*, pp. 400–401.

68. Braestrup, *Big Story*, vol. 1, pp. 162, 184, 531.

69. Ibid., pp. 531 (quotation), 492, 716 (quotation). Warner, *Certain Victory*, p. 205. Marc Leepson, "Viet Nam War Reconsidered," *Editorial Research Reports*, Mar. 1983, p. 195.

70. *Economist*, May 13, 1972, p. 34. Douglas Pike, quoted in Warner, *Certain Victory*, p. 183.

71. Braestrup, *Big Story*, vol. 1, p. 765.

72. *Pentagon Papers*, vol. 3, p. 480. See esp. McMaster, *Dereliction of Duty*; and Berman, *Planning a Tragedy*.

73. Donald Voiught, "American Culture and American Arms: The Case of Viet Nam," in Hunt and Shultz, *Unconventional War*. Krepinevich, *Army and Viet Nam*.

74. Thompson, *No Exit from Viet Nam*, p. 53; Krepinevich, *Army and Viet Nam*, p. 197; Edward N. Luttwak, *The Pentagon and the Art of War* (New York: Simon and Schuster, 1984), p. 32.

75. On Soviet involvement in the Vietnam conflict, see Douglas Pike, *Vietnam and the Soviet Union: Anatomy of an Alliance* (Boulder, Colo.: Westview, 1987); Robin Edmonds, *Soviet Foreign Policy 1962–1973: The Paradox of a Superpower* (New York: Oxford Univ. Press, 1975); Ilya Gaiduk, *The Soviet Union and the Viet Nam War* (Chicago: Ivan R. Dee, 1996); Leif Rosenberger, *Viet Nam and the Soviet Union: An Uneasy Alliance* (New York: Random House, 1986). The B-52s appeared above the Ho Chi Minh Trail according to a precise schedule, so that the NVA had plenty of time to take shelter. See "We Lied to You," *Economist*, Feb. 26, 1983. Soviet espionage in the United States also played its role in Hanoi's air defenses. Johnson is quoted in Richard M. Nixon, *RN: The Memoirs of Richard Nixon* (New York: Grosset and Dunlap, 1978), p. 431.

76. Douglas Pike, "Masters of Deceit" (Univ. of California, Berkeley, Calif., unpublished ms.), p. 31.

77. Thayer, *War without Fronts*, p. 85. *Pentagon Papers*, vol. 4, pp. 56, 116–20, 137, 168, 184, 223–24; see also Clodfelter, *Limits of Air Power*.

78. Clausewitz, *On War*, book 4, chap. 4.

79. Thompson and Frizzell, *Lessons of Viet Nam*, p. 77.

80. Luttwak, *Pentagon and the Art of War*, p. 42. For the dollar cost of killing

one soldier, see *New York Times*, Dec. 7, 1967. The destructiveness of the American way of war unfortunately antedates Vietnam. Consider Sherman's campaigns in Georgia and South Carolina, the bombing of nonmilitary targets in Europe and Japan in World War II, or the thorough liberation-devastation of Seoul.

81. For an excellent treatment of these and many other themes, Sorley's *Better War* is indispensable.

82. Taylor, *Swords and Plowshares*, p. 247. "Eisenhower added that Laos was the key to all southeast Asia" on January 19, 1961. Arthur Schlesinger, *A Thousand Days* (Boston: Houghton Mifflin, 1965), p. 163. Eisenhower said that the United States would have to act alone if necessary to close the Laotian invasion route. Johnson, *Vantage Point*, p. 51. The joint chiefs told President Kennedy they opposed putting ground troops in Laos—there were just too many problems with such a situation. See Colby, *Lost Victory*, p. 194. But Norman Hannah says the military opposed intervention in Laos to save Laos, not intervention in Laos to save South Vietnam. *Key to Failure*, p. 271. "Eisenhower turned out to have been right. . . . Even though Laos was a remote and landlocked country, the North Vietnamese, as feared and hated foreigners, could not have waged a guerrilla war on its soil. America could have fought there the sort of conventional war for which its army had been trained." Henry Kissinger, *Diplomacy* (New York: Simon and Schuster, 1994), p. 647.

83. This was the main concept for the invasion of France, developed by Alfred von Schlieffen, chief of the German General Staff from 1891 to 1905. Under the Schlieffen Plan, the French Army would be outflanked and then destroyed by a vast wheeling movement of the German Army's massive right (northern) wing across neutral Belgium.

84. Westmoreland, *Soldier Reports*, p. 148. True, the Polisario guerrillas were not the NVA, but then Morocco was not the United States. The quotation is in Palmer, *Twenty-Five–Year War*, pp. 182–86. Summers endorses General Palmer's conclusion that three divisions in Laos, with five along the DMZ, would have been sufficient to isolate the battlefield. Summers, *On Strategy*, pp. 122–23.

85. Johnson, *Vantage Point*, pp. 369, 370, my emphasis. "One further point which was a key element in the Viet Nam war and one which people do not realize was probably its turning point was the Laos Agreement of 1962. Because it kept the United States out of Laos and gave the North Vietnamese a free run it made the war almost unwinnable." Robert Thompson, "Regular Armies and Insurgency," in Haycock, *Regular Armies and Insurgency*, p. 17.

86. Shaplen, *Bitter Victory*, p. 158.

87. Hannah, *Key to Failure*, p. xxv.

88. Shaplen, *Bitter Victory*, pp. 148, 157; Douglas Pike, "Road to Victory," in *War in Peace*, vol. 5, edited by Robert Thompson (London: Orbis, 1984). Thompson, "Regular Armies and Insurgency," p. 18. Bundy is quoted in Hannah, *Key to Failure*, p. 183. Bunker is quoted in Hannah, *Key to Failure*, p. 217; Bunker urged President Johnson to invade Laos (pp. 236–37). Rostow is

quoted in Smith, *History of the Viet Nam War*, vol. 2, p. 102. See the discussion of an American barrier across Laos in Wirtz, *Tet Offensive*, pp. 120 ff.

89. Kolko, Anatomy of a War, pp. 482, 250. The quotation is in Callison, *Land to the Tiller*, p. 111. On the extent of Communist support in South Vietnam, see Robert A. Scalapino, "We Cannot Accept a Communist Seizure of Viet Nam," in the *New York Times Magazine*, Dec. 11, 1966, p. 46; the CBS survey is quoted in Fishel, *Viet Nam*, pp. 653, 659; Thompson, *No Exit from Viet Nam*, p. 65; Race, *War Comes to Long An*, p. 188; Howard R. Penniman, *Elections in South Viet Nam* (Washington, D.C.: American Enterprise Institute, 1972), p. 199; Duncanson, *Government and Revolution*, p. 13, estimates that the Communists had the support of one-fourth of the South Vietnamese. Thompson, *Peace Is Not at Hand*, p. 169. Malcolm Salmon, "After Revolution, Evolution," *Far Eastern Economic Review*, Dec. 12, 1975, pp. 32–34.

90. See Tien Hung Nguyen and Schechter, *Palace File*.

91. The quotation is in Le Gro, *Viet Nam from Ceasefire*, p. 88. Lewy, *America in Viet Nam*, p. 208; Van Tien Dung, *Our Great Spring Victory*, pp. 17–18; Dong Van Khuyen, *RVNAF*, pp. 287–88; Le Gro, *Viet Nam from Ceasefire*, pp. 84–87; Lomperis, *War Everyone Lost*, p. 75.

92. Giap, *How We Won the War*, p. 24.

93. The successful defense of Stalingrad against a furious Nazi assault (August 1942–January 1943) was the turning point of World War II in Europe.

94. Cao Van Vien, *Final Collapse*; Dawson, *55 Days*; Hosmer, Kellen, and Jenkins, *Fall of South Viet Nam*; Todd, *Cruel April*; Englemann, *Tears before the Rain*; Van Tien Dung, *Our Great Spring Victory*.

95. Chalmers Johnson offers this summary: "In terms of revolutionary strategy, communism has succeeded only when it has been able to co-opt a national liberation struggle, and it has failed whenever it was opposed to or isolated from a national liberation struggle, such as those in Israel, Algeria, Indonesia and Burma. Needless to add, even when supporting a war of national liberation, the communists have occasionally been defeated, as in Greece, Malaya, the Philippines, and Venezuela." *Autopsy on People's War*, p. 10.

96. See Anthony James Joes, *From the Barrel of a Gun*.

97. Dept. of the Army, "PROVN," Mar. 1966.

98. The quotations are in Hemingway, *Our War Was Different*, pp. 178, x. But see also William R. Corson, *The Betrayal* (New York: Norton, 1968). Lewy, *America in Viet Nam*, p. 116.

99. Westmoreland, *Soldier Reports*, p. 166.

100. See Harry Summers, *On Strategy*; Hannah, *Key to Failure*. Chen, "China's Involvement." Thompson, *Defeating Communist Insurgency*.

101. For the CAPs, see West, *Village*; West, *Small Unit Action*; Herrington, *Silence Was a Weapon*.

102. According to Liddell Hart: "Man has two supreme loyalties—to country and to family. And with most men the second, being more personal, is the stronger. So long as their families are safe they will defend their country, be-

lieving that by their sacrifice they are safeguarding their families also. But even the bonds of patriotism, discipline and comradeship are loosened when the family itself is menaced." B.H. Liddell Hart, *Strategy* (New York: Praeger, 1954), p. 153.

103. Clausewitz, *On War*, book 6, chap. 1. In *The Art of War*, Sun Tzu wrote, "Invincibility lies in the defense."

8. El Salvador: A Long War in a Small Country

1. By 1998 the population had increased to well over 6 million. On the relationship between poverty and the system of land ownership in El Salvador, see John Sheahan, *Patterns of Development in Latin America: Poverty, Repression, and Economic Strategy* (Princeton, N.J.: Princeton Univ. Press, 1987). For historical background on Central America, see Woodward, *Central America;* Thomas L. Karnes, *The Failure of Union: Central America, 1824–1975* (Chapel Hill: Univ. of North Carolina Press, 1976).

2. Dunkerly, *Power*, pp. 369–70. Dunkerley's book is ferociously hostile to Presidents Reagan and Duarte and indulgent toward the insurgents. But see also Fitch, *Political Consequences*. On "Focoism," see Regis Debray, *Revolution in the Revolution* (New York: Monthly Review, 1967); Daniel James, *Che Guevara* (London: Allen and Unwin, 1970).

3. Cynthia McClintock places great stress on the stolen 1972 elections as an explanation for the emergence of the FMLN several years later. *Revolutionary Movements in Latin America.*

4. Dunkerly, *Power*, p. 338. The headquarters of the FMLN was in Managua, Nicaragua.

5. LeMoyne, "El Salvador's Forgotten War," pp. 105–26.

6. The "final offensive" of the FMLN would fail in 1981 before any appreciable U.S. aid had arrived. Moreover, in neighboring Guatemala a similar insurgency was beaten without U.S. help. See Wickham-Crowley, *Guerrillas and Revolutions*, pp. 282 ff. Despite the importance of Carter's decision, there is hardly a mention of El Salvador in his memoirs or those of his national security advisor, Brzezinski, or his secretary of state, Vance. For that matter, President Reagan's secretary of state, George P. Shultz, and his secretary of defense, Caspar Weinberger, are almost equally reticent. See Jimmy Carter, *Keeping Faith: Memoirs of a President* (New York: Bantam Books, 1982); Zbigniew Brzezinski, *Power and Principle: Memoirs of a National Security Adviser 1977–1981* (New York: Farrar, Strauss, Giroux, 1983); Cyrus Vance, *Hard Choices* (New York: Simon and Schuster, 1983); Shultz, *Turmoil and Triumph;* Caspar Weinberger, *Fighting for Peace: Seven Critical Years at the Pentagon* (New York: Warner, 1990). Venezuelan personnel helped train some units of the Salvadoran armed forces. Interview with Col. John D. Waghelstein, *Senior Officers Oral History Program* (Carlisle Barracks, Pa.: U.S. Army Military History Institute, 1985).

7. See United Nations Economic Commission for Latin America, *Eco-*

nomic Survey of Latin America 1980 (Santiago, Chile: United Nations, 1982). Dunkerly, *Power,* p. 400.

8. "The Soviets saw the Sandinista victory as producing a domino effect in Central America. Operating mainly through Cuba and local Communists, Moscow sought to duplicate the Nicaraguan experience in El Salvador." Rothenberg, "Soviets and Central America."

9. Kissinger et al., *Report of the Bipartisan Commission* (hereafter cited as *Report).* See also "U.S. Policy in Central America: Consultant Papers for the Kissinger Commission," *AEI Foreign Policy and Defense Review* 5, no. 1 (1984).

10. *Report,* pp. 87 (Trotsky would doubtless agree), 84.

11. *Report,* pp. 4, 87.

12. *Report,* pp. 26–27, 25, 91; 126, 87.

13. *Report,* pp. 110–11, 13, 86, 37.

14. *Report,* pp. 11–12. This insight—that dictatorships do not protect their societies from Communism but instead prepare the way for it—was crucial, however overdue.

15. *Report,* pp. 110–11, 11, 113.

16. *Report,* p. 28.

17. *Report,* pp. 97, 104.

18. *Report,* pp. 109, 85.

19. All figures in this paragraph are adapted from Bacevich et al., *American Military Policy.*

20. Duarte, *My Story,* p. 19. And see Webre, *Duarte and the Christian Democratic Party.* Dunkerly stated that Duarte's victory in the presidential election stemmed in part from perceptions on the part of Salvadoran rightists that Duarte had Washington's blessing. *Power,* p. 409.

21. Dunkerly, *Power,* p. 424 n. See Garcia, "El Salvador."

22. See "Concerning Our Military Plans: The Military Strategy of the FMLN," a document captured near Perquin, El Salvador, translated and edited by Gabriel Marcella, U.S. Army War College, May 1986. Baloyra, "Negotiating War in El Salvador," p. 132. See Schwarz, *American Counterinsurgency Doctrine.* See Byrne, *El Salvador's Civil War,* p. 206, passim.

23. The minimum aim of the offensive was to bring the war into the hitherto quiescent capital, San Salvador, home to over one-quarter of the country's population. Guerrilla losses were high, and no popular uprising occurred. Yet the offensive produced a panic in many quarters (not least in Washington), reminiscent of the immediate aftermath of the 1968 Tet Offensive in Vietnam. It was during those turbulent days that Salvadoran army personnel executed six Jesuit priests, accusing them of being in sympathetic contact with the guerrillas, an episode that triggered great disquiet in the U.S. Congress.

24. Consult Sullivan, "Peace Came to El Salvador."

25. Schwarz, *American Counterinsurgency Doctrine,* p. 4, passim.

26. Ibid., p. 55.

27. Ibid., pp. 47–49. Nevertheless, land reform programs transferred more

than a fifth of agricultural land to small-farm families, which totaled about one-half million people. *El Salvador, 1979–1989: A Briefing Book on U.S. Aid and the Situation in El Salvador* (Washington, D.C.: Congressional Research Service, 1989), p. 10.

28. But of course that need not be the main or the only reason to hold elections: other reasons would include demonstrating that the insurgents lack popular support and that a peaceful road to change exists.

29. Roberto D'Aubuisson, founder of ARENA, publicly charged that his defeat in the 1984 presidential election was the result of CIA money and advice that went to Duarte's campaign. See, for example, *Washington Post*, May 3, 1984. With all due respect, I believe Benjamin Schwarz is simply wrong about the U.S. policy on elections: nothing did more to strengthen the anti-FMLN coalition inside and outside El Salvador than the free elections of 1982 and 1984, especially in Mexico, West Germany, and above all the U.S. Congress.

30. And Schwarz sometimes seems to come perilously close to this position.

31. Consult Waghelstein, *El Salvador;* Manwaring and Prisk, *El Salvador at War;* Sereseres, "Lessons." See also Evans, "El Salvador's Lessons."

32. Bacevich et al., *American Military Policy,* p. 5. Those authors were writing in 1988, "Observers generally concede that the FMLN—tough, competent, highly motivated—can sustain its current strategy indefinitely" (p. 6).

33. American-supplied helicopters, for one example, vastly improved the surveillance and response capabilities of the Salvadoran Army. U.S. aid also helped offset the deliberate guerrilla destruction of the economy.

34. Another factor is that Duarte and his Christian Democratic Party had ties with Christian Democratic Parties in Latin America and Europe. Guevara, *Guerrilla Warfare.* Goodwin and Skocpol, "Explaining Revolutions," p. 495.

35. It is not, however, the decisive question; see the discussion of the relative importance of numbers versus intensity during a civil war in Bergerud, *Dynamics of Defeat.*

36. If a popular rising did not occur because "the people" feared the guns of the government, does that not imply that either the FMLN was wantonly calling innocent civilians to their violent death or that the FMLN was unable to gauge popular sentiment—or both?

37. Johnson, in *Autopsy on People's War,* wrote, "Put crudely, we tend to work on the assumption that there is no such thing as bad peoples, only bad governments; and the very occurrence of revolutionary violence establishes a prima facie judgment in our minds in favor of the rebels and against the authorities" (p. 5). The pro-FMLN *Revolution in El Salvador: Origins and Evolution* by Tommie Sue Montgomery naively contrasts the many deplorable aspects of Salvadoran reality with the bright promises of the FMLN. Hannah Arendt, *On Revolution;* Grenier, "From Causes to Causers"; Goodwin and Skocpol, "Explaining Revolutions"; see also Forrest D. Colburn, *The Vogue of Revolution in Poor Countries* (Princeton, N.J.: Princeton Univ. Press, 1994); Eric Selbin, *Mod-*

ern Latin American Revolutions (Boulder, Colo.: Westview, 1993); and Desai and Eckstein, "Insurgency."

38. This is the very good question raised by Grenier in "From Causes to Causers."

39. Johnson, *Autopsy on People's War*, pp. 112–13. Many things in Batista's Cuba were unique in the Latin American context, and nothing more so than the army. Unlike Mexico or Colombia or Chile, Cuba had not won its independence from Spain; it had been granted independence by the United States after the Spanish-American War. The Cuban army was thus the result and not the cause of independence, possessing neither a heroic tradition nor counterguerrilla capabilities. Under Batista its high command became "a demoralized gaggle of corrupt, cruel and lazy officers without combat experience" (Hugh Thomas, *The Cuban Revolution* [New York: Harper and Row, 1977], p. 215). During the two-year conflict with Castro, this army, comprising 15,000 men, suffered 300 fatalities, less than three per week. When Batista fled Cuba on New Year's Eve 1958, many army units had not fired a single shot in battle. Before that, in May 1958, the Eisenhower administration imposed an arms embargo on Cuba. This move in effect placed the Batista government and the Castro guerrillas on the same moral plane and suggested that Washington wanted, or at least expected, the insurgents to win. It rocked the morale of Batista's cronies and swelled the ranks of his opponents. If Castro had had to face not an isolated Batista and his Khaki-clad mafia "army" but a government and army like that, for instance, of Colombia, much of the history of Latin American politics after 1958 would have been radically different. And finally, what happened to the Cuban middle class after Castro came to power served as an unmistakable warning duly noted throughout Latin America.

40. See the data on the social background of revolutionary elites and subelites in Wickham-Crowley, *Guerrillas and Revolutions*, esp. pp. 327 ff.; see also p. 285. The quotation is in Goodwin and Skocpol, "Explaining Revolutions," p. 492. LeMoyne, "El Salvador's Forgotten War." Actually, the FMLN had been forcing young men to join its ranks since the very early 1980s; that practice, aside from causing much resentment, resulted in desertions and defections, which often produced intelligence coups for the government. In 1986 mines caused nearly two-thirds of the casualties among the Salvadoran armed forces, compared to only 3 percent in 1984. Byrne, *El Salvador's Civil War*, p. 164 n. 19.

41. Wickham-Crowley, *Guerrillas and Revolutions*, p. 287.

42. Wickham-Crowley, *Guerrillas and Revolutions*; see also Charles Tilly, "Does Modernization Breed Revolution?" in *Comparative Politics* 5, no. 3 (Apr. 1973); Dix, "Why Revolutions Succeed and Fail," maintains that a broad negative coalition is necessary for successful revolution.

43. As Theda Skocpol emphasized in *States and Social Revolutions*.

44. See the interesting and useful collection of viewpoints in Manwaring and Prisk, *El Salvador at War*. See also Alfred B. Barr and Caesar D. Sereseres,

"U.S. Unconventional Warfare Doctrine, Policies, and Operations: Experiences and Lessons from Central America, 1980–1990," in *Saving Democracies: U.S. Intervention in Threatened Democratic States*, ed. Anthony James Joes (Westport, Conn.: Praeger, 1999), pp. 93–125.

9. Afghnistan: Cracking the Red Empire

1. David C. Isby, "Soviet Strategy and Tactics in Low Intensity Conflict," in Shultz et al., *Guerrilla Warfare and Counterinsurgency*, p. 330.

2. See Norris, *First Afghan War;* for good treatments of the pre-Soviet-invasion history of Afghanistan, see Dupree's widely praised *Afghanistan;* Poullada, "The Road to Crisis."

3. Before the invasion there were nearly 7 million Pushtuns; they are closely related to the Pathans of Pakistan, from whom they were divided in the nineteenth century by a British-imposed border; they lived mainly in the south and east, and almost all were Sunni Muslims. In the northeast were 2 million Tadzhiks. In the central massif lived 1 million Hazaras; they spoke a Persian dialect and were the largest Shi'a Muslim community in the country. A million Uzbeks and Turkomans lived in the north. In the west were about a million Persian-speaking Farsiwan, along with another million Aimaq. And there were many other groups. See Fletcher, *Afghanistan.*

4. See Collins, *Soviet Invasion of Afghanistan*, p. 50. Bradsher, *Afghanistan and the Soviet Union*, p. 80. See, for example, Vladimir Kuzichkin, *Inside the KGB: My Life in Soviet Espionage* (New York: Pantheon, 1990), p. 311. The former U.S. ambassador to Afghanistan, Robert Neumann, advised President Carter to cut off all U.S. aid to the new PDPA regime. Neumann later stated that the mild American reaction to the killing of Daoud contributed to the subsequent Soviet invasion. President Carter's national security adviser, Zbigniew Brzezinski, agrees with this view. Hammond, *Red Flag over Afghanistan*, p. 63.

5. Roy, "Afghan Communist Party." Anthony Arnold and Rosanne Klass, "Afghanistan's Divided Communist Party," in Klass, *Afghanistan.*

6. Amin Saikal and William Maley, introduction to Saikal and Maley, *Soviet Withdrawal*, p. 5. Bradsher, *Afghanistan and the Soviet Union*, chap. 5.

7. The quotation is in Elie Krakowski, "Afghanistan and Soviet Global Interests," in Klass, *Afghanistan*, p. 164. Amin, "Afghan Resistance," p. 380.

8. Amin had become president by killing his predecessor, Nur Mohammed Taraki, the first known member of the Afghan Communist Party. Soviet colonel Boyarinov, who led the assault on Amin's palace, was shot by his own troops.

9. As the quisling Kadar did in Hungary in 1956. Urban, *War in Afghanistan*, p. 47. Anatoly Dobrynin confirms this squalid deception in *In Confidence*, p. 445.

10. Babrak Karmal, born in 1929, was the founder of the Parcham faction. Son of an army general, he had attended Kabul University for a while. Collins,

Soviet Invasion of Afghanistan, p. 100; A. Rosul Amin, "The Sovietization of Afghanistan," in Klass, *Afghanistan,* p. 306.

11. Edward N. Luttwak, *The Grand Strategy of the Soviet Union* (New York: St. Martin's, 1983), p. 58.

12. The Brezhnev Doctrine included the publicly proclaimed insistence that once Communists had acquired governmental control of a country, by whatever means, the Soviet Union and other fraternal socialist states would never permit that country to have any other kind of government. (This had provided a doctrinal basis for the Warsaw Pact invasion of Czechoslovakia in 1968.) Martin Malia, in his impressive work *The Soviet Tragedy* (New York: Free Press, 1994), maintains that "the Afghan intervention was not dictated by geopolitical considerations, such as advancing a salient toward Middle East oil, as the West thought at the time, but by a senescent ideological concern for the inviolability of the frontiers of socialism" (p. 379). Arnold, *Afghanistan,* p. 133. For quotations concerning the Hitler-Stalin Pact of 1939, see Rosanne Klass, ed., *Afghanistan: The Great Game Revisited* (New York: Freedom House, 1987), p. 232.

13. On the planned incorporation of northern Afghanistan into the Soviet Union, see Bodansky, "Soviet Military Operations."

14. Collins, *Soviet Invasion of Afghanistan,* p. 26.

15. The quotations are in Krakowski, "Soviet Global Interests," pp. 162, 178; and Luttwak, *Grand Strategy,* p. 60. See Dobrynin, *In Confidence,* pp. 446–47; Cyrus Vance, secretary of state at the time, agrees with Dobrynin's view. *Hard Choices,* p. 388. Some in the Kremlin apparently feared that President Amin was getting ready to imitate Egypt's president Sadat and throw out his Soviet advisers. Kuzichkin, *Inside the KGB,* p. 315. Bradsher, *Afghanistan and the Soviet Union,* p. 156. According to Ambassador Dobrynin, top Soviet military leaders had opposed sending troops into Afghanistan. *In Confidence,* p. 444.

16. Louis Dupree, "Post-Withdrawal," in Saikal and Maley, *Soviet Withdrawal,* p. 31.

17. Isby, *War in a Distant Country,* p. 93.

18. Karp, *Seven Years,* p. 9. The quotations are in Brigot and Roy, *War in Afghanistan,* p. 74; and Isby, *War in a Distant Country,* p. 62. Kabul also purchased the adherence of certain tribes by exempting them from the draft. Most of those arrangements were purely tactical and hence temporary.

19. See Bradsher, *Afghanistan and the Soviet Union,* p. 294; Girardet, *Afghanistan: Soviet War,* p. 201; Amstutz, *First Five Years,* p. 122. See also Kakar, *Soviet Invasion and Afghan Response.*

20. Karp, *Eight Years,* p. 8; U.S. Department of State, *Afghanistan: Soviet Occupation and Withdrawal* (Washington, D.C.: U.S. Department of State, 1988).

21. Amstutz, *First Five Years,* p. 204.

22. Trottier and Karp, *Five Years of Occupation,* p. 6.

23. Amin, "Sovietization," p. 325.

24. Chaliand, "Bargain War," p. 330.

25. For insights into this general subject, see Roy, *Islam and Resistance.*

26. Amstutz, *First Five Years,* p. 152.

27. Arnold, *Afghanistan,* p. 98. Malhuret, "Report from Afghanistan."

28. Edwards, "Anti-Soviet Jihad," p. 24. Amstutz, *First Five Years,* p. 142. Girardet, *Afghanistan: Soviet War,* p. 125. Barnett R. Rubin, "Human Rights in Afghanistan," in Klass, *Afghanistan,* p. 345.

29. Girardet, *Afghanistan: Soviet War,* p. 63. Trottier and Karp, *Five Years of Occupation,* p. 5.

30. M. Siddieq Noorzoy, "Long-Term Soviet Economic Interests and Policies in Afghanistan," in Klass, *Afghanistan,* p. 91. Amstutz, *First Five Years,* p. 145.

31. Amstutz, *First Five Years,* pp. 150, 124. Van Hollen, *Three Years of Occupation,* p. 5.

32. Amstutz, *First Five Years,* pp. 186–87; Urban, *War in Afghanistan,* p. 69. Karp, *Six Years,* p. 7.

33. Chaliand, "Bargain War," p. 355.

34. Amstutz, *First Five Years,* p. 166. Sarin and Dvoretsky, *Afghan Syndrome,* pp. 108–12, 184. Van Hollen, *Three Years of Occupation,* p. 5.

35. Amstutz, *First Five Years,* pp. 183, 189. Girardet, *Afghanistan: Soviet War,* p. 141; Arnold, *Fateful Pebble,* p. 132. *New York Times,* Mar. 21, 1984, p. 7.

36. Karp, *Seven Years,* p. 9. Arnold, *Afghanistan,* p. 102. Van Hollen, *Three Years of Occupation,* p. 7.

37. Bodansky, "Soviet Military Operations." Allen and Muratoff, *Caucasian Battlefields,* chap. 3.

38. Both before and after the Basmachi Revolt, the Kremlin tried with fair success to maintain the divisions among their Central Asian subjects by encouraging the cultivation of local languages and dialects, with Russian as the sole lingua franca.

39. Jukes, "Soviet Armed Forces," p. 88. Soviet Muslim soldiers often defected to the mujahideen; Sarin and Dvoretsky, *Afghan Syndrome,* p. 88. For additional Russian perspectives, see Bocharov, *Russian Roulette;* Borovik, *Hidden War;* Oleg Yermakov, *Afghan Tales: Stories from Russia's Vietnam* (New York: Morrow, 1991). And on this topic Mark Galeotti's seductively written *Afghanistan* is indispensable. On the use of non-Russian troops, see Arnold, *Fateful Pebble.* See the table on ethnic casualties in Galeotti, *Afghanistan,* p. 28.

40. Karp, *Seven Years,* p. 10; Karp, *Eight Years,* p. 9.

41. Urban, *War in Afghanistan,* p. 176.

42. Bradsher, *Afghanistan and the Soviet Union,* p. 210. Jukes, "Soviet Armed Forces," p. 84.

43. Karp, *Eight Years,* p. 2. "Most Western estimates put Soviet troop strength at about 120,000 men." U.S. Department of State, *Afghanistan,* p. 5. Amstutz, *First Five Years,* pp. 168, 196.

44. Urban, *War in Afghanistan,* p. 129.

45. Cordesman and Wagner, *Lessons,* pp. 135, 127. Treatment for wounded soldiers improved as the war went on. Karp, *Six Years,* p. 8. On the lack of

initiative among officers, see Sarin and Dvoretsky, *Afghan Syndrome*. One must nevertheless acknowledge that numerous Soviet officers performed their duties well under the most trying circumstances.

46. Karp, *Six Years*, p. 7

47. Hosmer, "How Successful Has the Soviet Union Been?"

48. Soviet special forces were known generically in the West as Spetsnaz (*spetsialnoye naznachenie*); they impressed the mujahideen with their skill and daring, but they had relatively little effect on the war strategically. Karp, *Seven Years*, p. 11. Mark Galeotti was impressed with improvements in Soviet counterinsurgency techniques by the late 1980s, especially among elite units; *Afghanistan*, chap. 11.

49. Collins, *Soviet Invasion of Afghanistan*, p. 85. Girardet, *Afghanistan: Soviet War*, p. 42; Amstutz, *First Five Years*, p. 149. Urban, *War in Afghanistan*, p. 68. Van Hollen, *Three Years of Occupation*, p. 9.

50. Brigot and Roy, *War in Afghanistan*, p. 151. Cordesman and Wagner, *Lessons*, p. 175. The quotation is in U.S. Dept. of State, *Afghanistan*, p. 5.

51. Cordesman and Wagner, *Lessons*, p. 231 n, quotation on p. 177.

52. Bodansky, "Soviet Military Operations," p. 259, passim.

53. Dupree is quoted in Collins, *Soviet Invasion of Afghanistan*, p. 90. *New York Times*, Dec. 17, 1984, p. 1. See also the report by Amnesty International, *Afghanistan: Torture of Prisoners* (London: Amnesty International Publications, 1986). Girardet, *Afghanistan: Soviet War*. This method, "perfected" in Afghanistan, has been used also in Ethiopia and Cambodia. See Malhuret, "Report from Afghanistan," pp. 427 ff.

54. Girardet, *Afghanistan: Soviet War*, pp. 228, 219–20. Amstutz, *First Five Years*, pp. 175–76, 188. *Christian Science Monitor*, Oct. 26, 1988, p. 11; Malhuret, "Report from Afghanistan."

55. Malhuret, "Report from Afghanistan," p. 430; on this deeply disturbing topic of toy bombs, see also Girardet, *Afghanistan: Soviet War*, p. 213; Amstutz, *First Five Years*, p. 145; Arnold, *Afghanistan*, p. 99; Bradsher, *Afghanistan and the Soviet Union*, p. 211; *New York Times*, editorial, Dec. 10, 1985, p. 30.

56. Bradsher, *Afghanistan and the Soviet Union*, p. 279. The quotation is in Malhuret, "Report from Afghanistan," p. 430; see also the reports to the United Nations Commission on Human Rights by Felix Ermacora: "Human Rights in Afghanistan," UN Document nos. E/CN.4/1985/21, Feb. 19, 1985; A/40/843, Nov. 5, 1985; E/CN.4/1986/24, Feb. 17, 1986.

57. Collins, *Soviet Invasion of Afghanistan*, p. 59.

58. Amstutz, *First Five Years*, p. 132.

59. Ibid., pp. 132, 135, 128, 181. Bureau of Intelligence and Research, *Four Years of Occupation*, p. 2.

60. Trottier and Karp, *Five Years of Occupation*, p. 4. *New York Times*, Oct. 24, 1984, p. 1.

61. Amstutz, *First Five Years*, p. 140. Arnold, *Afghanistan*, p. 98. Trottier and Karp, *Five Years of Occupation*, p. 2.

62. Arnold, *Afghanistan*, p. 98.

63. Karp, *Eight Years*, p. 12. Rubin, "Fragmentation of Afghanistan," p. 158. Karp, *Seven Years*, p. 1. Urban, *War in Afghanistan*, p. 200.

64. Karp, *Eight Years*, pp. 6, 3, 5. On Western press coverage of raids into the USSR, see, for example, *New York Times*, Jan. 25, 1984, p. 1. Bradsher, *Afghanistan and the Soviet Union*, p. 276.

65. On Stingers, see, inter alia, Robert M. Gates, *From the Shadows* (New York: Simon and Schuster, 1996), pp. 349–50. Mark Galeotti downplays the effect of the Stinger in his *Afghanistan*.

66. *Christian Science Monitor*, Oct. 24, 1988. The quotations are in *Washington Post*, Dec. 15, 1985; and Van Hollen, *Three Years of Occupation*, p. 11. Girardet, *Afghanistan: Soviet War*, p. 248. Malhuret, "Report from Afghanistan." In his article "Afghanistan: Post-mortem," in the April 1989 *Atlantic*, Robert D. Kaplan wrote that foreign newsmen gave poor coverage to the Afghan war partly because there were no modern cities with good hotels close at hand.

67. At one point the Soviet High command contemplated sealing Afghanistan's borders with Pakistan and Iran with three hundred thousand troops, but nothing came of the idea. Kuzichkin, *Inside the KGB*, p. 349. Amin Saikal, "The Regional Politics of the Afghan Crisis," in Saikal and Maley, *Soviet Withdrawal*, p. 54. Collins, *Soviet Invasion of Afghanistan*, p. 153; on the bombing of villages inside Pakistan, see, for example, *New York Times*, Jan. 29, 1984, p. 1; Mar. 25, 1987, p. 1. Girardet, *Afghanistan: Soviet War*, p. 67. And see note 78. Farr and Merriam, *Afghan Resistance*, p. xii.

68. Bradsher, *Afghanistan and the Soviet Union*, p. 222.

69. Urban, *War in Afghanistan*, p. 97.

70. Karp, *Eight Years*, p. 22.

71. See Vertzberger, "Afghanistan in China's Policy," pp. 1–24; Holmes, "Afghanistan and Sino-Soviet Relations," pp. 122–42.

72. Amstutz, *First Five Years*, p. 216.

73. Amin, "Sovietization," p. 322.

74. Poullada, "Road to Crisis," p. 44, quotation on p. 48. Collins, *Soviet Invasion*, pp. 19, 20. Hammond, *Red Flag over Afghanistan*, pp. 26–28. In Secretary of State James Baker's memoirs, the word *Afghanistan* appears exactly two times. Granted, by his time Afghanistan had been overshadowed by the most momentous events.

75. Arnold, *Afghanistan*, p. 12. Collins, *Soviet Invasion*, p. 134.

76. Former USSR ambassador to Washington Anatoly Dobrynin writes that the Soviet leadership found Carter's statement "incredible," and we can certainly believe him. Dobrynin, *In Confidence*, p. 448. One wonders what President Carter thought of the Berlin Blockade, the Korean War, the Cuban Missile Crisis, or Vietnam.

77. Carter, *Keeping Faith*, p. 473.

78. Ibid., pp. 471–89, quotation on p. 483; Vance, *Hard Choices*, pp. 386–96; Brzezinski, *Power and Principle*, chap. 12. In fact, Carter had authorized help for

the resistance *before* the Soviet invasion; see Gates, *From the Shadows,* pp. 146–47. "The Soviet intervention and the sharp response of the United States proved a final turning point in Soviet-American relations." Dobrynin, *In Confidence,* p. 449.

79. "The Reagan Doctrine, as this strategy became known, sought to exploit vulnerabilities the Russians had created for themselves in the Third World; this latter-day effort to "roll back" Soviet influence would in time produce impressive results at minimum cost and risk to the United States." John Lewis Gaddis, *The United States and the End of the Cold War* (New York: Oxford Univ. Press, 1990), p. 124. See Jeane J. Kirkpatrick, *The Reagan Doctrine and U.S. Foreign Policy* (Washington, D.C.: Heritage Foundation, 1985); Mark Lagon, *The Reagan Doctrine* (Westport, Conn.: Praeger, 1994); James M. Scott, *Deciding to Intervene: The Reagan Doctrine and American Foreign Policy* (Durham, N.C.: Duke University Press, 1996); William Bode, "The Reagan Doctrine in Outline," and Angelo Codevilla, "The Reagan Doctrine: It Awaits Implementation," both in *Central America and the Reagan Doctrine,* ed. Walter F. Hahn (Boston: Univ. Press of America, 1987); Secretary of State George Shultz, "America and the Struggle for Freedom," *State Department Current Policy,* no. 659 (Feb. 1985).

80. Collins, *Soviet Invasion of Afghanistan,* p. 145. See Gates, *From the Shadows,* pp. 319–21.

81. Arnold, *Afghanistan,* p. 118; see *New York Times,* May 3, 1983; Nov. 28, 1984; *Wall Street Journal,* Apr. 9, 1984; *Washington Post,* Jan. 13, 1985; *Economist,* Jan. 19, 1985; Cordesman and Wagner, *Lessons,* pp. 20, 147. But in view of the eventual effect of the Afghan conflict on the Soviet empire, the Americans surely got their money's worth. John Ranelaugh, *The Agency: The Rise and Decline of the CIA* (New York: Simon and Schuster, 1986), p. 681; Amstutz, *First Five Years,* p. 210. President Reagan received a delegation of mujahideen leaders in the Oval Office in May 1986. Bradsher, *Afghanistan and the Soviet Union,* p. 278.

82. Jukes, "Soviet Armed Forces," p. 83; Cordesman and Wagner, *Lessons,* p. 165.

83. Cordesman and Wagner, *Lessons;* Jukes, "Soviet Armed Forces," p. 83. Of course, many dispute the official Soviet casualty figures; some authors believe that the Soviets lost between 40,000 and 50,000, from combat, disease, drugs, accidents, and suicide. See Arnold, *Fateful Pebble,* pp. 190 ff. Perhaps 730,000 Soviet troops passed through Afghanistan, only one soldier per four hundred Soviet citizens; five times more Soviet citizens died on the roads in one year in the 1980s than during the entire Afghan conflict; Galeotti, *Afghanistan,* pp. 28, 30, passim. Isby, *War in a Distant Country,* p. 65; Maley, "Geneva Accords," p. 16. Girardet, *Afghanistan: Soviet War,* p. 234.

84. John F. Shroder and Abduyl Tawab Assifi, "Afghan Mineral Resources and Soviet Exploitation," in Klass, *Afghanistan.*

85. The quotation is in Bennigsen, "Impact of the Afghan War," p. 295. Alexandre Bennigsen, "Mullahs, Mujahidin and Soviet Muslims," *Problems of*

Communism 33 (Nov.–Dec. 1984), pp. 28–45; see also the review article by Kemal Karpat, "Moscow and the 'Muslim Question,'" *Problems of Communism* 32 (Nov.–Dec. 1983), pp. 71–80; and Fuller, "Emergence of Central Asia."

86. U.S. Dept. of State, *Afghanistan*, p. 1. See also Gates, *From the Shadows*, p. 252.

87. Cordesman and Wagner, *Lessons*, p. 295. For a brief treatment of the Ukraine situation plus bibliography, see Anthony James Joes, *Guerrilla Warfare: A Historical, Biographical and Bibliographical Sourcebook* (Westport, Conn.: Greenwood, 1996), pp. 59–61, 263. "The Soviets learned three major lessons of modern war in much the same hard way the U.S. learned them in Viet Nam: First, it is virtually impossible to defeat a popular guerrilla army with secure sources of supply and a recovery area. Second, it is extremely difficult—if not impossible—to use modern weapons technology to cut off a guerrilla force from food and other basic supplies. Third, the success of pacification techniques depends on the existence of a popular local government, and the techniques must be seen as the actions of the local government and not of foreign military sources." Cordesman and Wagner, *Lessons*, p. 95.

88. Daley, "Gorbachev's Global Foreign Policy," pp. 496–513. An enlightening treatment of nonmilitary aspects of Soviet counterinsurgency in Afghanistan is Robbins, "Soviet Counterinsurgency in Afghanistan."

89. U.S. Dept. of State, *Afghanistan*, p. 2.

90. The quotation is in ibid., p. 5. See the account of relations between the United States and the USSR during this period in Shultz, *Triumph and Turmoil*, pp. 186–94.

91. Riaz Khan, *Untying the Afghan Knot: Negotiating Soviet Withdrawal* (Durham, N.C.: Duke Univ. Press, 1991), quotation on p. 1. Former secretary of state George P. Shultz exulted, "The Soviet withdrawal from Afghanistan was a tremendous triumph, one of the biggest events of Ronald Reagan's two terms and a turn of seminal significance in Soviet internal as well as external policies." *Triumph and Turmoil*, p. 1092. The resistance parties opposed the accords. They held that the Kabul regime, illegal and illegitimate, could not enter into any international agreement. In addition, they feared that the accords might foreshadow a lessening of world interest (such as it was) in their struggle. Ahmed Rashid, "Highway Lifeline," *Far Eastern Economic Review*, Oct. 26, 1989, p. 22.

92. Jukes, "Soviet Armed Forces," p. 83.

93. See chap. 7 of this volume.

94. Maley, "Geneva Accords," p. 13.

95. At this point one can only speculate about the degree to which their entanglement in Afghanistan restrained the Kremlin leaders from military intervention in Poland, and all that would have been triggered by such a move, in the early 1980s. And the unexpected and unsolved military problems encountered in Afghanistan undoubtedly account to a large degree for the Kremlin's reluctance to oppose the secession of the Soviet republics.

10. Implications and Provocations

1. In contrast to the Carolinas, strong points worked quite well for the British a century later in the South African War, mainly because in the latter conflict the British had an abundance of troops.

2. In the Philippines, with 116,000 square miles and 10 million inhabitants, U.S. forces reached (for a short time) 70,000, representing .09 percent of the U.S. population in 1900. In South Vietnam, with 67,000 square miles and 16 million inhabitants, U.S. forces eventually reached 580,000, .28 percent of the U.S. population in 1960.

3. See Anthony James Joes, "Continuity and Change." See Lieven, *Chechnya.*

4. Like the Vietcong, the Greek and Salvadoran insurgents enjoyed the inestimable benefits of foreign sanctuary and outside assistance. In the latter two cases, the governments survived not only because large elements of the population opposed a Communist takeover but also because the United States did not abandon them.

5. Thompson, *Peace Is Not at Hand,* p. 200 n. 66.

6. Recall that in the post–Spanish War Philippines, there was no indigenous government for the United States to support, either directly or indirectly. The Americans themselves assumed the role of government and hence had no choice but to confront and defeat armed rebellion. And in Nicaragua the number of Americans involved in counterinsurgent activities was always quite limited.

7. Countries with valuable experience in dealing with guerrillas include Britain, Colombia, El Salvador, France, Greece, Indonesia, Israel, Morocco, Peru, the Philippines, Portugal, Thailand, and Turkey, See Metz, *Counterinsurgency.*

8. Clausewitz, *On War,* book 8, chap. 4. Of course there are sound military reasons for choosing such a procedure as well.

9. Griffith, introduction to *Mao Tse-Tung on Guerrilla Warfare,* p. 34.

10. The best-known example of this method is the Morice Line between Algeria and Tunisia; the Moroccan "Hassan Line" also worked against insurgents in the former Spanish Sahara. Blockhouses served the British well against the Boers, and they served Chiang Kai-shek against the Maoists in the 1930s.

11. Some would include the resettlement of civilians in this list of nonviolent measures. That process worked effectively in British Malaya, but in many other conflicts it backfired in politically catastrophic ways. See Marston, "Resettlement."

12. Thompson, "Regular Armies and Insurgency," p. 10.

13. Clausewitz, *On War,* pp. 75, 87. The British Royal Commission is quoted in Thomas R. Mockaitis, "Low Intensity Conflict: The British Experience," *Conflict Quarterly* 13, no. 1 (1993), p. 10. Taruc, *He Who Rides the Tiger.* Latour, *Le martyre de L'Armée française,* p. 321. Leites, *Viet Cong Style,* p. 17. During the Algerian insurgency, the torture of prisoners by some elements of the French Army, for what seemed to some at the time the most compelling and justifying

of reasons, eventually contributed to the disruption of the officer corps and the granting of independence to Algeria. See Joes, *From the Barrel of a Gun,* chap. 7.

14. Sun Tzu said in *The Art of War:* "Treat captives well, and care for them." Mao Tse-tung insisted that his troops abstain from abusing prisoners.

15. See Joes, *Modern Guerrilla Insurgency,* pp. 26–27. In the words of Sun Tzu, "Pay heed to nourishing the troops" (*The Art of War*). During their Malayan conflict, the British commitment at its peak counted 40,000 regular troops (British, Commonwealth, Gurkha, and Malayan), plus 24,000 Federation Police, 37,000 Special Constables, and 250,000 Home Guards, for a grand total of 351,000, of whom 512 British and Commonwealth soldiers were killed. Edgar O'Ballance, *Malaya: The Communist Insurgent War* (Hamden, Conn.: Archon, 1966), pp. 164, 177.

16. The appalling behavior of Chinese troops in Tibet in the 1950s provoked a long and difficult guerrilla war there. And many decades later, the future of that unhappy land is still in question.

Bibliography

Acheson, Dean. *Present at the Creation*. New York: Norton, 1969.

Adams, Nina, and Alfred W. McCoy, eds. *Laos: War and Revolution*. New York: Harper and Row, 1970.

Aguinaldo, Emilio. *A Second Look at America*. New York: Robert Speller, 1957.

Alden, John Richard. *The South in the Revolution, 1763–1789*. Baton Rouge: Louisiana State Univ. Press, 1957.

Alexiev, Alexander. *Inside the Soviet Army in Afghanistan*. Santa Monica, Calif.: Rand, 1988.

Allen, W.E.D., and Paul Muratoff. *Caucasian Battlefields*. Cambridge: Cambridge Univ. Press, 1953.

Amin, Tahir. "Afghan Resistance: Past, Present and Future." *Asian Survey* 24 (Apr. 1984).

Amstutz, J. Bruce. *Afghanistan: The First Five Years of Soviet Occupation*. Washington, D.C.: National Defense Univ. Press, 1986.

Anderson, Bern. *By Sea and River: The Naval History of the Civil War*. Westport, Conn.: Greenwood, 1977.

Anderson, M., M. Arnstein, and H. Averch. *Insurgent Organization and Operations: A Case Study of the Viet Cong in the Delta, 1964–1966*. Santa Monica, Calif.: Rand, 1967.

Anderson, Troyer Steven. *The Command of the Howe Brothers during the American Revolution*. New York: Oxford Univ. Press, 1936.

Andrade, Dale. *Ashes to Ashes: The Phoenix Program and the Viet Nam War*. Lexington, Mass.: Lexington Books, 1990.

Andrews, William R. *The Village War: Vietnamese Communist Revolutionary Activity in Dinh Truong Province*. Columbia, Mo.: Univ. of Missouri Press, 1973.

Arnold, Anthony. *Afghanistan: The Soviet Invasion in Perspective*. Rev. ed. Stanford, Calif.: Hoover Institution, 1985.

———. *The Fateful Pebble: Afghanistan's Role in the Fall of the Soviet Empire*. Novato, Calif.: Presidio Press, 1993.

Asprey, Robert B. *War in the Shadows: The Guerrilla in History.* 2 vols. Garden City, N.Y.: Doubleday, 1975. [Revised 1994.]

Averch, Harvey, and John Koehler. *The Huk Rebellion in the Philippines: Quantitative Approaches.* Santa Monica, Calif.: Rand, 1970.

Averoff-Tossizza, Evangelos. *By Fire and Axe: The Communist Party and the Civil War in Greece, 1944–1949.* New Rochelle, N.Y.: Caratzas, 1978.

Bacevich, A.J., et al. *American Military Policy in Small Wars: The Case of El Salvador.* Washington, D.C.: Pergamon-Brassey's, 1988.

Bacevich, A.J. "Disagreeable Work: Pacifying the Moros, 1903-1906," *Military Review* (June 1982).

Baclagon, U.S. *Lessons from the Huk Campaign in the Philippines.* Manila: Colcol, 1960.

Baloyra, Enrique. "Negotiating War in El Salvador: The Politics of Endgame." *Journal of Interamerican Studies and World Affairs* 28, no. 1 (1986).

Barclay, C.N. "The Western Soldier versus the Communist Insurgent." *Military Review* 49 (Feb. 1969).

Barker, Elisabeth. *Macedonia: Its Place in Balkan Power Politics.* London: Royal Institute of International Affairs, 1950.

———. "Yugoslav Policy toward Greece 1947–1949. In *Studies in the History of the Greek Civil War 1945–1949,* ed. Lars Baerentzen, John O. Iatrides, and Ole L. Smith. Copenhagen: Museum Tusculanum, 1987.

———. "The Yugoslavs and the Greek Civil War of 1946–1949." In *Studies in the History of the Greek Civil War 1945–1949,* ed. Lars Baerentzen et al. Copenhagen: Museum Tusculanum, 1987.

Barnet, Richard J. *Intervention and Revolution: The United States in the Third World.* New York: World Publishing, 1968.

Barr, Alfred, and Caesar D. Sereseres. "U.S. Unconventional Warfare Doctrine, Policies and Operations: Experiences and Lessons from Cenral America, 1980–1990," in Anthony James Joes, ed., *Saving Democracies: U.S. Intervention in Threatened Democratic States* (Westport, Conn.: Praeger, 1999).

Barrett, John G. *The Civil War in North Carolina.* Chapel Hill: Univ. of North Carolina Press, 1963.

———. *Sherman's March through the Carolinas.* Chapel Hill: Univ. of North Carolina Press, 1956.

Barry, Michael. "Afghanistan: Another Cambodia?" *Commentary,* Aug. 1982.

Bashore, Boyd. "Dual Strategy for Limited War." In Franklin Mark Osanka, ed., *Modern Guerrilla Warfare.* Glencoe, Ill.,: Free Press, 1962. Also in *Military Review* 40 (May 1960).

Basler, Roy P., ed. *The Collected Works of Abraham Lincoln.* 9 vols. New Brunswick, N.J.: Rutgers Univ Press., 1953.

Bass, Robert D. *Gamecock: The Life and Times of General Thomas Sumter.* New York: Holt, Rinehart, and Winston, 1961.

———. *The Green Dragoon.* New York: Henry Holt, 1957.

———. *Swamp Fox.* New York: Henry Holt, 1959.

Baxter, James P., ed. *The British Invasion from the North [Journal of Lt. William Digby]*. 1887. Reprint, New York: Da Capo, 1970.

Beamer, Carl Brent. "Gray Ghostbusters: Eastern Theater Union Counterguerrilla Operations in the Civil War." Ph.D. diss., Ohio State Univ. Press, 1988.

Beckett, Ian F.W., ed. *The Roots of Counterinsurgency: Armies and Guerrilla Warfare 1900–1945*. London: Blandford, 1988.

Beckett, Ian F.W., and John Pimlott. *Armed Forces and Modern Counterinsurgency*. New York: St. Martin's, 1985.

Bell, J. Bowyer. *The Myth of the Guerrilla: Revolutionary Theory and Malpractice*. New York: Knopf, 1971.

———. "Revolutionary Insurgency." *Conflict* 9, no. 3 (1989).

Bennigsen, Alexandre. "The Impact of the Afghan War on Soviet Central Asia." In Klass, *Afghanistan*.

———. "Muslim Guerrilla Warfare in the Caucasus, 1918–1928." *Central Asian Survey* 2, no. 1 (1983).

———. *The Soviet Union and Muslim Guerrilla Wars 1920–1981*. Santa Monica, Calif.: Rand, 1981.

Bergerud, Eric M. *The Dynamics of Defeat: The Viet Nam War in Hau Nghia Province*. Boulder, Colo.: Westview, 1991.

Beringer, Richard E., Herman Hattaway, Archer Jones, and William N. Still Jr. *Why the South Lost the Civil War*. Athens: Univ. of Georgia Press, 1986.

Berman, Larry. *Planning a Tragedy: The Americanization of the War in Viet Nam*. New York: Norton, 1982.

Bernstein, Carl. "Arms for Afghanistan." *New Republic,* July 18, 1981.

Betancourt, Ernesto F. *Revolutionary Strategy: A Handbook for Practitioners*. New Brunswick, N.J.: Transaction, 1991.

Billings-Yun, Melanie. *Decision against War: Eisenhower and Dien Bien Phu*. New York: Columbia Univ., 1988.

Bird, Harrison. *March to Saratoga*. New York: Oxford Univ., 1963.

Blair, Anne. *Lodge in Vietnam*. New Haven, Conn.: Yale Univ. Press, 1995.

Blank, Stephen, et al. *Responding to Low Intensity Conflict Challenges*. Maxwell Air Force Base, Alabama: Air Univ. Press, 1990.

Blasier, Cole. *The Hovering Giant: U.S. Responses to Revolutionary Change in Latin America*. Pittsburgh: Univ. of Pittsburgh Press, 1976.

Blaufarb, Douglas. *The Counterinsurgency Era: United States Doctrine and Performance 1950 to the Present*. New York: Free Press, 1977.

Blount, James H. *The American Occupation of the Philippines 1898–1912*. New York: Putnam's, 1913.

Bocharov, Gennady. *Russian Roulette: Afghanistan through Russian Eyes*. New York: HarperCollins, 1990.

Bodansky, Yossef. "The Bear on the Chessboard: Soviet Military Gains in Afghanistan." *World Affairs* 5, no. 3 (1982–1983).

———. "Soviet Military Operations in Afghanistan." In Klass, *Aghanistan*.

Bodard, Lucien. *The Quicksand War: Prelude to Viet Nam.* Boston: Little, Brown, 1967.

Bode, William R. "The Reagan Doctrine." *Strategic Review,* winter 1986.

Bonner, Arthur. *Among the Afghans.* Durham, N.C.: Duke Univ. Press, 1987.

Boorman, Howard L., and Scott Boorman, "Chinese Communist Insurgent Warfare." *Political Science Quarterly,* June 1966.

Borovik, Artyom. *The Hidden War: A Russian Journalist's Account of the Soviet War in Afghanistan.* New York: Atlantic Monthly, 1990.

Bowler, R. Arthur. *Logistics and the Failure of the British Army in America, 1775–1783.* Princeton, N.J.: Princeton Univ. Press, 1975.

Bradford, James C., ed. *Crucible of Empire: The Spanish-American War and Its Aftermath.* Annapolis, Md.: Naval Institute Press, 1993.

Bradsher, Henry S. *Afghanistan and the Soviet Union.* Durham, N.C.: Duke Univ. Press, 1985.

Braestrup, Peter. *Big Story.* 2 vols. Boulder, Colo.: Westview, 1977.

———. *Vietnam as History.* Washington, D.C.: Univ. Press of America, 1984.

Breihan, Carl W. *Quantrill and His Civil War Guerrillas.* New York: Promontory, 1959.

Brigot, André, and Olivier Roy. *The War in Afghanistan.* New York: Harvester-Wheatsheaf, 1988.

Brimmell, J.H. *Communism in South East Asia: A Political Analysis.* London: Oxford Univ. Press, 1959.

Browne, Malcolm W. *The New Face of War.* New York: Bobbs-Merrill, 1965.

Brownlee, Richard S. *Gray Ghosts of the Confederacy: Guerrilla Warfare in the West, 1861–1865.* Baton Rouge: Louisiana State Univ. Press, 1958.

Broxup, Marie. "The Soviets in Afghanistan: The Anatomy of a Takeover." *Central Asian Survey* 1, no. 4 (1983).

Bui Diem. *In the Jaws of History.* Boston: Houghton Mifflin, 1987.

Bunker, Ellsworth. *The Bunker Papers: Reports to the President from Viet Nam, 1967–1973.* Ed. Douglas Pike. 3 vols. Berkeley: Univ. of California Press, 1990.

Bureau of Intelligence and Research. *Afghanistan: Four Years of Occupation.* Washington, D.C.: U.S. Department of State, 1983.

Burks. R.V. "Statistical Profile of the Greek Communist." *Journal of Modern History* 27 (1955).

Buttinger, Joseph. *A Dragon Defiant: A Short History of Viet Nam.* New York: Praeger, 1972.

———. *The Smaller Dragon: A Political History of Viet Nam.* New York: Praeger, 1958.

———. *Viet Nam: A Dragon Embattled.* 2 vols. New York: Praeger, 1967.

———. *Viet Nam: A Political History.* New York: Praeger, 1968.

Byrne, Hugh. *El Salvador's Civil War: A Study of Revolution.* Boulder, Colo.: Lynne Rienner, 1996.

Cable, Larry E. *Conflict of Myths: The Development of American Counterinsurgency Doctrine and the Viet Nam War.* New York: New York Univ. Press, 1986.

———. *Unholy Grail: The U.S. and the Wars in Viet Nam.* London: Routledge, 1991.

Callahan, North. *Daniel Morgan: Ranger of the Revolution.* New York: Holt, Rinehart, and Winston, 1961.

Callison, Charles Stuart. *Land to the Tiller in the Mekong Delta.* Lanham, Md.: Univ. Press of America, 1983.

Callwell, C.E. *Small Wars: Their Principles and Practice.* 1906. Reprint, Wakefield, Eng.: EP Publishing, 1976.

Campbell, Arthur. *Guerrillas: A History and Analysis from Napoleon's Time to the 1960s.* New York: John Day, 1968.

Cantwell, Thomas R. "The Army of South Viet Nam: A Military and Political History, 1955–1975." Ph.D. diss., Univ. of New South Wales, 1989.

Cao Van Vien. *The Final Collapse.* Washington, D.C.: U.S. Army Center of Military History, 1983.

Cao Van Vien and Dong Van Khuyen. *Reflections on the Viet Nam War.* Washington, D.C.: U.S. Army Center of Military History, 1980.

Cao Van Vien et al., *The U.S. Advisor.* Washington, D.C.: U.S. Army Center of Military History, 1980.

Carp, E. Wayne. *To Starve the Army at Pleasure: Continental Army Administration and American Political Culture 1775–1783.* Chapel Hill: Univ. of North Carolina Press, 1984.

Carver, George. "The Faceless Viet Cong." *Foreign Affairs* 44 (1966).

Carver, Michael. *War since 1945.* New York: Putnam's, 1981.

Castel, Albert. *William Clarke Quantrill: His Life and Times.* New York: Frederick Fell, 1962.

Catton, Bruce. *The Army of the Potomac.* 3 vols. Garden City, N.Y.: Doubleday, 1951–1953.

———. *The Centennial History of the Civil War.* 3 vols. Garden City, N.Y.: Doubleday, 1961–1965.

Central Intelligence Agency (CIA). *Intelligence in the War of Independence.* Washington, D.C.: Central Intelligence Agency, 1976. See also subsequent versions of this work.

Chaliand, Gerard. "The Bargain War in Afghanistan." In Chaliand, *Guerrilla Strategies.*

———. *Report from Afghanistan.* New York: Viking, 1982.

———, ed. *Guerrilla Strategies: Revolutionary Warfare and Counterinsurgency.* Berkeley: Univ. of California Press, 1982.

Chapman, William. *Inside the Philippine Revolution: The New People's Army and Its Struggle for Power.* New York: Norton, 1987.

Charters, David. "Coup and Consolidation: The Soviet Seizure of Afghanistan." *Conflict Quarterly,* spring 1981.

Chen Jian. "China's Involvement in the Viet Nam War, 1964–1969." *China Quarterly*, no. 142, June 1995.

———. *Mao and the Chinese Revolution*. London: Oxford Univ. Press, 1965.

Chorley, Katherine. *Armies and the Art of Revolution*. London: Faber and Faber, 1943.

Churchill, Winston. *Triumph and Tragedy*. Vol. 6 of *The Second World War*. Boston: Houghton Mifflin, 1953.

Cincinnatus [pseud.]. *Self-Destruction: The Disintegration and Decay of the United States Army during the Viet Nam Era*. New York: Norton, 1981.

Clausewitz, Carl von. *On War*. Ed. and Trans. Michael Howard and Peter Paret. Princeton, N.J.: Princeton Univ. Press, 1976.

Clinton, Henry. *The American Rebellion: Sir Henry Clinton's Narrative of His Campaigns, 1775–1782*. Ed. William B. Willcox. New Haven, Conn.: Yale Univ. Press, 1954.

Clodfelter, Mark. *The Limits of Air Power: The American Bombing of North Viet Nam*. New York: Free Press, 1989.

Clutterbuck, Richard L. *The Long, Long War: Counterinsurgency in Malaya and Viet Nam*. New York: Praeger, 1966.

Cohen, Eliot A. "Constraints on America's Conduct of Small Wars." *International Security*, fall 1984.

———. "Dynamics of Military Intervention." In *Foreign Military Intervention: The Dynamics of Protracted Conflict*, ed. Ariel E. Levite, Bruce W. Jentleson, and Larry Berman. New York: Columbia Univ. Press, 1992.

Colby, William. *Lost Victory*. Chicago: Contemporary Books, 1989.

Collins, James Lawton. *The Development and Training of the South Vietnamese Army, 1950–1972*. Washington, D.C.: Department of the Army, 1975.

Collins, Joseph J. "The Soviet Invasion of Afghanistan: Methods, Motives and Ramifications." *Naval War College Review*, Nov. 1980.

———. *The Soviet Invasion of Afghanistan: A Study in the Use of Force in Soviet Foreign Policy*. Lexington, Mass.: Lexington Books, 1985.

———. "Soviet Military Performance in Afghanistan: A Preliminary Assessment." *Comparative Strategy* 4 (1983).

Commager, Henry Steele, ed. *The Defeat of the Confederacy*. New York: Van Nostrand, 1964.

Condit, Doris M. *Case Study in Guerrilla War: Greece during World War II*. Washington, D.C.: Department of the Army, 1961.

Condit, Doris M., and Bert H. Cooper Jr., eds. *Challenge and Response in Internal Conflict*. 2 vols. Washington, D.C.: American Univ. Press, 1967–1968.

Connelley, William Elsey. *Quantrill and the Border Wars*. 1909. Reprint, New Yok: Pageant, 1956.

Cooper, Chester L. *The Lost Crusade: America in Viet Nam*. New York: Dodd, Mead, 1970.

Cordesman, Anthony H., and Abraham R. Wagner. *The Lessons of Modern War.* Vol. 2, *The Afghan and Falklands Conflicts.* Boulder, Colo.: Westview, 1990.

Cornish, Dudley Taylor. *The Sable Arm.* New York: Longmans, Green, 1956.

Corr, Edwin G., and Stephen Sloan, eds., *Low-Intensity Conflict: Old Threats in a New World.* Boulder, Colo.: Westview, 1992.

Cosmas, Graham A. *An Army for Empire: The United States Army in the Spanish-American War.* Columbia, Mo.: Univ. of Missouri Press, 1971.

Cross, James Eliot. *Conflict in the Shadows: The Nature and Politics of Guerrilla War.* Garden City, N.Y.: Doubleday, 1963.

Crozier, Brian. *The Rebel: A Study of Post-War Insurrections.* Boston: Beacon, 1960.

Current, Richard Nelson. *Lincoln's Loyalists: Union Soldiers from the Confederacy.* New York: Oxford Univ. Press, 1992.

Currey, Cecil B. *Edward Lansdale: The Unquiet American.* Boston: Houghton Mifflin, 1988.

———. *Victory at any Cost.* Washington, D.C.: Brassey's, 1997.

Curtis, Edward E. *The Organization of the British Army in the American Revolution.* New Haven, Conn.: Yale Univ. Press, 1926.

Daalder, Ivo H. "The United States and Military Intervention in Internal Conflict." In *The International Dimensions of Internal Conflict,* ed. Michael Brown. Cambridge, Mass.: MIT Press, 1996.

Daley. Tad. "Afghanistan and Gorbachev's Global Foreign Policy." *Asian Survey* 29 (May 1989).

Daskal, Steven E. "The Insurgency Threat and Ways to Defeat It." *Military Review* 66 (Jan. 1986).

Davidson, Phillip B. *Secrets of the Viet Nam War.* Novato, Calif.: Presidio Press, 1990.

———. *Viet Nam at War: The History, 1946–1975.* Novato, Calif.: Presidio Press, 1988.

Davidson, W. Phillips. *Some Observations on Viet Cong Operations in the Villages.* Santa Monica, Calif.: Rand, 1968.

Davis, Leonard. *Revolutionary Struggle in the Philippines.* London: Macmillan, 1989.

Davis, William C. *A Government of Our Own: The Making of the Confederacy.* New York: Free Press, 1994.

Dawson, Alan. *55 Days: The Fall of South Viet Nam.* Englewood Cliffs, N.J.: Prentice-Hall, 1977.

Degenhardt, Henry W., ed. *Revolutionary and Dissident Movements: An International Guide.* London: Longmans, 1988.

DeMond, Robert O. *The Loyalists in North Carolina during the Revolution.* 1940. Reprint, Hamden, Conn.: Archon Books, 1964.

Department of the Army. "A Program for the Pacification and Long-Term Development of South Viet Nam" (PROVN). Washington, D.C.: Department of the Army, 1966.

Department of Defense. *Casebook on Insurgency and Revolutionary Warfare: 23 Summary Accounts.* Washington, D.C.: American Univ. Press, 1962.

Desai, Raj, and Harry Eckstein. "Insurgency: The Transformation of Peasant Rebellion." *World Politics* 42 (July 1990).

Devillers, Philippe. *Histoire du Viet-Nam de 1940 à 1952.* 3d ed. Paris: Editions du Seuil, 1952.

Devillers, Philippe, and Jean Lacouture. *End of a War: Indochina 1954.* Trans. by Alexander Lieven and Adam Roberts. New York: Praeger, 1969.

Dix, Robert H. "Why Revolutions Succeed and Fail." *Polity* 16, no. 3 (1984).

Dixon, Cecil A., and Otto Heilbrunn. *Communist Guerrilla Warfare.* New York: Praeger, 1962.

Dobrynin, Anatoly. *In Confidence.* New York: Random House, 1995.

Dommen, Arthur. *Conflict in Laos.* New York: Praeger, 1964.

Donald, David, ed. *Why the North Won the Civil War.* Baton Rouge: Louisiana State Univ. Press, 1960.

Dong Van Khuyen. *The RVNAF.* Washington, D.C.: U.S. Army Center of Military History, 1980.

Donnell, John C. *Viet Cong Recruitment: Why and How Men Join.* Santa Monica, Calif.: Rand, 1975.

Dowdey, Clifford. *Lee.* Boston: Little, Brown, 1965.

Downie, Richard Duncan. *Learning from Conflict: The U.S. Military in Viet Nam, El Salvador, and the Drug War.* Westport, Conn.: Praeger, 1998.

Duarte, José Napoleon. *Duarte: My Story.* New York: Putnam's, 1986.

Duiker, William J. *The Communist Road to Power in Viet Nam.* Boulder, Colo.: Westview, 1981.

Dull, Jonathan R. *The French Navy and American Independence: A Study of Arms and Diplomacy 1774–1787.* Princeton, N.J.: Princeton Univ. Press, 1975.

Duncanson, Dennis J. *Government and Revolution in Viet Nam.* New York: Oxford Univ. Press, 1968.

Dunkerly, James. *Power in the Isthmus: A Political History of Modern Central America.* New York: Verso, 1988.

Dunn, Peter M. "The American Army: The Viet Nam War." In Beckett and Pimlott, *Armed Forces and Modern Counter-Insurgency.*

———. *The First Viet Nam War.* New York: St. Martin's, 1985.

Dupree, Louis. *Afghanistan.* Princeton, N.J.: Princeton Univ. Press, 1973.

Eaton, Clement. *A History of the Southern Confederacy.* New York: Free Press, 1954.

———. *Jefferson Davis.* New York: Free Press, 1977.

Eban, Martin. *Lin Piao.* New York: Stein and Day, 1970.

Eckstein, Harry, ed. *Internal War.* Glencoe, Ill.: Free Press, 1964.

Edwards, David Busby. "Origins of the Anti-Soviet Jihad." In Farr and Merriam, *Afghan Resistance.*

Ellis, John. *A Short History of Guerrilla Warfare.* London: Ian Allen, 1975.

Ely, Paul. *Lessons of the War in Indochina*. Vol. 2. Translation from French. Santa Monica, Calif.: Rand, 1967.

———. *Memoires: L'Indochine dans la tourmente*. Paris: Plon, 1964.

Englehardt, Michael J. "America Can Win, Sometimes: U.S. Success and Failure in Small Wars." *Conflict Quarterly* 9 (1989).

———. "Democracies, Dictatorships and Counterinsurgency: Does Regime Type Really Matter?" *Conflict Quarterly* 12 (1992).

Englemann, Larry. *Tears before the Rain: An Oral History of the Fall of South Viet Nam*. New York: Oxford Univ. Press, 1990.

Ermacora, Felix. "Report on the Situation of Human Rights in Afghanistan." UN Document nos. E/CN.4/1985/21, Feb. 19, 1985; A/40/843, Nov. 5, 1985; E/CN.4/1986/24, Feb. 17, 1986.

Escott, Paul D. *After Secession: Jefferson Davis and the Failure of Confederate Nationalism*. Baton Rouge: Louisiana State Univ. Press, 1978.

Evans, Ernest. "El Salvador's Lessons for Future U.S. Interventions." *World Affairs* 160 (summer 1997).

Fairbairn, Geoffrey. *Revolutionary Guerrilla Warfare: The Countryside Version*. Harmondsworth, Eng.: Penguin, 1974.

Fall, Bernard. *Hell in a Very Small Place*. Philadelphia: Lippincott, 1967.

———. *Street without Joy*. Harrisburg, Penn.: Stackpole, 1964.

———. *The Two Viet Nams: A Political and Military Analysis*. 2d ed., rev. New York: Praeger, 1967.

Farr, Grant M., and John G. Merriam, eds. *Afghan Resistance: The Politics of Survival*. Boulder, Colo.: Westview, 1987.

Faust, Drew Gilpin. *The Creation of Confederate Nationalism: Ideology and Identity in the Civil War South*. Baton Rouge: Louisiana State Univ. Press, 1988.

Fellman, Michael. *Inside War: The Guerrilla Conflict in Missouri during the American Civil War*. New York: Oxford Univ. Press, 1989.

Ferguson, Clyde R. "Functions of the Partisan-Militia in the South during the American Revolution: An Interpretation." In *The Revolutionary War in the South: Power, Conflict and Leadership*, ed. W. Robert Higgins. Durham, N.C.: Duke Univ. Press, 1979.

Filiberti, Edward J. "The Roots of U.S. Counterinsurgency Doctrine." *Military Review* 68 (Jan. 1988).

Fishel, Wesley. *Viet Nam: Anatomy of a Conflict*. Itasca, Ill.: Peacock, 1968.

Fitch, John S. *The Political Consequences of U.S. Military Assistance to Latin America*. Carlisle, Pa: U.S. Army War College, 1977.

Fleming, Thomas J. *Beat the Last Drum: The Siege of Yorktown*. New York: St. Martin's, 1963.

Fletcher, Arnold. *Afghanistan: Highway of Conquest*. Ithaca, N.Y.: Cornell Univ. Press, 1965.

Ford, Ronnie E. *Tet 1968: Understanding the Surprise*. London: Frank Cass, 1995.

Frederickson, George M. *Why the Confederacy Did Not Fight a Guerrilla War after the Fall of Richmond*. Gettysburg, Pa: Gettysburg College Press, 1996.

Freidel, Frank B. *The Splendid Little War.* Boston: Little, Brown, 1958.

FRUS. See U.S. Department of State.

Fuller, Graham. "The Emergence of Central Asia." *Foreign Affairs* 69, no. 2 (1990).

Fuller, J.F.C. *A Military History of the Western World.* Vol. 2, *From the Defeat of the Spanish Armada to the Battle of Waterloo.* New York: Da Capo, 1955.

Funston, Frederick. *Memories of Two Wars: Cuban and Philippine Experiences.* New York: Scribner's, 1911.

Gaddis, John Lewis. *Strategies of Containment.* New York: Oxford Univ. Press, 1982.

Galeotti, Mark. *Afghanistan: The Soviet Union's Last War.* Portland, Oreg.: Frank Cass, 1995.

Gallagher, Gary W., ed. *Fighting for the Confederacy: The Personal Reflections of General Edward Porter Alexander.* Chapel Hill: Univ. of North Carolina Press, 1989.

———. *The Confederate War.* Cambridge, Mass.: Harvard Univ. Press, 1997.

———. *Lee: The Soldier.* Lincoln, Nebr.: Univ. of Nebraska Press, 1996.

Gallucci, Robert L. *Neither Peace nor Honor: The Politics of American Military Policy in Viet Nam.* Baltimore: Johns Hopkins Univ. Press, 1975.

Galula, David. *Counter-Insurgency Warfare: Theory and Practice.* New York: Praeger, 1964.

Gann, Lewis H. *Guerrillas in History.* Stanford, Calif.: Hoover Institution Press, 1971.

Garcia, José. "El Salvador: Recent Elections in Historical Perspective." In *Elections and Democracy in Central America,* ed. John Booth and Mitchell Seligson. Chapel Hill: Univ. of North Carolina Press, 1989.

Gardner, Hugh. *Guerrilla and Counterguerrilla Warfare in Greece 1941–1945.* Washington, D.C.: Department of the Army, 1962.

Garland, Albert N., ed. *A Distant Challenge: The U.S. Infantryman in Viet Nam, 1967–1972.* 1969. Reprint, Nashville, Tenn.: Battery Press, 1983.

Garthoff, Raymond L. *How Russia Makes War.* London: Allen and Unwin, 1954.

Gates, John Morgan. *Schoolbooks and Krags: The United States Army in the Philippines 1898–1902.* Westport, Conn.: Greenwood, 1973.

Gelb, Leslie, and Richard K. Betts. *The Irony of Viet Nam.* Washington, D.C.: Brookings Institution, 1979.

Gerson, Noel B. *The Swamp Fox: Francis Marion.* Garden City, N.Y.: Doubleday, 1967.

Ghaus, Abdul Samad. *The Fall of Afghanistan: An Insider's Account.* London: Pergamon-Brassey's, 1988.

Giap, General. *See* Vo Nguyen Giap.

Gilbert, Gustav. "Counterinsurgency." *Military Review* 45 (April 1965).

Girardet, Edward. *Afghanistan: The Soviet War.* New York: St. Martin's, 1985.

———. "Russia's War in Afghanistan." *Central Asian Survey* 2, no. 1 (1983).

Girling, John L.S. *America and the Third World: Revolution and Intervention.* London: Routledge and Kegan Paul, 1980.

————. *People's War: Conditions and Consequences in China and South East Asia.* New York: Praeger, 1969.

Glatthaar, Joseph T. *Forged in Battle: The Civil War Alliance of Black Soldiers and White Officers.* New York: Meridian, 1991.

Goldwert, Marvin. *The Constabulary in the Dominican Republic and Nicaragua.* Gainesville: Univ. of Florida Press, 1962.

Goodman, Allan E. *An Institutional Profile of the South Vietnamese Officer Corps.* Santa Monica, Calif.: Rand, 1970.

————. *The Lost Peace: America's Search for a Negotiated Settlement of the Viet Nam War.* Stanford, Calif.: Hoover Institution Press, 1978.

————. *Politics in War: The Bases of Political Community in South Viet Nam.* Cambridge, Mass.: Harvard Univ. Press, 1973.

Goodwin, Jeff, and Theda Skocpol, "Explaining Revolutions in the Contemporary Third World." *Politics and Society* 17, no. 4 (1989).

Graff, Henry F., ed. *American Imperialism and the Philippine Insurrection.* Boston: Little, Brown, 1969.

Grant, Thomas A. "Little Wars, Big Problems: The United States and Counterinsurgency in the Postwar World." Ph.D. diss., Univ. of California, Irvine, 1990.

Greenberg, Lawrence M. *The Hukbalahap Insurrection: A Case Study of a Successful Anti-Insurgency Operation in the Philippines, 1946–1955.* Washington, D.C.: U.S. Army Center of Military History, 1986.

Greene, George Washington. *The Life of Nathanael Greene.* 3 vols. Cambridge, Mass.: Hurd and Houghton, 1871.

Greene, Thomas. *Comparative Revolutionary Movements.* Englewood Cliffs, N.J.: Prentice-Hall, 1984.

Greene, T.N., ed. *The Guerrilla—And How to Fight Him.* New York: Praeger, 1962.

Gregorie, Anne King. *Thomas Sumter.* Columbia, S.C.: R.L. Bryan, 1931.

Grenier, Yvon. "From Causes to Causers: The Etiology of Salvadoran Internal War Revisited." *Journal of Conflict Studies* 16 (fall 1996).

Griffith, Samuel B. *Mao Tse-Tung on Guerrilla Warfare.* New York: Praeger, 1961.

————. *Peking and People's War.* New York: Praeger, 1966.

Grintner, Laurence E. "How They Lost: Doctrines, Strategies and Outcomes of the Viet Nam War." *Asian Survey* 15, no. 12 (1975).

Gruber, Ira D. "Britain's Southern Strategy." In *The Revolutionary War in the South: Power, Conflict and Leadership*, ed. W. Robert Higgins. Durham, N.C.: Duke Univ. Press, 1979.

Guevara, Ernesto. *Guerrilla Warfare.* New York: Vintage, 1960.

Gurtov, Melvin. *Hanoi on War and Peace.* Santa Monica, Calif.: Rand, 1967.

Gurtov, Melvin, and Konrad Kellen. *Viet Nam: Lessons and Mislessons.* Santa Monica, Calif.: Rand, 1969.

Gwynn, Charles. *Imperial Policing.* New York: St. Martin's, 1934.

Hammer, Ellen J. *A Death in November: America in Viet Nam 1963.* New York: Dutton, 1987.

————. "South Viet Nam: The Limits of Political Action." *Pacific Affairs* 35 (1962).

————. *The Struggle for Indochina 1940–1955.* Stanford, Calif.: Stanford Univ. Press, 1966.

Hammer, Kenneth M. "Huks in the Philippines." In Osanka, *Modern Guerrilla Warfare.*

Hammond, Thomas T. *Red Flag over Afghanistan: The Communist Coup, the Soviet Invasion, and the Consequences.* Boulder, Colo.: Westview, 1984.

Hannah, Norman B. *The Key to Failure: Laos and the Viet Nam War.* Lanham, Md.: Madison Books, 1987.

Harmon, Christopher. "Illustrations of Learning in Counterinsurgency Warfare." *Comparative Strategy* 11 (1992).

Harsh, Joseph L. *Confederate Tide Rising: Robert E. Lee and the Making of Southern Strategy, 1861–1862.* Kent, Ohio: Kent State Univ. Press, 1998.

Hart, Douglas M. "Low Intensity Conflict in Afghanistan: The Soviet View." *Survival* 24 (March–April 1982).

Hattaway, Herman, and Archer Jones. *How the North Won: A Military History of the Civil War.* Urbana: Univ. of Illinois, 1991.

Haycock, Ronald, ed. *Regular Armies and Insurgency.* London, Croom Helm, 1979.

Heilbrunn, Otto. *Partisan Warfare.* London, Allen and Unwin, 1962.

Heiman, Leo. "Guerrilla War: An Analysis." *Military Review* 43 (1963).

Hemingway, Al. *Our War Was Different: Marine Combined Action Platoons in Viet Nam.* Annapolis, Md.: Naval Institute Press, 1994.

Henderson, Darryl. *Why the Viet Cong Fought: A Study of Motivation and Control in a Modern Army in Combat.* Westport, Conn.: Greenwood, 1979.

Hennessy, Michael A. *Strategy in Viet Nam: The Marines and Revolutionary Warfare in I Corps, 1965–1972.* Westport, Conn.: Praeger, 1997.

Herring, George C. *America's Longest War.* 2d ed. New York: Knopf, 1986.

Herring, George C., and Richard H. Immerson. "Eisenhower, Dulles, and Dien Bien Phu: 'The Day We Didn't Go to War' Revisited." *Journal of American History* 72 (Sept. 1985).

Herrington, Stuart A. *Peace with Honor?* Novato, Calif.: Presidio Press, 1983.

————. *Silence Was a Weapon: The Viet Nam War in the Villages.* Novato, Calif.: Presidio Press, 1982.

Heymann, Hans, and William Whitson. *Can and Should the United States Preserve a Military Capability for Revolutionary Conflict?* Santa Monica, Calif.: Rand, 1972.

Higginbotham, Don. *The War of American Independence.* New York: Macmillan, 1971.

————, ed. *Military Analysis of the Revolutionary War.* Millwood, N.Y.: KTO Press, 1977.

Higham, Robin, ed. *A Guide to the Sources of British Military History.* London: Routledge and Kegan Paul, 1972.

————. *A Guide to the Sources of United States Military History.* Hamden, Conn.: Archon, 1975.

Hoang Ngoc Lung. *The General Offensives of 1968–1969.* Washington, D.C.: U.S. Army Center of Military History, 1981.

Hoang Van Chi. *From Colonialism to Communism: A Case History of North Viet Nam.* New York: Praeger, 1964.

Ho Chi Minh. *Ho Chi Minh on Revolution.* New York: Praeger, 1967.

Hoffman, Bruce. *'Holy Terror': The Implications of Terrorism Motivated by a Religious Imperative.* Santa Monica, Calif.: Rand, 1993.

Hoffmann, Ronald, Thad W. Tate, and Peter J. Albert, eds. *An Uncivil War: The Southern Backcountry during the American Revolution.* Charlottesville: Univ. of Virginia, 1985.

Holmes, Leslie. "Afghanistan and Sino-Soviet Relations." In Saikal and Maley, *Soviet Withdrawal.*

Honey, P.J. *North Viet Nam Today: Profile of a Communist Satellite.* New York: Praeger, 1962.

Horn, Keith W. *Battle for Hue: Tet 1968.* Novato, Calif.: Presidio Press, 1983.

Hosmer, Stephen T. *The Army's Role in Counterinsurgency and Insurgency.* Santa Monica, Calif.: Rand, 1990.

———. *Constraints on U.S. Strategy in Third World Conflicts.* New York: Crane, Russak, 1988.

———. "How Successful Has the Soviet Union Been in Third World Protracted Conflict?" In Shultz et al., *Guerrilla Warfare and Counterinsurgency.*

Hosmer, Stephen T., Konrad Kellen, and Brian M. Jenkins. *The Fall of South Viet Nam.* New York: Crane, Russak, 1980.

Hosmer, Stephen T., and Thomas W. Wolfe. *Soviet Policy and Practice toward Third World Conflicts.* Lexington, Mass.: Lexington Books, 1983.

Humes, Thomas William. *The Loyal Mountaineers of Tennessee.* 1888. Reprint, Spartanburg, S.C.: Reprint Company, 1974.

Hung P. Nguyen. "Communist Offensive Strategy and the Defense of South Viet Nam." In Matthews and Brown, *Assessing the Viet Nam War.*

Hunt, Richard A. *Pacification: The American Struggle for Viet Nam's Hearts and Minds.* Boulder, Colo.: Westview, 1995.

Hunt, Richard A., and Richard H. Shultz Jr., eds. *Lessons from an Unconventional War.* New York: Pergamon, 1982.

Huntington, Samuel P. "Patterns of Intervention: America and the Soviets in the Third World." *National Interest* 7 (spring 1987).

Hurley, Vic. *Swish of the Kris: The Story of the Moros.* New York: Dutton, 1936.

Huynh Kim Khanh. *Vietnamese Communism 1925–1945.* Ithaca, N.Y.: Cornell Univ., 1982.

Iatrides, John O. "Perceptions of Soviet Involvement in the Greek Civil War 1945–1949." In *Studies in the History of the Greek Civil War 1945–1949,* ed. Lars Baerentzen et al. Copenhagen: Museum Tusculanum, 1987.

———. *Revolt in Athens.* Princeton, N.J.: Princeton Univ., 1972.

———, ed. *Greece in the 1940s: A Nation in Crisis.* Hanover, N.H.: Univ. Press of New England, 1981.

Idriess, Ion L. *Guerrilla Tactics.* Sydney: Angus and Robertson, 1942.

Isaacs, Arnold R. *Without Honor: Defeat in Viet Nam and Cambodia.* New York: Vintage, 1984.

Isby, David C. *War in a Distant Country: Afghanistan, Invasion and Resistance.* London: Arms and Armour, 1989.

Janke, Peter. *Guerrilla and Terrorist Organizations: A World Directory and Bibliography.* New York: Macmillan, 1983.

Joes, Anthony James. "Continuity and Change in Guerrilla War: The Spanish and Afghan Cases." *Journal of Conflict Studies* 16, no. 2 (1996).

————. *From the Barrel of a Gun: Armies and Revolutions.* Washington, D.C.: Pergamon-Brassey's, 1986.

————. *Guerrilla Conflict Before the Cold War.* Westport, Conn.: Praeger, 1996.

————. *Modern Guerrilla Insurgency.* Westport, Conn.: Praeger, 1992.

————. *The War for South Viet Nam.* New York: Praeger, 1989.

Johnson, Chalmers. *Autopsy on People's War.* Berkeley: Univ. of California, 1973.

————. "Civilian Loyalties and Guerrilla Conflict." *World Politics* 17 (1964).

————. *Peasant Nationalism and Communist Power.* Stanford, Calif.: Stanford Univ., 1961.

Johnson, Lyndon B. *The Vantage Point.* Holt, Rinehart, Winston, 1971.

Johnston, Henry P. *The Yorktown Campaign of Cornwallis.* New York: Harper, 1881.

Joint Low-Intensity Conflict Project, *Analytical Review of Low-Intensity Conflict.* Fort Monroe, Va: U.S. Army, 1986.

Jomini, Antoine Henri. *The Art of War.* Trans. G.H. Mendell and W.P. Craighill. 1862. Reprint, Westport, Conn.: Greenwood, n.d.

Jones, Archer. *The Art of War in the Western World.* New York: Oxford Univ., 1987.

Jones, Gregg. *Red Revolution: Inside the Philippine Guerrilla Movement.* Boulder, Colo.: Westview, 1989.

Jones, Howard. *"A New Kind of War": America's Global Strategy and the Truman Doctrine in Greece.* New York: Oxford Univ. Press, 1989.

Jones, Virgil Carrington. *Grey Ghosts and Rebel Raiders.* New York: Henry Holt, 1956.

Jornacion, George W. "The Time of the Eagles: United States Army Officers and the Pacification of the Philippine Moros." Ph.D. diss., Univ. of California, Los Angeles, 1973.

Jukes, Geoffrey. "The Soviet Armed Forces and the Afghan War." In Saikal and Maley, *Soviet Withdrawal.*

Jumper, Roy, and Marjorie Weiner Normand. "Viet Nam." In *Government and Politics in Southeast Asia,* ed. George Kahin. Ithaca, N.Y.: Cornell Univ., 1964.

Kahn, Riaz. *Untying the Afghan Knot: Negotiating Soviet Withdrawal.* Durham, N.C.: Duke Univ., 1991.

Kakar, M. Hasan. *Afghanistan: The Soviet Invasion and the Afghan Response 1979–1982.* Berkeley: Univ. of California, 1995.

Kammann, William. *A Search for Stability: United States Diplomacy toward Nicaragua 1925–1933.* South Bend, Ind.: Notre Dame Univ., 1968.

Karnes, Thomas L. *The Failure of Union: Central America 1824–1960.* Chapel Hill: Univ. of North Carolina, 1961.

Karp, Craig. *Afghanistan: Eight Years of Soviet Occupation.* Washington, D.C.: U.S. Department of State, 1987.

———. *Afghanistan: Seven Years of Soviet Occupation.* Washington, D.C.: U.S. Department of State, 1986.

———. *Afghanistan: Six Years of Soviet Occupation.* Washington, D.C.: U.S. Department of State, 1985.

Katz, Mark. "Anti-Soviet Insurgencies: Growing Trend or Passing Phase?" *Orbis* 30 (summer 1986).

———. *The Third World and Soviet Military Thought.* Baltimore: Johns Hopkins Univ., 1982.

Katzenbach, Edward L., and Gene Z. Hanrahan. "The Revolutionary Strategy of Mao Tse-tung." *Political Science Quarterly* 70 (Sept. 1955).

Kecskemeti, Paul. *Insurgency as a Strategic Problem.* Santa Monica, Calif.: Rand, 1967.

Keegan, John. *A History of Warfare.* New York: Knopf, 1993.

Kellen, Konrad. *A Profile of the PAVN Soldier in Viet Nam.* Santa Monica, Calif.: Rand, 1966.

———. *A View of the VC.* Santa Monica, Calif.: Rand, 1969.

Kennan, George F. *Memoirs 1925–1950.* 2 vols. Boston: Little, Brown, 1967.

Kerby, Robert L. "Why the Confederacy Lost." *Review of Politics* 35 (July 1973).

Kerkvliet, Benedict J. *The Huk Rebellion: A Study of Peasant Revolt in the Philippines.* Berkeley: Univ. of California, 1977.

Kessler, Richard J. *Rebellion and Repression in the Philippines.* New Haven, Conn.: Yale Univ. Press, 1989.

Khrushchev, Nikita. *Memoirs.* Boston: Little, Brown, 1970.

Kissinger, Henry, et al. *Report of the Bipartisan Commission on Central America.* Washington, D.C.: U.S. Government Printing Office, 1984.

Klare, Michael T., and Peter Kornbluh, eds. *Low Intensity Warfare: Counterinsurgency, Proinsurgency and Antiterrorism in the Eighties.* New York: Pantheon, 1988.

Klass, Rosanne, ed. *Afghanistan: The Great Game Revisited.* New York: Freedom House, 1987.

Knorr, Klaus. "Unconventional Warfare: Strategy and Tactics in Internal Political Strife." *Annals of the American Academy of Political and Social Science* 341 (May 1962).

Koehler, John. *Explaining Dissident Success: The Huks in Central Luzon.* Santa Monica, Calif.: Rand, 1972.

Kolko, Gabriel. *Anatomy of a War: Viet Nam, the United States, and the Modern Historical Experience.* New York: Pantheon, 1985.

Komer, Robert W. *Bureaucracy at War: U.S. Performance in the Vietnam Conflict.* Boulder, Colo., Westview, 1986.

———. *Bureaucracy Does Its Thing: Institutional Constraints on US-GVN Performance in Viet Nam.* Santa Monica, Calif.: Rand, 1972.

———. "Impact of Pacification on Insurgency in South Viet Nam." *Journal of International Affairs* 25, no. 1 (1971).

Kousoulas, D. George. "The Guerrilla War the Communists Lost." *U.S. Naval Institute Proceedings* 89 (1963).

———. *Modern Greece.* New York: Scribner's, 1974.

———. *Revolution and Defeat: The Story of the Greek Communist Party.* London : Oxford Univ. Press, 1965.

Krakowski, Ellie D. "Afghanistan: The Forgotten War." *Central Asian Survey* 4, no. 2 (1985).

Krepinevich, Andrew F., Jr. *The Army and Viet Nam.* Baltimore: Johns Hopkins Univ. Press, 1986.

Krulak, Victor N., ed. *Guerrilla Warfare.* Annapolis, Md.: U.S. Naval Institute Press, 1964.

Lachia, Eduardo. *The Huks: Philippine Agrarian Society in Revolt.* New York: Prager, 1971.

Lacouture, Jean. *Ho Chi Minh: A Political Biography.* Trans. Peter Wiles. London: Penguin, 1968.

Lambert, Robert Stansbury. *South Carolina Loyalists in the American Revolution.* Columbia: Univ. of South Carolina Press, 1987.

Lam Quang Thi. *Autopsy: The Death of South Viet Nam.* Phoenix: Sphinx, 1986.

Lancaster, Donald. *The Emancipation of French Indochina.* London: Oxford Univ. Press, 1961.

Langley, Lester D. *The Banana Wars: The United States Intervention in the Caribbean, 1898–1934.* Chicago: Dorsey, 1985.

Lanning, Michael Lee, and Dan Gragg. *Inside the VC and the NVA.* New York: Fawcett Columbine, 1992.

Lansdale, Edward G. *In the Midst of Wars: An American's Mission to Southeast Asia.* New York: Harper and Row, 1972.

———. "Viet Nam: Do We Understand Revolution?" *Foreign Affairs,* Oct. 1964.

———. "Viet Nam—Still the Search for Goals." *Foreign Affairs,* Oct. 1968.

Laqueur, Walter. *Guerrilla: A Historical and Critical Study.* Boston: Little, Brown, 1976.

———. *The Guerrilla Reader: A Historical Anthology.* New York: New American Library, 1977.

Larkin, John A. "Early Guerrilla Struggle in the Philippines." *Peasant Studies* 19 (1991).

Lee, Henry. *Memoirs of the War in the Southern Department of the United States.* Ed. Robert E. Lee. 1869. Reprint, New York: Arno Press, 1969.

Leech, Margaret. *In the Days of McKinley.* New York: Harper and Row, 1959.

Leeper. Reginald. *When Greek Meets Greek*. London: Chatto and Windus, 1950.

Le Gro, William E. *Viet Nam from Ceasefire to Capitulation*. Washington, D.C.: U.S. Army Center of Military History, 1981.

Leites, Nathan. *The Viet Cong Style of Politics*. Santa Monica, Calif.: Rand, 1969.

Leites, Nathan, and Charles Wolf Jr. *Rebellion and Authority: An Analytical Essay on Insurgent Conflicts*. Chicago: Markham, 1970.

LeMoyne, James. "El Salvador's Forgotten War." *Foreign Affairs* 68 (summer 1989).

Leroy, James A. *The Americans in the Philippines*. New York: Houghton Mifflin, 1914.

Lessons from the Viet Nam War. London: Royal United Services Institution, 1969.

Lewis, John Wilson, ed. *Peasant Rebellion and Communist Revolution in Asia*. Stanford, Calif.: Stanford Univ., 1974.

Lewy, Guenter. *America in Viet Nam*. New York: Oxford Univ. Press, 1978.

————. "Some Political-Military Lessons of the Viet Nam War." In Matthews and Brown, *Assessing the Viet Nam War*.

Lieven, Anatol. *Chechnya: Tombstone of Russian Power*. New Haven, Conn.: Yale Univ. Press, 1998.

Lind, Michael. *Viet Nam: The Necessary War*. New York: Free Press, 1999.

Lindholm, Richard W., ed. *Viet Nam: The First Five Years*. East Lansing: Michigan State Univ., 1959.

Lindsay, Franklin. "Unconventional Warfare." *Foreign Affairs* 40 (Jan. 1962).

Linn, Brian McAlister. *The Philippine War, 1899–1902*. Lawrence, Kans.: Univ. Press of Kansas, 2000.

————. *The U.S. Army and Counterinsurgency in the Philippine War, 1899–1902*. Chapel Hill: Univ. of North Carolina, 1989.

Lin Piao. *Long Live the Victory of People's War*. Peking: Foreign Language Press, 1965.

Liu, F.F. *A Military History of Modern China, 1924–1949*. Princeton, N.J.: Princeton Univ. Press, 1956.

Lockhart, Greg. *Nation in Arms: The Origins of the People's Army of Viet Nam*. Boston: Allen and Unwin, 1989.

Lodge, Henry Cabot. *The Storm Has Many Eyes*. New York: Norton, 1973.

Logevall, Fredrik. *Choosing War: The Lost Chance for Peace and the Escalation of War in Vietnam*. Berkeley: Univ. of California Press, 1999.

Lomperis, Timothy J. *From People's War to People's Rule: Insurgency, Intervention and the Lessons of Viet Nam*. Chapel Hill: Univ. of North Carolina Press, 1996.

————. *The War Everyone Lost—And Won: America's Intervention in Viet Nam's Twin Struggles*. Baton Rouge: Louisiana State Univ. Press, 1984.

Long, A.L. *Memoirs of Robert E. Lee*. Secaucus, N.J.: Blue and Grey Press, 1983.

Lonn, Ella. *Desertion during the Civil War*. 1928. Reprint, Gloucester, Mass.: Peter Smith, 1966.

Low Intensity Conflict Field Manual No. 100-20. Washington, D.C.: Department of the Army, 1981.

Lucas, Marion Brunson. *Sherman and the Burning of Columbia.* College Station: Texas A&M Univ. Press, 1976.

Macauley, Neil. *The Sandino Affair.* Chicago: Quadrangle, 1967.

MacDonald, Peter. *Giap: The Victor in Viet Nam.* New York: Norton, 1993.

Mack, Andrew. "Why Big Nations Lose Small Wars: The Politics of Asymmetric Conflict." *World Politics* 27 (Jan. 1975).

Mackesy, Piers. *The War for America, 1775–1783.* Cambridge, Mass.: Harvard Univ. Press, 1965.

Maechling, Charles. "Insurgency and Counterinsurgency: The Role of Strategic Theory." *Parameters* 14 (autumn 1984).

Magno, José, and A. James Gregor. "Insurgency and Counterinsurgency in the Philippines." *Asian Survey* 26 (May 1986).

Maley, William. "The Geneva Accords of April 1988." In Saikal and Maley, *Soviet Withdrawal.*

Malhuret, Claude. "Report from Afghanistan." *Foreign Affairs* 62 (winter 1984).

Mallin, Jay. *Strategy for Conquest: Communist Documents on Guerrilla Warfare.* Coral Gables, Fla.: Univ. of Miami Press, 1970.

Maneli, Mieczyslaw. *War of the Vanquished.* Trans. M. de Gorcey. New York: Harper and Row, 1971.

Mangold. Tom. *The Tunnels of Cu Chi.* New York: Random House, 1985.

Manwaring, Max G., ed. *Uncomfortable Wars: Toward a New Paradigm of Low-Intensity Conflict.* Boulder, Colo.: Westview, 1991.

Manwaring, Max G., and Courtney Prisk, eds. *El Salvador at War: An Oral History.* Washington, D.C. National Defense Univ. Press, 1988.

Mao Tse-tung. *Basic Tactics.* Trans. Stuart Schram. New York: Praeger, 1966.

———. *On the Protracted War.* Peking: Foreign Languages Press, 1954.

———. *Report on an Investigation of the Peasant Movement in Hunan.* 1927. Reprint, Peking: Foreign Languages Press, 1967.

———. *Selected Military Writings.* Peking: Foreign Languages Press, 1966.

Marr, David G. *The Viet Nam Tradition on Trial 1920–1945.* Berkeley: Univ. of California Press, 1981.

Marston, R. "Resettlement as a Counter-Revolutionary Technique." *Royal United Services Institute for Defence Studies* 124, no. 4 (1979).

Martin, Mike. *Afghanistan: Inside a Rebel Stronghold.* Dorset, Eng.: Blandford, 1984.

Matthews, Lloyd J., and Dale E. Brown, eds. *Assessing the Viet Nam War.* Washington, D.C.: Pergamon-Brassey's, 1987.

May, Glenn Anthony. *Battle for Batangas: A Philippine Province at War.* New Haven, Conn.: Yale Univ. Press, 1991.

———. "Why the United States Won the Philippine-American War, 1899–1902." *Pacific Historical Review* 52 (Nov. 1983).

Mazower, Mark. *Inside Hitler's Greece: The Experience of Occupation 1941–1944.* New Haven, Conn.: Yale Univ. Press, 1993.

McAlister, John T. *Viet Nam: The Origins of Revolution.* Garden City, N.Y.: Doubleday Anchor, 1971.

McClintock, Cynthia. *Revolutionary Movements in Latin America: El Salvador's FMLN and Peru's Shining Path.* Washington, D.C.: U.S. Institute of Peace, 1998.

McCoy, James. *Secrets of the Viet Cong.* New York: Hippocrene, 1992.

McCrady, Edward. *The History of South Carolina in the Revolution, 1780–1783.* 1902. Reprint, New York: Paladin, 1969.

McGarvey, Patrick J. *Visions of Victory: Selected Vietnamese Communist Military Writings 1965–1968.* Stanford, Calif.: Hoover Institution Press, 1969.

McKuen, John. *The Art of Counter-Revolutionary Warfare.* London: Faber and Faber, 1966.

McMaster, H.R. *Dereliction of Duty.* New York: HarperCollins, 1997.

McNeill, William H. *Greece: American Aid in Action.* New York: Twentieth Century Fund, 1957.

McPherson, James M. *Battle Cry of Freedom: The Civil War Era.* New York: Oxford Univ. Press, 1988.

———. "Lincoln and the Strategy of Unconditional Surrender." In *Lincoln, the War President,* ed. Gabor S. Boritt. New York: Oxford Univ. Press, 1992.

Megee, Vernon. "The Genesis of Air Support in Guerrilla Operations." *United States Naval Institute Proceedings* 91 (June 1965).

Metz, Steven. *Counterinsurgency.* Carlisle, Pa.: U.S. Army War College, 1995.

Miller, Stuart Creighton. *"Benevolent Assimilation": The American Conquest of the Philippines, 1899–1903.* New Haven, Conn.: Yale Univ. Press, 1982.

Millett, Allan R. *Semper Fidelis: The History of the United States Marine Corps.* New York: Macmillan, 1980.

Millett, Richard. *Guardians of the Dynasty.* Maryknoll, N.Y.: Orbis, 1977.

Mockaitis, Thomas R. *British Counterinsurgency 1919–1960.* New York: St. Martin's, 1990.

Monaghan, Jay. *Civil War on the Western Border 1854–1865.* Boston: Little, Brown, 1955.

Moore, Albert Burton. *Conscription and Conflict in the Confederacy.* 1924. Reprint, New York: Hillary House, 1963.

Morgan, H. Wayne, ed. *Making Peace with Spain: The Diary of Whitelaw Reid.* Austin: Univ. of Texas, 1965.

Mosby, John S. *The Memoirs of Colonel John S. Mosby.* New York: Kraus Reprint Co., 1969.

Moyar, Mark. *Phoenix and the Birds of Prey: The CIA's Secret Campaign to Destroy the Viet Cong.* Annapolis, Md.: Naval Institute Press, 1997.

Munro, Dana G. *Intervention and Dollar Diplomacy in the Caribbean, 1900–1921.* Princeton, N.J.: Princeton Univ. Press, 1964.

Murdock, Eugene C. *One Million Men: The Civil War Draft in the North.* Westport, Conn.: Greenwood, 1971.

Murphy, Orville. *Charles Gravier, Comte de Vergennes: French Diplomacy in the Age of Revolution, 1717-1787.* Albany N.Y.: State Univ. of New York Press, 1982.

Murray, J.C. "The Anti-Bandit War." Reprinted in Greene, *The Guerrilla—And How to Fight Him.*

Nasution, Abdul H. *Fundamentals of Guerrilla Warfare.* 1953. Reprint, New York: Praeger, 1965.

Navarre, Henri. *Agonie de l'Indochine.* Paris: Plon, 1958.

Nelson, Paul David. *General Horatio Gates.* Baton Rouge: Louisiana State Univ. Press, 1976.

Nelson, William H. *The American Tory.* Oxford: Oxford Univ. Press, 1961.

Nevins, Allan. *Ordeal of the Union: A House Dividing, 1852–1857.* New York: Scribner's, 1947.

———. *The Statesmanship of the Civil War.* New York: Macmillan, 1953.

———. *The War for the Union.* 4 vols. New York: Scribner's, 1959–1971.

Ngo Quang Truong. *The Easter Offensive of 1972.* Washington, D.C.: U.S. Army Center of Military History, 1980.

———. *Territorial Forces.* Washington, D.C.: U.S. Army Center of Military History, 1981.

Nguyen Tien Hung and Jerrold Schecter. *The Palace File: Viet Nam Secret Documents.* New York: Haper and Row, 1986.

Nickerson, Hoffman. *The Turning Point of the Revolution.* 2 vols. Fort Washington, N.Y.: Kennikat Press, 1928.

Nighswonger, William A. *Rural Pacification in Viet Nam.* New York: Praeger, 1966.

Nixon, Richard. *No More Viet Nams.* New York: Arbor House, 1985.

Nolting, Frederick. *From Trust to Tragedy: The Political Memoirs of Frederick Nolting, Kennedy's Ambassador to Diem's Viet Nam.* New York: Praeger, 1988.

Norris, James A. *The First Afghan War.* Cambridge: Cambridge Univ. Press, 1967.

O'Ballance, Edgar. *The Greek Civil War.* London: Faber and Faber, 1966

———. *The Indo-China War 1945–1954.* London: Faber and Faber, 1964.

Oberdorfer, Don. *Tet!* Garden City, N.Y.: Doubleday, 1971.

O'Neill, Bard E. *Insurgency and Terrorism: Inside Modern Revolutionary Warfare.* Washington, D.C.: Brassey's, 1990.

O'Neill, Bard E., William Weston, and Donald Alberts, eds. *Insurgency in the Modern World.* Boulder, Colo.: Westview, 1980.

O'Neill, Robert. *General Giap.* New York: Praeger, 1969.

———. *The Strategy of General Giap since 1964.* Canberra: Australian National Univ., 1969.

Orlov, Alexander. *Handbook of Intelligence and Guerrilla Warfare.* Ann Arbor, Mich.: Univ. of Michigan Press, 1963.

Osanka, Franklin Mark, ed. *Modern Guerrilla Warfare: Fighting Communist Guerrilla Movements, 1941–1961.* Glencoe, Ill.: Free Press, 1962.

O'Sullivan, Noel K., ed. *Revolutionary Theory and Political Reality.* New York: St. Martin's, 1983.

O'Sullivan, Patrick, and Jesse W. Miller. *The Geography of Warfare*. New York: St. Martin's, 1983.

Paget, Julian. *Counter-Insurgency Campaigning*. London: Faber and Faber, 1967.

Palmer, Bruce, Jr. *The 25-Year War: America's Military Role in Viet Nam*. Lexington: Univ. Press of Kentucky, 1984.

Palmer, Dave Richard. *Summons of the Trumpet*. San Rafael, Calif.: Presidio Press, 1978.

Paludan, Phillip Shaw. *Victims: A True Story of the Civil War*. Knoxville: Univ. of Tennessee Press, 1981.

Pancake, John S. *This Destructive War: The British Campaign in the Carolinas, 1780–1782*. University: Univ. of Alabama Press, 1985.

Papagos, Alexander. "Guerrilla Warfare." In Osanka, *Modern Guerrilla Warfare*. Also in *Foreign Affairs* 30 (Jan. 1952).

Paret, Peter, and John Shy. *Guerrillas in the 1960s*. New York: Praeger, 1962.

Parrish, R.D. *Combat Recon: My Year with the ARVN*. New York: St. Martin's, 1991.

Paschall, Rod. "Marxist Counterinsurgencies." *Parameters* 16, no. 2 (1986).

Pauker, Guy. *Sources of Insurgency in Developing Countries*. Santa Monica, Calif.: Rand, 1973.

Paul, Roland. "Laos: Anatomy of an American Involvement." *Foreign Affairs*, Apr. 1971.

The Pentagon Papers. Gravel Edition. 5 vols. Boston: Beacon Press, 1971.

People's Army of Viet Nam, *Viet Nam: The Anti-U.S. Resistance War for National Salvation*. Hanoi: PAVN Publishing House, 1980.

Perkins, Dexter. *The United States and the Caribbean*. Cambridge, Mass.: Harvard Univ. Press, 1966.

Perkins, James Breck. *France in the American Revolution*. Boston: Houghton Mifflin, 1911.

Perkins, Whitney T. *Constraint of Empire: The United States and Caribbean Interventions*. Westport, Conn.: Greenwood, 1981.

Peterson, Michael E. *The Combined Action Platoons: The U.S. Marines' Other War in Viet Nam*. New York: Praeger, 1989.

Phelan, John Leddy. *The Hispanization of the Philippines*. Madison: Univ. of Wisconsin Press, 1967.

Pierce, Richard A. *Russian Central Asia 1867–1917: A Study in Colonial Rule*. Berkeley: Univ. of California Press, 1960.

Pike, Douglas. *History of Vietnamese Communism 1925–1976*. Stanford, Calif.: Hoover Institution, 1978.

———. *PAVN: People's Army of Viet Nam*. Novato, Calif.: Presidio Press, 1986.

———. *Viet Cong*. Cambridge, Mass.: MIT Press, 1966.

———. *The Viet Cong Strategy of Terror*. Cambridge, Mass.: MIT Press, 1970.

Pimlott, John, ed. *Viet Nam: The History and the Tactics*. New York: Crescent, 1982.

Pomeroy, William J. *Guerrilla and Counter-Guerrilla Warfare.* New York: International Publishers, 1964.

———. "The Philippine Peasantry and the Huk Revolt." *Journal of Peasant Studies* 5, no. 4 (1978).

———, ed. *Guerrilla Warfare and Marxism.* New York: International Publishers, 1968.

Poullada, Leon B. "Afghanistan and the United States: The Crucial Years." *Middle East Journal* 35, no. 2 (1981).

———. "Road to Crisis, 1919–1980." In Klass, *Afghanistan.*

Prados, John. *Blood Road: The Ho Chi Minh Trail and the Vietnam War.* New York: Wiley, 1999.

———. *The Hidden History of the Vietnam War.* Chicago: Ivan R. Dee, 1995.

Pratt, Julius. *America's Colonial Experiment.* New York: Prentice-Hall, 1950.

———. *Expansionists of 1898.* Baltimore: Johns Hopkins Univ. Press, 1951.

Prochau, William. *Once Upon a Distant War: Young War Correspondents and the Early Viet Nam Battles.* New York: Times Books, 1995.

Pustay, John S. *Counterinsurgency Warfare.* New York: Free Press, 1965.

Race, Jeffrey. *War Comes to Long An: Revolutionary Conflict in a Vietnamese Province.* Berkeley: Univ. of California Press, 1972.

Radu, Michael. *The New Insurgencies: Anticommunist Guerrillas in the Third World.* New Brunswick, N.J.: Transaction, 1990.

Ramage, James A. *Gray Ghost: The Life of John Singleton Mosby.* Lexington, Ky.: Univ. Press of Kentucky, 1999.

Randle, Robert E. *Geneva, 1954.* Princeton, N.J.: Princeton Univ. Press, 1969.

Rankin, Hugh F. *Francis Marion: The Swamp Fox.* New York: Crowell, 1973.

Regional Conflict Working Group. *Commitment to Freedom: Security Assistance as a U.S. Policy Instrument in the Third World.* Washington, D.C.: U.S. Government Printing Office, 1988.

———. *Supporting U.S. Strategy for Third World Conflict.* Washington, D.C.: U.S. Government Printing Office, 1988.

"Revolutionary War: Western Response." Special issue. *Journal of International Affairs* 25, no. 1 (1971).

Rice, Edward E. *Wars of the Third Kind: Conflict in Underdeveloped Countries.* Berkeley: Univ. of California Press, 1988.

Richardson, James. "The Huk Rebellion." *Journal of Contemporary Asia* 8, no. 2 (1978).

Richter, Heinz. *British Intervention in Greece: From Varkiza to Civil War.* London: Merlin, 1985.

Robbins, James S. "Soviet Counterinsurgency Strategy in Afghanistan 1979–1989." Ph.D. diss., Tufts Univ., 1991.

Robinson, Donald. *The Dirty Wars.* New York: Delacorte, 1968.

Robinson, Thomas W. *A Politico-Military Biography of Lin Piao.* Santa Monica, Calif.: Rand, 1971.

Rolph, Hammond. "Vietnamese Communism and the Protracted War." *Asian Survey* 12 (1972).

Romulo, Carlos P. *Crusade in Asia.* New York: John Day, 1955.

Rosen, Stephen. "Viet Nam and the American Theory of Limited War." *International Security* 7 (1982).

Rothenberg, Morris. "The Soviets and Central America." In *Central America: Anatomy of Conflict,* ed. Robert Leiken. New York: Pergamon, 1984.

Roy, Olivier. *Islam and Resistance in Afghanistan.* Cambridge: Cambridge Univ. Press, 1986.

———. *The Lessons of the Soviet-Afghan War.* Adelphi Paper 259. London: International Institute of Strategic Studies, 1991.

———. "The Origins of the Afghan Communist Party." *Central Asian Survey* 7 (1988).

Royster, Charles. *A Revolutionary People at War: The Continental Army and American Character, 1775–1783.* Chapel Hill: Univ. of North Carolina Press, 1979.

Rubin, Barnett R. "The Fragmentation of Afghanistan." *Foreign Affairs* 68 (winter 1989–1990).

———. *To Die in Afghanistan.* New York: Helsinki Watch and Asia Watch, 1985.

Rubin, Barnett R., and Jeri Laber. *A Nation Is Dying: Afghanistan under the Soviets 1979–1987.* Chicago: Northwestern Univ. Press, 1988.

Russell, Diana E.H. *Rebellion, Revolution and Armed Force.* New York: Academic Press, 1974.

Ryan, Nigel. *A Hitch or Two in Afghanistan.* London: Weidenfeld and Nicolson, 1983.

Rywkin, Michael. *Russia in Central Asia.* New York: Collier, 1963.

Saikal, Amin, and William Maley, eds. *The Soviet Withdrawal from Afghanistan.* Cambridge: Cambridge Univ. Press, 1989.

Sanger, Richard H. *Insurgent Era.* Washington, D.C.: Potomac Books, 1967.

Sansom, Robert L. *The Economics of Insurgency in the Mekong Delta of Viet Nam.* Cambridge, Mass.: MIT Press, 1970.

Santoli, Al. *Everything We Had: An Oral History of the Viet Nam War by Thirty-Three American Soldiers Who Fought It.* New York: Random House, 1981.

Sarin, Oleg, and Lev Dvoretsky. *The Afghan Syndrome: The Soviet Union's Viet Nam.* Novato, Calif.: Presidio Press, 1993.

Sarkesian, Sam. *Ameria's Forgotten Wars: The Counterrevolutionary Past and Lessons for the Future.* Westport, Conn.: Greenwood, 1984.

Scaff, Alvin H. *The Philippine Answer to Communism.* Stanford, Calif.: Stanford Univ. Press, 1955.

Schell, Jonathan. *The Village of Ben Suc.* New York: Random House, 1967.

Schott, Joseph L. *The Ordeal of Samar.* Indianapolis: Bobbs-Merrill, 1965.

Schram, Stuart. *Mao Tse-Tung.* Harmondsworth, Eng.: Penguin, 1966.

Schultz, Duane P. *Quantrill's War.* New York: St. Martin's, 1996.

Schwartzstein, Stuart J.D. "Chemical Warfare in Afghanistan." *World Affairs* 145, no. 3 (1982–1983).

Schwarz, Benjamin. *American Counterinsurgency Doctrine and El Salvador: The Frustrations of Reform and the Illusions of Nation Building*. Santa Monica, Calif.: Rand, 1991.

Scigliano, Robert. *South Viet Nam: Nation under Stress*. Boston: Houghton Mifflin, 1964.

Scott, Andrew M. *Insurgency*. Chapel Hill: Univ. of North Carolina, 1970.

Scott, Harriet, and William Scott. *The Soviet Art of War*. Boulder, Colo.: Westview, 1982.

Scott, James M. *Deciding to Intervene: The Reagan Doctrine and American Foreign Policy*. Durham, N.C.: Duke Univ. Press, 1996.

Selden, Mark. *The Yenan Way in Revolutionary China*. Cambridge: Cambridge Univ. Press, 1971.

Serafis, Stefanos. *Greek Resistance Army: The Story of ELAS*. London: Birch Books, 1951.

Sereseres, Caesar. "Lessons from Central America's Revolutionary Wars, 1972–1984." In *The Lessons of Recent Wars in the Third World*, ed. Robert E. Harkavy and Stephanie G. Neuman. Lexington, Mass.: Lexington Books, 1985.

Sexton, William Thaddeus. *Soldiers in the Sun*. Harrisburg, Penn.: Military Service Publishing Company, 1939.

Shafer, D. Michael. *Deadly Paradigms: The Failure of U.S. Counterinsurgency Policy*. Princeton, N.J.: Princeton Univ. Press, 1988.

Shahrani, M. Nazif, and Robert L. Canfield, eds. *Revolutions and Rebellions in Afghanistan*. Berkeley: Univ. of California Press, 1986.

Shaplen, Robert. *Bitter Victory*. New York: Harper and Row, 1986.

———. *The Lost Revolution: The U.S. in Viet Nam 1946–1966*. New York: Harper and Row, 1966.

———. *The Road from War: Vietnam, 1965-1971*. New York: Harper and Row, 1970.

Sharp, U.S. Grant. *Strategy for Defeat: Viet Nam in Retrospect*. San Rafael, Calif.: Presidio Press, 1978.

Sharp, U.S. Grant, and William Westmoreland. *Report on the War in Viet Nam*. Washington, D.C.: U.S. Government Printing Office, 1968.

Sheehan, Neil. *A Bright Shining Lie: John Paul Vann and America in Viet Nam*. New York: Random House, 1988.

Sheikh, Ali T. "Not the Whole Truth: Media Coverage of the Afghan Conflict." *Conflict Quarterly* 10, no. 4 (1990).

Short, Anthony. *The Origins of the Viet Nam War*. London: Longmans, 1989.

Shultz, George P. *Triumph and Turmoil: My Years as Secretary of State*. New York: Scribner's, 1993.

Shultz, Richard H., Jr. "Breaking the Will of the Enemy in the Viet Nam War." *Journal of Peace Research* 15, no. 2 (1978).

———. "Coercive Force and Military Strategy: Deterrence Logic and the Cost-Benefit Model of Counterinsurgency Warfare." *Western Political Quarterly* 32 (1979).

———. The Low-Intensity Conflict Environment of the 1990s. *Annals of the American Academy of Political and Social Science* 157 (Sept. 1991).

Shultz, Richard H., Jr., et al, eds. *Guerrilla Warfare and Counterinsurgency: U.S.-Soviet Policy in the Third World.* Lexington, Mass.: Lexington Books, 1989.

Shy, John. *A People Numerous and Armed.* Oxford: Oxford Univ. Press, 1976.

Shy, John, and Thomas Collier. "Revolutionary Warfare." In *Makers of Modern Strategy,* ed. Peter Paret. Princeton, N.J.: Princeton Univ. Press, 1986.

Siepel, Kevin H. *Rebel: The Life and Times of John Singleton Mosby.* New York: St. Martin's, 1983.

Singh, Baljit, and Ko-Wang Mei. *Theory and Practice of Modern Guerrilla Warfare.* New York: Asia Publishing House, 1971.

Skocpol, Theda. "What Makes Peasants Revolutionary?" *Comparative Politics* 14 (1982).

Smedley, Agnes. *The Great Road: The Life and Times of Chu Teh.* New York: Monthly Review, 1956.

Smith, Paul H. *Loyalists and Redcoats: A Study in British Revolutionary Policy.* Chapel Hill: Univ. of North Carolina Press, 1964.

Smith, R.B. *An International History of the Vietnam War,* vol. 1, *Revolution vs. Containment, 1955-1961.* New York: St. Martin's, 1983.

———. *An International History of the Vietnam War,* vol. 2, *The Kennedy Strategy.* New York: St. Martin's, 1985.

Smith, W. Wayne. "An Experiment in Counterinsurgency: The Assessment of Confederate Sympathizers in Missouri." *Journal of Southern History* 35 (1969).

Smythe, Donald. *Guerrilla Warrior: The Early Life of John J. Pershing.* New York: Scribner's, 1973.

Social Science Research Bureau of Michigan State University. *Problems of Freedom: South Viet Nam since Independence.* Glencoe, Ill.: Free Press, 1961.

Sorley, Lewis. *A Better War: The Unexamined Victories and the Final Tragedy of America's Last Years in Viet Nam.* New York: Harcourt Brace, 1999.

———. *Thunderbolt: General Creighton Abrams and the Army of His Times.* New York: Simon and Schuster, 1992.

Spector, Ronald H. *Advice and Support: The Early Years 1941–1960.* Washington, D.C.: U.S. Army Center of Military History, 1983.

Spencer, Floyd. *War and Postwar Greece.* Washington, D.C.: Library of Congress, 1952.

Stanley, Peter W., ed. *Reappraising an Empire: New Perspectives on Philippine-American History.* Cambridge, Mass.: Harvard Univ. Press, 1984.

Stanton, Shelby. *Green Berets at War: U.S. Army Special Forces in Southeast Asia, 1956–1975.* Novato, Calif.: Presidio Press, 1985.

———. *The Rise and Fall of an American Army: U.S. Ground Forces in Viet Nam 1965–1973.* Novato, Calif.: Presidio Press, 1985.

Starner, Frances Lucille. *Magsaysay and the Philippine Peasantry: The Agrarian*

Impact on Philippine Politics 1953–1956. Berkeley: Univ. of California Press, 1961.

Staudenmaier, William C., and Alan Sabrossky. "A Strategy of Counter-Revolutionary War." *Military Review* 65 (Feb. 1985).

Stavrakis, Peter J. *Moscow and Greek Communism 1944–1949*. Ithaca, N.Y.: Cornell Univ. Press, 1989.

Stevens, Richard. *The Trail*. New York: Garland, 1992.

Stimson, Henry L. *American Policy in Nicaragua*. New York: Scribner's, 1927.

Stone, William L. *The Campaign of Lieut. Gen. John Burgoyne and the Expedition of Lieut. Col. Barry St. Leger*. 1877. Reprint, New York: Da Capo, 1970.

Storey, Moorfield. *Conquest of the Philippines by the United States, 1898–1925*. New York: Putnam's, 1926.

Sturtevant, David R. "Filipino Peasant Rebellions Examined: Lessons from the Past." *CALC Report* 12, no. 3 (1986).

———. *Popular Uprising in the Philippines, 1840–1940*. Ithaca, N.Y.: Cornell Univ. Press, 1976.

"Subnational Conflict." Special issue. *World Affairs* 146 (winter 1983–1984).

Sullivan, Joseph O. "How Peace Came to El Salvador." *Orbis* 38 (winter 1994).

Summers, Harry G. *On Strategy: A Critical Analysis of the Viet Nam War*. Novato, Calif.: Presidio Press, 1982.

———. "Principles of War and Low-Intensity Conflict." *Military Review* 65 (1985).

Sun Tzu, *The Art of War*. Trans. Samuel B. Griffith. New York: Oxford Univ. Press, 1963.

Sutherland, Daniel E. "Guerrillas: The Real War in Arkansas." *Arkansas Historical Quarterly* 52 (1993).

Tanham, George K. *Communist Revolutionary Warfare: From the Viet Minh to the Viet Cong*. Rev. ed. New York: Praeger, 1967.

———. "Some Insurgency Lessons from Southeast Asia." *Orbis* 16 (1972).

———. *Trail in Thailand*. New York: Crane, Russak, 1974.

Tanham, George K., and Dennis J. Duncanson. "Some Dilemmas of Counterinsurgency." *Foreign Affairs*, Oct. 1969.

Taruc, Luis. *Born of the People*. 1953. Reprint, Westport, Conn.: Greenwood, 1973.

———. *He Who Rides the Tiger*. New York: Praeger, 1967.

Tatum, Georgia Lee. *Disloyalty in the Confederacy*. Chapel Hill: Univ. of North Carolina Press, 1934.

Taylor, John R.M. *The Philippine Insurrection against the United States: A Compilation of Documents with Notes and Introduction*. 5 vols. Pasay City, Philippines: Eugenio Lopez Foundation, 1971–1973.

Taylor, Maxwell D. *Swords and Plowshares*. New York: Norton, 1972.

Thane, Elswyth. *The Fighting Quaker: Nathanael Greene*. New York: Hawthorn, 1972.

Thaxton, Ralph. "On Peasant Revolution and National Resistance: Towards a

406 ■ Bibliography

Theory of Peasant Mobilization and Revolutionary War with Special Reference to Modern China." World Politics 30, no. 1 (1977).

Thayer, Charles W. *Guerrilla.* New York: Harper and Row, 1965.

Thayer, Theodore. *Nathanael Greene: Strategist of the American Revolution.* New York: Twayne, 1960.

Thayer, Thomas C. *War without Fronts: The American Experience in Viet Nam.* Boulder, Colo.: Westview, 1985.

Thies, Wallace J. *When Governments Collide: Coercion and Diplomacy in the Viet Nam Conflict 1964–1968.* Berkeley: Univ. of California Press, 1980.

Thompson, Loren B., ed. *Low-Intensity Conflict: The Pattern of Warfare in the Modern World.* Lexington, Mass.: Lexington Books, 1989.

Thompson, Robert. *Defeating Communist Insurgency: The Lessons of Malaya and Viet Nam.* New York: Praeger, 1966.

———. *No Exit from Viet Nam.* New York: David McKay, 1969.

———. *Peace Is Not at Hand.* New York: David McKay, 1974.

———. *Revolutionary War in World Strategy.* New York: Taplinger, 1970.

Thompson, W. Scott, and Donaldson D. Frizzell, eds. *The Lessons of Viet Nam.* New York: Crane, Russak, 1977.

Thornton, Thomas P. "The Emergence of Communist Revolutionary Doctrine." In *Communism and Revolution: The Strategic Uses of Political Violence,* ed. Cyril E. Black and Thomas P. Thornton. Princeton, N.J.: Princeton Univ. Press, 1964.

Todd, Olivier. *Cruel April: The Fall of Saigon.* New York: Norton, 1990.

Tran Dinh Tho. *Pacification.* Washington, D.C.: U.S. Army Center of Military History, 1980.

Tran Van Don. *Our Endless War.* San Rafael, Calif.: Presidio Press, 1978.

Tran Van Tra. *Concluding the 30–Years War.* Roslyn, Va.: Foreign Broadcast Information Service, 1983.

Trinquier, Roger. *Modern Warfare: A French View of Counterinsurgency.* New York: Praeger, 1964. Published in French in 1961.

Trottier, Paul, and Craig Karp. *Afghanistan: Five Years of Occupation.* Special Report no. 120. Washington, D.C.: U.S. State Department, 1984.

Truong Chinh [pseud.]. *Primer for Revolt.* New York: Praeger, 1963.

———. *The Resistance Will Win.* Hanoi: Foreign Languages Publishing House, 1960.

Truong Nhu Tang. *A Viet Cong Memoir.* New York: Harcourt, 1987.

Tsoucalas, Constantine. *The Greek Tragedy.* Baltimore: Penguin, 1969.

Turley, Gerald H. *The Easter Offensive.* Novato, Calif.: Presidio Press, 1985.

Turley, William S. *Vietnamese Communism in Comparative Perspective.* Boulder, Colo.: Westview, 1980.

Turner, Robert F. *Vietnamese Communism: Its Origins and Development.* Stanford, Calif.: Hoover Institution, 1975.

Urban, Mark. *War in Afghanistan.* New York: St. Martin's, 1988.

U.S. Army Special Warfare Center. *Readings in Guerrilla Warfare.* Fort Bragg, N.C., 1960.

U.S. Department of State. *Foreign Relations of the United States (FRUS).* Washington, D.C.: U.S. Government Printing Office, 1919–1991.

U.S. Marine Corps. *Small Wars Manual.* Washington, D.C.: U.S. Government Printing Office, 1940.

U.S. Naval Institute. *Studies in Guerrilla Warfare.* Annapolis, Md.: U.S. Naval Institute Press, 1963.

U.S. Senate Committee on the Philippines. *Hearings: Affairs in the Philippine Islands.* 57th Congress, 2d session, 1902.

Valeriano, Napoleon, and Charles T.P. Bohannan. *Counter-Guerrilla Operations: The Philippine Experience.* New York: Praeger, 1962.

VanDeMark, Brian. *Into the Quagmire: Lyndon Johnson and the Escalation of the Viet Nam War.* New York: Oxford Univ. Press, 1991.

Van der Kroef, Justus. "Aquino and the Communists: A Philippine Strategic Stalemate?" *World Affairs* 151 (winter 1988–1989).

———. *Aquino's Philippines: The Deepening Security Crisis.* London: Institute for the Study of Conflict, 1988.

Vandiver, Frank E. *Black Jack: The Life and Times of General John J. Pershing.* College Station: Texas A&M Univ. Press, 1977.

Van Fleet, James A. "How We Won in Greece." *Balkan Studies* 8 (1967).

Van Hollen, Eliza. *Afghanistan: Three Years of Occupation.* Washington, D.C.: U.S. Department of State, 1982.

Van Tien Dung. *Our Great Spring Victory.* New York: Monthly Review, 1977.

Vertzberger, Yaacov. "Afghanistan in China's Policy." *Problems of Communism* 31 (May–June 1982).

Vickery, Michael. *Cambodia, 1975–1982.* Boston: South End, 1984.

Vo Nguyen Giap. *Dien Bien Phu.* Hanoi: Foreign Languages Publishing House, 1964.

———. *How We Won the War.* Philadelphia: Recon, 1976.

———. *The Military Art of People's War.* New York: Monthly Review, 1970.

———. *People's War, People's Army.* New York: Praeger, 1962.

Waghelstein, John. *El Salvador: Observations and Experiences in Counterinsurgency.* Carlisle, Pa.: U.S. Army War College, 1985.

———. "Post–Viet Nam Counterinsurgency Doctrine." *Military Review* 65 (1985).

Wainhouse, Edward R. "Guerrilla War in Greece, 1946–1949: A Case Study." *Military Review* 37 (June 1957).

Walker, Thomas W. "Nicaragua: The Somoza Family Regime." In *Latin American Politics and Development,* ed. Howard J. Wiarda and Harvey F. Kline. Boston: Houghton Mifflin, 1979.

Wallace, Willard M. *Appeal to Arms: A Military History of the American Revolution.* New York: Harper, 1951.

Walt, Lewis W. *Strange War, Strange Strategy.* New York: Funk and Wagnalls, 1970.

Walton, John. *Reluctant Rebels.* New York: Columbia Univ. Press, 1984.

Ward, Christopher. *The War of the Revolution.* 2 vols. New York: Macmillan, 1952.

Ware, Lewis B., ed. *Low Intensity Conflict in the Third World.* Maxwell Air Force Base, Ala.: Air Univ. Press, 1988.

Waring, Alice N. *The Fighting Elder: Andrew Pickens.* Columbia: Univ. of South Carolina Press, 1962.

Warner, Denis. *Certain Victory: How Hanoi Won the War.* Kansas City, Kans.: Sheed, Andrews, and McMeel, 1978.

———. *The Last Confucian.* New York: Macmillan, 1963

Weatherbee, Donald P. *The United Front in Thailand: A Documentary Analysis.* Columbia: Univ. of South Carolina, 1970.

Webre, Stephen. *José Napoleon Duarte and the Christian Democratic Party in Salvadoran Politics 1960–1972.* Baton Rouge: Louisiana State Univ. Press, 1979.

Weigley, Russell F. "American Strategy: A Call for a Critical Strategic History." In *Reconsiderations on the Revolutionary War,* ed. Don Higginbotham. Westport, Conn.: Greenwood, 1978.

———. *The American Way of War: A History of United States Military Strategy and Policy.* Bloomington: Indiana Univ. Press, 1977.

———. *The Partisan War: The South Carolina Campaign of 1780–1782.* Columbia: Univ. of South Carolina Press, 1970.

Welch, Richard E. *Response to Imperialism: The United States and the Philippine-American War.* Chapel Hill: Univ. of North Carolina Press, 1979.

Weller, Jac. *Fire and Movement: Bargain-Basement War in the Far East.* New York: Crowell, 1967.

———. "Irregular but Effective: Partizan Weapons Tactics in the American Revolution, Southern Theatre." In *Military Analysis: An Anthology,* ed. the editors of *Military Affairs.* Millwood, N.Y.: KTO Press, 1977.

Wert, Jeffrey D. *Mosby's Rangers.* New York: Simon and Schuster, 1990.

Wesley, Charles H. *The Collapse of the Confederacy.* New York: Russell and Russell, 1937.

West, F.J., Jr. *Small Unit Action in Viet Nam.* Quantico, Va.: U.S. Marine Corps, 1967.

———. *The Village.* New York: Harper and Row, 1972.

Westmoreland, William. *A Soldier Reports.* Garden City, N.Y.: Doubleday, 1976.

Wheeler, Geoffrey. *The Modern History of Soviet Central Asia.* London: Weidenfeld and Nicolson, 1964.

Wickham-Crowley, Timothy. *Guerrillas and Revolutions in Latin America: A Comparative Study of Insurgents and Regimes since 1956.* Princeton, N.J.: Princeton Univ. Press, 1991.

Wickwire, Franklin, and Mary Wickwire. *Cornwallis: The American Adventure.* Boston: Houghton Mifflin, 1970.

Wildman, Edwin. *Aguinaldo*. Boston: Lothrop, 1901.

Wiley, Bell Irvin. *The Life of Johnny Reb: The Common Soldier of the Confederacy*. 1943. Reprint, Baton Rouge: Louisiana State Univ. Press, 1970.

————. *The Road to Appomattox*. 1956. Reprint, New York: Atheneum, 1983.

Willcox, William B. *Portrait of a General: Sir Henry Clinton in the War of Independence*. New York: Knopf, 1964.

Wimbush, S. Endeus, and Alex Alexiev. *Soviet Central Asian Soldiers in Afghanistan*. Santa Monica, Calif.: Rand, 1984.

Winters, Francis X. *The Year of the Hare*. Athens: Univ. of Georgia Press, 1997.

Wirtz, James J. *The Tet Offensive: Intelligence Failure in War*. Ithaca, N.Y.: Cornell Univ. Press, 1991.

Wittner, Lawrence S. *American Intervention in Greece 1943–1949*. New York: Columbia Univ. Press, 1982.

Wolf, Charles, Jr. *Insurgency and Counterinsurgency: New Myths and Old Realities*. Santa Monica, Calif.: Rand, 1965.

————. *The Logic of Failure: A Viet Nam "Lesson."* Santa Monica, Calif.: Rand, 1971.

Wolf, Eric. *Peasant Wars of the Twentieth Century*. New York: Harper and Row, 1969.

Wolff, Leon. *Little Brown Brother: How the United States Purchased and Pacified the Philippine Islands at the Century's Turn*. New York: Doubleday, 1961.

Woodhouse, C.M. *The Struggle for Greece 1941–1949*. London: Hart-Davis, MacGibbon, 1976.

Woodward, Ralph Lee. *Central America: A Nation Divided*. New York: Oxford Univ. Press, 1976.

Young, Kenneth. *The Greek Passion*. London: J.M. Dent, 1969.

Zasloff, Joseph J. *Origins of the Insurgency in South Viet Nam, 1954–1960: The Role of the Southern Viet Minh Cadres*. Santa Monica, Calif.: Rand, 1967.

Zimmerman, William, and Robert Axelrod. "The 'Lessons' of Viet Nam and Soviet Foreign Policy." *World Politics* 34, no. 1 (1981).

Zotos, Stephanos. *Greece: The Struggle for Freedom*. New York: Crowell, 1967.

Index